CONSTRUCTING THE AMERICAN PAST

A SOURCEBOOK OF A PEOPLE'S HISTORY
VOLUME ONE TO 1877

Elliott J. Gorn
Randy Roberts
Susan Schulten
Terry D. Bilhartz

NEW YORK   OXFORD
OXFORD UNIVERSITY PRESS

Oxford University Press is a department of the University of Oxford.
It furthers the University's objective of excellence in research, scholarship,
and education by publishing worldwide. Oxford is a registered trade mark
of Oxford University Press in the UK and certain other countries.

Published in the United States of America by
Oxford University Press
198 Madison Avenue, New York, NY 10016,
United States of America.

Library of Congress Cataloging-in-Publication Data

Names: Gorn, Elliott J., 1951- editor of compilation. | Roberts, Randy, 1951-
    editor of compilation. | Schulten, Susan, editor of compilation.
Title: Constructing the American past : a sourcebook of a people's history /
    Elliot J. Gorn, Randy Roberts, Susan Schulten.
Other titles: Sourcebook of a people's history
Description: Eighth edition. | New York, NY : Oxford University Press, [2018]
    | Audience: "Constructing the American Past asks students to become
    historians. This volume-volume sourcebook is a series of "case studies" of
    particular episodes or events in American History."—Provided by publisher.
Identifiers: LCCN 2017026453 | ISBN 9780190280956 (v. 1 : pbk.)/9780190280963 (v. 2 : pbk.)
Subjects: LCSH: United States—History—Sources. | United
    States—History—Textbooks.
Classification: LCC E173 .C69 2018 | DDC 973—dc23 LC record available at https://lccn.loc.
gov/2017026453

9 8 7 6 5 4 3
Printed by Sheridan Books, Inc., United States of America

TABLE OF CONTENTS

CHAPTER 5   **Forming a More Perfect Union: The Constitution
and the Bill of Rights**   *83*

CHAPTER **8**   The Upheaval of Westward Expansion   *143*

HISTORICAL CONTEXT   *143*

THE DOCUMENTS

ABOUT THE EDITORS

ELLIOTT J. GORN

Elliott J. Gorn is Joseph Gagliano Professor of History at Loyola University Chicago. After taking his bachelor's degree from UC Berkeley and PhD from Yale, he taught at Alabama, Miami of Ohio, Purdue, Brown, and the University of Helsinki. He is author of *The Manly Art: Bare-Knuckle Prize Fighting in America, Mother Jones: The Most Dangerous Woman in America*, and *Dillinger's Wild Ride: The Year that Made Public Enemy Number One*. Gorn's research has been supported by grants from the Guggenheim Foundation, the National Endowment for the Humanities, the Stanford Humanities Center and the Huntington Library. He is finishing a book about the 1955 murder of Emmett Till.

RANDY ROBERTS

Randy Roberts is Distinguished Professor of History at Purdue University. He took his bachelor's degree from Mansfield University in Pennsylvania and his PhD at Louisiana State University. He is author or co-author of ten books, including *Blood Brothers: The Fatal Friendship Between Muhammad Ali and Malcolm X, Where the Domino Fell: America and Vietnam, 1945–1990, Papa Jack: Jack Johnson and the Era of White Hopes*, and *John Wayne, American*. Roberts has won numerous teaching awards, including the Carnegie Foundation's "Professor of the Year Award" for the state of Indiana. He specializes in teaching military history, sports history, and popular culture. He has served frequently as a consultant and on-camera commentator for PBS, HBO, and the History Channel.

SUSAN SCHULTEN

Susan Schulten is professor of history at the University of Denver, where she has taught since 1996. She earned her B.A. from U.C. Berkeley and PhD from University of Pennsylvania. Schulten is the author of *Mapping the Nation: History and Cartography in Nineteenth-Century America* (www.mappingthenation.com) and *The Geographical Imagination in America, 1880– 1950*. From 2010 to 2014, she contributed regularly to the *New York Times* "Disunion" series, which commemorated the sesquicentennial of the American Civil War. Her work has been supported by the Guggenheim Foundation and the National Endowment for the Humanities. Her current project—a history of America through 100 maps—is forthcoming from the University of Chicago Press.

TERRY D. BILHARTZ

Terry Bilhartz taught at Sam Houston State University for nearly forty years. A graduate of Dallas Baptist College, he took a Master's degree from Emory University and his PhD from George Washington University, then began full-time teaching in 1977. He conducted research at Vanderbilt, Stanford, and the University of Connecticut, and in the course of his career he authored or co-authored over fifty books and articles, including *Urban Religion and the Second Great Awakening, Francis Asbury's America, Images of Texas in the Nation*, and *Sacred Words: A Source Book on the Great Religions of the World*. Terry passed away unexpectedly on December 12, 2014. He was 64. Terry was always a joy to work with, and we hope this new edition of *Constructing the American Past* continues to reflect his passion for teaching history.

INTRODUCTION

What was it like back then? What did people think and believe? What motivated them to laugh and cry, fight and die? How did people live? Were their homes comfortable? Were their workdays long? Were their diets sufficient? How did they worship, if at all? These questions and hundreds more surface instantly when historians and students ponder the past. Indeed, the question "What was it like back then?" is fundamental to any person with a sense of curiosity. It also lies at the core of the historical profession. Using a wide range of sources, historians try to "construct" what life was like in the past.

The process of construction is challenging. Since the sources needed to answer any important historical question are frequently incomplete, contradictory, or evasive, the writing of history can never be as precise as we would like. Imagine putting together a picture puzzle that is supposed to contain 1,000 pieces, but half of them have been lost. With effort and imagination, you might be able to reconstruct the general outlines of the picture. The process is roughly akin to historical inquiry. Hard work, analytical ability, and imagination—these come into play in both ventures.

Constructing the American Past asks you to become your own historian. This volume is a series of "case studies," of particular episodes or events in American history. The "Historical Context" essay that introduces each chapter sets the stage for the issues at hand. The essay is followed by a selection of primary documents, including maps, broadsides, diaries, letters, newspaper articles, trial records, memoirs, political pamphlets—the basic stuff that historians use to construct the past, the materials on which historians base their interpretations and build their narratives.

All historical sources have biases, but some are more reliable than others. The historian's task—your task—is to sort through contradictory evidence and come up with a plausible account of what happened and why. But equally important, documents come from people, and people disagree in their fundamental values and beliefs. You want to get "underneath" the sources, think about what sorts of assumptions their authors made, consider why people believed and acted as they did, and ponder why history is so frequently contested ground. Remember above all that being a historian—constructing the past—is interpretive work; history is more an art than a science.

That's what makes doing history exciting. Every historian has a story of working in an archive, feeling sleepy and bored, when something leaps off the page. Maybe a paragraph written by someone who has been dead 100 years boldly states a new idea; or a diary turns up and reveals the inner life of someone who seemed so unknowable; or an eyewitness account of clashing armies makes the battlefield come alive. Doing history can be as exciting as any act of discovery and exploration. And as you will see, *everything* has a history.

For example, we may take for granted our Bill of Rights—the first ten amendments to the Constitution, enumerating the rights of citizens—but as Chapter 5 shows, the Founders did not agree at all on the need for a Bill of Rights, let alone a new Constitution. The written rights of free speech, a free press, and free assembly had to be argued over, fought for. Another example: what was it like to be at a religious revival at the beginning of the nineteenth century? Who attended them and why? Chapter 6 on the Second Great Awakening offers eyewitness accounts and shows how religious fervor spilled over into a range of reforms, including temperance and antislavery movements. Or again, what was it like emigrating to America in 1850? Where did the immigrants come from, how did they live, and how did Americans welcome or reject them?

This eighth edition of *Constructing the American Past*, volume 1, includes our most extensive revisions to date. Chapters 7 and 12 are entirely new, designed to address the problems of immigration and emancipation, respectively. In the other chapters, significant new materials have been added. The growth of slavery and the centrality of race is now evident in chapters related to the Revolution, the Constitution, westward expansion, labor, women's experience, and the violent aftermath of the Civil War. The diversity of female experience is apparent not just in the chapter on antebellum women's voices, but in several others as well. The relationship between evangelical revivals and social reform is explored in an enlarged chapter on the Second Great Awakening, while material on the Indian policies of President Andrew Jackson complicates his reputation as a leader for the common man. In-depth coverage of Texas independence and the subsequent war with Mexico underscores the dilemmas brought by westward expansion. The new chapter on immigration explores the history of nativism, while the second new chapter on emancipation in the Civil War demonstrates the role not just of President Lincoln, but of slaves, abolitionists, and the military. Throughout the text, new images and maps have been included to provoke discussion and convey the visual dimension of the past. Above all, our goal has been to stimulate conversation and critical thinking about key issues in the American past. Note that the language in some of these documents is powerful, even offensive, but we have preserved as it originally appeared so that the sources may speak for themselves.

Since the last edition of *Constructing the American Past* was published, one of our co-editors, Terry Bilhartz, passed away. For over twenty years, the three of us worked together, edited, argued, and constructed these volumes. We miss Terry. He was a fine historian and a great collaborator. But we welcome our new co-editor, Susan Schulten of the

University of Denver. Susan has brought enormous energy and great ideas to this latest edition of *Constructing the American Past*. She truly has revitalized this project.

We have had considerable help preparing this edition. First Brian Wheel, and then Charles Cavaliere at Oxford University Press guided us through the editorial process. Katherine Schnakenberg at Oxford gave us thorough and prompt help negotiating permission to reprint primary sources from countless archives. Patricia Berube carefully supervised the final stages of editing. Three graduate students at Loyola University Chicago served as research assistants: Chelsea Denault, Hope Shannon, and Sebastian Wuepper; editorial assistance was also provided by Sam Anderson.

Several outside readers have strengthened our work. We acknowledge with gratitude the comments we received from Cindy Hahamovitch, University of Georgia, Louis Haas at Middle Tennessee State University, Damon Eubank at Cambellsville University, and two reviewers who wished to remain anonymous.

Many of the events and documents in this collection were first used in our own class-rooms. In that spirit we dedicate this collection to our students, past, present, and future, who have taught us so much about teaching.

Elliott J. Gorn
Randy Roberts
Susan Schulten
Terry D. Bilhartz

CHAPTER 1

CONTACT AND CONQUEST: THE MEETING OF OLD AND NEW WORLDS

HISTORICAL CONTEXT

On "Discovery Day" in 1892, the citizens of the United States were in a festive mood. Along parade routes, at neighborhood picnics, and in town squares, flag-waving Americans celebrated the four-hundredth anniversary of Columbus's voyage by watching soldiers, politicians, and other dignitaries march by, swaying to the music of brass bands, and applauding local leaders who extolled the exploits of the "Admiral of the Ocean Sea."

In large cities, the festivities were more elaborate. In New York, for example, the editors of the *New York Times* used hyperbole to describe the opening of the Columbian Celebration: "Young America Leads Off—First Of The Great Parades Of Columbus Week—Solid Masses Of Humanity Line The Route—The City Hidden Under Flags And Bunting." The next day, the editors wrote, "Before Two Million Eyes—The Great Parade Of War Ships And River Craft—Spectators Hide The Water Front From Sight." On the third day, the headlines screamed, "The Climax Of The Week—All Past Parade Records Sent To The Rear—Cascades Of Gay Colors Everywhere—The Avenues Packed With Vast Throngs By Sunrise And Filled To Their Utmost Capacity All Day And Night—Model Work By The Police In Handling The Greatest Crowd New-York Ever Held."

The quadricentennial parties in New York City, as spectacular as they were, could not match the size or duration of the festivities in Chicago. On October 21, 1892, Chicago's World Columbian Exposition—an event destined to attract about 40 percent of the U.S. population!—held its dedication-day ceremonies. Cardinal James Gibbons declared,

> Four hundred years ago Columbus discovered this American continent, and therefore, we are primarily indebted to him for the land which we enjoy in peace and security. Columbus united the skill and daring of a navigator with the zeal of an apostle, and in his voyage of exploration he was not only impelled by the desire of enriching his sovereign with the wealth of new dominions, but he was also inspired by the lofty ambition of carrying the light of the Gospel to a people that were buried in the darkness of idolatry. . . . Fervent

should be our gratitude since we possess the fruits of his labors and of his victory. But not for this earthly possession only should we be thankful, more for the precious boon of constitutional liberty which we inherit.[1]

Gibbons's words characterized most of the commemorations of Columbus in 1892. For millions of late–nineteenth-century Americans, hailing Columbus was synonymous with celebrating the progress of humanity, the opening of the American frontier, the triumph of Western technology, the advance of Christianity, and the spread of democratic institutions.

One hundred years later, Americans prepared for the five-hundredth anniversary of the Columbus voyage. This time, however, reflections on the era of Old and New World contact evoked different reactions. There were plenty of parades and patriotic speeches. But there were also some discordant notes. In Denver, Colorado, a scheduled Columbus Day parade was called off to prevent a clash between the marchers and Native American protesters. In Berkeley, California, the city council renamed October 12 "Indigenous People's Day" and dedicated the site of a planned Turtle Island Monument, which was to commemorate a Native American story of creation. In Columbus, Ohio (the world's largest city named for Columbus), groups of Native Americans held a memorial service in a park about two blocks from a full-scale model of the *Santa Maria*. In New York City, the National Council of Churches announced that 1992 should be a time not of celebration, but of repentance for an "invasion and colonization with legalized occupation, genocide, economic exploitation, and a deep level of institutional racism and moral decadence."

Americans in 1992 remembered an unpopular war in Vietnam, our long struggles against Jim Crow discrimination and racism, and the ugly stain of numerous "ethnic cleansings" around the world. They looked at the past differently from U.S. citizens of 1892. History itself had not changed, but assessments of its consequences surely had. With a greater sensitivity to a Native American point-of-view and to environmental concerns, more recent interpretations of history often emphasize the negative side of the Columbian exchange. Contact brought not "progress" so much as disease, starvation, and enslavement. It wreaked havoc on the cultures and environment of the western hemisphere, and it resulted in the death of tens of millions of people, most directly by diseases from which indigenous peoples had no immunity. Indeed, according to the interpretation offered by historian David E. Stannard in *American Holocaust: Columbus and the Conquest of the New World*, the "European and white American destruction of the native peoples of the Americas was the most massive act of genocide in the history of the world."

This chapter focuses on the era of initial contact between the peoples of Europe and the Americas. It was a period of discovery and disease, of exploration and exploitation, of colonization and conquest. We include excerpts from Columbus's narrative of his first voyage; from the works of Bartolomé de Las Casas, the controversial "Protector of the Indians"; and from Aztec accounts of the coming of the Spanish. The first two sources, although among the most significant texts describing the period of encounter, are both products of European minds, and they tell us as much about Old World perceptions and ambitions as they do about New World realities. Consequently, do not be too quick to accept at face value the assertions stated in the texts. Rather, question the sources thoroughly, always asking why these words were written and how much of the testimony is trustworthy. While no full narratives exist that reveal how the indigenous peoples of the Caribbean reacted to those early days of contact, other voices give us hints of how they experienced the coming of Europeans. The Aztec chroniclers left moving accounts of the clash between the two peoples.

Columbus had a simple but expensive idea: to reach the eastern world by sailing west. While European monarchs coveted the profits that could be made from finding a waterway to the Orient, most gave little consideration to Columbus's plan. They rejected his scheme, not because they believed the earth to be flat, but because their advisers told them that the earth was quite large and that to reach the East by sailing west, one would have to travel some 10,000 miles across dangerous Atlantic waters. Columbus, however, believing the earth to be much smaller than scholars estimated, insisted that Japan was only about 2,400 miles from the Canary Islands. If given the opportunity, Columbus promised not only to prove the calculations of the scholars wrong, but also to find a waterway to the riches of Asia.

Several developments worked to Columbus's advantage. In searching for a southern sea lane to India in 1488, Portuguese mariners sailed 5,000 miles down the African coastline to the tip of that continent. These explorations— while confirming the possibility of reaching the East by sailing south—also demonstrated that such a trip would be longer and costlier than had been anticipated. This discovery made a westward journey to the East appear more attractive. Furthermore, in January 1492, the Spanish Christians defeated the Moorish Muslims in Granada, thereby ending years of warfare in southern Spain. The Spaniards also banished all Jews from the land. Once freed from the expense of this costly civil war, the Spanish monarchs, Ferdinand and Isabella, now had the luxury of gambling their fortunes on Columbus's scheme. They supplied Columbus with three ships and a crew, an elaborate title, and a diplomatic passport intended to introduce him to the kings he expected to meet in the Orient. In return for this sponsorship, the Spanish Crown was to receive 90 percent of all income gained from the enterprise.

Although it was not required or even customary for Spanish sea captains at this time to keep a travel log, Columbus decided to document his historic search for the Orient. Writing for his monarchs but with an eye to history, Columbus produced a narrative of the voyage, a document that included a prologue detailing the objectives of the mission as well as daily journal entries describing the preparation of the fleet, the outward voyage, landfall, exploration, and the homeward journey. On returning to Spain, Columbus presented his narrative to Queen Isabella, who copied it, kept the original, and returned the copy to Columbus. The original was subsequently lost, and Columbus's copy passed on his death to his eldest son, and later to Luis, one of his grandsons. Although Luis had permission to publish the journal, he never did, and some scholars have been led to conclude that he sold it to subsidize his legendary debauchery. At any rate, both the original and the only known copy of Columbus's journal disappeared before the historic text could be published.

Fortunately, however, in the 1530s, Bartolomé de Las Casas came into contact with one of the copies of the journal while he was conducting research for his own *History of the Indies*. Las Casas took extensive notes from the journal, summarizing portions of it and copying other sections word for word. Las Casas's transcription, which itself was not published until 1825, is the closest we are likely to get to Columbus's original 1492–1493 narrative.

In addition to providing us with the only extant version of Columbus's journal, Las Casas also left a passionate description of the consequences of the first half-century of Spanish colonization. Las Casas became interested in the peoples of the New World at an early age. In 1493, while only eight years old, he saw Columbus parade through the streets of Seville during a triumphant tour showcasing the first voyage. Six months later, Las Casas's father and three of his uncles sailed on the second of Columbus's four transatlantic voyages. As a young teenager, Las Casas received from his father an unusual souvenir gift: a Taino boy, a servant who was subsequently freed and returned to the Indies on the order of Queen Isabella. In 1502, Las Casas made the first of what would be ten trips across the Atlantic. Initially as a *doctrinero* (or teacher of Christian doctrine to the Indians) and later as the first Roman Catholic priest ordained in the New World, Las Casas began to see the moral inequities within a colonial system that granted Spanish settlers—in return for promising to instruct the natives in Christian doctrine—the right to the fields, mines, and labor of Native American subjects. Between 1514, when Las Casas first spoke against the horrors of Spanish exploitation, and his death in 1564, he carried on a gallant if frustrating crusade for Native American rights.

While reading the following documents, rethink the meaning of the "Age of Contact and Conquest." Recreate the moment of encounter. In what ways were the Old and New Worlds and their peoples alike and different? What did the word *discovery* mean to Columbus and the subsequent colonists, and what did it mean to the Native Americans who encountered alien peoples invading their lands? Also, reflect on the consequences of the Spanish colonization efforts. How did the Spanish justify colonization, and how valid were these justifications?

INTRODUCTION TO DOCUMENTS 1 AND 2

The following are excerpts from the writings of the Spanish monarchs, Ferdinand and Isabella, and Christopher Columbus. The first document, "Privileges and Prerogatives Granted by Their Catholic Majesties," offers insights into what the Spanish monarchs expected Columbus to accomplish on his maiden voyage. The second document is taken from the prologue and journal of Columbus's first voyage, as it comes down to us from Las Casas. Recall that Columbus found land as he had anticipated, when about 2,400 miles out into the Atlantic. The people and environs he encountered, however, were not what he expected. While he anticipated the busy ports and elegantly robed subjects that had been described in the writings of Marco Polo about the Far East, he instead found naked strangers and few signs of commerce. His words suggest a bewildered man struggling to reconcile the known with the unknown. Trying to take in and report all that he sees, Columbus describes the peoples he encounters as innocent and loving, good potential Christians but also remarks how easily they might be enslaved. (Note: *Grand Khan* and *Cathay* refer to Asia.)

1. PRIVILEGES AND PREROGATIVES GRANTED BY THEIR CATHOLIC MAJESTIES TO CHRISTOPHER COLUMBUS (1492)

Image 1.1 Woodcut accompanying Christopher Columbus's 1493 letter

This woodcut depicts King Ferdinand at left, and Columbus as the little figure in the boat meeting the much larger inhabitants of Hispaniola. In much medieval and early modern art, the size of the figures in artistic renderings implied something about the relationship of the figure to God and the viewer. Often, saints and other important people were depicted as larger than commoners. What do you think this artist was implying by making the Taino Indians larger than Columbus and approximately the same size as King Ferdinand?

Source: Library of Congress.

FERDINAND and ELIZABETH, by the Grace of God, King and Queen of Castile, of Leon, of Aragon, of Sicily, of Granada, of Toledo, of Valencia, of Galicia, of Majorca, of Minorca, of Sevil, of Sardinia, of Jaen, of Algarve, of Algezira, of Gibraltar, of the Canary Islands. . . ,

For as much of you, Christopher Columbus, are going by our command, with some of our vessels and men, to discover and subdue some Islands and Continent in the ocean, and it is hoped that by God's assistance, some of the said Islands and Continent in the ocean will be discovered and conquered by your means and conduct, therefore it is but just and reasonable, that since you expose yourself to such danger to serve us, you should be rewarded for it. And we being willing to honor and favor You for the reasons aforesaid: Our will is, That you, Christopher Columbus, after discovering and conquering the said Islands and Continent in the said ocean, or any of them, shall be our Admiral of the said Islands and Continent you shall so discover and conquer; and that you be our Admiral, Vice-Roy, and Governor in them, and that for the future, you may call and style yourself, D. Christopher Columbus, and that your sons and successors in the said employment, may call themselves Dons, Admirals, Vice-Roys, and Governors of them; and that you may exercise the office of Admiral, with the charge of Vice-Roy and Governor of the said Islands and Continent, which you and your Lieutenants shall conquer, and freely decide all causes, civil and criminal, appertaining to the said employment of Admiral, Vice-Roy, and Governor, as you shall think fit in justice, and as the Admirals of our kingdoms use to do; and that you have power to punish offenders; and you

and your Lieutenants exercise the employments of Admiral, Vice-Roy, and Governor, in all things belonging to the said offices, or any of them; and that you enjoy the perquisites and salaries belonging to the said employments, and to each of them, in the same manner as the High Admiral of our kingdoms does. . . .

GIVEN at Granada, on the 30th of April, in the year of our Lord, 1492.

I, The King, I, the Queen.[2]

2. JOURNAL OF CHRISTOPHER COLUMBUS'S FIRST VOYAGE (1492)

. . . [I]n this present year of 1492, after your Highnesses had given an end to the war with the Moors who reigned in Europe, and had finished it in the very great city of Granada, where in this present year, on the second day of the month of January, by force of arms, I saw the royal banners of your Highnesses placed on the towers of Alhambra, which is the fortress of that city, and I saw the Moorish King come forth from the gates of the city and kiss the royal hands of your Highness, and of the Prince my Lord, and presently in that same month, acting on the information that I had given to your Highnesses touching the lands of India, and respecting a Prince who is called *Grand Can*, which means in our language King of Kings, how he and his ancestors had sent to Rome many times to ask for learned men of our holy faith to teach him, and how the Holy Father had never complied insomuch that many people believing in idolatries were lost by receiving doctrine of perdition: Your Highnesses, as Catholic Christians and Princes who love the holy Christian faith, and the propagation of it, and who are enemies to the sect of Mahoma and to all idolatries and heresies, resolved to send me, Cristobal Colon, to the said parts of India to see the said princes, and the cities and lands, and their disposition, with a view that they might be converted to our holy faith; and ordered that I should not go by land to the eastward, as had been customary, but that

I should go by way of the west, whither up to this day, we do not know for certain that any one has gone.

Thus, after having turned out all the Jews from all your kingdoms and lordships, in the same month of January, your Highnesses gave orders to me that with a sufficient fleet I should go to the said parts of India, and for this they made great concessions to me, and ennobled me, so that henceforward I should be called Don, and should be Chief Admiral of the Ocean Sea, perpetual Viceroy and Governor of all the islands and continents that I should discover and gain, and that I might hereafter discover and gain, and that I might hereafter discover and gain in the Ocean Sea, and that my eldest son should succeed, and so on from generation to generation for ever.

I left the city of Granada on the 12th day of May, in the same year of 1492, being Saturday, and came to the town of Palos, which is a seaport; where I equipped three vessels well suited for such service; and departed from that port, well supplied with provisions and with many sailors, on the 3[d] day of August of the same year, being Friday, half an hour before sunrise, taking the route to the islands of Canaria, belonging to your Highnesses, which are in the said Ocean Sea, that I might thence take my departure for navigating until I should arrive at the Indies, and give the letters of your Highnesses to those princes, so as to comply with my orders. As part of my duty I thought it well to write an account of all the voyage very punctually, noting from day to day all that I should do and see, and that should happen, as will be seen further on. . . .*

WEDNESDAY, 10TH OF OCTOBER

The course was W.S.W., and they went at the rate of 10 miles an hour, occasionally 12 miles, and sometimes 7. During the day and night they made 59 leagues, counted as no more than 44. Here the people could endure no longer. They complained of the length of the voyage. But the Admiral cheered them up in the best way he could, giving them good hopes of the advantages they might gain from it. He added that, however much they might complain, he had to go to the Indies, and that he would go on until he found them, with the help of our Lord.

THURSDAY, 11TH OF OCTOBER

The course was W.S.W., and there was more sea than there had been during the whole of the voyage. They saw sandpipers, and a green reed near the ship. Those of the caravel *Pinta* saw a cane and a pole, and they took up another small pole which appeared to have been worked with iron; also another bit of cane, a land-plant, and a small board. The crew of the caravel *Nina* also saw signs of land, and a small branch covered with berries. Everyone breathed afresh and rejoiced at these signs. The run until sunset was 26 leagues.

After sunset the Admiral returned to his original west course, and they went along at the rate of 12 miles an hour. Up to two hours after midnight they had gone 90 miles, equal to 22½ leagues. As the caravel *Pinta* was a better sailer, and went ahead of the Admiral, she found the land, and made the signals ordered by the Admiral. The land was first seen by a sailor named Rodrigo de Triana. But the Admiral, at ten in the previous night, being on the castle of the poop, saw a light, though it was so uncertain that he could not affirm it was land. He called Pero Gutierrez, a gentleman of the King's bedchamber, and said that there seemed to be a light, and that he should look at it. He did so, and saw it. The Admiral said the

same to Rodrigo Sanchez of Segovia, whom the King and Queen had sent with the fleet as inspector, but he could see nothing, because he was not in a place whence anything could be seen. After the Admiral had spoken he saw the light once or twice, and it was like a wax candle rising and falling. It seemed to few to be an indication of land; but the Admiral made certain that land was close. When they said the *Salve*, which all the sailors were accustomed to sing in their way, the Admiral asked and admonished the men to keep a good look-out on the forecastle, and to watch well for land; and to him who should first cry out that he saw land, he would give a silk doublet, besides the other rewards promised by the Sovereigns, which were 10,000 maravedis to him who should first see it. At two hours after midnight the land was sighted at a distance of two leagues. They shortened sail, and lay by under the mainsail without the bonnets. The vessels were hove to, waiting for daylight; and on Friday they arrived at a small island of the Lucayos, called, in the language of the Indians, *Guanahani*. Presently they saw naked people. The Admiral went on shore in the armed boat, and Martin Alonson Pinzon, and Vicente Yanez, his brother, who was captain of the *Nina*. The Admiral took the royal standard, and the captains went with two banners of the green cross, which the Admiral took in all the ships as a sign, with an F and a Y and a crown over each letter, one on one side of the cross and the other on the other. Having landed, they saw trees very green, and much water, and fruits of diverse kinds. The Admiral called to the two captains, and to the others who leaped on shore, and to Rodrigo Escovedo, secretary of the whole fleet, and to Rodrigo Sanchez of Segovia, and said that they should bear faithful testimony that he, in presence of all, had taken, as he now took, possession of the said island for the King and for the Queen, his Lords making the declarations that are required, as is more largely set forth in the testimonies which were then made in writing.

Presently many inhabitants of the island assembled. What follows is in the actual words of the Admiral in his book of the first navigation and discovery of the Indies. "I," he says, "that we might form great friendship, for I knew that they were a people

---

* Columbus at times refers to himself in the third person.

who could be more easily freed and converted to our holy faith by love than by force, gave to some of them red caps, and glass beads to put round their necks, and many other things of little value, which gave them great pleasure, and made them so much our friends that it was a marvel to see. They afterwards came to the ship's boats where we were, swimming and bringing us parrots, cotton threads in skeins, darts, and many other things; and we exchanged them for other things that we gave them, such as glass beads and small bells. In fine, they took all, and gave what they had with good will. It appeared to me to be a race of people very poor in everything. They go as naked as when their mothers bore them, and so do the women, although I did not see more than one young girl. All I saw were youths, none more than thirty years of age. They are very well made, with very handsome bodies, and very good countenances. Their hair is short and coarse, almost like the hairs of a horse's tail. They wear the hairs brought down to the eyebrows, except a few locks behind, which they wear long and never cut. They paint themselves black, and they are the colour of the Canarians, neither black nor white. Some paint themselves white, others red, and others of what colour they find. Some paint their faces, others the whole body, some only round the eyes, others only on the nose. They neither carry nor know anything of arms, for I showed them swords, and they took them by the blade and cut themselves through ignorance. They have no iron, their darts being wands without iron, some of them having a fish's tooth at the end, and others being pointed in various ways. They are all of fair stature and size, with good faces, and well made. I saw some with marks of wounds on their bodies, and I made signs to ask what it was, and they gave me to understand that people from other adjacent islands came with the intention of seizing them, and that they defended themselves. I believed, and still believe, that they come from the mainland to take them prisoners. They should be good servants and intelligent, for I observed that they quickly took in what was said to them, and I believe that they would easily be made Christians, as it appeared to me that they had no religion. I, our Lord being pleased, will take hence, at the time of my departure, six natives for your Highnesses, that they may learn to speak. I saw no beast of any kind excepts parrots, on this island.

SATURDAY, 13TH OF OCTOBER

. . . They came to the ship in small canoes, made out of the trunk of a tree like a long boat, and all of one piece, and wonderfully worked, considering the country. They are large, some of them holding 40 to 45 men, others smaller, and some only large enough to hold one man. They are propelled with a paddle like a baker's shovel, and go at a marvelous rate. If the canoe capsizes they all promptly begin to swim, and to bale it out with calabashes that they take with them. They brought skeins of cotton thread, parrots, darts, and other small things which it would be tedious to recount, and they give all in exchange for anything that may be given to them. I was attentive, and took trouble to ascertain if there was gold. . . . This island is rather large and very flat, with bright green trees, much water, and a very large lake in the centre, without any mountain, and the whole land so green that it is a pleasure to look on it. The people are very docile, and for the longing to possess our things, and not having anything to give in return, they take what they can get, and presently swim away.

SUNDAY, 14TH OF OCTOBER

At dawn I ordered the ship's boat and the boats of the caravels to be got ready, and I went along the coast of the island to the N.N.E., to see the other side, which was on the other side to the east, and also to see the villages. Presently I saw two or three, and the people all came to the shore, calling out and giving thanks to God. Some of them brought us water, others came with food, and when they saw that I did not want to land, they got into the sea, and came swimming to us. We understood that they asked us if we had come from heaven. One old man came into the boat, and others cried out, in loud voices, to all the men and women, to come and see the men who had come from heaven, and to bring them to eat at drink. Many came, including women, each bringing something, giving thanks to God, throwing themselves on the ground and shouting to us to come on shore. But I was afraid to land, seeing an extensive reef of rocks which surrounded the island, with deep water between it and the shore forming a port large enough for as many ships as there are in Christendom, but with a very narrow entrance. . . . I saw a piece of land which appeared like an island, although it is not one, and on it there were six houses. It might be converted into an island in two days, though I do not see that it would be necessary, for these people are very simple as regards the use of arms, as your Highnesses will see from the seven that I caused to be taken, to bring home and learn our language and return; unless your Highnesses should order them all to be brought to Castille, or to be kept as captives on the same island; for with fifty men they can all be subjugated and made to do what is required of them. Close to the above peninsula there are gardens of the most beautiful trees I ever saw, and with leaves as green as those of Castille in the month of April and May, and much water. I examined all that port, and afterwards I returned to the ship and made sail. I saw so many islands that I hardly knew how to determine to which I should go first. Those natives I had with me said, by signs, that there were so many that they could not be numbered, and they gave the names of more than a hundred. At last I looked out for the largest, and resolved to shape a course for it, and so I did. It will be distant five leagues from this of *San Salvador*, and the others some more, some less. All are very flat, and all are inhabited. The natives make war on each other, although these are very simple-minded and handsomely formed people.

TUESDAY, 30TH OF OCTOBER

He left the Rio de Mares and steered N.W., seeing a cape covered with palm trees to which he gave the name of *Cabo de Palmas*, after having made good 15 leagues. The Indians on board the caravel *Pinta* said that beyond that cape there was a river, and that from the river to *Cuba* it was four days' journey. The captain of the *Pinta* reported that he understood from that, that this *Cuba* was a city, and that the land was a great continent trending far to the north. The king of that country, he gathered, was at war with the Gran Can. . . . The Admiral resolved to reach the Grand Can, who he thought was here or at the city of Cathay, which belongs to him, and is very grand, as he was informed before leaving Spain.

SUNDAY, 4TH OF NOVEMBER

. . . The Admiral showed the Indians some specimens of cinnamon and pepper he had brought from Castille, and they knew it, and said, by signs, that there was plenty in the vicinity, pointing to the S.E. He also showed them gold and pearls, on which certain old men said that there was an infinite quantity

in a place called *Bohio*, and that the people wore it on their necks, ears, arms, and legs, as well as pearls. He further understood them to say that there were great ships and much merchandise, all to the S.E. He also understood that, far away, there were men with one eye, and others with dogs' noses who were cannibals, and that when they captured an enemy they beheaded him and drank his blood.

The Admiral then determined to return to the ship and wait for the return of the two men he had sent, intending to depart and seek for those lands, if his envoys brought some good news touching what he desired.

TUESDAY, 6TH OF NOVEMBER

They saw many kinds of trees, herbs, and sweet-smelling flowers; and birds of many different kinds, unlike those of Spain, except the partridges, geese, of which there are many, and singing nightingales. They saw no quadrupeds except the dogs that do not bark. The land is very fertile, and is cultivated with yams and several kinds of beans different from ours, as well as corn. There were great quantities of cotton gathered, spun, and worked up. In a single house they saw more than 500 *arrobas*, and as much as 4,000 *quintals* could be yielded every year. The Admiral said that "it did not appear to be cultivated, and that it bore all the year round. It is very fine, and has a large boll. All that was possessed by these people they gave at a very low price, and a great bundle of cotton was exchanged for the point of a needle or other trifle. They are a people, says the Admiral, guileless and unwarlike. Men and women go as naked as when their mothers bore them. It is true that the women wear a very small rag of cotton-cloth, and they are of a very good appearance, not very dark, less so than the Canarians. I hold, most serene Princes, that if devout religious persons were here, knowing the language, they would all turn Christians. I trust in our Lord that your Highnesses will resolve upon this with much diligence, to bring so many great nations within the Church, and to convert them; as you have destroyed those who would not confess the Father, the Son, and the Holy Ghost. And after your days, all of us being mortal, may your kingdoms and lordships, with the will and disposition to increase the holy Christian religion as you have done hitherto. Amen!"

"To day I got the ship afloat, and prepared to depart on Thursday, in the name of God, and to steer S.E. in search of gold and spices, and to discover land."

These are the words of the Admiral, who intended to depart on Thursday, but, the wind being contrary, he could not go until the 12th of November.[3]

INTRODUCTION TO DOCUMENTS 3 AND 4

The third document comes from a Catholic priest who dared to challenge the justice of Spanish conduct in the New World. Bartolomé de Las Casas wrote his *Very Brief Account of the Destruction of the Indies* in 1542 to be read aloud in a court called by the Holy Roman Emperor, Charles V, to consider Spanish colonial reforms. Las Casas's objective was to shock his audience with gruesome details of Spanish cruelty. His account was later translated into six European languages and was circulated widely by the enemies of Spain. The passages reprinted here were translated into English in 1589, and discussed the island of Hispaniola (modern-day Haiti and the Dominican Republic), which Columbus had earlier described in his journal. Document 4 is a map printed in Europe just at the time that Las Casas made his observations. It captures contemporary perceptions of the North American continent, and the ambitious hope of finding a passage to Asia.

3. *THE CRUELTIES OF THE SPANIARDS COMMITTED IN AMERICA* (1589)

BARTOLOMÉ DE LAS CASAS

AMERICA was discover'd and found out An. Dom. 1492 and the Year insuing inhabited by the Spaniards, and afterward a multitude of them travelled thither from Spain for the space of Nine and Forty Years. Their first attempt was on the Spanish Island, which indeed is a most fertile Soil, and at present in greatest Reputation for its Spatiousness and Length, containing in Circumference Six Hundred Miles: Nay, it is on all sides surrounded with an almost innumerable number of Islands, which we found so well peopled with Natives and Foreigners, that there is scarce any Region in the Universe fortified with so many Inhabitants: But the main Land or Continent, distant from this Island Two Hundred and Fifty Miles and upwards, extends itself above Ten Thousand Miles in Length near the Sea-shoar, which Lands are some of them already discover'd, and more may be found out in process of time. . . .

Now this infinite multitude of Men are by the Creation of God innocently simple, altogether void of and averse to all manner of Craft, Subtlety and Malice, and most Obedient and Loyal Subjects to their Native Sovereigns; and behave themselves very patiently, submissively and quietly toward the Spaniards, to whom they are subservient and subject; so that finally they live without the least thirst after revenge, laying aside all litigiousness, Commotion and hatred.

This is a most tender and effeminate people, and of so imbecile and unequal-balanced temper, that they are altogether incapable of hard labour. . . . This Nation is very Necessitous and Indigent, Masters of very slender Possessions, and consequently, neither Haughty, nor Ambitious. . . . They go naked, having no other Covering but what conceals their Pudends from publick sight. An hairy Plad, or loose Coat . . . . or a coarse woven Cloth . . . serves them for the warmest Winter Garment. They lye on a coarse Rug or Matt, and those that have the most plentiful Estate or Fortunes, the better sort, use Net-work, knotted at the four corners in lieu of Beds, which the Inhabitants of the Island of Hispaniola, in their own proper Idiom term Hammacks. . . , The Natives [are] tractable, and capable of Morality or Goodness, very apt to receive the instill'd Principles of the Catholick Religion; nor are they averse to Civility and good Manners, being not so much discompos'd by variety of Obstructions, as the rest of Mankind. . . . I myself have heard the Spaniards themselves (who dare not assume the Confidence to deny the good Nature predominant in them) declare, that there was nothing wanting in them for the acquisition of Eternal Beatitude, but the sole Knowledge and Understanding of the Deity.

The Spaniards first assaulted these innocent Sheep, so qualified by the Almighty, as is premention'd, like most cruel Tygers, Wolves and Lions hunger-starv'd, studying nothing, for the space of Forty Years, after their first Landing, but the Massacre of these Wretches, whom they have so inhumanely and barbarously butcher'd and harass'd with several kinds of Torments, never before known, or heard (of which you shall have some account in the following Discourse) that of Three Millions of Persons, which lived in Hispaniola itself, there is at present but the inconsiderable Remnant of scarce Three Hundred.

Nay the Isle of Cuba, which extends as far, as Valledolid in Spain is distant from Rome, lies now incultivated, like a Desert, and intomb'd in its own Ruins. You may also find the Isles of St. John [Puerto Rico], and Jamaica, both large and fruitful places, unpeopled and desolate. The Lucayan Islands on the North-side, adjacent to Hispaniola and Cuba, which are Sixty in number, or thereabout, together with those, vulgarly known by the name of the Gigantic Isles, and others, the most infertile whereof, exceeds the Royal Garden of Sevil in fruitfulness, a most healthful and pleasant Climat, is now laid waste and uninhabited; and whereas, when the Spaniards first arriv'd here, above Five Hundred Thousand Men dwelt in it, they are now cut off, some by slaughter, and others ravished away by Force and Violence, to work in the Mines of Hispaniola, which was destitute of Native Inhabitants. . . .

As to the firm Land, we are certainly satisfied, and assur'd, that the Spaniards by their barbarous and execrable Actions have absolutely depopulated Ten Kingdoms, of greater extent than all Spain, together with the Kingdoms of Arragon and Portugal, that is to say, above One Thousand Miles, which now lye wast and desolate, and are absolutely ruinated, when as formerly no other Country whatsoever was more populous. Nay we dare boldly affirm, that during the Forty years space, wherein they exercised their sanguinary and detestable Tyranny in these Regions, above Twelve Millions (computing Men, Women, and Children) have undeservedly perished; nor do I conceive that I should deviate from the Truth by saying that above Fifty Millions in all paid their last Debt due to Nature.

Those that arriv'd at these Islands from the remotest parts of Spain, and who pride themselves in the Name of Christians, steer'd Two courses principally, in order to the Extirpation, and Exterminating of this People from the face of the Earth. The first whereof was by raising an unjust, bloody, cruel War. The other, by putting all them to death, who hitherto, thirsted after their Liberty, or design'd (which the most Potent, Strenuous and Magnanimous Spirits intended) to recover their pristin Freedom, and shake off the Shackles of so injurious a Captivity. . . .

Now the ultimate end and scope that incited the Spaniards to endeavour the Extirpation and Desolation of this People, was Gold only; that thereby growing opulent in a short time, they might arrive at once at such Degrees and Dignities, as were no wayes consistent with their Persons.

Finally, in one word, their Ambition and Avarice, than which the heart of Man never entertained greater, and the vast Wealth of these Regions; the Humility and Patience of the Inhabitants (which made their approach to these Lands more facile and easie) did much promote the business: Whom they so despicably contemned, that they treated them (I speak of things which I was an Eye-Witness of, without the least fallacy) not as Beasts, which I cordially wished they would, but as the most abject dung and filth of the Earth; and so sollicitous they were of their Life and Soul, that the above-mentioned number of People died without understanding the true Faith or Sacraments . . . the Spaniards never received any injury from the Indians, but that they rather reverenced them as Persons descended from Heaven, until that they were compelled to take up Arms, provoked thereunto by repeated Injuries, violent Torments, and injust Butcheries.

OF THE ISLAND HISPANIOLA

In this Isle, which, as we have said, the Spaniards first attempted, the bloody slaughter and destruction of Men first began: for they violently forced away Women and Children to make them Slaves, and ill-treated them, consuming and wasting their Food . . . one individual Spaniard consumed more Victuals in one day, than would serve to maintain Three Families a Month, every one consisting of Ten Persons. Now being oppressed by such evil usage, and afflicted with such great Torments and violent Entertainment they began to understand, that such Men as these had not their Mission from Heaven; and therefore some of them conceal'd their Provisions and others their Wives and Children in lurking holes; but some, to avoid the obdurate and dreadful temper of such a Nation, sought their Refuge on the craggy tops of Mountains; for the Spaniards did not only entertain them with Cuffs, Blows, and wicked Cudgelling, but laid violent hands also on the Governours of Cities. . . . From which time they began to consider by what wayes and means they might expel the Spaniards out of their Countrey, and immediately took up Arms. But, good God, what Arms, do you imagine? Namely such, both Offensive and Defensive, as resemble Reeds wherewith Boys sport with one another, more than Manly Arms and Weapons.

Which the Spaniards no sooner perceived, but they, mounted on generous Steeds, well weapon'd with Lances and Swords, began to exercise their bloody Butcheries and Stratagems, and overrunning their Cities and Towns, spared no Age, or Sex, nay not so much as Women with Child, but ripping up their Bellies, tore them alive in pieces. They laid Wagers among themselves, who should with a Sword at one blow cut, or divide a Man in two; or which of them should decollate or behead a Man, with the greatest dexterity; nay farther, which should sheath his Sword in the Bowels of a Man with the quickest dispatch and expedition. They snatcht young Babes from the Mothers Breasts, and then dasht out the Brains of those Innocents against the Rocks; others they cast into Rivers scoffing and jeering them, and call'd upon the Bodies when falling with derision, the true testimony of their Cruelty, to come to them, and inhumanely exposing others to their Merciless Swords, together with the Mothers that gave them Life.

. . . I really believe, and am satisfied by certain undeniable conjectures, that at the very juncture of time, when all these outrages were committed in this Isle, the Indians were not so much as guilty of one single mortal sin of Commission against the Spaniards, that might deserve from any Man revenge or require satisfaction. And as for those sins, the punishment whereof God hath reserved to himself, as the immoderate desire of Revenge, Hatred, Envy or inward rancor of Spirit, to which they might be transported against such Capital Enemies as the Spaniards were, I judge that very few of them can be justly accused of them; . . . and this I can assure you, that the Indians had ever a just cause of raising War against the Spaniards, and the Spaniards on the contrary never waged a just War against them, but what was more injurious and groundless then any undertaken by the worst of Tyrants. . . .

The Warlike Engagements being over, and the Inhabitants all swept away, they divided among themselves the Young Men, Women and Children promiscuously reserved for that purpose, one obtained thirty, another forty, to this Man one hundred were disposed, to the other two hundred, and the more any one was in favor with the domineering Tyrant (whom they styled Governor) the more he became Master of, upon this pretence, and with this Proviso, that he should see them instructed in the Catholick Religion, when as they themselves to whom they were committed to be taught, and the care of their Souls intrusted to them were, for the major part Idiots, Cruel, Avaritious, infected and stained with all sorts of Vices. And this was the great care they had of them, they sent the Males to the Mines to dig and bring away the Gold, which is an intollerable Labor; but the Women they made use of to Manure and Till the ground, which is a toil most difficult even to Men of the strongest and most robust constitutions; allowing them no other food but Herbage, and such kind of unsubstantial nutriment, so that the Nursing Womens Milk was exsiccated and so dryed up, that the young Infants lately brought forth, all perished, and Females being separated from and debarred cohabitation with Men, there was no procreation. The Men died in Mines, hunger starved and oppressed with labor, and the Women perished in the Fields, harassed and broken with the like Evils and Calamities: Thus an infinite number of Inhabitants that formerly peopled this Island were exterminated and dwindled away to nothing by such Consumptions.[4]

4. SEBASTIAN MUNSTER, MAP OF THE NEW WORLD (1542)

Image 1.2 An early view of the Western Hemisphere

This is among the earliest maps of the New World, drawn by Sebastian Munster in 1542, the same year that Las Casas wrote his withering critique of Spanish treatment of the indigenous peoples. The map reflects contemporary assumptions about New World geography, particularly the belief that a large "Sea of Verrazano" cut into North America so deeply that it created a narrow isthmus that could easily be crossed on the way to Asia. Mexico City—or Tenoxtitlan as described in the Codex of Document 5—is here named "Temistitan," and mistakenly connected to the Gulf of Mexico. Munster's was perhaps the most widely known map of the New World in the early sixteenth century.

Source: Sebastian Munster, *Novae Insulae XVII Nova Tabula.* Courtesy Barry Lawrence Ruderman Antique Maps; www.raremaps.com.

There is no way to tell the story of the coming of Europeans in the words of Caribbean peoples, or those who lived in the present-day United States. Their impressions are lost to history. But written records have survived from the most powerful native group, the Aztecs. On November 8, 1519, Hernán Cortés, accompanied by 600 Spanish soldiers, as well as many indigenous allies, entered the Aztec capitol of Tenochtitlán (today, Ciudad de Mexico, Mexico City). On first seeing the city, Bernal Díaz del Castillo, one of the conquistadors, thought he must be dreaming; the temples and towers and fortresses all gleaming white were "a wonderful thing to behold." The Spaniards were greeted by Moctezuma (Montezuma), the Aztec king. Motecuhzoma believed that Cortés must be Quetzalcoatl, the god who it had been prophesied would return some day from across the waters. The following account was recorded in Nahuatl, the Aztec language, by students of the Franciscan friar Bernadino de Sahagún. Called the *Florentine Codex*, these narratives were taken down a few decades after the conquest and were based on the reminiscences of Aztecs who had lived through those events.

5. *THE AZTEC ACCOUNT OF THE SPANISH CONQUEST, FLORENTINE CODEX, AS COLLECTED BY BERNADINO DE SAHAGÚN*

[The Spaniards] had come to reach Xoloco . . . there-upon Moctezuma arrayed himself, attired himself, in order to meet them, and also a number of great lords [and] princes, his ruling men, his noblemen [arrayed themselves]. Thereupon they went to meet them. In gourd supports they set out precious flowers . . . wreaths for the head, garlands of flowers. And they bore golden necklaces, necklaces with pendants, plaited neck bands.

And already Moctezuma met them there in Uitzillan. Thereupon he gave gifts to the commandant, the commander of soldiers; he gave him flowers, he bejeweled him with necklaces, he hung garlands about him, he covered him with flowers, he wreathed his head with flowers. Thereupon he had the golden necklaces laid before him—all the kinds of gifts of greeting, with which the meeting was concluded. On some he hung necklaces.

Then [Cortes] said to Moctezuma: "Is this not thou? Art thou not he? Art thou Moctezuma?"

Moctezuma replied: "Indeed yes; I am he."

Thereupon he arose; he arose to meet him face to face. He inclined his body deeply. He drew him close. He arose firmly.

Thus he besought him: [Moctezuma] said to him: "O our lord, thou hast suffered fatigue, thou hast endured weariness. Thou hast come to arrive on earth. Thou hast come to govern thy city of Mexico; thou hast come to descend upon thy mat, upon thy seat, which for a moment I have watched for thee, which I have guarded for thee. For thy governors are departed—the rulers Itzoatl, Moctezuma the Elder, Axayacatl, Tizoc, Auitzotl, who yet a very short time ago had come to stand guard for thee, who had come to govern the city of Mexico. Under their protection thy common folk came. Do they yet perchance know it in their absence? O that one of them might witness, might marvel at what to me now hath befallen, at what I see quite in the absence of our lords. I by no means merely dream, I do not merely see in a dream, I do not see in my sleep; I do not merely dream that I see thee, that I look into thy face. I have been afflicted for some time. I have gazed at the unknown place whence thou hast come—from among the clouds, from among the mists. And so this. The rulers departed maintaining that thou wouldst come to visit thy city, that thou wouldst come to descend upon thy mat, upon thy seat. And now it hath been fulfilled; thou hast come; thou hast endured fatigue, thou hast endured weariness. Peace be with thee. Rest thyself. Visit thy palace. Rest thy body. May peace be with our lords."

. . . And when they had gone to arrive in the palace, when they had gone to enter it, at once they firmly seized Moctezuma. They continually kept him closely under observation; they never let him from their sight. With him was Itzquauhtzin. But the others just came forth [unimpeded].

And when this had come to pass, then each of the guns shot off. As if in confusion there was going off to one side, there was scattering from one's sight, a jumping in all directions. It was as if one had lost one's breath; it was as if for the time there was stupefaction, as if one were affected by mushrooms, as if something unknown were shown one. Fear prevailed. It was as if everyone had swallowed his heart. Even before it had grown dark, there was terror, there was astonishment, there was apprehension, there was a stunning of the people.

And when it dawned, thereupon were proclaimed all the things which [the Spaniards] required: white tortillas, roasted turkey hens, eggs, fresh water, wood, firewood, charcoal, earthen bowls, polished vessels, water jars, large water pitchers, cooking vessels, all manner of clay articles. This had Moctezuma indeed commanded.

But when he summoned forth the noblemen, no longer did they obey [Moctezuma]. They only grew angry. No longer did they come to him, no longer did they go to him. No longer was he heeded. But nevertheless he was not therefore neglected; he was given all that he required—food, drink, and water [and] fodder for the deer.

And when [the Spaniards] were all settled, they thereupon inquired of Moctezuma as to all the city's treasure—the devices, the shields. Much did they importune him; with great zeal they sought gold. And Moctezuma thereupon went leading the Spaniards. They went surrounding him, scattered about him; he went among them, he went in their lead; they went each holding him, each grasping him. And when they reached the storehouse, a place called Teocalco, thereupon were brought forth all the brilliant things; the quetzal feather head fan, the devices, the shields, the golden discs, the devils' necklaces, the golden nose crescents, the golden leg bands, the golden arm bands, the golden forehead bands.

Thereupon was detached the gold which was on the shields and which was on all the devices. And as all the gold was detached, at once they ignited, set fire to, applied fire to all the various precious things [which remained]. They all burned. And the gold the Spaniards formed into separate bars. And the green stone, as much as they saw to be good they took. . . . And the Spaniards walked everywhere; they went everywhere taking to pieces the hiding places, storehouses, storage places. They took all, all that they saw which they saw to be good.

. . . And afterwards [Pedro de Alvarado] thereupon inquired about the Feast of Uitzilopochtli: what sort of feast day it was. He wished to marvel at it, he wished to see what it was, how it was done. Thereupon Moctezuma commanded those of his governors who could enter. They brought forth the word.

And when the word had come forth there from where Moctezuma was enclosed, thereupon the women who had fasted for a year ground up the amaranth, the fish amaranth, there in the temple courtyard. The Spaniards came forth. They were elaborately attired in battle gear; they were arrayed for battle, arrayed as warriors. They came to [the women]: they came among them; they circled about them; they looked at each one, they looked into the faces of each of the grinding women. And when it had come to pass that they came looking at them, thereupon they entered the great palace. As was known, it was said that at the time they would have slain the men if many of us warriors had been assembled.

[The following events took place when Cortes was away from Tenochtitlan, and the Spanish soldiers were under the command of Pedro de Alvarado.]

And when the Feast of Toxcatl had arrived, toward sundown they began to give man's form to [Uitzilopochtli's amaranth seed dough image]. They formed it like a man, they gave it the look of a man, they gave it the appearance of a man. And that of which they made its body was only amaranth seed dough, a dough, a dough of fish amaranth seed. They laid it out on a framework of sticks; these were thorny sticks and sticks forming angles. . . .

And when dawn broke, when it was already the feast day, when it was early morning, already those who had made vows to him uncovered his face. Before him they formed a row; they offered him incense; before him they laid, on all sides, gifts—fasting foods, rolls of amaranth seed dough. But when this was done, not now did they take him up, not now did they lift him up to Itepeyoc. And all the men, the young seasoned warriors, were each as if diligently engaged, as if content, in proceeding with the feast, in observing the feast, in order to make the Spaniards see it, to make them wonder at it, to show it to them. . . .

And when this was happening, when already the feast was being observed, when already there was dancing, when already there was singing, when already there was song with dance, the singing resounded like waves breaking.

When it was already time, when the moment was opportune for the Spaniards to slay them, thereupon they came forth. They were arrayed for battle. They came everywhere to block each of the ways leading out [and] leading in. . . . No one could go out.

And when this had been done, thereupon they entered the temple courtyard to slay them. Those whose task it was to slay them went only afoot, each with his leather shield, some, each one, with his iron-studded shield, and each with his iron sword. Thereupon they surrounded the dancers. Thereupon they went among the drums. Then they struck the drummer's arms; they severed both his hands; then they struck his neck. Far off did his neck [and head] go to fall. Then they all pierced the people with iron lances and they struck them each with iron swords. Of some they slashed open their backs: then their entrails gushed out. Of some they cut their heads to pieces; they absolutely pulverized their heads; their heads were absolutely pulverized. And some they struck on the shoulder; they split openings, they broke openings in their bodies. Of some they struck repeatedly the shanks; of some they struck repeatedly the thighs; of some they struck the belly; then their entrails gushed forth. And when in vain one would run, he would only drag his intestines like something raw as he tried to escape. Nowhere could he go.

Image 1.3 Representations from the Florentine Codex

The Spanish massacre of the Aztecs in the main temple, Tenochtitlan.

Source: Arthur J. O. Anderson and Charles E. Dibble, translators, *Florentine Codex: General History of the Things of New Spain,* Fray Bernardino de Sahagun (School of American Research and the University of Utah, 1975).

And him who tried to go out they there struck; they stabbed him.

But some climbed the wall; they were able to escape. Some entered the *calpulli* [buildings]; there they escaped. And some escaped [the Spaniards] among [the dead]; they got in among those really dead, only by feigning to be dead. They were able to escape. But if one took a breath, if they saw him, they stabbed him.

And the blood of the brave warriors ran like water; it was as if it lay slippery. And a foul odor rose and spread from the blood. And the intestines were as if dragged out. And the Spaniards went everywhere as they searched in the *calpulli* [buildings]. Everywhere they went making thrusts as they searched, in case someone had taken refuge. They went everywhere. They went taking to pieces all places in the *calpulli* [buildings] as they searched.

And when [the massacre] became known, thereupon there was shouting: "O brave warriors, O Mexicans, hasten here! Let there be arraying—the devices, the shields, the arrows! Come! Hasten here! Already they have died, they have perished, they have been annihilated, O Mexicans, O brave warriors!" Thereupon there was an outcry, already there was shouting, there was shrieking with hands striking the lips. Quickly there was a marshaling of forces; it was as if the brave warriors each were determined; they bore the arrows and the shields with them. Thereupon there was fighting. They shot at them with arrows with barbed points, with spears, and with tridents. And they cast at them barb-pointed arrows with broad, obsidian points. It was as if a mass of deep yellow reeds spread over the Spaniards.

And the Spaniards then enclosed themselves behind the stone [walls]. And the Spaniards also shot the Mexicans with iron arrows and fired the guns at them. And then they placed Moctezuma in irons.[5]

POSTSCRIPT

The Aztecs were formidable opponents. It took the Spanish nearly two years to conquer them, as the native warriors inflicted heavy casualties and sometimes drove their enemies before them. But greed, superior technology, and the European diseases that ravaged the indigenous population finally did their work.

QUESTIONS

1. Contrast the celebrations of "Discovery Day" in 1892 and "Columbus Day" in 1992. How do you explain the differences?

2. Compare the ways Columbus and Las Casas described the environment and peoples of the New World. How do you account for the similarities and differences in their observations?

3. To what degree did religion influence Spanish exploration and colonization? How might contemporary views of geography have shaped their actions and approaches to the New World?

4. In what ways did the Spanish conquest of the New World affect the political, economic, social, agricultural, and dietary patterns of the two continents?

5. Using all three sources, retell the story of Columbus as if you were living in the Caribbean when the Spanish arrived.

6. What label—*hero, villain, victim, product of his time*, or some other term—best captures your feelings about each of the following: (a) Columbus, (b) Las Casas, and (c) Motecuhzoma? Justify your responses.

ADDITIONAL READING

An older yet still insightful and entertaining biography of Columbus is Samuel Eliot Morrison's *Admiral of the Ocean Sea* (1942). The definitive edition of the journal of the first voyage is Oliver Dunn and James E. Kelley, eds., *The Diario of Christopher Columbus's First Voyage to America, 1492–93* (1989). An interesting introduction to Las Casas, as well as a translation of his writings, is in George Sanderlin, ed., *Bartolomé de Las Casas* (1971). An excellent study that details the important biological consequences produced by the interaction of the European and Native American cultures is Alfred W. Crosby Jr.'s *The Columbian Exchange* (1972). Also of interest are the three short volumes produced for the Quincentennial by the American Historical Association: James Axtell, *Imagining the Other: First Encounters in North America* (1991); William D. Phillips Jr., *Before 1492: Christopher Columbus's Formative Years* (1992); and Karen Ordahl Kupperman, *North America and the Beginnings of European Colonization* (1992). On North America before Columbus, see Alvin M. Josephy, *America in 1492: The World of the Indian Peoples Before the Arrival of Columbus* (1992); Francis Jennings, *The Founders of America* (1993); Alice B. Kehoe, *North American Indians* (1992); Alvin M. Josephy, Jr., *500 Nations: An Illustrated History of North American Indians* (1995); and Charles C. Mann, *1491* (2005).

ENDNOTES

1. *New York Times*, October 13, 1892, p. 11.
2. Francis Newton Thorpe, *The Federal and State Constitutions, Colonial Charters, and Other Organic Laws of the States, Territories, and Colonies now or heretofore forming the United States of America* (Government Printing Office, 1909), pp. 39–40.
3. Christopher Columbus, *The Journal of Christopher Columbus (during his first voyage, 1492–93)* and documents relating to the voyages of John Cabot and Gaspar Corte Real. Translated with notes and an introduction by Clements R. Markham (London: Printed for the Hakluyt Society, 1893).
4. (Barth. De Las) Casas, Narratio, etc., "Popery truly display'd in its bloody colours" (London: Printed for R. Hewson, 1689).
5. From Arthur J. O. Anderson and Charles E. Dibble, translators, *Florentine Codex: General History of the Things of New Spain*, Fray Bernardino de Sahagun (School of American Research and the University of Utah, 1975), book 12, part 13, pp. 43–44, 47–48 49–50, 51–52, 53, 55–56.

CHAPTER 2

THE FOUNDING OF VIRGINIA AND MASSACHUSETTS BAY COLONIES

HISTORICAL CONTEXT

Historians search for clues about past events, ideas, or people, discounting some evidence to piece together a meaningful story. Occasionally the stories we tell evoke broad, enduring emotional responses. These accounts are passed forward from generation to generation and become engrained in the collective memory of a people, entering the realm of "myth." In labeling a story a myth, we are not saying that it is necessarily untrue. Rather, we simply mean that the story has become a traditional tale, shared by all members of a community, that purports to explain the origins, customs, and institutions of a people.

Stories of the early English settlements have become American myths. Most of us can recall accounts about Jamestown, the first permanent English colony in America, and Captain John Smith, the savior of the colony, who himself was saved by the pleas of the Algonquian princess Pocahontas, a beautiful maiden who later converted to Christianity and married another English settler. From childhood, we also remember stories of the Pilgrims who settled near Plymouth Rock and later joined with the local natives to give thanks for their first fall harvest. These memories, while not necessarily incorrect, are highly selective. In Virginia, for example, stories of *first* English efforts to settle the land named for the "virgin" Queen Elizabeth begin, not in Jamestown in 1607, but in the failed colonies of Roanoke (today, part of North Carolina) in the 1580s. Only after the Roanoke settlers mysteriously disappeared did Jamestown become Britain's first permanent New World colony. Moreover, as a business enterprise, Jamestown was a financial disaster that cost investors their fortunes and colonists their lives. Similarly, in New England, the inspirational stories of the Pilgrims of Plymouth are only a footnote to the much larger story of the Puritans who later settled Massachusetts Bay and left a complex legacy.

This chapter includes descriptions of life in Virginia and in Massachusetts Bay during the first half-centuries of attempted British settlement. In reading the documents written by those who participated in these historic ventures, try to identify the principal concerns of the settlers. To what degree do these descriptions correspond to your preconceived notions? How do you explain the discrepancies?

DYING AND SURVIVING IN VIRGINIA

For nearly a century following Columbus's first voyage, Spain was the dominant nation on earth. Midway into Queen Elizabeth's reign, however, the English monarch quietly gave two half-brothers, Humphrey Gilbert and Walter Raleigh, permission to establish an English settlement in any land not actually possessed by a "Christian prince." In the careful wording of this license, Elizabeth avoided directly challenging Philip II, who had claimed all of North America for Spain, but who actually possessed as his northernmost outpost only a lonely fort in Saint Augustine, Florida. The English queen did not worry herself about affronting the chieftains of the indigenous peoples of North America.

In 1583, Gilbert attempted to plant an English outpost in Newfoundland. The harsh environment there forced an early return to England for additional supplies, during which Gilbert was lost at sea. Undaunted, Raleigh sent a 1584 exploration party to find a more suitable and warmer settlement location. After this advance party under the command of Philip Amadas and Arthur Barlowe had explored the Chesapeake Bay area of North America, Raleigh sent about 100 would-be English colonists, most of whom were soldiers, to the region, now renamed "Virginia." The colonists built a fort at Roanoke Island on the Carolina Outer Banks. Within a year, this effort failed, but in 1587, a second group made up of 155 English recruits, including seventeen women and eleven children, reestablished the settlement at Roanoke. England's war against the Spanish Armada delayed the resupply of Roanoke, and when help finally arrived in 1590, the island was abandoned and the settlers had vanished.

The twice-failed venture at Roanoke demonstrated how risky and expensive colonization was. Future settlements would be undertaken not by individual promoters such as Gilbert or Raleigh, but by joint-stock companies, the forerunners of the modern-day corporation. These companies, which generally secured from the Crown special trading privileges, raised funds to support the enterprise by selling shares to investors who preferred to divide among themselves the financial risks as well as the anticipated profits. One of these joint-stock companies consisted of merchants from London, who in 1606 received from King James I rights to colonize in Virginia. After recruiting about 140 colonists, the London investors sent three ships to the Chesapeake region. In April 1607, those who survived the passage selected an encampment on a peninsula about sixty miles up a river. They chose the site, calling it "Jamestown" in honor of their king, because it had a deep-water shoreline and an abundance of trees and game, and could be readily defended from Spanish attack. Unfortunately, Jamestown lacked adequate freshwater springs, and the high ground rimming its shores made much of the peninsula a marshland—an ideal habitat for malaria-bearing mosquitoes. The Spanish never attacked, but the mosquitoes and Native Americans did. By the time a second shipment of supplies arrived in January 1608, only thirty-eight of the original group remained alive. Later English recruits swelled the population to about 500, but all save sixty of these died during the "Starving Time" of the winter of 1609–1610.

Many of the earliest settlers were gentlemen, who expected to lead rather than work, or servants and tradesmen, who were accustomed to labor but did not consider farming their line of work. Having come to Virginia with unrealistic expectations, they found the environment unfamiliar and hostile. Ill prepared and ill supplied, they quickly lost both health and spirit. The dictatorial controls of such leaders as John Smith and Sir Thomas Dale kept the colony afloat for a while, but even during the best of times, survival—not the pursuit

Image 2.1 Pomeiock Village

This drawing by John White, an English artist who accompanied Sir Walter Raleigh's party to America in 1585, depicts the typical Algonquian village of Pomeiock. Many Eastern groups of Native Americans settled in semi-permanent villages like this one, composed of domed houses made from woven mats and bark and surrounded by a defensive wooden palisade.

Source: 1585 John White, Courtesy Library of Congress

of happiness—was the only realistic goal. In the worst of times, some resorted to cannibalism in order to survive.

The colony endured largely because the stockholders back home refused to concede defeat. Although always short of the capital needed to fund the project adequately, the company kept sending new recruits in the hope of making a return on its investment. By the second decade of the venture, the great majority of the immigrants came as "indentured servants;" that is, as bound laborers who, in exchange for the price of passage, legally committed themselves to work a set number of years (generally four to seven) for their masters.

In a desperate search for profits, the stockholders in England tried many tactics. They censored colonial publications, lied about life in Virginia, and brought Pocahontas to England (and to her death!) to promote their enterprise. To encourage more migration to the colony, they recruited shiploads of unmarried English women and auctioned them off for tobacco as wives for the Virginia bachelors. To bring order to the colony, they invoked martial law, and when they deemed it to be to their financial advantage, they instituted a House of Burgesses that gave the Virginians some say in local affairs—subject, of course, to the veto of the company. However, after an Indian uprising of 1622 killed one-third of the white population in Virginia, even the most optimistic of the investors fell into despair. By 1624, when King James finally revoked the company's charter, the stockholders had lost about 100,000 pounds, an equivalent of $15 million in today's currency. Jamestown was the first permanent English colony in the New World, but it also was a death trap and a financial bust.

INTRODUCTION TO DOCUMENTS 1 AND 2

The first two documents are taken from a collection of narratives published in 1589 by Richard Hakluyt, a friend of Raleigh's colonization ventures (spelling and grammar have been modernized). Although the documents were written by Englishmen with European biases and were edited to fit the propaganda needs of Raleigh, the texts are important, for they provide us with the first view of North America before English occupation. The excerpts from Arthur Barlowe's "Narrative of the 1584 Voyage" describe the landscape and peoples of the North American seacoast at the time of contact, though Barlowe's description is as much an English fantasy of Eden as a real description of native people. The much darker selections from Thomas Harriot's *A Brief and True Report of the New Found Land of Virginia* detail sympathetic observations of the inner life and beliefs of the native peoples. What can such an account tell us about these early interactions between the English and natives? Harriot's descriptions of the mysterious epidemics that marked his travels also inform us of one of the appalling results of contact: the spread of European diseases among the aboriginal populations. Compare Harriot and Barlowe's descriptions of contact in Virginia with Columbus's initial impressions of the Caribbean. In what ways are the accounts similar and different?

1. "NARRATIVE OF THE 1584 VOYAGE"

ARTHUR BARLOWE

The first voyage made to the coasts of America, with two boats, were [by] Captains Master Philip Amadas and Master Arthur Barlowe, who discovered part of the country now called Virginia, in 1584: Written by one of the said Captains and sent to Sir Walter Raleigh, knight, at whose charge and direction the voyage was set forth.

On the 27th day of April, in the year of our redemption 1584, we departed the west of England with two boats well furnished with men and victuals. . . .

On the tenth of May we arrived at the Canaries, and on the tenth of June in this present year, we were fallen with the Islands of the West Indies. . . .

The next day there came upon us divers boats, and in one of them, the King's brother, accompanied with forty or fifty men, very handsome and goodly people, and in their behavior as mannerly and civil as any of Europe. His name was Granganimeo, and the King is called Wingina, the country Wingandacoa (and now by her Majesty, Virginia). . . .

The King is greatly obeyed, and his brothers and children reverenced. The King himself was sorely wounded in a fight which he had with the King of the next country. . . . A day or two after this, we fell to trading with them, exchanging some things that we had for chamous leather, elk and deer skins. When we showed him all our packet of merchandise, of all the things that he saw, a bright tin dish most pleased him. He presently took it up, clapt it before his breast, and afterward made a hole in the brim thereof, and hung it about his neck, making signs that it would defend him against his enemies arrows. Those people maintain a deadly and terrible war with the people and King adjoining.

[The people] are of color yellowish, and their hair black for the most, and yet we saw children that had very fine auburn and chestnut color hair. . . . No people in the world carry more respect to their King, Nobility and Governors than these do. The King's brother's wife, when she came to us, as she did many times, was always followed with forty or fifty women. . . .

The King's brother had great liking of our armor, a sword, and divers other things which we had, and offered to lay a great box of pearl in exchange for them. But we refused it for this time because we would not make them know that we esteemed it until we had understood in what places of the country the pearl grew (which now your worship does very well understand). He was very just in his promise, for many times we delivered him merchandise upon his word and always he came within the day and performed his promise. He sent us every day a brace or two of fat bucks, conies, hares, fish, the best of the world. He sent us divers kinds of fruits, melons, walnuts, cucumbers, gourds, peas, and divers roots, and fruits very excellent good, and of their country corn, which is very white, fair and well tasted and grows three times in five months. In May they sow, in July they reap; in June they sow, in August they reap; in July they sow, in September they reap. They only cast the corn into the ground, breaking a little of the soft turf with a wooden mattock or pick ax. We proved the soil and put some of our peas into the ground. In ten days they were of fourteen inches high. They have also beans very fair, of divers colors and wonderful plenty, some growing naturally and some in their gardens. And so have they both wheat and oats. . . .

The following evening we came to an island which they call Roanoke. [It was] distant from the harbor by which we entered, seven leagues. At the north end thereof, there was a village of nine houses, built of cedar and fortified round about with sharp trees to keep out their enemies. The entrance into it made it like a turnpike very artificially. When we came towards it, standing near unto the waters side, the wife of Grangyno, the King's brother, came running out to meet us very cheerfully and friendly. Her husband was not then in the village. Some of her people she commanded to draw our boat on the shore for the beating of the billow. Others she appointed to carry us on their backs to the dry ground and others to bring our oars into the house for fear of stealing. When we were come into the outer room, having five rooms in her house, she caused us to sit down by a great fire, and after took off our clothes and washed them and dried them again. Some of the women pulled off our stockings and washed them. Some washed our feet in warm water, and she herself took great pains to see all things ordered in the best manner she could, making great haste to dress some meat for us to eat. . . . We were entertained with all love and kindness, and with as much bounty, after their manner, as they could possibly devise. We found the people most gentle, loving and faithful, void of all guile and treason, and such as lived after the manner of the golden age. The earth brings forth all things in abundance as in the first creation, without toil or labor. . . .[1]

2. "A BRIEF AND TRUE REPORT OF THE NEW FOUND LAND OF VIRGINIA" (1588)

THOMAS HARRIOT

Within a few days after our departure from every . . . town, the people began to die very fast, and many in short space, in some towns about twenty, in some [forty] and in one six score, which in truth was very many in respect of their numbers. . . . The disease also so strange, that they neither knew what it was, nor how to cure it, the like by report of the oldest men in the country never happened before, time out of mind. A thing especially observed by us, as also by the natural inhabitants themselves.

Insomuch that when some of the inhabitants which were our friends, and especially the Wiroans Wingina, had observed such effects in four or five towns to follow their wicked practices, they were persuaded that it was the work of our God through our means, and that we by him might kill and slay whom we would without weapons, and not come near them. . . .

This marvelous accident in all the country wrought so strange opinions of us, that some people could not tell whether to think us gods or men, and the rather because that all the space of their sickness, there was no man of ours known to die, or that was especially sick. They noted also that we had no women amongst us, neither that we did care for any of theirs.

Some therefore were of opinion that we were not borne of women, and therefore not mortal, but that we were men of an old generation many years past, then risen again to immortality. Some would likewise seem to prophecy, that there were more of our generation yet to come, to kill theirs and take their places, as some thought the purpose was, by that which was already done.[2]

INTRODUCTION TO DOCUMENTS 3–7

The following documents depict life in Jamestown. Documents 3 and 4 were written by two of the fortunate survivors of the colony's early years: George Percy and John Smith (again, the spelling and grammar of these documents have been modernized). Percy's 1607 observations describe the tenuous relationships between the English and their Algonquian neighbors. Smith's account detail the "Starving Time" of 1609, and his cartographic representation of the colony, are presented in Documents 4 and 5. Between 1610 and 1616, the company attempted to restore order by imposing severe regulations upon the colonists. Document 6 describes these stern rules and punishments, which constitute the first English body of laws in the western hemisphere. Ask yourself why these particular rules were devised, and why the punishments were so severe. After 1617, company reforms gave more freedoms to the colonists and resulted in a rising population of English settlers. For many, however, life remained difficult. The final document in this section is a letter written in 1623 by a young indentured servant to his family back in England.

3. "DISCOURSE" (1607)

GEORGE PERCY

About four o'clock in the morning, we described [detected] the land of Virginia. The same day we entered into the Bay of Chesapeake directly, without any let or hindrance. There we landed and discovered a little way, but we could find nothing worth speaking of but fair meadows and goodly tall trees. With such fresh waters running through the woods, I was almost ravished at the first sight thereof.

At night, when we were going abroad, there came the savages creeping upon all fours from the hills like bears, with their bows in their mouths. [They] charged us [looking] very desperately in their faces, hurt Captain Gabrill Archer in both his hands and a sailor in two very dangerous places of the body. After they had spent their arrows, and felt the sharpness of our shot, they retired into the woods with a great noise. . . .

On the twenty-ninth day we set up a cross at Chesapeake Bay, and named that place Cape Henry. On the thirtieth, we came with our ships to Cape Comfort where we saw five savages running on the shore. Presently the Captain caused the shallop to be manned. Rowing to the shore, the Captain called to them in a sign of friendship, but they were at first very timorsome [fearful] until they saw the Captain lay his hand on his heart. Upon that, they laid down their bows and arrows and came very boldly to us, making signs to come ashore to their town, which is called by the savages Kecoughtan. We coasted to their town, rowing over a river running into the main. The savages swam over with their bows and arrows in their mouths.

When we came over to the other side, there were many other savages which directed us to their town where we were entertained by them very kindly. When we came first ashore, they made a doleful noise, laying their faces to the ground, scratching the earth with their nails. We thought they had been at their idolatry. When they ended their ceremonies, they went into their houses and brought out mats and laid [them] upon the ground. The chiefest of them sat all in a rank. The meanest sort brought us such dainties as they had: bread which they make of maize or guinea wheat. They would not suffer us to eat unless we sat down, which we did on a mat right against them. After we were well satisfied, they gave us of their tobacco, which they took in an artificial pipe made of earth like ours are, but far bigger, with the bowl fashioned together with a piece of fine copper. After they had feasted us, they showed us, in welcome, their manner of dancing, which was in this fashion. One of the savages was standing in the midst singing, beating one hand against another. All the rest were dancing about him, shouting, howling, and stamping against the ground with many antic tricks and faces, making noise like so many wolves or devils. One thing of them I observed: when they were in their dance, they kept stroke with their feet just one with another. But with their hands, heads, faces and bodies, every one of them had a separate gesture. They continued for the space of half an hour. When they had ended their dance, the Captain gave them beads and other trifling jewels. They hang through their ears fowls' legs. They shave the right side of their heads with a shell. On the left side they wear an ell long tied up with an artificial knot, with many fowls feathers sticking in it. They go altogether naked, but their privates are covered with beasts skins beset commonly with little bones or beasts teeth. Some paint their bodies black, some red, with artificial knots of sundry lively colors, very beautiful and pleasing to the eye, in a braver fashion than they in the West Indies. . . .

At Port Cottage in our voyage up the river, we saw a savage boy about the age of ten years with a head of hair of perfect yellow and a reasonable white skin, which is a miracle amongst all savages.[3]

4. "GREAT WAS OUR FAMINE" (1609)

JOHN SMITH

. . . As for corn, provision and contribution from the savages, we had nothing but mortal wounds, with clubs and arrows; as for our hogs, hens, goats, sheep, horse, or what lived, our commanders, officers and savages daily consumed them, some small proportions sometimes we tasted, till all was devoured; then swords, arms, pieces, or anything, we traded with the savages, whose cruel fingers were so oft imbrued in our blood, that what by their cruelty, our Governor's indiscretion, and the loss of our ships, of five hundred within six months after Captain Smith's* departure, there remained not past sixty men, women and children, most miserable and poor creatures; and those were preserved for the most part, by roots, herbs, acorns, walnuts, berries, now and then a little fish: they that had starch in these extremities, made no small use of it; yea, even the very skins of our horses. Nay, so great was our famine, that a savage we slew, and buried, the poorer sort took him up again and ate him, and so did diverse one another boiled and stewed with roots and herbs: and one amongst the rest did kill his wife, powdered [i.e., salted] her, and had eaten part of her before it was known, for which he was executed, as he well deserved; now whether she was better roasted, boiled or carbonadoed [i.e., grilled], I know not, but of such a dish as powdered wife I never heard of. This was that time, which still to this day we called the starving time; it were too vile to say, and scarce to be believed, what we endured: but the occasion was our own, for want of providence, industry, and government, and not the barrenness and defect of the country, as is generally supposed; for till then in three years, for the numbers were landed us, we had never from England provision sufficient for six months, though it seemed by the bills of loading sufficient was sent us, such a glutton is the sea, and such good fellows the mariners; we as little tasted of the great proportion sent us, as they of our want and miseries, yet notwithstanding they ever overswayed and ruled the business, though we endured all that is said, and chiefly lived on what this good country naturally afforded; yet had we been even in paradise itself with these governors, it would not have been much better with us; yet there was amongst us, who had they had the government as Captain Smith appointed, but that they could not maintain it, would surely have kept us from those extremities of miseries. This in ten days more, would have supplanted us all with death.

But God that would not this country should be unplanted, sent Sir Thomas Gates, and Sir George Sommers with one hundred and fifty people most happily preserved by the Bermudas to preserve us. . . .[4]

5. JOHN SMITH'S MAP OF VIRGINIA (1624)

This was one of the earliest and most influential maps of the Chesapeake Bay, first printed in 1612. It is oriented with north at right and west at the top, mimicking the perspective of Europeans who came from east to west and moved into the interior. Smith's map was the first accurate representation of the terrain and its features, and it was used to encourage future settlements. Ironically, the map depicts successful settlement—note for instance the monarchical seal—even though the colony of Jamestown failed to survive. Smith himself was careful to note the extent of his geographical knowledge with crosses, beyond which he relied on native sources.

---

* Note that Smith writes in the third person.

Image 2.2 John Smith's map of Virginia (1624)

Captain John Smith's map of Virginia was first published in London in 1612, depicting a settled and successful colony that was quite at odds with the reality at Jamestown.

Source: Library of Congress

6. FROM *LAWS DIVINE, MORAL AND MARTIAL* (1611)

1. First since we owe our highest and supreme duty, our greatest, and all our allegiance to him, from whom all power and authority is derived, and flows as from the first, and only fountain, and being especial soldiers impressed in this sacred cause, we must alone expect our success from him, who is only the blesser of all good attempts, the king of kings, the commander of commanders, and Lord of Hosts, I do strictly command and charge all captains and officers, of what quality or nature soever, whether commanders in the field, or in town, or towns, forts or fortresses, to have a care that the Almighty God be duly and daily served. . . .

6. Every man and woman duly twice a day upon the first tolling of the bell shall upon the working days repair unto the church, to hear divine service upon pain of losing his or her day's allowance for the first omission, for the second to be whipped, and for the third to be condemned to the galleys for six months. Likewise no man or woman shall dare to violate or break the Sabbath

by any gaming, public, or private abroad, or at home, but duly sanctify and observe the same, both himself and his family, by preparing themselves at home with private prayer, that they may be the better fitted for the public, according to the commandments of God. . . .

9. No man shall commit the horrible, and detestable sins of sodomy upon pain of death; and he or she that can be lawfully convicted of adultery shall be punished with death. No man shall ravish or force any woman, maid or Indian, or other, upon pain of death, and know the[e] that he or she, that shall commit fornication, and evident proof made thereof, for their first fault shall be whipped, for their second they shall be whipped, and for their third they shall be whipped three times a week for one month, and ask public forgiveness in the assembly of the congregation. . . .

13. No manner of person whatsoever . . . shall detract, slander, calumniate, murmur, mutiny, resist, disobey, or neglect the commandments, either of the Lord Governor, and Captain General, the Lieutenant General, the Marshal, the Council, or any authorized captain, commander or public officer, upon pain for the first time so offending to be whipped several times, and upon his knees to acknowledge his offense, with asking forgiveness upon the Sabbath day in the assembly of the congregation, and for the second time so offending to be condemned to the galley for three years: and for the third time so offending to be punished with death. . . .

15. No man of what condition soever shall barter, truck, or trade with the Indians, except he be thereunto appointed by lawful authority, upon pain of death.

16. No man shall rifle or despoil, by force or violence, take away anything from any Indian coming to trade, or otherwise, upon pain of death. . . .

20. No captain, master, mariner, or sailor, or what officer else belonging to any ship, or ships, now within our river, or hereafter which shall arrive, shall dare to bargain, exchange, barter, truck, trade, or sell, upon pain of death, unto any one landman member of this present colony, any provisions of what kind soever, above the determined valuations, and prices, set down and proclaimed, and sent therefore unto each of your several ships, to be fixed upon your main mast, to the intent that want of due notice, and ignorance in this case, be no excuse, or plea, for any one offender herein. . . .

23. No man shall embezzle, lose, or willingly break, or fraudulently take away, either spade, shovel, hatchet, axe, mattock, or other tool or instrument upon pain of whipping.

25. Every man shall have an especial and due care, to keep his house sweet and clean, as also so much of the street, as lieth before his door, and especially he shall so provide, and set his bedstead whereon he lieth, that it may stand three feet at least from the ground, as he will answer the contrary at a martial court. . . .

31. What man or woman soever, shall rob any garden, public or private, being set to weed the same, or willfully pluck up therein any root, herb, or flower, to spoil and waste or steal the same, or rob any vineyard, or gather up the grapes, or steal any ears of the corn growing, whether in the ground belonging to the same fort or town where he dwelleth, or in any other, shall be punished with death. . . .[5]

7. AN INDENTURED SERVANT DESCRIBES LIFE IN VIRGINIA IN A LETTER TO HIS PARENTS, 1623

RICHARD FRETHORNE

*L*oving and kind father and mother:
My most humble duty remembered to you, hoping in God of your good health, as I myself am at the making hereof. This is to let you understand that I your child am in a most heavy case by reason of the nature of the country, [which] is such that it causeth much sickness, [such] as the scurvy and the bloody flux and divers other diseases, which maketh the body very poor and weak. And when we are sick there is nothing to comfort us; for since I came out of the ship I never ate anything

but peas, and loblollie (that is, water gruel). As for deer or venison I never saw any since I came into this land. There is indeed some fowl, but we are not allowed to go and get it, but must work hard both early and late for a mess of water gruel and a mouthful of bread and beef. A mouthful of bread for a penny loaf must serve for four men which is most pitiful. [You would be grieved] if you did know as much as I [do], when people cry out day and night—Oh! that they were in England without their limbs—and would not care to lose any limb to be in England again, yea, though they beg from door to door. For we live in fear of the enemy every hour, yet we have had a combat with them on the Sunday before Shrovetide, and we took two alive and made slaves of them. But it was by policy, for we are in great danger; for our plantation is very weak by reason of the death and sickness of our company. For we came but twenty for the merchants, and they are half dead just; and we look every hour when two more should go. Yet there came some four other men yet to live with us, of which there is but one alive; and our Lieutenant is dead, and [also] his father and his brother. And there was some five or six of the last year's twenty, of which there is but three left, so that we are fain to get other men to plant with us; and yet we are but 32 to fight against 3,000 if they should come. . . .

And I have nothing to comfort me, nor is there nothing to be gotten here but sickness and death, except [in the event] that one had money to lay out in some things for profit. But I have nothing at all—no, not a shirt to my back but two rags (2), nor no clothes but one poor suit, nor but one pair of shoes, but one pair of stockings, but one cap, [and] but two bands. My cloak is stolen by one of my own fellows, and to his dying hour [he] would not tell me what he did with it; but some of my fellows saw him have butter and beef out of a ship, which my cloak, I doubt [not], paid for. So that I have not a penny, not a penny worth, to help me to either spice or sugar or strong waters, without the which one cannot live here. . . . I do protest unto you that I have eaten more in [one] day at home than I have allowed me here for a week. . . .

And [I] saith that if you love me you will redeem me suddenly, for which I do entreat and beg. And if you cannot get the merchants to redeem me for some little money, then for God's sake get a gathering or entreat some good folks to lay out some little sum of money in meal and cheese and butter and beef. Any eating meat will yield great profit. Oil and vinegar is very good; but, father, there is great loss in leaking. But for God's sake send beef and cheese and butter, or the more of one sort and none of another. . . . And look whatsoever you send me—be it never so much—look, what[ever] I make of it, I will deal truly with you. I will send it over and beg the profit to redeem me; and if I die before it come, I have entreated Goodman Jackson to send you the worth of it, who hath promised he will. . . . Good father, do not forget me, but have mercy and pity my miserable case. I know if you did but see me, you would weep to see me. . . . Wherefore, for God's sake, pity me. I pray you to remember my love to all my friends and kindred. I hope all my brothers and sisters are in good health, and as for my part I have set down my resolution that certainly will be; that is, that the answer of this letter will be life or death to me. Therefore, good father, send as soon as you can; and if you send me anything let this be the mark.[6]

INTRODUCTION TO DOCUMENTS 8, 9, AND 10

Jamestown's early struggles finally came to an end, and the two essential ingredients were tobacco and slaves. Before too many years, England developed an insatiable appetite for Virginia tobacco. But who would cultivate it? The horrific mortality in early Jamestown, the unwillingness of "gentlemen" colonists to work hard, the tribulations of indentured servants like Richard Frethorne made for an unreliable labor force. A fortuitous solution presented itself. In 1620, colonist John Rolfe wrote to Edwin Sandys, treasurer of the Virginia Company, that a Dutch man-of-war (an armed boat) left off twenty Negroes in Jamestown in exchange for resupplying the ship. The Africans' precise legal status was unclear, but by the 1660s and probably before, blacks and their descendants were mostly slaves for life. What do documents 8, 9 and 10 tell us about who would and would not be a slave? Why did the first law specify that bondage of a child would be determined "according to the condition of the mother?" How does religion figure in? What do the laws tell us about sex? About power? About violence? Once again, the spelling has been modernized.

---

8. "NEGRO WOMEN'S CHILDREN TO SERVE ACCORDING TO THE CONDITION OF THE MOTHER" (DECEMBER 1662)

AN ACT BY THE VIRGINIA GENERAL ASSEMBLY

WHEREAS some doubts have arisen whether children got by any Englishman upon a negro woman should be slave or free, *Be it therefore enacted and declared by this present grand assembly*, that all children born in this country shall be held bond or free only according to the condition of the mother, *And* that if any Christian shall commit fornication with a negro man or woman, he or she so offending shall pay double the fines imposed by the former act.[7]

9. "AN ACT DECLARING THAT THE BAPTISM OF SLAVES DOTH NOT EXEMPT THEM FROM BONDAGE" (SEPTEMBER 1667)

VIRGINIA GENERAL ASSEMBLY

WHEREAS some doubts have risen whether children that are slaves by birth, and by the charity and piety of their owners made partakers of the blessed sacrament of baptism, should by virtue of their baptism be made free; *It is enacted and declared by this grand assembly, and the authority thereof,* that the conferring of baptism doth not alter the condition of the person as to his bondage or freedom; that divers masters, freed from this doubt, may more carefully endeavor the propagation of Christianity by permitting children, though slaves, or those of greater growth if capable to be admitted to that sacrament.[8]

10. "AN ACT CONCERNING SERVANTS AND SLAVES" (OCTOBER 1705)

VIRGINIA GENERAL ASSEMBLY

. . . And if any slave resist his master, or owner, or other person, by his or her order, correcting such slave, and shall happen to be killed in such correction, it shall not be accounted felony; but the master, owner, and every such other person so giving correction, shall be free and acquit of all punishment and accusation for the same, as if such incident had never happened: And also, if any negro, mulatto, or Indian, bond or free, shall at any time, lift his or her hand, in opposition against any Christian, not being negro, mulatto, or Indian, he or she so offending shall, for every such offence, proved by the oath of the party, receive on his or her bare back, thirty lashes, well laid on; cognizable by a justice of the peace for that county wherein such offence shall be committed.[9]

THE PURITANS OF MASSACHUSETTS BAY

Six hundred miles up the coast from Jamestown was the region affectionately dubbed "New England" by Captain John Smith. Many of the early migrants to this area came for religious purposes. The first English subjects to settle there were the famous "Pilgrims," labeled such because of their pilgrimages in search of a place where they could practice their distinct form of Christianity. After denouncing the Church of England as an ungodly institution, these future Pilgrims were harassed by Anglicans in their hometown of Scrooby, England, and sought refuge abroad. In 1607, they sailed for Leyden, Holland, where they lived for about a dozen years until a group of merchants from Plymouth, England, offered them a deal. The Plymouth merchants, holding a charter from James I that allowed them to establish a commercial enterprise similar to the Jamestown venture, promised to transport these "Puritan Separatists" to America in return for their labor. An agreement was reached, the *Mayflower* sailed, and shortly before Christmas 1620, the Pilgrims landed near a rock named after the city of their sponsors.

A decade after the settlement of Plymouth, a second, larger wave of Puritan immigrants arrived in New England. Like the Pilgrims, the Massachusetts Bay Puritans disliked the theology, government, and lack of discipline within the Church of England. Unlike the Separatist Pilgrims, however, these Puritans believed that the Anglican Church was still God's church and could be purified. When political circumstances in England frustrated their attempts at reform, Puritan leaders devised an ambitious plan to establish a model "Christian commonwealth" in Massachusetts Bay. Confident that it was the nature of God to punish sin and reward obedience, these Non-Separatist Puritans hoped to save their church and nation from impending calamity by setting an example for Old England to imitate.

For these visionaries, the New World was a New Canaan, and they were God's chosen people sent on an errand into the wilderness. Their goal was not worldly success but the establishment of a colony dedicated to the glory of God. (Of course, there was a contradiction here—wouldn't God smile on such a Commonwealth, and wouldn't God's people prosper, and wouldn't that very prosperity become a problem?) Creating a Godly commonwealth was not easy. Maintaining it was even harder. The seriousness of the Puritan's mission encouraged them to suppress dissent, to limit voting rights to church members, to punish moral laxity among both believers and nonbelievers, to demand hard labor from everyone, and to prevent extravagance. Nonetheless, the Puritans were not simply "puritanical" prigs. For instance, they did not prohibit seasonal times of feasting and merriment or condemn the drinking of beer or wine in moderation. They also rejected the doctrine that sex was intended solely for procreation. Rather, they viewed sex within marriage as a gift from God to be enjoyed. They discouraged all extramarital affairs—punishing severely adulterous and homosexual relationships—but they treated premarital sex, which was common, with considerable leniency. They also permitted divorces for those whose spouses were impotent, too long absent, or cruel.

If not repressed zealots, they were not flawless citizens or compassionate neighbors either. Holding fast to the Calvinistic doctrine that all humans were sinful and deserved damnation but that God in His mercy had "predestined" some for salvation, the Puritans relegated the non-elect to a subordinate status on earth and to eternal affliction in hell. They also viewed their Native American neighbors as cultural inferiors, assuming them to be the descendants of one of the Ten Lost Tribes of Israel, whose original white skin coloring had been darkened naturally by the sun and unnaturally by degenerate customs. This interpretation encouraged Puritan missionaries to translate the Bible into the Algonquian language and to seek Christian converts among the natives. New England missionaries won fewer Indians to Christianity than the Jesuits did in New France, largely because the Puritans held high and rigid standards that included a knowledge of complex theological issues and a prescribed conversion experience.

Despite their concern about the salvation of the Algonquian peoples, at times the Puritans turned violently against their neighbors. A deadly confrontation erupted in 1675 between the Wampanoag chieftain Metacomet (known among the Puritans as King Philip) and the descendants of the Plymouth Pilgrims. The ensuing struggle, dubbed by the English "King Philip's War," had a devastating impact on the region's population and morale. Within two years, nearly 10 percent of the adult white male and 30 percent of the Native American population had died in the fighting or from the disease and starvation that followed.

King Philip's War forced the Puritans to reexamine themselves and their mission. In the first half-century of settlement, New England had prospered in many ways. Virtually everyone in the region could read and write, an achievement unequaled by other seventeenth-century cultures. The average adult life expectancy in New England was about sixty-five years, more than ten years longer than in Old England and twenty years longer than in Virginia. Longer life meant more working years and the potential for more money; it meant longer marriages and more children. But for Puritans on a holy mission, prosperity had its drawbacks. From the outset, non-Puritans who came to New England for commercial reasons threatened the religious values of the founders. With the passing years, these enterprising emigrants were joined by increasing numbers of second- and third-generation New Englanders who also preferred pursuing earthly rather than heavenly treasures. For the pious remnant, the alarming drop in church membership and the disconcerting tendency to place economic gain above community concerns were signs of spiritual declension.

In the latter decades of the seventeenth century, Puritan preachers railed against the waning piety of their times and called the people to public and private repentance. Meanwhile, political troubles in England compounded their anxieties. In 1684, Charles II revoked the charter of Massachusetts Bay. In 1691, the English Crown assumed the role of appointing the governor of the colony and forced Massachusetts to drop the religious qualification for the right to vote in colonial elections. With power now in the hands of the Crown and colonial merchants, concerned Puritans could not help but wonder if their misfortunes were punishments from God. Had He forsaken the people of New England? Had they, builders of a prosperous colony mightily concerned with success, forsaken God? Was there still hope for their redemption?

The following documents touch on a variety of topics, including the original purpose of the colony; community and family life in New England; and Puritan–Indian conflicts. As you read each selection, try to identify both the changing and the unchanging elements within the Puritan experience. What was it that united and divided the people of Massachusetts Bay? To what did they give their highest allegiance, family, religion, business, education, township, colony, country? And how did they react when what they valued was threatened? In probing these facets of the New England mind and soul, you may discover that the mysterious world of the seventeenth century is not so foreign to us after all.

INTRODUCTION TO DOCUMENT 11

In 1630, while aboard the flagship *Arbella*, Governor John Winthrop wrote and delivered "A Model of Christian Charity." Although the document reads like a Puritan sermon, Winthrop was not a minister, and his intent was not simply to present a Sabbath day religious homily. Rather, as Governor of Massachusetts Bay, Winthrop took the occasion to articulate the hopes, fears, and dreams of the colony's organizers. His speech was an elaborate statement about how people must act, socially and economically, for the colony to succeed. What is the essence of Winthrop's message? In particular, what was his attitude toward the prospects of success—both individual and collective—in Massachusetts Bay?

11. "A MODEL OF CHRISTIAN CHARITY" (1630)

JOHN WINTHROP

God Almighty, in his most holy and wise providence, hath so disposed of the condition of mankind, as in all times some must be rich, some poor, some high and eminent in power and dignity, others mean and in subjection.

THE REASON HEREOF

First, to hold conformity with the rest of his works. Being delighted to show forth the glory of his wisdom in the variety and difference of the creatures. . . .

Secondly, that he might have the more occasion to manifest the work of his Spirit. First, upon the wicked, in moderating and restraining them: so that the rich and mighty should not eat up the poor, nor the poor and despised rise up against their superiors and shake off their yoke. Secondly, in the regenerate, in exercising his graces in them: as in the great ones, their love, mercy, gentleness, temperance etc.; in the poor and inferior sort, their faith, patience, obedience etc.

Thirdly, that every man might have need of other, and from hence they might be all knit more nearly together in the bond of brotherly affection. From hence it appears plainly that no man is made more honorable than another, or more wealthy etc., out of any particular and singular respect to himself, but for the glory of his creator and the common good of the creature, man. . . .

QUESTION: What rule must we observe in lending?
ANSWER: Thou must observe whether thy brother hath present or probable or possible means of repaying thee; if there be none of these, thou must give him according to his necessity, rather than lend him as he requires. If he hath present means of repaying thee, thou art to look at him, not as an act of mercy, but by way of commerce, wherein thou art to walk by the rule of Justice. But if his means of repaying thee be only probable or possible, then is he an object of thy mercy—thou must lend him, though there be danger of losing it.

QUESTION: What rule must we observe in forgiving?
ANSWER: Whether thou didst lend by way of commerce or in mercy, if he have nothing to pay thee [thou] must forgive him. . . .

Thus stands the cause between God and us. We are entered into covenant with him for this work, we have taken out a commission, the Lord hath given us leave to draw our own articles, we have professed to enterprise these actions, upon these and those ends, we have hereupon besought him of favor and blessing. Now if the Lord shall please to hear us, and bring us in peace to the place we desire, then hath he ratified this covenant and sealed our commission, [and] will expect a strict performance of the articles contained in it. But if we shall neglect the observation of these articles, which are the ends we have propounded, and, dissembling with our God, shall fall to embrace this present world and prosecute our carnal intentions, seeking great things for ourselves and our posterity, the Lord will surely break out in wrath against us, be revenged of such a perjured people and make us know the price of the breach of such a covenant.

Now the only way to avoid this shipwreck, and to provide for our posterity, is to follow the counsel of Micah: to do justly, to love mercy, to walk humbly with our God. For this end, we must be knit together in this work as one man, we must entertain each other in brotherly affection, we must be willing to abridge ourselves of our superfluities, for the supply of others' necessities, we must uphold a familiar commerce together in all meekness, gentleness, patience and liberality; we must delight in each other, make others' conditions our own, rejoice together, mourn together, labor and suffer together, always having before our eyes our commission and community in the work, our community as members of the same body. So shall we keep the unity of the spirit in the bond of peace. The Lord will be our God, and delight to dwell among us as his own people, and will command a blessing upon us in all our ways, so that we shall see much more of his wisdom, power, goodness and truth, than formerly we have been acquainted with. We shall find that the God of Israel is among us, when ten of us shall be able to resist a thousand of our enemies; when he shall make us a praise and glory that men shall say of succeeding plantations: "the Lord make it like that of New England." For we must consider that we shall be as a city upon a hill: The eyes of all people are upon us, so that if we shall deal falsely with our God in this work we have undertaken, and so cause him to withdraw his present help from us, we shall be made a story and a by-word through the world: we shall open the mouths of enemies to speak evil of the ways of God and all professors for God's sake. We shall shame the faces of many of God's worthy servants, and cause their prayers to be turned into curses upon us, till we be consumed out of the good land whither we are going.

INTRODUCTION TO DOCUMENTS 12 AND 13

Notwithstanding Winthrop's call for Christian unity, not all settlers to Massachusetts embraced either his mission or methods. The following documents express the opinions of two of Winthrop's adversaries, Anne Hutchinson and Robert Keayne. Hutchinson was a pious Puritan woman who accused the colonial ministers of teaching that one can get to heaven by doing good works. Puritans rejected this teaching, insisting that salvation comes from grace through faith, not through good works. For accusing the ministers of this false teaching, Hutchinson was brought to court and tried for sedition in 1637. Document 12 contains some excerpts from her trial. How did Hutchinson defend her understanding of divine truth, and why was she banished from Massachusetts?

Document 13 contains excerpts from the last will and testament of the eminently successful New England merchant Robert Keayne. Throughout his career, Keayne was hounded by Puritan authorities, who claimed that he had secured his wealth by corrupt practices, which included lending money for excessive interest, selling goods at rates determined by market factors, and pursuing his own self-interest rather than the common good of the community. For these practices, Keayne was brought before the court and fined £200. In the following passages, Keayne defends himself against the charges of price-gouging and of failing to support the common good. Compare Keayne's defense with Winthrop's address to the Puritans aboard the *Arabella*. Do you think Keayne's capitalistic business practices and Winthrop's Puritan mission were compatible? Did Keayne threaten the colony in the same way that Hutchinson did?

12. EXCERPTS FROM THE TRIAL OF ANNE HUTCHINSON (NOVEMBER 1637)

Mr. Winthrop, governor: Mrs. Hutchinson, you are called here as one of those that have troubled the peace of the commonwealth and the churches here; you are known to be a woman that hath had a great share in the promoting and divulging of those opinions that are causes of this trouble, and to be nearly joined not only in affinity and affection with some of those the court had taken notice of and passed censure upon, but you have spoken divers things as we have been informed very prejudicial to the honour of the churches and ministers thereof, and you have maintained a meeting and an assembly in your house that hath been condemned by the general assembly as a thing not tolerable nor comely in the sight of God nor fitting for your sex. . . .

MRS. HUTCHINSON: If you please to give me leave I shall give you the ground of what I know to be true. Being much troubled to see the falseness of the constitution of the church of England, I had like to have turned separatist; where-upon I kept a day of solemn humiliation and pondering of the things; this scripture was brought upon me—he that denies Jesus Christ to be come in the flesh is the antichrist—This I considered of and in considering found that the papists did not deny him to be come in the flesh, nor we did not deny him—who then was antichrist? Was the Turk antichrist only? The Lord knows that I could not open scripture; he must by his prophetical office open it unto me. So after that being unsatisfied in the things, the Lord was pleased to bring this scripture out of the Hebrews. He that denies the testa-ment denies the testator, and in this did open unto me and give me to see that those which did not teach the new covenant had the spirit of antichrist, and upon this he did discover the ministry unto me and ever since, I bless the Lord, he hath let me see which was the clear ministry and which the wrong. Since that time I confess I have been more choice and he hath left me to distinguish between the voice of my beloved and the voice of Moses, the voice of John Baptist and the voice of the antichrist, for all those voices are spoken of in scripture. Now if you do condemn me for speaking what in my conscience I know to be truth I must commit myself unto the Lord.

MR. NOWEL: How do you know that that was the spirit?

MRS. HUTCHINSON: How did Abraham know that it was God that bid him offer his son, being a breach of the sixth commandment?

DEP. GOV: By an immediate voice.

MRS. HUTCHINSON: So to me by an immediate revelation.

DEP. GOV: How! an immediate revelation.

MRS. HUTCHINSON: By the voice of his own spirit to my soul. . . . You have power over my body but the Lord Jesus hath power over my body and soul, and assure yourselves thus much, you do as much as in you lies to put the Lord Jesus Christ from you, and if you go on in this course you begin you will bring a curse upon you and your posterity, and the mouth of the Lord hath spoken it.

After more testimony, the court rendered its verdict.

GOVERNOR: Mrs. Hutchinson, the sentence of the court you hear is that you are banished from out of our jurisdiction as being a woman not fit for our society, and are to be imprisoned till the court shall send you away.

MRS. HUTCHINSON: I desire to know wherefore I am banished?

GOVERNOR: Say no more, the court knows wherefore and is satisfied.[10]

13. FROM *THE APOLOGIA OF ROBERT KEAYNE* (1653)

[My attempts] to promote the good of this place have been answered by diverse herewith unchristian, un-charitable and unjust reproaches and slanders since I came hither, as if men had the liberty of their tongues to reproach any that were not beneficial to them, . . . as if no punishment had been sufficient to expiate my offense, for selling a good bridle for 2s[hillings] that now worse are sold without offense for 3 . . . and so in all other things proportionably as selling gold buttons for two shilling nine pence a dozen that cost above 2 in London and yet were never paid for them that complained. These were the great matters in which I had offended, when my self have often seen and heard offenses, complaints and crimes of a high nature against God and men such as filthy uncleanness, fornications, drunkenness, fearful oaths, quarreling, mutinous Sabbath breakings thefts, forgeries, and such like which hath passed with fines or censures so small or easy as hath not been worth the naming or regarding.

I did submit to the censure, I paid the fine to the uttermost, which is not nor hath been done by many (nor so earnestly required as mine was) though for certain and not supposed offenses of far higher nature which I can make good not by hearsay only but in my own knowledge. Yea offenses of the same kind and which was so greatly aggravated and with such indignation pursued by some, as if no censure could be too great or too severe, as if I had not been worthy to have lived upon the earth . . . are not only now common almost in every shop and warehouse but even then and ever since with a higher measure of excess, yea even by some of them that were most zealous and had their hands and tongues deepest in my censure,

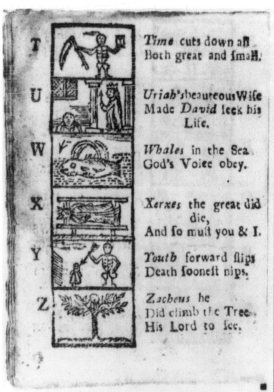

Image 2.3 Illustrated alphabet from the *New England Primer*, 1721

The Puritans believed that the word of God must come to each individual by reading the Bible, so they considered literacy essential. *"The New England Primer,"* with its didactic style and moral lessons, was the main textbook for children. This page is from the 1721 edition, though it was first published in the 1690s.

Source: Library of Congress

since of buyers which they were then, they are turned sellers and peddling merchants themselves so that they are become no offenses now nor worthy questioning nor taking notice of in others. Yea contrary to their own promises instead of gains there was apparent loss without any gains to the seller, and the oppression lay justly and truly on the buyer's hand rather than on the seller, but then the country being all buyers and few sellers though it would not be seen on that side then, for if the lion will say the lamb is a fox, it must be so, the lamb must be content to leave it. . . . Yet I have borne this patiently and without disturbance or troubling the Court with any petitions for remission or abatement of the fine, . . . because the more innocently that I suffer, the more patiently have I borne it, leaving my cause therein to the Lord. [In the end, Keane suggested if the Court chose to rescind his fine, that the money be given to Harvard College or to some "other more good or public use or service."][11]

INTRODUCTION TO DOCUMENT 14

The most popular literary genre of late colonial times was the captivity narrative, accounts of whites being taken by Native Americans. The first and perhaps the best of the Puritan captivity narratives was written by Mary Rowlandson, the wife of a clergyman who was captured during King Philip's War. Published in 1682, it sold quickly and went through some thirty future editions, preparing the way for many other captivity stories, which also became the bestsellers of their day. This narrative was popular in part because it was a thrilling personal-adventure story placed in an exotic context. But for the Puritans, it was also a religious epic that described how God had punished but not forgotten His people. The personal story of Rowlandson was in microcosm the story of all Puritans whom God tested then redeemed. While offering some insights into the culture of the Algonquians, these selections from Rowlandson's *The Sovereignty and Goodness of God* reveal even more about the New England mind and the tensions within a conflicted Puritan society.

14. FROM *THE SOVEREIGNTY AND GOODNESS OF GOD* (1682)

MARY ROWLANDSON

Now is that dreadful hour come that I have often heard of (in time of war as it was the case of others), but now mine eyes see it. Some in our house were fighting for their lives, others wallowing in their blood, the house on fire over our heads, and the bloody heathen ready to knock us on the head if we stirred out. Now might we hear mothers and children crying out for themselves and one another, "Lord, what shall we do?" Then I took my children (and one of my sisters, hers) to go forth and leave the house, but as soon as we came to the door and appeared, the Indians shot so thick that the bullets rattled against the house as if one had taken an handful of stones and threw them so that we were fain to give back. We had six stout dogs belonging to our garrison, but none of them would stir although another time, if any Indian had come to the door, they were ready to fly upon him and tear him down. The Lord hereby would make us the more to acknowledge His hand and to see that our help is always in Him. But out we must go, the fire increasing and coming along behind us roaring, and the Indians gaping before us with their guns, spears, and hatchets to devour us. No sooner were we out of the house, but my brother-in-law [John Divoll] (being before wounded, in defending the house, in or near the throat) fell down dead; whereat the Indians scornfully shouted, halloed, and were presently upon him, stripping off his clothes. The bullets flying thick, one went through my side, and the same (as would seem) through the bowels and hand of my dear child in my arms. One of my elder sister's children, named William [Kerley], had then his leg broken, which the Indians perceiving, they knocked him on the head. Thus were we butchered by those merciless heathen, standing amazed, with the blood running down to our heels.

. . . The Indians laid hold of us, pulling me one way and the children another, and said, "Come go along with us." I told them they would kill me. They answered, if I were willing to go along with them they would not hurt me.

Oh, the doleful sight that now was to behold at this house! "Come, behold the works of the Lord, what desolation He has made in the earth." Of thirty-seven persons who were in this one house none escaped either present death or a bitter captivity save only one, who might say as he, Job 1:15, "And I only am escaped alone to tell the news." There were twelve killed, some shot, some stabbed with their spears, some knocked down with their hatchets. When we are in prosperity, oh, the little that we think of such dreadful sights, and to see our dear friends and relations lie bleeding out their heart-blood upon the ground! There was one who was chopped into the head with a hatchet and stripped naked, and yet was crawling up and down. It is a solemn sight to see so many Christians lying in their blood, some here and some there, like a company of sheep torn by wolves, all of them stripped naked by a company of hellhounds, roaring, singing, ranting and insulting, as if they would have torn our very hearts out. Yet the Lord by his almighty power preserved a number of us from death, for there were twenty-four of us taken alive and carried captive.

I had often before this said that if the Indians should come I should choose rather to be killed by them than taken alive, but when it came to the trial, my mind changed; their glittering weapons so daunted my spirit that I chose rather to go along with those (as I may say) ravenous beasts than that moment to end my days.

Thus nine days I sat upon my knees with my babe in my lap till my flesh was raw again; my child being even ready to depart this sorrowful world, they bade me carry it out to another wigwam (I suppose because they would not be troubled with such spectacles), whither I went with a heavy heart, and down I sat with the picture of death in my lap. About two hours in the night my sweet babe like a lamb departed this life on Feb. 18, 1675, it being about six years and five months old. It was nine days from the first wounding in this miserable condition without any refreshing of one nature or other except a little cold water. I cannot but take notice how at another time I could not bear to be in the room where any dead person was, but now the case is changed; I must and could lie down by my dead babe side by side all the night after. I have thought since of the wonderful goodness of God to me in preserving me in the use of my reason and senses in that distressed time that I did not use wicked and violent means to end my own miserable life. . . .

In my travels an Indian came to me and told me if I were willing, he and his squaw would run away and go home along with me. I told him no. I was not willing to run away but desired to wait God's time that I might go home quietly and without fear. And now God hath granted me my desire. O, the wonderful power of God that I have seen and the experience that I have had! I have been in the midst of those roaring lions and savage bears that feared neither God nor man nor the devil, by night and day, alone and in company, sleeping all sorts together, and yet not one of them ever offered me the least abuse of unchastity to me in word or action. Though some are ready to say I speak it for my own credit, I speak it in the presence of God and to His glory. God's power is as great now and as sufficient to save as when He preserved Daniel in the lion's den or the three children in the fiery furnace. I may well say as his Psal. 107:12, "Oh, give thanks unto the Lord for He is good, for His mercy endureth forever." Let the redeemed of the Lord say so whom He hath redeemed from the hand of the enemy, especially that I should come away in the midst of so many hundreds of enemies quietly and peaceably and not a dog moving his tongue. . . .

Now I see the Lord had His time to scourge and chasten me. The portion of some is to have their afflictions by drops, now one drop and then another, but the dregs of the cup, the wine of astonishment, like a sweeping rain that leaveth no food, did the Lord prepare to be my portion. Affliction I wanted and affliction I had, full measure (I thought) pressed down and running over. Yet I see when God calls a person to anything and through never so many difficulties, yet He is fully able to carry them through and make them see and say they have been gainers thereby. And I hope I can say in some measure, as David did, "It is good for me that I have been afflicted."[12]

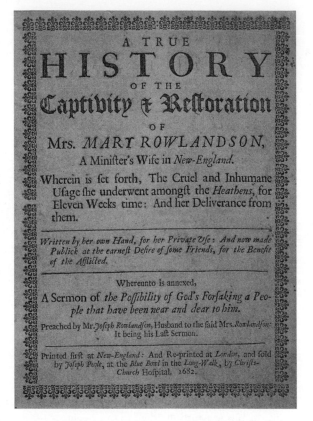

Image 2.4 From Mary Rowlandson's captivity narrative (1682)

How do you explain the wide and enduring appeal of Rowlandson's captivity narrative? What does the cover here reveal about Rowlandson's intent in writing it, and the document's contemporary use among readers?

Source: Courtesy University of Pennsylvania Special Collections Library.

QUESTIONS

1. Compare the motivations for establishing Virginia and Massachusetts Bay. Do the outcomes reflect these differences?
2. Compare the descriptions of Native Americans in the writings of Rowlandson, Columbus, Las Casas, Barlowe, and Percy. How do you explain the similarities and the differences?
3. Do the rules instituted at Jamestown in 1611 resemble the kind of order that Winthrop hoped to establish in Massachusetts Bay?
4. Were Jamestown and Massachusetts Bay successful colonies? Explain your answer.
5. Both Keane and Hutchinson were singled out for their deviant behavior in Massachusetts Bay. Why were they understood to pose such a threat to the viability of the colony?

ADDITIONAL READING

David B. Quinn and Alison M. Quinn's *The First Colonists* (1982) and Karen Ordahl Kupperman's *Captain John Smith* (1988) provide excellent introductions to the writings of some of the most colorful figures in early Virginia. An often-asked question is addressed in J. A. Leo Lemay's *Did Pocahontas Save Captain John Smith?* (1992). Other interesting studies discussing race relations in Virginia include Ben C. McCary, *Indians in Seventeenth Century Virginia* (1992); Kathleen M. Brown, *Good Wives, Nasty Wenches, Anxious Patriarchs* (1996); and Hugh Thomas, *The Slave Trade* (1997). An excellent introduction to the study of Winthrop and New England Puritanism is Edmund S. Morgan's *The Puritan Dilemma: The Story of John Winthrop* (1985). Other insightful examinations into Puritan culture include Harry S. Stout, *The New England Soul: Preaching and Religious Culture* (1986); Stephen Innes, *Creating the Commonwealth: The Economic Culture of Puritan New England* (1995); and David Hall, *Worlds of Wonder, Days of Judgment: Popular Religious Belief in Early New England (1989)*. The female Puritan experience is vividly discussed in Lyle Koehler's *A Search for Power: The "Weaker Sex" in Seventeenth-Century New England* (1980) and Amanda Porterfield's *Female Piety in Puritan New England: The Emergence of Religious Humanism* (1992). For discussions of Puritan–Indian relations, see James Axtell, *The European and the Indian: Essays in the Ethnohistory of Colonial North America* (1981). For the nearby settlement at Plymouth Plantation, see Nathaniel Philbrick, *Mayflower* (2005).

ENDNOTES

1. In Richard Hakluyt, *The principall navigations, voyages and discoveries of the English nation made by sea or over land* (London, 1589).
2. Ibid.
3. Lyon Gardiner Tyler, ed., *Narratives of Early Virginia, 1606–1625* (New York: Scribner's, 1907), pp. 9–12, 17.
4. John Smith, "What happened in the first Government after the Alteration in the Time of Captain George Piercie, their Governor." 1609.
5. William Strachey, *For the Colony in Virginea Britannia. Laws divine, moral, and martial &c.* (London: W. Burre, 1612). Courtesy Newberry Library, Chicago.
6. Richard Frethorne, letter to his father and mother, March 20, April 2–3, 1623, in Susan Kingsbury, ed., *The Records of the Virginia Company of London* (Washington, D.C.: Government Printing Office, 1935), v.4, pp. 58–62.
7. William Waller Hening, ed., *The Statutes at Large; Being a Collection of All the Laws of Virginia from the First Session of the Legislature, in the Year 1619* (New York: R. & W. & B. Bartow, 1823), v.2, p. 170.
8. Hening, ed., *The Statutes at Large*, v.2, p. 260.
9. Ibid., v.3, pp. 447–463.
10. *The History of the Province of Massachusets-Bay, from the Charter of King William and Queen Mary in 1691, until the year 1750. By Mr. Hutchinson, Lieutenant Governor of the Province.* V. II (London: J. Smith, 1768), Appendix II, pp. 482, 508–509, 520.
11. First published in *A Report of the Record Commissioners of the City of Boston Containing Miscellaneous Papers* (Boston: Rockwell and Churchill, 1886), pp. 27–30.
12. Mary Rowlandson, *A Narrative of the Captivity and Restoration of Mrs. Mary Rowlandson* (1682).

CHAPTER 3

EIGHTEENTH-CENTURY VOICES

HISTORICAL CONTEXT

Before 1776, most colonists thought of themselves as English. They were proud of England, proud to be part of the Empire. True, Germans, Africans, Scots, Native Americans, and others retained many of their old ways. But more than those of any other single group, English language, religion, customs, and folkways predominated from Florida to Maine. Alongside colonists' pride in their Englishness, however, a growing sense of American identity was emerging. Perhaps it was inevitable that 100 years of settlement and 3,000 miles of distance would engender feelings of American distinctiveness. The mixing of so many diverse peoples on fresh and abundant land caused the French immigrant Michel-Guillaume Jean de Crèvecoeur (who anglicized his name to J. Hector St. John Crèvecoeur) to ask, "What, then, is the American, this new man?"

The eighteenth-century was filled with both adherence to tradition—the rights of Englishmen and commonwealth ideals, for example—and a sense of change, of individuals and societies shaping themselves to bold new concepts of human aspiration. This second strand was part of something called "the Enlightenment." The Enlightenment was more a tendency or trend in the thinking of both Europeans and Americans than an organized intellectual movement. In its most optimistic form, on the eve of the American Revolution, the Enlightenment was characterized by faith in progress and in humankind's ability to control its own fate.

Many Enlightenment thinkers, such as Benjamin Franklin, were deists. They believed that God created the world, but then God left men and women alone to work out their own destinies. There were natural moral laws, boundaries of good and evil, but these had to be discovered and implemented by people acting on their own behalf. Enlightenment thought tended toward the concrete and particular, the empirical and experimental; it was a sensibility rooted in the day-to-day life of the world, not in metaphysics. Science, technology, and progress were closely associated with the Enlightenment, and the discoveries of the natural world made by men like Galileo in astronomy, Newton in physics, and Linnaeus in biology were hallmarks of Enlightenment thought. Moreover, it was believed that the same scientific procedures that allowed clear-cut classification schemes in botany or zoology, or that demonstrated the operation of natural physical laws, could yield equally rational plans for ordering human affairs.

Even as Enlightenment ideals gained adherents, however, a great religious awakening was sweeping through the colonies, causing growing numbers of people to monitor constantly the condition of their eternal souls and to find in sermons and the Bible their guides to living. Yet, by the second half of the eighteenth century, many of the most influential Americans—in politics, commerce, and diplomacy—were inclined to hold religion at arm's length, and to tread lightly over things like church ritual, the Revealed Word, and specific ideas about heaven and hell. They especially rejected the notion of an ever-present God who watched over and judged people according to some cosmic plan. Such individuals placed their faith in the human community and worked hard to build up institutions that promoted culture, learning, prosperity, and health.

In this chapter, we explore the writings of several Americans who lived at the dawn of the Enlightenment, but who were also affected by the Great Awakening. By the eighteenth century, the colonies from New England to the Carolinas were well established. All might still suffer economic setbacks, epidemics, and Indian uprisings, but there was no doubt they had become permanent settlements. Tens of thousands of settlers and their descendants found themselves embedded in relatively stable relationships of power and dependence.

Of course, there were differences between the settlements. The heirs of the Puritans still held considerable influence in New England, the cities of the middle colonies were growing rapidly from the profits of shipping and trading, and the southern colonies had developed their own plantation life based on chattel slavery. We must not draw these distinctions too sharply though; slavery existed throughout the colonies, trade out of Boston and Charleston rivaled that of New York and Philadelphia, and Protestantism was hegemonic everywhere.

All of the colonies had developed social structures that gave great wealth, power, or prestige to some families and none of those advantages to others. The privileged people of the eighteenth century were almost invariably white, male, and Protestant. To be sure, most who fit that description were not rich or powerful, but the great majority who attained independent wealth and status were. To be propertyless, an African slave, Native American, a woman, was to be socially disadvantaged. Above all, the rich and powerful among the colonists thought of themselves as Englishmen. Three thousand miles of water that separated them from the mother country made them keen to maintain their Englishness. And even as they pushed Native Americans off the land, enslaved Africans, and subordinated women, white men increasingly insisted on their freedom to define themselves.

This chapter includes writings from five eighteenth-century colonials. Consider how each illuminates the forces at work in the era. William Byrd II, Jonathan Edwards, and Benjamin Franklin became very influential in the decades before the American Revolution. All were shaped by Enlightenment ideas. Byrd, who in many ways recreated an Old World patriarchal life like that of the landed gentry of England, began each day reading texts that included Greek and Latin secular works, foundation documents of Enlightenment thought. While attending Yale, Edwards, America's greatest religious thinker of the century, was influenced by John Locke's *Essay Concerning Human Understanding*, which argued that human knowledge came to us through our senses, through our direct experience of the world, not through innate ideas implanted before birth. And, of course, Franklin, the experimental scientist, became the leading figure in the American Enlightenment.

The ideas of the Enlightenment, however, must be seen alongside the religious fervor of the Great Awakening, which directly shaped Edwards's life and that of the two others featured in this chapter, Sarah Osborne, and Olaudah Equiano. How—and why—does each detail their evangelical awakening? All five writers identified as Christian, so consider the way that faith and concepts of a virtuous life governed their actions. All five, moreover, were sufficiently aware of their circumstances and position that they wrote accounts of their lives. To whom were they writing and why?

Despite the similarities, there were, of course, important differences between these individuals, particularly differences of position and power. The comfortable lives of men like Byrd were built on the backs of African slaves. Note how Byrd casually writes of "my people," assuming his right to their labor. Equiano details the pain of enslavement and separation from loved ones in Africa, as well as the estrangement he felt in the colonies. Also, consider Jonathan Edwards's musings on his relationship to God, then read the words of Sarah Osborn, who is equally pious and writing in the same Protestant idiom, yet her words reflecting very different—and especially female—concerns as a mother and a widow.

INTRODUCTION TO DOCUMENTS 1 AND 2

William Byrd II (1674–1744) of Westover, Virginia, was the oldest of this group. He was the son of William Byrd I, who built the family fortune on Indian trade and plantation agriculture. By the time young William inherited the estate in 1704, Virginia's seventeenth-century scramble for wealth that we read about in Chapter 2 had settled into a more stable pattern. Dominating that society was a small number of elite families like the Byrds, whose wealth was based on owning the most fertile lands. They farmed that land intensively with the use of African and African American slaves to produce a profitable staple crop such as tobacco.

It was not just wealth but gentility that the southern elite craved. By the early eighteenth century, the great families had built large mansions and modeled their lives on the English rural gentry. At age ten, William Byrd was sent to England and then Holland for his education, since the colonies were not yet able to provide young men of good families with the polish of an Old World gentleman. Byrd returned in 1692 at age eighteen and quickly became one of the leading lights of the landed aristocracy. Charming and learned, with powerful friends in England and America, Byrd was one of the youngest members of the Virginia House of Burgesses (the colonial legislature) and a member of the Council of State. He served his colony as a colonel in the militia and as an agent in London, and he was elected a Fellow of the Royal Society, an elite scholarly organization of which he was very proud. His marriage to Lucy Parke in 1706 ratified his place among Virginia's social elite.

Byrd's diary was not discovered, decoded, and published until 1941. He probably kept this journal from early in the century almost until he died in 1744. However, only a few selected years have been found. He kept the diary using a shorthand writing system. Byrd's daily entries are brief, roughly a paragraph long; they reveal little of his inner life, emotions, and feelings. But in their sheer regularity, they tell us much about how he lived his life, what he valued, and how he interacted with others. "I danced my dance," he wrote. His dance was a set of exercises to be done indoors when the weather was inclement, but that phrase can also be taken as a metaphor for Byrd's everyday transactions. Byrd often refers to "my people," meaning not only his family, but also those who labored on his plantation, both Africans and whites. As you read, consider how Byrd interacts with others, and how he saw his role as patriarch of Westover Plantation.

Byrd's diary is followed by excerpts from the extraordinary life of Olaudah Equiano, who was born in Africa, then kidnapped and sold into slavery at the age of eleven. The first part is his introduction to British readers, followed by a short account of his life as a slave in Virginia. Soon thereafter, Equiano was bought by a British naval officer, and served on slave ships and in the British Navy. Equiano sailed the world, and by the age of twenty-one had purchased his own freedom.

The next excerpt in Equiano's memoir is his account of his conversion to Christianity in 1774, which can be usefully compared to the similar accounts by Edwards and Osborne later in this chapter. Equiano's experiences in the American colonies led him to become an increasingly vocal opponent of slavery. Indeed, it was this conviction—as well as his Christian faith—that moved him to write an account of his life in the 1780s. The *Narrative* was published in London in 1789 and New York two years later and became a crucial text in the young abolitionist movement in England, and—several decades later—in the United States.

1. THE DIARIES OF WILLIAM BYRD (1709–1719)

Nov. 2, 1709—I rose at 6 o'clock and read a chapter in Hebrew and some Greek in Lucian. I said my prayers and ate milk for breakfast, and settled some accounts, and then went to court where we made an end of the business. We went to dinner about 4 o'clock and I ate boiled beef again. In the evening I went to Dr. [Barret's] where my wife came this afternoon. Here I found Mrs. Chiswell, my sister Custis, and other ladies. We sat and talked till about 11 o'clock and then retired to our chambers. I played at [r-m] with Mrs. Chiswell and kissed her on the bed till she was angry and my wife also was uneasy about it, and cried as soon as the company was gone. I neglected to say my prayers, which I should not have done, because I ought to beg pardon for the lust I had

for another man's wife. However I had good health, good thoughts, and good humor, thanks be to God Almighty. . . .

July 30, 1710—I rose at 5 o'clock and wrote a letter to Major Burwell about his boat which Captain Broadwater's people had brought round and sent Tom with it. I read two chapters in Hebrew and some Greek in Thucydides. I said my prayers and ate boiled milk for breakfast. I danced my dance. I read a sermon in Dr. Tillotson and then took a little [nap]. I ate fish for dinner. In the afternoon my wife and I had a little quarrel which I reconciled with a flourish. Then she read a sermon in Dr. Tillotson to me. It is to be observed that the flourish was performed on the billiard table. I read a little Latin. In the evening

Image 3.1 Hans Hyssing portrait of William Byrd II, c.1724
This portrait of Byrd was most likely painted while he was living in England, after the death of his first wife. Byrd is featured as man of comfort and gentility, though his diary reveals the complexity of his life at Westover plantation.
Source: Courtesy Virginia Historical Society

we took a walk about the plantation. I neglected to say my prayers but had good health, good thoughts, and good humor, thanks be to God. This month there were many people sick of fever and pain in their heads; perhaps this might be caused by the cold weather which we had this month, which was indeed the coldest that ever was known in July in this country. Several of my people have been sick, but none died, thank God. . . .

Nov. 13, 1710—I rose at 7 o'clock and said a short prayer. Then I took a little walk about the plantation. I ate toast and cider for breakfast. Colonel Digges sent for a white negro for us to see who except the color was featured like other negroes. She told us that in her country, which is called Aboh near Calabar there were many whites as well as blacks. We played at dice till about 12 o'clock and then we [went] to Williamsburg, but I was so dusted with dirt that I was forced to change my clothes. Yesterday Mr. Ingles had a child burnt to death by fire taking hold of its clothes. We went to the capitol and stayed there about two hours and then I went and dined with the Governor where I ate roast mutton. I had a letter from home which told me all was well except a negro woman who ran away and was found dead. I said my prayers and had good thoughts, good health, and good humor, thank God Almighty.

Dec. 22, 1710—I rose about 8 o'clock but read nothing because the sloop came and I was busy in loading her and in punishing Johnny and scolding at S-k-f-r for bringing goods for Mr. Tullitt contrary to my orders. About 10 o'clock I sent her away. It rained this morning. I ate boiled milk for breakfast. I neglected to say my prayers. I settled several things which took up all the morning. Some of the sick people grew better and some others fell sick. I ate raspberries for dinner. In the afternoon my wife and I played at billiards and I laid her down and rogered her on the [trestle]. About 4 o'clock Mr. Bland came on his way to Williamsburg but I persuaded him to stay all night. We sat and talked all the evening. I neglected to say my prayers but had good thoughts, good health, and good humor, thank God Almighty.

Dec. 31, 1710—I rose at 5 o'clock and read a chapter in Hebrew and four leaves in Lucian. I said my prayers and ate boiled milk for breakfast. My daughter was very sick all night and vomited a great deal but was a little better this morning. All my sick people were better, thank God, and I had another girl come down sick from the quarters. I danced my dance. Then I read a sermon in Dr. Tillotson and after that walked in the garden till dinner. I ate roast venison. In the afternoon I looked over my sick people and then took a walk about the plantation. The weather was very warm still. My wife walked with me and when she came back she was very much indisposed and went to bed. In the evening I read another sermon in Dr. Tillotson. About 8 o'clock the wind came to northwest and it began to be cold. I said my prayers and had good health, good thoughts, and good humor, thank God Almighty.

Some night this month I dreamed that I saw a flaming sword in the sky and called some company to see it but before they could come it was disappeared, and about a week after my wife and I were walking and we discovered in the clouds a shining cloud exactly in the shape of a dart and seemed to be over my plantation but it soon disappeared likewise. Both these appearances seemed to foretell some misfortune to me which afterwards came to pass in the death of several of my negroes after a very unusual manner. My wife about two months since dreamed she saw an angel in the shape of a big woman who told her the time was altered and the seasons were changed and that several calamities would follow that confusion. God avert his judgment from this poor country.

Feb. 6, 1711—(In Williamsburg) . . . About 7 o'clock the company went in coaches from the Governor's house to the capitol where the Governor opened the ball with a French dance with my wife. Then I danced with Mrs. Russell and then several others and among the rest Colonel Smith's son, who made a sad freak. Then we danced country dances for an hour and the company was carried into another room where was a very fine collation of sweetmeats. The Governor was very gallant to the ladies and very courteous to the gentlemen. About 2 o'clock the company returned in the coaches and because the drive was dirty the Governor carried the ladies into their coaches. . . . Colonel Carter's family and Mr. Blair were stopped by the unruliness of the horses and Daniel Wilkinson was so gallant as to lead the horses himself through all the dirt and rain to Mr. Blair's house. . . . It rained all day and all night. The President had the worst clothes of anybody there.

Feb. 27, 1711—I rose at 6 o'clock and read two chapters in Hebrew and some Greek in Lucian. I said my prayers and ate boiled milk for breakfast. I danced my dance and then went to the brick house to see my people pile the planks and found them all idle for which I threatened them soundly but did not whip them. The weather was cold and the wind at northeast. I wrote a letter to England. Then I read some English till 12 o'clock when Mr. Dunn and his wife came. I ate boiled beef for dinner. In the afternoon Mr. Dunn and I played at billiards. Then we took a long walk about the plantation and looked over all my business. In the evening my wife and little Jenny had a great quarrel in which my wife got the worst but at last by the help of the family Jenny was overcome and soundly whipped. At night I ate some bread and cheese. I said my prayers and had good health, good thoughts, and good humor, thank God Almighty.

March 4, 1711— . . . My [wife] continued still disordered in her back and belly. However she went to church with Mrs. Dunn in the coach and I walked there. Mr. Anderson gave us a good sermon. After church nobody came home with us. Little Peter came from above and brought news another negro died, which makes 17 this winter; God's will be done. Several others are sick. The Lord have mercy on them, and spare them if it be His will. . . .

April 30, 1711—I rose at 5 o'clock and said a short prayer and then drank two dishes of chocolate. Then I took my leave about 6 o'clock and found it very cold. I met with nothing extraordinary in my journey and got home about 11 o'clock and found all well, only my wife was melancholy. We took a walk in the garden and pasture. We discovered that by the contrivance of Nurse and Anaka Prue got in at the cellar window and stole some strong beer and cider and wine. I turned Nurse away upon it and punished Anaka. I ate some fish for dinner. In the afternoon I caused Jack and John to be whipped for drinking at John [Cross] all last Sunday. In the evening I took a walk about the plantation and found things in good order. At night I ate some bread and butter. I said my prayers and had good health, good thoughts, and good humor, thank God Almighty. The weather was very cold for the season. I gave my wife a powerful flourish and gave her great ecstasy and refreshment.

June 23, 1711— . . . My wife was indisposed and was threatened with miscarriage. I again persuaded to bleed but she could not be persuaded to it. . . . I had a small quarrel with my wife because she would not be bled but neither good words nor bad could prevail against her fear which is very uncontrollable.

June 25, 1711— . . . My wife grew worse and after much trial and persuasion was let blood when it was too late. Captain Stith came about some [n-l] he said he lent my father 20 years ago. Mr. Rogers came also about Mrs. Parker's business. My wife grew very ill which made [me] weep for her. I ate roast mutton for dinner. In the afternoon my wife grew worse and voided a prodigious quantity of blood. I settled some accounts till the evening and then took a walk about the plantation. Before I returned my wife sent for me because she was very weak and soon after I came she was delivered of a false conception and then grew better. I sent for Mrs. Hamlin who came presently. I said my prayers and had good health, good thoughts, and good humor, thank God Almighty.

June 26, 1711— . . . My wife was extremely mended and very cheerful, thank God. I settled some accounts till dinner. I ate some boiled mutton for dinner. In the afternoon I took a nap by my wife and then went and read some French. I lent my wife some pictures to divert her. . . . In the evening I took a walk about the plantation and drank some warm milk from the cow. I said my prayers and had good health, good thoughts, and good humor, thank God Almighty.[1]

[*The following passages are from Byrd's London Diary. Byrd lived in England for a few years after the death of his wife.*]

Oct. 4, 1718—I rose about 7 o'clock and read a chapter in Hebrew and some Greek. I said my prayers and had boiled milk for breakfast. The weather was cold and clear, the wind west. About 11 o'clock came Mrs. Wilkinson and brought me some linen. Then I went into the City and dined with old Mr. Perry who gave me several letters from Virginia. I ate some cold roast beef. After dinner I received a hundred pounds and then went to visit Dick Perry who was exceedingly bad of the gout. Here I drank tea and about 4 o'clock went to Molly Cole's and sat with her half an hour. Then I went home and wrote a letter into the country and then looked in at the play. Then I went to visit Mrs. A-l-n and committed uncleanness with the maid because the mistress was not at home. However, when the mistress came I rogered her and about 12 o'clock went home and ate a plum cake for supper. I neglected my prayers, for which God forgive me.

May 13, 1719—I rose about 8 o'clock and read a chapter in Hebrew and some Greek in Lucian. I said my prayers, and had milk for breakfast. The weather was cold and cloudy, the wind west, and it blew violently. I danced my dance and about 11 o'clock went to the Duke of Argyll's but he was from home. Then to Mrs. Southwell's where I sat about an hour. Then I returned home and wrote two letters to Virginia and put several things in order till 2 o'clock when I was angry with my man about my dinner. I ate some veal cutlets. After dinner I put several things in order till 5 o'clock and then I went to the widow Pierson's, where I stayed till 9 o'clock and then went to Will's where I had two dishes of chocolate. Then I went to my kind Mrs. Smith where I met a fine young woman, with whom I ate some rabbit fricassee and then we went to bed together and I rogered her three times and neglected my prayers.[2]

2. THE INTERESTING NARRATIVE OF THE LIFE OF OLAUDAH EQUIANO (1790)

To the Lords Spiritual and Temporal, and the Commons of the Parliament of Great Britain My Lords and Gentlemen,

Permit me, with the greatest deference and respect, to lay at your feet the following genuine narrative; the chief design of which is to excite in your august assemblies a sense of compassion for the miseries which the Slave-Trade has entailed on my unfortunate countrymen. By the horrors of that trade I was first torn away from all the tender connections that were naturally dear to my heart; but these, through the mysterious ways of Providence, I ought to regard as infinitely more than compensated by the introduction I have thence obtained to the knowledge of the Christian religion, and of a nation which, by its liberal sentiments, its humanity, the glorious freedom of its government, and its proficiency in arts and sciences, has exalted the dignity of human nature.

OLAUDAH EQUIANO, or GUSTAVUS VASSA
October 30, 1790

We were not many days in the merchant's custody, before we were sold after their usual manner, which is this: On a signal given (as the beat of a drum), the buyers rush at once into the yard where the slaves are confined, and make choice of that parcel they like best. The noise and clamor with which this is attended, and the eagerness visible in the countenances of the buyers, serve not a little to increase the apprehension of terrified Africans, who may well be supposed to consider them as the ministers of that destruction to which they think themselves devoted. In this manner, without scruple, are relations and friends separated,

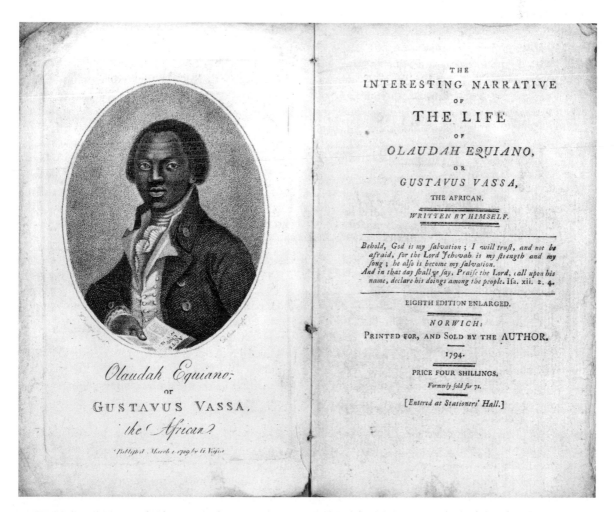

Image 3.2 Frontispiece and title page to *The Interesting Narrative of the Life of Olaudah Equiano, or Gustavus Vassa, the African* (Norwich, 1794)
Source: Library of Congress

most of them never to see each other again. I remember, in the vessel in which I was brought over, in the men's apartment, there were several brothers, who, in the sale, were sold in different lots; and it was very moving on this occasion, to see and hear their cries at parting. O, ye nominal Christians! might not an African ask you—Learned you this from your God, who says unto you, Do unto all men as you would men should do unto you? It is not enough that we are torn from our country and friends, to toil for your luxury and lust of gain? Must every tender feeling be likewise sacrificed to your avarice? Are the dearest friends and relations, now rendered more dear by their separation from their kindred, still to be parted from each other, and thus prevented from cheering the gloom of slavery, with the small comfort of being together, and mingling their sufferings and sorrows? Why are parents to lose their children, brothers their sisters, and husbands their wives? Surely, this is a new refinement in cruelty, which, while it has no advantage to atone for it, thus aggravates distress, and adds fresh horrors even to the wretchedness of slavery.

. . . We were landed up a river a good way from the sea, about Virginia county, where we saw few or none of our native Africans, and not one soul who could talk to me. I was a few weeks weeding grass and gathering stones in a plantation; and at last all my companions were distributed different ways, and only myself was left. I was now exceedingly miserable, and thought myself worse off than any of the rest of my companions, for they could talk to each other, but I had no person to speak to that I could understand. In this state, I was constantly grieving and pining, and wishing for death rather than anything else. While I was in this plantation, the gentleman, to whom I suppose the estate belonged, being unwell, I was one day sent for to his dwelling-house to fan him; when I came into the room where he was I was very much affrighted at some things I saw, and the more so as I had seen a black woman slave as I came through the house, who was cooking the dinner, and the poor creature was cruelly loaded with various kinds of iron machines; she had one particularly on her head, which locked her mouth so fast that she could scarcely speak; and could not eat nor drink. I was much astonished and shocked

at this contrivance, which I afterwards learned was called the iron muzzle. Soon after I had a fan put in my hand, to fan the gentleman while he slept; and so I did indeed with great fear. While he was fast asleep I indulged myself a great deal in looking about the room, which to me appeared very fine and curious. The first object that engaged my attention was a watch which hung on the chimney, and was going. I was quite surprised at the noise it made, and was afraid it would tell the gentleman anything I might do amiss; and when I immediately after observed a picture hanging in the room, which appeared constantly to look at me, I was still more affrighted, having never seen such things as these before. At one time I thought it was something relative to magic; and not seeing it move, I thought it might be some way the whites had to keep their great men when they died, and offer them libations as we used to do our friendly spirits. In this state of anxiety I remained till my master awoke, when I was dismissed out of the room, to my no small satisfaction and relief. . . .

On the morning of the 6th of October [1774] (I pray you to attend), all that day, I thought I should either see or hear something supernatural. I had a secret impulse on my mind of something that was to take place, which drove me continually for that time to a throne of grace. It pleased God to enable me to wrestle with him, as Jacob did: I prayed that if sudden death were to happen, and I perished, it might be at Christ's feet.

In the evening of the same day, as I was reading and meditating on the fourth chapter of Acts, twelfth verse, under the solemn apprehensions of eternity, and reflecting on my past actions, I began to think I had lived a moral life, and that I had a proper ground to believe I had an interest in the divine favor; but still meditating on the subject, not knowing whether salvation was to be had partly for our own good deeds or solely as the sovereign gift of God; in this deep consternation the Lord was pleased to break in upon my soul with his bright beams of heavenly light; and in an instant, as it were, removing the veil, and letting light into a dark place, I saw clearly with an eye of faith, the crucified Saviour bleeding on the cross on mount Calvary; the scriptures became an unsealed book; I saw myself a condemned criminal under the law, which came with its full force to my conscience, and when "the commandment came sin revived, and I died." I saw the Lord Jesus Christ in his humiliation, loaded and bearing my reproach, sin, and shame. I then clearly perceived that by the deeds of the law no flesh could be justified. I was then convinced that by the first Adam sin came, and by the second Adam (the Lord Jesus Christ) all that are saved must be made alive . . .

Now ever leading providential circumstance that happened to me, from the day I was taken from my parents to that hour, was then in my view, as if it had

but just then occurred. I was sensible of the invisible hand of God, which guided and protected me, when in truth I knew it not: still the Lord pursued me, although I slighted and disregarded it; this mercy melted me down. When I considered my poor wretched state I wept, seeing what a great debtor I was to sovereign free grade. Now the Ethiopian was willing to be saved by Jesus Christ, the sinner's only surety, and also to rely on none other person or thing for salvation. Self was obnoxious, and good works he had none, for it is God that worketh in us both to will and to do.[3]

INTRODUCTION TO DOCUMENTS 3 AND 4

Jonathan Edwards (1703–1758) was born in East Windsor, Connecticut, the son of pastor Timothy Edwards and grandson of the renowned Puritan minister Solomon Stoddard from Northampton, Massachusetts. When he was still twelve years old, in 1716, Jonathan entered the newly founded Yale College. His training, of course, was centered heavily in theology; he received his Artium Baccalaureatus (A.B.) degree in 1720 and his Magister Artium (M.A.) in 1723, and he became a tutor at the college the following year.

The following passage describes Edwards's conversion when he was about eighteen years old. He had been religious as a child, but this memoir, written when Edwards was in his late thirties, looks back twenty years to describe that moment around age eighteen when he felt the presence of God in a deep, emotional way. The description of Edwards's conversion is one of the great testaments of faith in the English language. More precisely, he describes his surrender to the Calvinist concept of the absolute sovereignty of God. In 1727, a few years after the events described here, Edwards married Sarah Pierpont of New Haven, who became well known (some said notorious) for the emotional fervor of her faith. In the years after his conversion, Edwards's writings developed the connection between religious conviction and deep personal feeling as the touchstone of faith for his congregants.

Around the time that he wrote this memoir, Edwards had been ordained associate pastor of his grandfather's old congregation in Northampton. Between 1735 and 1737, Edwards's preaching ignited a local revival movement in his church that not only brought in vast numbers of new members but also attracted interest throughout the colonies. Edwards's preaching was an early local manifestation of what came to be called the Great Awakening. The outpouring of divine grace soon spread, especially as the Rev. George Whitefield of England began to preach in the colonies toward the end of the decade. Whitefield brought a new style to the pulpit: He preached in fields and in town squares, he told stories of real people saved and damned, and he beat his breast while sinners cried out and groaned for salvation. In the following excerpt from his memoirs, Edwards describes his own conversion experience.

During the same Great Awakening that Edwards helped ignite, a young woman named Sarah Osborne pondered her own experience of God. We know of Osborne's life through her remarkable memoir, published in 1799. In it, Osborne details her tumultuous times, from her sharp conflicts with her parents as a teenager, through her young marriage and loss of her husband, and later the death of her only son. Osborne also lived in Rhode Island during the upheaval of the French and Indian War, and later in her life took the unusual step for a woman of leading prayer groups. For this—and especially for including African Americans in these gatherings—Osborne was much criticized, but she was convinced of the importance of spreading the Gospel. In fact, most of those individuals converting to evangelical Christianity in the eighteenth century were women.

Looking back, Osborne used her memoir to discern the meaning of her life, and decided that her misfortunes were but challenges from God to strengthen her faith. Like that of Equiano and Edwards, Osborne's memoir is also important evidence of the Great Awakening, the outpouring of faith that emphasized an emotional and direct experience of God and salvation. And like Edwards—as well as Equiano and Franklin—we see a growing appreciation of the individual as an agent of change in the modern world.

---

3. FROM *THE MEMOIRS OF REV. JONATHAN EDWARDS*

The first instance, that I remember, of that sort of inward, sweet delight in God and divine things, that I have lived much in since, was on reading those words. 1 Tim. i. 17. *Now unto the King eternal, immortal, invisible, the only wise God, be honour and glory for ever and ever. Amen.* As I read the words, there came into my soul, and was as it were diffused through it, a sense of the glory of the Divine Being; a new sense, quite different from any thing I ever experienced before. Never any words of Scripture seemed to me as these words did. I thought with myself, how excellent a Being that was, and how happy I should be, if I might enjoy that God, and be rapt up to him in heaven; and be as it were swallowed up in him for ever! I kept saying, and as it were singing, over these words of Scripture to myself; and went to pray to God that I might enjoy him; and prayed in a manner quite different from what I used to do, with a new sort of affection. But it never came into my thought, that there was any thing spiritual, or of a saying nature, in this.

From about that time I began to have a new kind of apprehensions and ideas of Christ, and the work of redemption, and the glorious way of salvation by him. An inward, sweet sense of these things, at times, came into my heart; and my soul was led away in pleasant views and contemplations of them. And

my mind was greatly engaged to spend my time in reading and meditating on Christ, on the beauty and excellency of his person, and the lovely way of salvation by free grace in him. I found no books so delightful to me, as those that treated of these subjects. Those words Cant. ii. 1. used to be abundantly with me, *I am the rose of Sharon, and the lily of the valleys.* The words seemed to me sweetly to represent the loveliness and beauty of Jesus Christ. The whole book of Canticles used to be pleasant to me, and I used to be much in reading it, about that time; and found from time to time an inward sweetness, that would carry me away in my contemplations. This I know not how to express otherwise, than by a calm, sweet abstraction of soul from all the concerns of this world; and sometimes a kind of vision, or fixed ideas and imaginations, of being alone in the mountains, or some solitary wilderness, far from all mankind, sweetly conversing with Christ, and wrapt and swallowed up in God. The sense I had to divine things, would often of a sudden kindle up, as it were, a sweet burning in my heart, an ardour of soul, that I know not how to express.

Not long after I first began to experience these things, I gave an account to my father of some things that had passed in my mind. I was pretty much affected by the discourse we had together; and when the discourse was ended, I walked abroad alone, in a solitary place in my father's pasture, for contemplation. And as I was walking there, and looking upon the sky and clouds, there came into my mind so sweet a sense of the glorious *majesty* and *grace* of God, as I know not how to express—I seemed to see them both in a sweet conjunction; majesty and meekness joined together. it was a sweet, and gentle, and holy majesty; and also a majestic meekness; an awful sweetness; a high, and great, and holy gentleness.

After this my sense of divine things gradually increased, and became more and more lively, and had more of that inward sweetness. The appearance of every thing was altered; there seemed to be, as it were, a calm, sweet cast or appearance of divine glory, in almost every thing. God's excellency, his wisdom, his purity, and love, seemed to appear in every thing; in the sun, moon, and stars; in the clouds and blue sky; in the grass, flowers, trees; in the water and all nature; which used greatly to fix my mind. I often used to sit and view the moon for a long time; and in the day, spent much time in viewing the clouds and sky, to behold the sweet glory of God in these things: in the mean time singing forth, with a low voice, my contemplations of the Creator and Redeemer. And scarce any thing, among all the works of nature, was so sweet to me as thunder and lightning: formerly nothing had been so terrible to me. Before, I used to be uncommonly terrified with thunder, and to be struck with terror when I saw a thunder-storm rising; but now, on the contrary, it rejoiced me. I felt God, if I may so speak, at the first appearance of a thunderstorm; and used to take the opportunity, at such times, to fix myself in order to view the clouds, and see the lightnings play, and hear the majestic and awful voice of God's thunders, which oftentimes was exceedingly entertaining, leading me to sweet contemplations of my great and glorious God. While thus engaged, it always seemed natural for me to sing or chant forth my meditations; or, to speak my thoughts in soliloquies with a singing voice.

I felt then great satisfaction as to my good state; but that did not content me. I had vehement longings of soul after God and Christ, and after more holiness, wherewith my heart seemed to be full, and ready to break; which often brought to my mind the words of the psalmist, Ps. cxix. 28. *My soul breaketh for the longing it hath*. I often felt a mourning and lamenting in my heart, that I had not turned to God sooner, that I might have had more time to grow in grace. My mind was greatly fixed on divine things; almost perpetually in the contemplation of them. I spent most of my time in thinking of divine things, year after year, often walking alone in the woods, and solitary places, for meditation, soliloquy, and prayer, and converse with God; and it was always my manner, at such times, to sing forth my contemplations. I was almost constantly in ejaculatory prayer, wherever I was. Prayer seemed to be natural to me, as the breath by which the inward burnings of my heart had vent. The delights which I now felt in the things of religion, were of an exceedingly different kind from those before mentioned, that I had when a boy; and what I had no more notion of, than one born blind has of pleasant and beautiful colours. They were of a more inward, pure, soul-animating, and refreshing nature. Those former delights never reached the heart; and did not arise from any sight of the divine excellency of the things of God; or any taste of the soul-satisfying and life-giving good there is in them.

My sense of divine things seemed gradually to increase, till I went to preach at New York; which was about a year and a half after they began: and while I was there I felt them very sensibly, in a much higher degree than I had done before. My longings after God and holiness were much increased. Pure and humble, holy and heavenly, Christianity appeared exceedingly amiable to me. I felt a burning desire to be, in every thing, a complete Christian; and conformed to the blessed image of Christ; and that I might live, in all things, according to the pure, sweet, and blessed rules of the gospel. . . .

While at New York, I sometimes was much affected with reflections on my past life, considering how late it was before I began to be truly religious; and how wickedly I had lived till then: and once so as to weep abundantly, and for a considerable time together.

On January 12, 1723, I made a solemn dedication of myself to God, and wrote it down; giving up myself, and all that I had, to God; to be for the future in no respect my own; to act as one that had no right to himself, in any respect. And solemnly vowed to take God for my whole portion and felicity, looking on nothing else as any part of my happiness, nor acting as it were; and his law for the constant rule of my obedience;

engaging to fight with all my might against the world, the flesh, and the devil, to the end of my life. But I have reason to be infinitely humbled, when I consider how much I have failed of answering my obligation.

I had, then, abundance of sweet religious conversation, in the family where I lived, with Mr. John Smith, and his pious mother. My heart was knit in affection to those in whom were appearances of true piety; and I could bear the thoughts of no other companions, but such as were holy, and the disciples of the blessed Jesus. I had great longings for the advancement of Christ's kingdom in the world; and my secret prayers used to be, in great part, taken up in praying for it. If I heard the least hint of any thing that happened in any part of the world, that appeared, in some respect or other, to have a favourable aspect on the interests of Christ's kingdom, my soul eagerly catched at it, and it would much animate and refresh me. . . .

I very frequently used to retire into a solitary place on the banks of Hudson's river, at some distance from the city, for contemplation on divine things and secret converse with God; and had many sweet hours there. Sometimes Mr. Smith and I walked there together, to converse on the things of God; and our conversation turned much on the advancement of Christ's kingdom in the world, and the glorious things that God would accomplish for his church in the latter days. I had then, and at other times, the greatest delight in the Holy Scriptures of any book whatsoever. Oftentimes in reading it every word seemed to touch my heart. I felt a harmony between something in my heart, and those sweet and powerful words. I seemed often to see so much light exhibited by every sentence, and such a refreshing food communicated, that I could not get along in reading; often dwelling long on one sentence, to see the wonders contained in it; and yet almost every sentence seemed to be full of wonders.[4]

4. FROM *THE MEMOIRS OF THE LIFE OF MRS. SARAH OSBORN*

In the process of time, I was married to Mr. Samuel Wheaten, being in my eighteenth year, October 21, 1731, and went with my husband, the next winter, to see his friends in the country; where I stayed almost five months; and was almost all the time under strong [religious] convictions. Oh, how I did sweat and tremble for fear my convictions should wear off again, and plead with God to set home strong convictions, and never, never suffer them to cease, till they ended in a sound and saving conversion. . . .

After I came home, I met with much affliction in many respects. It seemed to me that the whole world were in arms against me. I thought I was the most despised creature living upon the earth. I used to pray to God in secret to relieve me; but did not, as I ought, see his hand in permitting it so to be, as a just punishment for my vile sins: And therefore was not humbled under it as I ought; but let nature rise and acted very imprudently, in many respects. I was then with

child, and often lamented that I was to bring a child into such a world of sorrow: But some times found a disposition to dedicate my babe to God, while in the womb; and did so, at all seasons of secret prayer. And after it was born, my husband being at sea, I could not rest till I had solemnly given it up to God in baptism. And I thought that I did indeed give up both myself and it to God.

I met with many trials in my lying in, it being an extreme cold season. My child was born on Oct. 27, 1732. The next spring, my husband returned home; but went to sea again, and died abroad in November 1733. I was then in my twentieth year. The news of my husband's death came to me on the first of the next of April. . . . But God appeared wonderfully for my support. I saw his hand, and was enabled to submit with patience to his will. I daily looked round me, to see how much heavier the hand of God was laid on some others, than it was on me, where they were left with a large number of children, and much involved in debt. And I had but one to maintain; and though poor, yet not involved. Others, I saw, as well as myself, had their friends snatched from them by sudden accidents. The consideration of these things, together with the thoughts of what I deserved, stilled me so, that though the loss of my companion, whom I dearly loved, was great; yet the veins of mercy, which I saw running though all my afflictions, were so great likewise, that, with Job, I could say, "The Lord gave, and the Lord hath taken away, and blessed be the name of the Lord."

. . . As before this affliction every one seemed to be enemies to me, so from that time, all became friends. My parents treated me very tenderly; and God inclined every one who saw me to be kind to me. My brother was come into New England: And being a single man, we went to housekeeping together. But in three months after he married, and I soon found it would not do to live as before; and began to be thoughtful how I should do. I could see no way in which I could get a living. All doors seemed to be shut. But I verily believed that God would point out a way for me. And accordingly, the very day I came to a resolution to move as soon as I could, a stranger to my case, who kept a school a little way off, came to me, and told me that she only waited for a fair wind to go to Carolina; and, if it would suit me, I should have her chamber and scholars; which I joyfully accepted. Thus the widow's God remarkable provided for me. This was on Nov. 19, 1734. I was then placed in a family, who discovered a great deal of affection for me; and in all respects used me as tenderly as if I had been a near relation. . . .

These were happy days—But now how shall I speak! Oh, that I may do it with a heart truly broken for my sins! After all this, I began to grow more conformed to the world. Things which, when I was thus lively, appeared insipid, and indeed odious to me,

began to grow more tolerable, and by degrees in a measure pleasant. And depraved nature and Satan together pleaded for them thus, That there was a time for all things; and singing and dancing now and then, with a particular friend, was an innocent diversion.

. . . [I] continued thus till March 1741. And then it pleased God to return Mr. Tennent to us again, and he preached twenty-one sermons here. But while he was here, I was more than ever distressed. I had lost the sensible manifestations of Christ's love. . . . And [Mr. Tennent] struck directly at those things, for which I had so foolishly and wickedly pleaded Christian example, such as singing songs, dancing and foolish jesting, which is not convenient. He said, he would not say there was no such thing as a dancing Christian, but he had a very mean opinion of such as could bear to spend their time so, when it is so short, and the work for eternity so great. Then, and not till then, was I fully convinced what prodigal wasters of precious time such things were. And, through grace, I have abhorred them all ever since.

Thus I sunk by degrees lower and lower, till I had at last almost lost all sense of my former experiences. I had only the bare remembrance of them, and they seemed like dreams or delusion; at some times. At others again, I had some revivals. . . . But I knew I was a dreadful backslider, and had dealt treacherously with God. . . .

In Sept. 1740, God in mercy sent his dear servant [George] Whitefield here, which in some measure stirred me up. But why Mr. [Gilbert] Tennent came soon after, it pleased God to bless his preaching so to me, that it roused me. But I was all the winter after exercised with dreadful doubts and fears about my state. I questioned the truth of all I had experienced, and feared I had never yet passed through the pangs of the new birth, or ever had one spark of grace.[5]

INTRODUCTION TO DOCUMENT 5

Benjamin Franklin was much more clearly a child of the Enlightenment than the others in this chapter. Indeed, as he recounts, it was the religious disagreements between his parents that fostered his own doubts about religion. Nonetheless, Franklin's ancestors were devout, and he probably inherited more from them than he acknowledged. If he rejected their otherworldliness, he embraced their notion of stewardship. Many Protestants came to believe that people should work hard, not because they wanted money and goods, but because success could be a sign of God's grace, an indication that a heavenly future was in store. Franklin might not pin his hopes for salvation on worldly success, but he agreed with the old Puritans that mere wealth was not a worthy goal in life, that those who prospered were obliged to use their gifts to benefit others. Restraint, good temper, a sense of communal obligation, reason, rational discourse, and the spreading of wisdom—these were the real goals of life, and money's purpose was to serve those ends.

Franklin was born in Boston in 1706, the tenth and youngest son of Josiah Franklin, an English immigrant to Boston. At age ten, after a few years of schooling, Benjamin entered his father's trade of tallow chandler. He hated the candle- and soap-making shop and soon was apprenticed to his half-brother James as a printer. Ben's rebelliousness emerged again; the brothers quarreled often, and in 1723, Franklin left for Philadelphia. He found employment as a printer and, by age twenty-three, opened his own shop. Soon he entered a common-law marriage with Deborah Reed, whose husband had deserted her. As Franklin's memoir reveals, he was very active in the affairs of his community. He experimented with electricity and produced one invention after another; he organized friends into a reading and debating society in Philadelphia; he joined others in founding a subscription library, a university, and a town fire department. When he retired from business a wealthy middle-aged man, he devoted even more time to public affairs, especially to the cause of American independence and the governance of the new nation.

Franklin embodied the spirit of success and optimism, accomplishment and energy that we like to think of as distinctly American. He was the consummate man of acts. But it is in the context of his own times, the eighteenth century, that he is best understood. Franklin composed his memoirs as an older man looking back over his youth; these passages were written in 1771 and 1784 and then published in the early nineteenth century. Like Edwards, Osborne, and Equiano, Franklin was able to reflect on the arc of his life and shape the story as he saw fit. An autobiography is never just a retelling of events; authors have audiences in mind, and they hope to persuade, to impart some lesson or moral, or to explain or justify or exonerate themselves. What does this selection reveal about Franklin's view of his own legacy?

---

5. FROM *THE MEMOIRS OF BENJAMIN FRANKLIN*

Before I enter upon my public appearance in business, it may be well to let you know the then state of my mind, with regard to my principles and morals, that you may see how far those influenced the future events of my life. My parents had early given me religious impressions, and brought me through my childhood piously in the dissenting way. But I was scarce fifteen, when, after doubting by turns several points, as I found them disputed in the different books I read, I began to doubt of the revelation itself. Some books against Deism fell into my hands. . . . It happened that they wrought an effect on me quite contrary to what was intended by them; for the arguments of the Deists which were quoted to be refuted appeared to me much stronger than the refutations; in short, I soon became a thorough Deist. . . .

I grew convinced that *truth, sincerity,* and *integrity,* in dealings between man and man, were of the utmost importance to the felicity of life; and I formed written resolutions (which still remain in my journal book) to practise them ever while I lived. Revelation had indeed no weight with me as such; but I entertained an opinion, that though certain actions might not be bad, *because* they were forbidden by it, or good *because* it commanded them; yet probably those actions might be forbidden *because* they were bad for us, or commanded *because* they were beneficial to us, in their own natures, all the circumstances of things considered. And this persuasion, with the kind hand of Providence, or some guardian angel, or accidental favourable circumstances and situations, or all together, preserved me through this dangerous time of youth and the hazardous situations I was sometimes in among strangers, remote from the eye and advice of my father; free from any *wilful* gross immorality or injustice, that might have been expected from my want of religion; I say *wilful*, because the instances I have mentioned had something of *necessity* in them, from my youth, inexperience, and the knavery of others: I had therefore a tolerable character to begin the world with; I valued it properly, and determined to preserve it.

I should have mentioned before, that in the autumn of the preceding year, I had formed most of my ingenious acquaintance into a club for mutual improvement, which we called the JUNTO; we met on Friday evenings. The rules that I drew up required that every member in his turn should produce one or more queries on any point of morals, politics, or natural philosophy, to be discussed by the company; and once in three months produce and read an essay of his own writing, on any subject he pleased. Our debates were to be under the direction of a president, and to be conducted in the sincere spirit of inquiry after truth, without fondness for dispute, or desire of victory; and to prevent warmth, all expressions of positiveness in opinions, or direct contradiction, were after some time made contraband, and prohibited under small pecuniary [penalties]. . . .

About this time there was a cry among the people for more paper-money; only fifteen thousand pounds being extant in the province, and that soon to be sunk. The wealthy inhabitants opposed any addition; being against all paper currency, from the apprehension that it would depreciate, as it had done in New England, to the injury of all creditors. We had discussed this point in our junto, where I was on the side of an addition. . . . Our debates possessed me so fully of the subject, that I wrote

and printed an anonymous pamphlet on it, entitled *"The Nature and Necessity of a Paper Currency."* It was well received by the common people in general; but the rich men disliked it, for it increased and strengthened the clamour for more money; and they happening to have no writers among them that were able to answer it, their opposition slackened, and the point was carried by a majority in the house. My friends there, who considered I had been of some service, thought fit to reward me, by employing me in printing the money; a very profitable job, and a great help to me: this was another advantage gained by my being able to write. . . .

I now opened a small stationer's shop: I had in it blanks of all kinds; the correctest that ever appeared among us. I was assisted in that by my friend Brientnal: I had also paper, parchment, chapmen's books, &c. One Whitemash, a compositor I had known in London, an excellent workman, now came to me, and worked with me constantly and diligently; and I took an apprentice, the son of Aquila Rose.

. . . I began now gradually to pay off the debt I was under for the printing house. In order to secure my credit and character as a tradesman, I took care not only to be in *reality* industrious and frugal, but to avoid the appearances to the contrary. I dressed plain, and was seen at no places of idle diversion: I never went out a fishing or shooting: a book indeed sometimes debauched me from my work, but that was seldom, was private, and gave no scandal: and to show that I was not above my business, I sometimes brought home the paper I purchased at the stores, through the streets on a wheelbarrow. Thus being esteemed an industrious, thriving young man, and paying duly for what I bought, the merchants who imported stationery solicited my custom; others proposed supplying me with books, and I went on prosperously. . . .

. . . At the time I established myself in Pennsylvania, there was not a good bookseller's shop in any of the colonies to the southward of Boston. In New York and Philadelphia, the printers were indeed stationers, but they sold only paper, &c. almanacs, ballads, and a few common school-books. Those who loved reading were obliged to send for their books from England: the members of the Junto had each a few. We had left the alehouse, where we first met, and hired a room to hold our club in. I proposed that we should all of us bring our books to that room; where they would not only be ready to consult in our conferences, but become a common benefit, each of us being at liberty to borrow such as he wished to read at home. This was accordingly done, and for some time contented us: finding the advantage of this little collection, I proposed to render the benefit from the books more common, by commencing a public subscription library. . . . The books were imported; the library was open one day in the week for lending them to subscribers, on their promissory notes to pay double the value if not duly returned. The institution soon manifested its utility, was imitated by other towns, and in other provinces. The libraries were augmented by donations; reading became fashionable; and our people having no public amusements to divert their attention from study, became better acquainted with books, and in a few years were observed by strangers to be better instructed, and more intelligent than people of the same rank generally are in other countries. . . .

This library afforded me the means of improvement by constant study, for which I set apart an hour or two each day; and thus repaired in some degree the loss of the learned education my father once intended for me. Reading was the only amusement I allowed myself. I spent no time in taverns, games, or frolics of any kind; and my industry in my business continued as indefatigable as it was necessary. I was indebted for my printing house, I had a young family coming on to be educated, and I had two competitors to contend with for business, who were established in the place before me. My circumstances however grew daily easier. My original habits of frugality continuing, and my father having among his instructions to me when a boy, frequently repeated a Proverb of Solomon, *"seest thou a man diligent in his calling, he shall stand before kings, he shall not stand before mean men."* I thence considered industry as a means of obtaining wealth and distinction, which encouraged me; though I did not think that I should ever literally stand before kings, which however has since happened; for I have stood before five, and even had the honour of sitting down with one, (the king of Denmark,) to dinner.

We have an English proverb that says,

He that would thrive,
Must ask his wife.

It was lucky for me that I had one as much disposed to industry and frugality as myself. She assisted me cheerfully in my business, folding and stitching pamphlets, tending shop, purchasing old linen rags for the paper makers, &c. We kept no idle servants, our table was plain and simple, our furniture of the cheapest. For instance, my breakfast was for a long time bread and milk, (no tea) and I ate it out of a twopenny earthern porringer, with a pewter spoon: but mark how luxury will enter families, and make a progress in spite of principle; being called one morning to breakfast, I found it in a china bowl, with a spoon of silver. They had been bought for me without my knowledge by my wife, and had cost her the enormous sum of three and twenty shillings; for which she had no other excuse or apology to make, but that she thought *her* husband deserved a silver spoon and china bowl as well as any of his neighbours. This was the first appearance of plate and china in our house, which afterwards, in a course of years, as our wealth increased, augmented gradually to several hundred pounds in value.

I had been religiously educated as a Presbyterian; but though some of the dogmas of that persuasion, such as *the eternal decrees of God, election, reprobation, &c.* appeared to me unintelligible, and I early absented myself from the public assemblies of the sect, (Sunday being my studying day). I never was without some religious principles: I never doubted, for instance, the existence of a Deity, that he made the world, and governed it by his providence; that the most acceptable service of God was the doing good to man; that our souls are immortal; and that all crimes will be punished, and virtue rewarded, either here or hereafter; these I esteemed the essentials of every religion, and being to be found in all the religions we had in our country, I respected them all, though with different degrees of respect, as I found them more or less mixed with other articles, which, without any tendency to inspire, promote, or confirm morality, served principally to divide us, and make us unfriendly to one another. . . . I had some years before composed a little liturgy, or form of prayer, for my own private use, (viz. in 1728), entitled *Articles of Belief and*

Acts of Religion. I returned to the use of this, and went no more to the public assemblies. My conduct might be blameable, but I leave it without attempting further to excuse it; my present purpose being to relate facts, and not to make apologies for them.

It was about this time I conceived the bold and arduous project of arriving at *moral perfection:* I wished to live without committing any fault at any time, and to conquer all that either natural inclination, custom, or company, might lead me into. As I knew, or thought I knew, what was right and wrong, I did not see why I might not *always* do the one and avoid the other. . . .

. . . I included under thirteen names of virtues, all that at that time occurred to me as necessary or desirable; and annexed to each a short precept, which fully expressed the extent I gave to its meaning.

These names of *virtues,* with their precepts, were,

1. *Temperance.*—Eat not to dulness: drink not to elevation.
2. *Silence.*—Speak not but what may benefit others or yourself: avoid trifling conversation.
3. *Order.*—Let all your things have their places: let each part of your business have its time.
4. *Resolution.*—Resolve to perform what you ought: perform without fail what you resolve.
5. *Frugality.*—Make no expense, but to do good to others or yourself: that is waste nothing.
6. *Industry.*—Lose no time: be always employed in something useful: cut off all unnecessary actions.
7. *Sincerity.*—Use no hurtful deceit: think innocently and justly: and, if you speak, speak accordingly.
8. *Justice.*—Wrong none by doing injuries, or omitting the benefits that are your duty.
9. *Moderation.*—Avoid extremes: forbear resenting injuries so much as you think they deserve.
10. *Cleanliness.*—Tolerate no uncleanliness in body, clothes, or habitation.
11. *Tranquillity.*—Be not disturbed at trifles, nor at accidents common or unavoidable.
12. *Chastity.*—Rarely use venery, but for health or offspring; never to dulness or weakness, or the injury of your own or another's peace or reputation.
13. *Humility.*—Imitate *Jesus* and *Socrates.* . . .

I made a little book, in which I allotted a page for each of the virtues. I ruled each page with red ink, so as to have seven columns, one for each day of the week, marking each column with a letter for the day. I crossed these columns with thirteen red lines, marking the beginning of each line with the first letter of one of the virtues; on which line, and in its proper column, I might mark by a little black spot, every fault I found upon examination to have been committed respecting that virtue, upon that day.

I determined to give a week's strict attention to each of the virtues successively. Thus in the first week, my great guard was to avoid every the least offence against *Temperance;* leaving the other virtues to their ordinary chance, only marking every evening the faults of the day. Thus, if in the first week I could keep my first line marked T. clear of spots, I supposed the habit of that virtue so much strengthened, and its opposite weakened, that I might venture extending my attention to include the next; and for the following week keep both lines clear of spots. Proceeding thus to the last, I could get through a course complete in thirteen weeks, and four courses in a year. . . .

And conceiving God to be the fountain of wisdom, I thought it right and necessary to solicit his assistance for obtaining it; to this end I formed the following little prayer, which was prefixed to my tables of examination, for daily use.

O powerful goodness! bountiful father! merciful guide! Increase in me that wisdom which discovers my truest interest: Strengthen my resolution to perform what that wisdom dictates: Accept my kind offices to thy other children, as the only return in my power for thy continual favours to me.

The precept of *Order,* requiring that *every part of my business should have its allotted time,* one page in my little book contained the following scheme of employment for the twenty-four hours of a natural day.

I entered upon the execution of this plan for self-examination, and continued it with occasional intermissions for some time. I was surprised to find myself so much fuller of faults than I had imagined; but I had the satisfaction of seeing them diminish. . . .

It may be well my posterity should be informed, that to this little artifice with the blessing of God, their ancestor owed the constant felicity of his life down to his 79th year, in which this is written. What reverses may attend the remainder is in the hand of Providence: but if they arrive, the reflection on past happiness enjoyed, ought to help his bearing them with more resignation. To *Temperance* he ascribes his long continued health, and what is still left to him of a good constitution. To *Industry* and *Frugality,* the early easiness of his circumstances, and acquisition of his fortune, with all that knowledge that enabled him to be an useful citizen and obtained for him some degree of reputation among the learned. To *Sincerity* and *Justice,* the confidence of his country, and the honourable employs it conferred upon him: and to the joint influence of the whole mass of the virtues, even in the imperfect state he was able to acquire them, all that evenness of temper and that cheerfulness in conversation which makes his company still sought for, and agreeable even to his young acquaintance: I hope therefore that some of my descendants may follow the example and reap the benefit.

It will be remarked that, though my scheme was not wholly without religion, there was in it no mark of any of the distinguishing tenets of any particular sect; I had purposely avoided them; for being fully persuaded of the utility and excellency of my method, and that it might be serviceable to people in all religions, and intending some time or other to publish it, I would not have any thing in it, that should prejudice any one, of any sect, against it. I proposed writing a little comment on each virtue, in which I would have shown the advantages of possessing it, and the mischiefs attending its opposite vice; I should have called my book *The Art of Virtue,* because it would have shown the means and manner of obtaining virtue, which would have distinguished it

from the mere exhortation to be good, that does not instruct and indicate the means; but is like the apostle's man of verbal charity, who without showing to the naked and hungry, how or where they might get clothes or victuals, only exhorted them to be fed and clothed. James ii. 15, 16. . . .

My list of virtues contained at first but twelve: but a Quaker friend having kindly informed me that I was generally thought proud; that my pride showed itself frequently in conversation; that I was not content with being in the right when discussing any point, but was overbearing, and rather insolent; (of which he convinced me by mentioning several instances) I determined to endeavour to cure myself if I could of this vice or folly among the rest; and I added *Humility* to my list, giving an extensive meaning to the word. I cannot boast of much success in acquiring the *reality* of this virtue, but I had a good deal with regard to the appearance of it. I made it a rule to forbear all direct contradiction to the sentiments of others, and all positive assertion of mine own. I even forbid myself, agreeably to the old laws of our Junto, the use of every word or expression in the language that imported a fixed opinion; such as *certainly, undoubtedly, &c.* and I adopted instead of them, *I conceive, I apprehend,* or *I imagine,* a thing to be so, or so; or it so *appears to me at present.*

. . . In reality there is perhaps no one of our natural passions so hard to subdue as *Pride;* disguise it, struggle with it, stifle it, mortify it as much as one pleases, it is still alive, and will every now and then peep out and show itself; you will see it perhaps often in this history. For even if I could conceive that I had completely overcome it, I should probably be *proud of my humility.*[6]

QUESTIONS

1. How would you characterize the relationship between William Byrd and Lucy Parke Byrd? If Lucy had kept a diary, how do you think she might have described the same events?
2. How did each of these authors think about their relationship to God? Do Equiano, Edwards, and Osborne describe their conversion and their faith in similar terms?
3. Whom do you think Byrd, Edwards, Equiano, Osborn, and Franklin had in mind as they wrote about their lives? Why did each of them record their life experiences? What message did they hope to convey to their readers?
4. How did each conceptualize and live out a virtuous life? What were their guides for living? What experiences brought them satisfaction and shame?

ADDITIONAL READING

On the origins of regional differences in American culture, read David Hackett Fischer's *Albion's Seed: Four British Folkways in America* (1989). Henry May's *The Enlightenment in America* (1976) is a classic work on the subject; for the southern colonies, see Allan Kulikoff, *Tobacco and Slaves: The Development of Southern Cultures in the Chesapeake, 1680–1800* (1986). On individuals see, see Pierre Marambaud, *William Byrd of Westover, 1674–1744* (1971); James Walvin, *An African's Life: The Life and Times of Olaudah Equiano, 1745–1797* (1998); Patricia J. Tracey, *Jonathan Edwards, Pastor: Religion and Society in Eighteenth Century Northampton* (1980); Ronald William Clark, *Benjamin Franklin: A Biography* (1983); Catherine Brekus, *Sarah Osborne's World: The Rise of Evangelical Christianity in Early America* (2013). More recent works on Ben Franklin include Gordon Wood, *The Americanization of Benjamin Franklin* (2005), and Walter Isaacson, *Benjamin Franklin, An American Life* (2004). On African Americans in the colonies, see Peter Wood, *Black Majority* (1974), and Michael Gomez, *Exchanging Our Country Marks* (1998). Peter Kolchin, *American Slavery* (1993) compares slave systems in the colonies, the Caribbean, Brazil, and Russia. Edward Countryman's *Americans* (1991) makes note of the diversity of early America. Richard White, *The Middle Ground* (1991), examines the cultural interactions of the Great Lakes region.

ENDNOTES

1. Louis B. Wright and Marion Tinling, eds., *The Secret Diary of William Byrd of Westover, 1709–1712* (Richmond, VA: Dietz Press, 1941).
2. Louis B. Wright and Marion Tinling, eds., *The London Diary, 1717–1721, and Other Writings* (New York: Oxford University Press, 1958).
3. *The Interesting Narrative of the Life of Olaudah Equiano, or Gustavus Vassa, the African, written by himself* (London, 1790), pp. iii; 280–283.
4. *Memoirs of the Rev. Jonathan Edwards, A.M.*, by John Hawksley (London: Printed for James Black, 1815), pp. 50–57, 60–61.
5. *Memoirs of the Life of Mrs. Sarah Osborn, who died at Newport, Rhode Island, on the Second Day of August 1796.* By Samuel Hopkins (Worcester, MA: 1799). Courtesy Library of Congress.
6. *The Memoirs of Benjamin Franklin, written by himself* (Philadelphia: McCarty & Davis, 1837).

CHAPTER 4

WHAT KIND OF REVOLUTION? JUSTIFICATIONS FOR REBELLION

HISTORICAL CONTEXT

The great question confronting the English subjects who lived in America during the decade of the 1770s was this: Under what circumstances are rebellions against established authority justified? After months of intense debate, during which many ideas were presented, considered, and rejected, Americans declared the colonies to "be free and independent states." With this declaration, they launched the first national rebellion against colonial rule in modern times. But while the nature of this rebellion was understood by some to be a defense of liberty, others saw it as an unnecessary disruption that threatened the rights of Englishmen in America.

The American War of Independence began first in people's minds. Before a shot was fired, the colonists had to break the laws that governed them and to deny the right of those who had ruled them to do so any longer—in short, to reject what they had accepted for decades. Their *intellectual* work of justifying rebellion has inspired other people around the world for over 200 years. Yet because winners write history, Americans today rarely stop to consider the arguments against rebellion that were made in the 1770s. This chapter restores that sense of contingency by showing that independence was anything but inevitable.

Years of controversy between the colonies and England divided the colonists into several schools of thought. On one side were the militants, who vowed never to yield to British pretensions. In the middle were the moderates, who, while denouncing British encroachments on their liberties, saw benefits from their association with England and favored policies of conciliation. On the other side were the Tories, who desired to remain loyal to the Crown and often argued that threats to that English liberty came from the rebels themselves. These groups were roughly equal in number.

When the First Continental Congress opened session in September 1774, the delegates debated and then rejected a plan of compromise proposed by Joseph Galloway of Pennsylvania. In its stead, the militants within the Congress pushed through a Declaration of Rights and Grievances that denied England's right to tax the colonists and demanded the repeal of several Acts viewed by the delegates as "intolerable." The ensuing spring, the British Parliament considered these demands but ultimately rejected a plan of reconciliation and voted instead to send more troops to quell the growing resistance in America.

With the militants in control on both sides of the Atlantic, the stage was set for confrontation. On April 18, 1775, General Thomas Gage dispatched 700 British soldiers from Boston to capture colonial leaders and arms at Concord, Massachusetts. The Boston Committee of Correspondence immediately sent Paul Revere and two other patriots to warn the colonists of the British movements. At dawn the following morning, seventy "Minutemen"—about half the adult males in Lexington—encountered the British regulars at a bridge along the road to Concord. Guns flashed, men fell, and a war began.

Three weeks later, colonial delegates to the Second Continental Congress gathered in Philadelphia. This body promptly resolved to undertake "the defense of American liberty." It created an army and appointed George Washington as commander-in-chief. These initial actions, however, did not include a demand for independence. Rather, for the next fifteen months, the chief objective of the delegates to the Congress was to secure the repeal of parliamentary legislation they considered oppressive. They wanted, they said, not independence, but the constitutional liberties due all Englishmen, including those who lived in America.

As the rebellion continued, however, hopes for reconciliation evaporated. Late in the summer of 1775, British king George III issued the Proclamation for Suppressing Rebellion and Sedition and then hired mercenary soldiers to help crush the revolt. Meanwhile, Lord Dunmore, the Royal Governor of Virginia, placed his colony under martial law, issued a proclamation that offered freedom to slaves and indentured servants who joined the Loyalist army, and ordered the bombing of Norfolk. Early in 1776, another royal governor, Josiah Martin, also raised a force of 1,500 Scottish Highlanders in an attempt to seize control of North Carolina. Such actions by the king and his men provoked many planters from the South as well as patriots from the North to demand a final break with Great Britain.

Perhaps the individual most influential in arousing public sentiment for independence was Thomas Paine. As a recent English immigrant who had been in America scarcely a year, Paine was an unlikely person to assume this role. Born in 1737, the son of a poor Quaker father and an Anglican mother, Paine had known poverty and hardship from birth. In his youth, Paine had lived an unsettled life, finding temporary employment as a sailor, a teacher, a tobacconist, a grocer, and an exciseman. His two unhappy marriages were brief—the first ending with the death of his wife and the second in legal separation. A working man with a lively intellectual curiosity, Paine often championed the causes of England's laboring classes.

In 1774, without work or money, Paine left for the New World. Armed with a letter of introduction from Benjamin Franklin, he found employment with a Philadelphia printer and rapidly rose in prominence, securing in February 1775 the editorship of the *Pennsylvania Magazine*. During the ensuing months, Paine published several promising pieces, including "African Slavery in America," an article that described slavery as "murder, robbery, lewdness and barbarity." Another essay, "A Serious Thought," included the bold prediction that "the Almighty will finally separate America from Britain." In these works, we see flashes of Paine's literary genius, a genius that became fully manifest in January 1776 with the publication of his electrifying masterpiece, *Common Sense.*

The influence of this pamphlet can hardly be exaggerated. Written in a simple, plain, and direct style, easily read and understood by all, *Common Sense* became an instant hit, selling 120,000 copies in three months and more than half a million copies altogether. Newspapers across the colonies printed extended excerpts from *Common Sense* and summarized its arguments in favor of independence. Virtually everyone in the colonies either read *Common Sense* or heard it discussed in public forums, as Paine's words appealed across classes and regions. Paine's brilliant piece of propaganda helped transform reluctant rebels into republican revolutionaries inflamed with a passion for independence.

As Americans discussed *Common Sense* in town meetings and taverns, colonial assemblies debated the desirability of independence. In April 1776, North Carolina became the first colony to empower its delegates to the Second Continental Congress to support "independency." A month later, a Virginia convention passed a resolution instructing its delegates to introduce to the Congress a motion declaring the colonies to be "free and independent States, absolved from all allegiance to, or dependence on, the Crown or Parliament of Great Britain." In early June, Richard Henry Lee presented the Virginia Resolution to the Congress, and John Adams of Massachusetts seconded the motion. When moderate delegates questioned the wisdom of declaring independence before the people of the middle colonies demanded it, the Congress decided to postpone debate on the resolution until July 1, hoping that a three-week delay would produce a more united front. In the interim, the Congress appointed a committee, composed of Thomas Jefferson, John Adams, Benjamin Franklin, Robert Livingston, and Roger Sherman, to draft a document proposing a rationale for independence.

The Committee of Five selected the thirty-three-year-old Jefferson to write the preliminary draft of the Declaration. Despite his youth, Jefferson was the obvious choice. He was a Virginian, and according to protocol, it was proper for a delegate from the colony that had introduced the resolution to draft the formal declaration. Moreover, Jefferson was an eloquent writer. He labored for about two weeks on his preliminary draft, showing it privately to Adams and Franklin (who offered a few suggestions) before bringing it back to the committee for further revisions.

On July 1, as agreed upon, the Congress reopened debate on the Virginia Resolution. Nine colonies expressed support for the resolution, and two (Pennsylvania and South Carolina) opposed the motion. The delegation from Delaware was evenly split, however, and New York's delegation refused to vote until it received specific instructions on the matter from home. With only nine affirmative votes, the Congress decided to defer the decision.

By the next morning, however, circumstances had changed considerably. On July 2, 1776, the Congress voted unanimously—twelve colonies in favor, none opposed, with New York abstaining—to sever all ties with England and become free and independent states.

Having made the critical decision, the Congress began debate on the wording of the formal declaration that would announce the birth of a nation. For two days the Congress examined, line by line, the document drafted by Jefferson and revised by the Committee of Five. After making a number of modifications, on July 4, the Congress officially promulgated the Declaration of Independence.

Image 4.1 Congress Voting Independence (c.1800)

This print, taken from a painting by Robert Edge Pine and Edward Savage, depicts John Adams, Roger Sherman, Robert Livingston, and Thomas Jefferson presenting a draft of the Declaration of Independence to Congress. Benjamin Franklin, the fifth member of the draft committee, is seated in the center-left foreground. The painting is considered the most authentic depiction of the event, free of dramatic embellishment.

Source: Courtesy Historical Society of Pennsylvania

INTRODUCTION TO DOCUMENTS 1–4

By 1774, the British Parliament's power to regulate trade and tax goods had been challenged with boycotts, the destruction of property, and the intimidation of customs officials by organized mobs. When Bostonians threw chests of East India Company tea into the harbor rather than pay taxes on it, Parliament reacted by closing the port of Boston, sending soldiers to enforce order, exempting those soldiers from local civil laws, tightening colonial control over the Massachusetts legislature, banning town meetings, and installing a British general, Thomas Gage, as the new royal governor. In response to these Intolerable Acts, as some called them, the colonies sent delegates to what became known as the First Continental Congress. Rather suddenly, thirteen separate disputes with England found a single, although extralegal, forum.

The issues that confronted the Continental Congress give us a good sense of how divided people were ideologically. The first document here is an excerpt from Joseph Galloway's "Plan of Union." Galloway was a moderate from Pennsylvania, and he sought some way to reconcile the colonists' desire to rule their own destinies with their status as British subjects. The Congress rejected his plan of union, demanding instead the repeal of the Intolerable Acts. Given that Galloway's peaceful solution had widespread support, why is he not remembered alongside Paine and Franklin as a hero of the era?

Just weeks after Galloway issued his plan, fifty-one women gathered in Edenton, North Carolina, to boycott tea and other British products. News of their "tea party" spread quickly, as it was the earliest instance of female political action in support of independence. Document 2 satirizes their act from a British perspective, a negative portrait of women in the traditionally male sphere of politics. Yet opposition to the revolution was not limited to Britain. Document 3 is the Reverend Samuel Seabury's January 1775 call to the New York legislature to resist radical ideas and express loyalty to the Crown and Parliament. On the other side, Benjamin Franklin wrote personally to Galloway from London in February 1775, explaining the limits of his own moderation. In all of these documents, note how charged the rhetoric had become, an indication of the political polarization of the moment and the emotional depth of the issues. Note especially how Franklin contrasted England's "extreme corruption" with America's "glorious public virtue."

1. PLAN OF UNION (1774)

JOSEPH GALLOWAY

SEPTEMBER 28, 1774

Resolved, That the Congress will apply to His Majesty for a redress of grievances, under which his faithful subjects in America labour; and assure him, that the Colonies hold in abhorrence the idea of being considered independent communities on the British Government, and most ardently desire the establishment of a Political Union, not only among themselves, but with the mother State, upon those principles of safety and freedom which are essential in the constitution of all free governments, and particularly that of the British Legislature; And as the Colonies from their local circumstances, cannot be represented in the Parliament of Great Britain, they will humbly propose to His Majesty, and his two Houses of Parliament, the following plan, under which the strength of the whole Empire may be drawn together on any emergency, the interests of both countries advanced, and the rights and liberties of America secured.

A Plan of a proposed Union between Great Britain and the Colonies . . .

That a British and American Legislature, for regulating the administration of the general affairs of America, be proposed and established in America, including all the said colonies; within and under which government, each colony shall retain its present constitution and powers of regulating and governing its own internal police in all cases whatsoever.

That the said government be administered by a President-General to be appointed by the King, and a Grand Council to be chosen by the representatives of the people of the several colonies in their respective Assemblies, once in every three years. . . .

That the Grand Council shall meet once in every year, if they shall think it necessary, and oftener, if occasions shall require, at such time and place as they shall adjourn to at the last preceding meeting, or as they shall be called to meet at, by the President-General on any emergency.

That the Grand Council shall have power to choose their Speaker, and shall hold and exercise all the like rights, liberties, and privileges as are held and exercised by and in the House of Commons of Great Britain.

That the President-General shall hold his office during the pleasure of the King, and his assent shall be requisite to all acts of the Grand Council, and it shall be his office and duty to cause them to be carried into execution.

That the President-General, by and with the advice and consent of the Grand Council, hold and exercise all the legislative rights, powers, and authorities, necessary for regulating and administering all the general police and affairs of the colonies. . . .

That the said President-General and Grand Council be an inferior and distinct branch of the British Legislature, united and incorporated with it for the aforesaid general purposes; and that any of the said general regulations may originate, and be formed and digested, either in the Parliament of Great Britain or in the said Grand Council; and being prepared, transmitted to the other for their approbation or dissent; and that the assent of both shall be requisite to the validity of all such general acts and statutes. . . .[1]

2. "A SOCIETY OF PATRIOTIC LADIES" (1775)

Plate V.

A SOCIETY of PATRIOTIC LADIES,
AT
EDENTON in NORTH CAROLINA.

Image 4.2 "A Society of Patriotic Ladies" (1775) In 1774, fifty-one women gathered to protest tea and other British exports in Edenton, North Carolina, prompting this satire of the event in a London newspaper a few months later. Women are portrayed with masculine qualities, interfering with the realm of male responsibility while neglecting their own work as mothers. Note the role of men as well as an African-American servant. Why might the Edenton Tea Party have caused such a stir? Was this the type of political behavior that Reverend Seabury was so concerned about?

Source: London: Printed for R. Sayer and J. Bennett, March 25, 1775. Library of Congress.

3. "AN ALARM TO THE LEGISLATURE" JANUARY 17, 1775

SAMUEL SEABURY

Honourable Gentlemen,

When you reflect upon the present confused and distressed state of this, and the other colonies, I am persuaded, that you will think no apology necessary for the liberty I have taken, of addressing you on that subject. The unhappy contention we have entered into with our parent state, would inevitably be attended with many disagreeable circumstances, with many and great inconveniences to us, even were it conducted on our part, with *propriety* and *moderation*. What then must be the case, when all proper and moderate measures are *rejected?* When not even the *appearance* of decency is regarded? When nothing seems to be consulted, but how to perplex, irritate, and affront, the *British Ministry, Parliament, Nation and King?* When every scheme that tends to *peace*, is branded with *ignominy;* as being the machination of slavery! When nothing is called Freedom but Sedition! Nothing Liberty but Rebellion! . . .

When the Delegates had met at Philadelphia, instead of settling a reasonable plan of accommodation with the parent country, they employed themselves in censuring acts of the British parliament, which were principally intended to prevent *smuggling,* and all *illicit trade;*—in writing addresses to the people of *Great-Britain,* to the inhabitants of the *colonies in general,* and to those of the *province of Quebec,* in *particular;* with the *evident design* of making them *dissatisfied with their present government;* and of *exciting clamours,* and raising *seditions* and *rebellions* against the *state;*—and in exercising a *legislative authority over all the colonies.* They had the insolence to proclaim themselves a full and free representation of his Majesty's faithful subjects in all the colonies from Nova-Scotia to Georgia"; and, as such, have laid a *tax* on all those colonies, viz. the *profits* arising from the *sales of all goods* imported from Great-Britain, Ireland, &c. during the months of December and January: Which *tax* is to be employed for the *relief* of the *Boston poor.* . . .

Behold, Gentlemen, behold the wretched state to which we are reduced! A *foreign power* is brought in to *govern this province.* Laws made at *Philadelphia,* by factious men from *New-England, New-Jersey, Pennsylvania, Maryland, Virginia,* and the *Carolinas,* are imposed upon us by the most *imperious menaces.* Money is levied upon us without the *consent* of our *representatives:* which very *money,* under colour of relieving the *poor* people of Boston, it is too *probable* will be employed to *raise an army against the King.* Mobs and riots are encouraged, in order to *force* submission to the *tyranny of the Congress.* . . .

Act now, I beseech you, as you ever have done, as the faithful representatives of the people; as the real guardians of their Rights and Liberties. Give them deliverance from the tyranny of the *Congress* and *Committees:* Secure them against the horrid carnage of a *civil war:* And endeavour to obtain for them a free and permanent constitution. . . .

Be assured, Gentlemen, that a very great majority of your constituents disapprove of the late violent proceedings, and will support you in the pursuit of more *moderate measures,* as soon as You have *delivered* Them from the *tyranny of Committees,* from the *fear of violence,* and the *dread of mobs.* Recur boldly to your good, old, legal and successful way of proceeding, by *petition* and *remonstrance.*

Address yourselves to the *King* and the *two Houses of Parliament.* Let your representations be *decent* and *firm,* and principally directed to obtain a *solid American Constitution;* such as *we* can *accept* with *safety,* and *Great-Britain* can *grant* with *dignity.* Try the experiment, and you will assuredly find that our most gracious Sovereign and both Houses of Parliament will readily *meet* you in the *paths of peace.*

Only shew your *willingness* towards an accommodation, by *acknowledging the supreme legislative authority of Great-Britain*, and I dare confidently pronounce the attainment of whatever you with *propriety*, can *ask*, and the legislature of Great-Britain with *honour concede.*[2]

4. BENJAMIN FRANKLIN, LETTER TO JOSEPH GALLOWAY, FEBRUARY 25, 1775

Dear Friend, In my last I mentioned to you my showing your plan of union to Lords Chatham and Camden. I now hear that you had sent it to Lord Dartmouth. . . .

I have not heard what objections were made to the plan in the Congress, nor would I make more than this one, that, when I consider the extreme corruption prevalent among all orders of men in this old, rotten state, and the glorious public virtue so predominant in our rising country, I cannot but apprehend more mischief than benefit from a closer union. I fear they will drag us after them in all the plundering wars which their desperate circumstances, injustice, and rapacity may prompt them to undertake; and their widewasting prodigality and profusion is a gulf that will swallow up every aid we may distress ourselves to afford them.

Here numberless and needless places, enormous salaries, pensions, perquisites, bribes, groundless quarrels, foolish expeditions, false accounts or no accounts, contracts and jobs, devour all revenue, and produce continual necessity in the midst of natural plenty. I apprehend, therefore, that to unite us intimately will only be to corrupt and poison us also. . . .

. . . However, I would try anything, and bear anything that can be borne with safety to our just liberties, rather than engage in a war with such relations, unless compelled to it by dire necessity in our own defence.

But should that plan be again brought forward, I imagine that before establishing the union, it would be necessary to agree on the following preliminary articles.

(1) The Declaratory Act; (2) all Acts of Parliament, or parts of Acts laying duties on the colonies; (3) all Acts of Parliament altering the charters, or constitutions, or laws of any colony; (4) all Acts of Parliament restraining manufactures; to be repealed. (5) Those parts of the Navigation Acts, which are for the good of the whole Empire, such as require that ships in the trade should be British or Plantation built, and navigated by three fourths British subjects, with the duties necessary for regulating commerce, to be re-enacted by both Parliaments. (6) Then, to induce the Americans to see the regulating Acts faithfully executed, it would be well to give the duties collected in each colony to the treasury of that colony, and let the Governor and Assembly appoint the officers to collect them, and proportion their salaries. Thus the business will be cheaper and better done, and the misunderstandings between the two countries, now created and fomented by the unprincipled wretches generally appointed from England, be entirely prevented.

These are hasty thoughts submitted to your consideration.

You will see the new proposal of Lord North, made on Monday last, which I have sent to the committee. Those in [the English] administration, who are for violent measures, are said to dislike it. The others rely upon it as a means of dividing, and by that means subduing us. But I cannot conceive that any colony will undertake to grant a revenue to a government that holds a sword over their heads with a threat to strike the moment they cease to give or do not give so much as it is pleased to expect. In such a situation, where is the right of giving our own property freely or the right to judge of our own ability to give? It seems to me the language of a highwayman who, with a pistol in your face, says: "Give me your purse, and then I will not put my hand into your pocket. But give me all your money, or I will shoot you through the head." With great and sincere esteem, I am, etc.,

B. Franklin.[3]

INTRODUCTION TO DOCUMENT 5

The convening of the First Continental Congress in 1774 was an enormous step in the thinking of the colonists. If Patrick Henry went further than most in declaring himself an American more than a Virginian, he nonetheless captured the drift of events. The Continental Congress was only one quasi-governmental body among countless others throughout the colonies, all of which were completely unauthorized by British law. In 1775 and 1776, extralegal institutions raised money, passed legislation, and gathered armed militia. And the radicals had effectively ended trade with Britain. With the bloody day in Lexington and Concord, when scores of British and colonial troops fell, and then with the convening of the Second Continental Congress, the die of rebellion was cast.

Yet what was the meaning of these events? Why were people fighting and dying? Thomas Paine helped provide some answers. The following is an excerpt from his *Common Sense*. In reading this document, consider how eighteenth-century men and women from various social groups would respond to his arguments. What were Paine's ideas about the origins of law, government, and community? How did the English monarchy deviate from these origins? Pay particular attention to the metaphors that Paine used to make his case. Finally, consider how moderates such as Galloway might have responded to Paine's arguments.

---

5. *COMMON SENSE* (1776)

THOMAS PAINE

. . . Mankind being originally equals in the order of creation, the equality could only be destroyed by some subsequent circumstance: the distinctions of rich and poor may in a great measure be accounted for, and that without having recourse to the harsh ill-sounding names of oppression and avarice. . . . But there is another and greater distinction for which no truly natural or religious reason can be assigned, and that is the distinction of men into KINGS and SUBJECTS. Male and female are the distinctions of nature, good and bad the distinctions of heaven; but how a race of men came into the world so exalted above the rest, and distinguished like some new species, is worth inquiring into, and whether they are the means of happiness or of misery to mankind.

In the early ages of the world, according to the scripture chronology there were no kings; the consequence of which was, there were no wars; it is the pride of kings which throws mankind into confusion. . . .

In the following pages I offer nothing more than simple facts, plain arguments, and common sense: and have no other preliminaries to settle with the reader, than that he will divest himself of prejudice and pre-possession, and suffer his reason and his feelings to determine for themselves: that he will put on, or rather that he will not put off, the true character of a man, and generously enlarge his views beyond the present day. . . .

The sun never shone on a cause of greater worth. 'Tis not the affair of a city, a country, a province, or a kingdom; but of a continent—of at least one eighth part of the habitable globe. 'Tis not the concern of a day, a year, or an age; posterity are virtually involved in the contest, and will be more or less affected even to the end of time, by the proceedings now. Now is the seed-time of continental union, faith and honor. The least fracture now will be like a name engraved with the point of a pin on the tender rind of a young oak; the wound would enlarge with the tree, and posterity read it in full grown characters. . . .

I have heard it asserted by some, that as America has flourished under her former connection with Great Britain, the same connection is necessary towards her future happiness, and will always have the same effect. Nothing can be more fallacious than this kind of argument. We may as well assert that because a child has thrived upon milk, that it is never to have meat, or that the first twenty years of our lives is to become a precedent for the next twenty. But even this is admitting more than is true; for I answer roundly, that America would have flourished as much, and probably much more, had no European power taken any notice of her. The commerce by which she hath enriched herself are the necessaries of life, and will always have a market while eating is the custom of Europe.

I challenge the warmest advocate for reconciliation to show a single advantage that this continent can reap by being connected with Great Britain. I repeat the challenge; not a single advantage is derived. Our corn will fetch its price in any market in Europe, and our imported goods must be paid for, buy them where we will.

But the injuries and disadvantages which we sustain by that connection, are without number; and our duty to mankind at large, as well as to ourselves, instruct us to renounce the alliance: because, any submission to, or dependence on, Great Britain, tends directly to involve this continent in European wars and quarrels, and set us at variance with nations who would otherwise seek our friendship, and against whom we have neither anger nor complaint. As Europe is our market for trade, we ought to form no partial connection with any part of it. It is the true interest of America to steer clear of European contentions, which she never can do, while, by her dependence on Britain, she is made the makeweight in the scale of British politics.

Europe is too thickly planted with kingdoms to be long at peace, and whenever a war breaks out between England and any foreign power, the trade of America goes to ruin, *because of her connection with Britain.* The next war may not turn out like the last, and should it not, the advocates for reconciliation now will be wishing for separation then, because neutrality in that case would be a safer convoy than a man of war. Every thing that is right or reasonable pleads for separation. The blood of the slain, the weeping voice of nature cries, 'TIS TIME TO PART. Even the distance at which the Almighty hath placed England and America is a strong and natural proof that the authority of the one over the other, was never the design of heaven. The time likewise at which the continent was discovered, adds weight to the argument, and the manner in which it was peopled, increases the force of it. The Reformation was preceded by the discovery of America: As if the Almighty graciously meant to open a sanctuary to the persecuted in future years, when home should afford neither friendship nor safety. . . .

Small islands not capable of protecting themselves are the proper objects for government to take under their care; but there is something absurd, in supposing a Continent to be perpetually governed by an island. In no instance hath nature made the satellite larger than its primary planet; and as England and America, with respect to each other, reverse the common order of nature, it is evident that they belong to different systems. England to Europe: America to itself.

. . . As I have always considered the independency of this continent, as an event which sooner or later must arrive, so from the late rapid progress of the continent to maturity, the event cannot be far off. Wherefore, on the breaking out of hostilities, it was not worth the while to have disputed a matter which time would have finally redressed, unless we meant to be in earnest: otherwise it is like wasting an estate on a suit at law, to regulate the trespasses of a tenant whose lease is just expiring. No man was a warmer wisher for a reconciliation than myself, before the fatal nineteenth of April, 1775, but the moment the event of that day was made known, I rejected the hardened, sullen-tempered Pharaoh of England for ever; and disdain the wretch, that with the pretended title of FATHER OF HIS PEOPLE can unfeelingly hear of their slaughter, and composedly sleep with their blood upon his soul. . . .

But where, say some, is the king of America? I'll tell you, friend, he reigns above, and doth not make havoc of mankind like the royal brute of Great Britain. Yet that we may not appear to be defective even in earthly honors, let a day be solemnly set apart for proclaiming the charter; let it be brought forth placed on the divine law, the Word of God; let a crown be placed thereon, by which the world may know, that so far as we approve of monarchy, that in America the law is king. For as in absolute governments the king is law, so in free countries the law ought to be king; and there ought to be no other. But lest any ill use should afterwards arise, let the crown at the conclusion of the ceremony be demolished, and scattered among the people whose right it is.

A government of our own is our natural right: and when a man seriously reflects on the precariousness of human affairs, he will become convinced, that it is infinitely wiser and safer, to form a Constitution of our own in a cool deliberate manner, while we have it in our power, than to trust such an interesting event to time and chance. . . . Ye that oppose independence now, ye know not what ye do: ye are opening a door

to eternal tyranny, by keeping vacant the seat of government. There are thousands and tens of thousands, who would think it glorious to expel from the continent, that barbarous and hellish power, which hath stirred up the Indians and the Negroes to destroy us; the cruelty hath a double guilt, it is dealing brutally by us, and treacherously by them.

To talk of friendship with those in whom our reason forbids us to have faith, and our affections wounded through a thousand pores instruct us to detest, is madness and folly. Every day wears out the little remains of kindred between us and them; and can there be any reason to hope, that as the relationship expires, the affection will increase, or that we shall agree better when we have ten times more and greater concerns to quarrel over than ever?

Ye that tell us of harmony and reconciliation, can ye restore to us the time that is past? Can ye give to prostitution its former innocence? neither can ye reconcile Britain and America. The last cord now is broken, the people of England are presenting addresses against us. There are injuries which nature cannot forgive; she would cease to be nature if she did. As well can the lover forgive the ravisher of his mistress, as the continent forgive the murders of Britain. . . . O! ye that love mankind! Ye that dare oppose not only the tyranny but the tyrant, stand forth! Every spot of the old world is overrun with oppression. Freedom hath been hunted round the globe. Asia and Africa have long expelled her. Europe regards her like a stranger, and England hath given her warning to depart. O! receive the fugitive, and prepare in time an asylum for mankind.[4]

INTRODUCTION TO DOCUMENT 6

Notwithstanding Paine's persuasive pen, not everyone agreed with his assertions. For American Loyalists, it was the rebels, not the King who were waging war against basic English liberties. One Englishman who articulated this position was John Wesley, an Anglican minister beloved both in England and the colonies by all who called themselves "Methodists." A lifelong Tory (according to Wesley, a Tory was "one who believes God, not the people, to be the origin of all civil power"), Wesley was an outspoken critic of the rebellion. When asked to deliver a "charity sermon" for the benefit of the widows and orphans of the early victims of the war, Wesley wrote and later published "National Sins and Miseries." Compare the argument and rhetoric of this sermon with Paine's *Common Sense.* How do they come to such different conclusions, given that both insist that they are relying on "reason"? And what does Wesley mean when he observes that "reason is lost in rage"? What was it about the revolution that so disturbed him?

6. "A SERMON PREACHED AT ST. MATTHEW'S, BETHNAL GREEN, ON SUNDAY, NOV. 12, 1775"

JOHN WESLEY

Let not anyone think this is but a small calamity which is fallen upon our land. If you saw, as I have seen, in every county, city, town, men who were once of a calm, mild, friendly temper, mad with party zeal, foaming with rage against their quiet neighbours, ready to tear out one another's throats, and to plunge their swords into each other's bowels; if you had heard men who once feared God and honoured the king now breathing out the bitterest invectives against him, and just ripe, should any occasion offer, for treason and rebellion; you would not then judge this to be a little evil, a matter of small moment, but one of the heaviest judgments which God can permit to fall upon a guilty land.

Such is the condition of Englishmen at home. And is it any better abroad? I fear not. From those who are now upon the spot I learn that in our colonies, also, many are causing the people to drink largely of the same deadly wine; thousands of whom are there inflamed more and more, till their heads are utterly turned, and they are mad to all intents and purposes. Reason is lost in rage; its small still voice is drowned by popular clamour. Wisdom is fallen in the streets. And where is the place of understanding? It is hardly to be found in these provinces. Here is *slavery,* real slavery indeed, most properly so called. For the regular, legal, constitutional form of government is no more. Here is real, not imaginary, bondage; not the shadow of English liberty is left. Not only no *liberty of the press* is allowed—none dare print a page or a line unless it be exactly conformable to the sentiments of our lords, the people—but no *liberty of speech.* Their "tongue" is not "their own." None must dare to utter one word either in favour of King George, or in disfavour of the idol they have set up—the new, illegal, unconstitutional government, utterly unknown to us and to our forefathers. Here is no *religious liberty;* no liberty of conscience from them that "honour the King," and whom consequently a sense of duty prompts them to defend from the vile calumnies continually vented against him. Here is no *civil liberty;* no enjoying the fruit of their labour any further than the populace pleases. A man has no security for his trade, his house, his property, unless he will swim with the stream. Nay, he has no security for his life if his popular neighbour has a mind to cut his throat. For there is no law, and no legal magistrate to take cognizance of offenses. There is the gulf of tyranny—of arbitrary power on one hand, and of anarchy on the other. And, as if all this were not misery enough, see likewise the fell monster, war! But who can describe the complicated misery which is contained in this? Hark! The cannons roar! A pitchy cloud covers the face of the sky. Noise, confusion, terror, reign over all! Dying groans are on every side. The bodies of men are pierced, torn, hewed in pieces; their blood is poured on the earth like water! Their souls take their flight into the eternal world; perhaps into everlasting misery. The ministers of grace turn away from the horrid scene; the ministers of vengeance triumph. Such already has been the face of things in that once happy land where peace and plenty, even while banished from great part of Europe, smiled for near a hundred years.

And what is it which drags on these poor victims into the field of blood? It is a great phantom which stalks before them, which they are taught to call, "liberty"! It is this which breathes

> . . . into their hearts stern love of war,
> And thirst of vengeance, and contempt of death.

Real liberty, meantime, is trampled underfoot, and is lost in anarchy and confusion.

But which of these warriors all the while considered the wife of his youth, that is now left a disconsolate widow—perhaps with none that careth for her; perhaps deprived of her only comfort and support, and not having where to lay her head? Who considered his helpless children, now desolate orphans, it may be, crying for bread, while their mother has nothing left to give them but her sorrows and her tears?[5]

INTRODUCTION TO DOCUMENTS 7, 8, AND 9

Even as Paine and Wesley penned their tirades against the evils of tyranny, events in Virginia were forcing Patriots and Loyalists alike to reflect upon the condition of that group of Americans most robbed of human freedoms. On November 7, 1775, Lord Dunmore issued a proclamation for the colony of Virginia that offered freedom to any slave who agreed to join the fight for the British side. This proclamation caused an immediate stir, and in mid-December, the Virginia colonial assembly responded with its own proclamation threatening strict punishment for slaves deserting to the British. The following documents include Lord Dunmore's "Proclamation," a published letter about the proclamation, and Virginia's official reaction to the proclamation. What do these documents reveal about American and British attitudes toward slavery and liberty? Does Dunmore's proclamation complicate your sense of the American Revolution as a war for freedom? How do you think southern planters and African-American slaves would have responded to this debate?

7. LORD DUNMORE'S PROCLAMATION FOR THE COLONY OF VIRGINIA (1775)

BY HIS EXCELLENCY THE RIGHT HONORABLE JOHN EARLE OF DUNMORE, HIS MAJESTY'S LIEUTENANT AND GOVERNOR GENERAL OF THE COLONY AND DOMINION OF VIRGINIA, AND VICE ADMIRAL OF THE SAME

A PROCLAMATION

As I have ever entertained Hopes, that an Accommodation might have taken Place between Great-Britain and this Colony, without being compelled by my Duty to this most disagreeable but now absolutely necessary Step, rendered so by a Body of armed Men unlawfully assembled, firing on His Majesty's

Tenders, and the formation of an Army, and that Army now on their March to attack his Majesty's Troops and destroy the well disposed subjects of the Colony. To defeat such treasonable Purposes, and that all such Traitors, and their Abettors, may be brought to Justice, and that the Peace, and good Order of this Colony may be again restored, which the ordinary Course of the Civil Law is unable to effect; I have thought fit to issue this my Proclamation, hereby declaring, that until the aforesaid good Purpose can be obtained, I do in Virtue of the Power and Authority to ME given, by His MAJESTY, determine to execute Martial Law, and cause the same to be executed throughout this Colony: and to ****** the Peace and good Order may the sooner be restored, I do require every Person capable of bearing Arms, to resort to His Majesty's Standard, or be looked upon as Traitors to His Majesty's Crown and Government, and thereby become liable to the Penalty the Law inflicts upon such Offenses; such as forfeiture of Life, confiscation of Lands, &. &. And I do hereby further declare all indented [*sic*] Servants, Negroes, or others, (appertaining to Rebels,) free that are able and willing to bear Arms, they joining His Majesty's Troops as soon as may be, for the more speedily reducing this Colony to a proper Sense of their Duty, to His Majesty's Crown and Dignity . . . .
Given under my Hand on board the Ship William by Norfolk, the 7th Day of November in the Sixteenth Year of His Majesty's Reign. Dunmore (God save the King.)

8. LETTER REGARDING DUNMORE'S PROCLAMATION FROM THE *VIRGINIA GAZETTE*, NOVEMBER 25, 1775

. . . The second class of people, for whose sake a few remarks upon this proclamation seem necessary, is the Negroes. They have been flattered with their freedom, if they be able to bear arms, and will speedily join Lord Dunmore's troops. To none then is freedom promised but to such as are able to do Lord Dunmore service: The aged, the infirm, the women and children, are still to remain the property of their masters, masters who will be provoked to severity, should part of their slaves desert them. Lord Dunmore's declaration, therefore, is a cruel declaration to the Negroes. He does not even pretend to make it out of any tenderness to them, but solely on his own account; and should it meet with success, it leaves by far the greater number at the mercy of an enraged and injured people. But should there be any amongst the Negroes weak enough to believe that Dunmore intends to do them a kindness, and wicked enough to provoke the fury of the Americans against their defenceless fathers and mothers, their wives, their women and children, let them only consider the difficulty of effecting their escape, and what they must expect to suffer if they fall into the hands of the Americans. Let them farther consider what must be their fate, should the English prove conquerors in this dispute. If we can judge of the future from the past, it will not be much mended. Long have the Americans, moved by compassion, and actuated by sound policy, endeavoured to stop the progress of slavery. Our Assemblies have repeatedly passed acts laying heavy duties upon imported Negroes, by which they meant altogether to prevent the horrid traffick; but their humane intentions have been as often frustrated by the cruelty and covetousness of a set of English merchants, who prevailed upon the King to repeal our kind and merciful acts, little indeed to the credit of his humanity. Can it then be supposed that the Negroes will be better used by the English, who have always encouraged and upheld this slavery, than by their present masters, who pity their condition, who wish, in general, to make it as easy and comfortable as possible, and who would willingly, were it in their power, or were they permitted, not only prevent any more Negroes from losing their freedom, but restore it to such as have already unhappily lost it. No, the ends of Lord Dunmore and his party being answered, they will either give up the offending Negroes to the rigour of the laws they have broken, or sell them in the West Indies, where every year they sell many thousands of their miserable brethren, to perish either by the inclemency of the weather, or the cruelty of barbarous masters. Be not then, ye Negroes, tempted by this proclamation to ruin yourselves. I have given you a faithful view of what you are to expect; and I declare, before GOD, in doing it, I have considered your welfare, as well as that of the country. Whether you will profit by my advice I cannot tell; but this I know, that whether we suffer or not, if you desert us, you most certainly will.[6]

9. BY THE REPRESENTATIVES OF THE PEOPLE OF THE COLONY AND DOMINION OF VIRGINIA, ASSEMBLED IN GENERAL CONVENTION, DECEMBER 14, 1775

A DECLARATION

Whereas Lord Dunmore, by his proclamation, dated on board the ship William, off Norfolk, the 7th day of November 1775, hath offered freedom to such abled-bodied slaves as are willing to join him, and take up arms, against the good people of this colony, giving thereby encouragement to a general insurrection, which may induce a necessity of inflicting the severest punishments upon those unhappy people, already deluded by his base and insidious arts; and whereas, by an act of the General Assembly now in force in this colony, it is enacted, that all negro or other slaves, conspiring to rebel or make insurrection, shall suffer death, and be excluded all benefit of clergy: We think it proper to declare, that all slaves who have been, or shall be, seduced, by his lordship's proclamation, or other arts, to desert their masters' service, and take up arms against the inhabitants of this colony, shall be liable to such punishment as shall hereafter be directed by the General Convention. And to that end all such, who have taken this unlawful and wicked step, may return in safety to their duty, and escape the punishment due to their crimes, we hereby promise pardon to them, they surrendering themselves to col. William Woodford, or any other commander of our troops, and not appearing in arms after the publication hereof. And we do farther earnestly recommend it to all humane and benevolent persons in this colony to explain and make known this our offer of mercy to those unfortunate people.

Edmund Pendleton, president.[7]

INTRODUCTION TO DOCUMENT 10

The war for independence had multiple causes: political, economic, and social. Document 10 is the title page of a published sermon that suggests that religion also played a role in the rebellion. What type of appeal might a sermon like this have had, and to whom?

10. "GOD ARISING AND PLEADING HIS PEOPLE'S CAUSE" (1777)

ABRAHAM KETELTAS

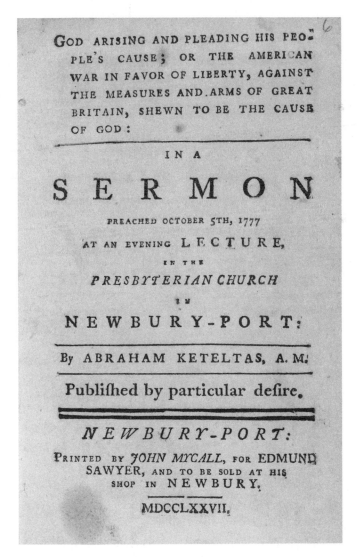

Image 4.3 Abraham Keteltas, "God Arising and Pleading His People's Cause; or The American War . . . Shewn to Be the Cause of God."

Compare the message of this sermon delivered in 1777 to that of Reverend Seabury two years earlier. How might religious arguments have been used to advance or limit the movement for independence?

Source: Newbury-Port: John Mycall for Edmund Sawyer, 1777. RB 80646. The Huntington Library, San Marino, California.

INTRODUCTION TO DOCUMENTS 11 AND 12

Just half a year after Paine published his stirring call for rebellion, the thirteen colonies declared themselves free and independent states. The following documents are taken from this period of decision. Document 11 contains selections from the letters of John and Abigail Adams that were written during 1776 while John was a delegate to the Second Continental Congress. Consider the advice that Abigail gave to John in these letters, and John's response. Also note his predictions about how future generations would celebrate July 2, 1776, the day that Congress first declared its independence from England. The spelling in the letters has been modernized.

Document 12 is the finalized draft of the Declaration of Independence, which was originally written by Thomas Jefferson in June 1776 and then edited and finally announced by Congress on July 4. This historic document consists of two parts: an introduction that justifies the abstract right of revolution and a much longer section listing specific grievances against George III that explains to the world why the colonists felt driven to exercise the inalienable rights outlined in the introduction. While the list of grievances was probably the section of greatest importance to the generation that fought the Revolution, the words contained in the preamble have inspired oppressed peoples all across the world for more than two centuries. Yet how might Galloway, Seabury, and Wesley have responded to the declaration when it was finalized?

11. CORRESPONDENCE OF ABIGAIL AND JOHN ADAMS

ABIGAIL ADAMS TO JOHN ADAMS
BRAINTREE, MARCH 31, 1776

I long to hear that you have declared an independency—and by the way in the new Code of Laws which I suppose it will be necessary for you to make I desire you would Remember the Ladies, and be more generous and favorable to them than your ancestors. Do not put such unlimited power into the hands of the Husbands. Remember all Men would be tyrants if they could. If particular care and attention is not paid to the Ladies we are determined to foment a Rebellion, and will not hold ourselves bound by any Laws in which we have no voice, or Representation.

That your Sex are Naturally Tyrannical is a Truth so thoroughly established as to admit of no dispute, but such of you as wish to be happy willingly give up the harsh title of Master for the more tender and endearing one of Friend. Why then, not put it out of the power of the vicious and the Lawless to use us with cruelty and indignity with impunity. Men of Sense in all Ages abhor those customs which treat us only as the vassals of your Sex. Regard us then as Beings placed by providence under your protection and in imitation of the Supreme Being make use of that power only for our happiness.[8]

JOHN ADAMS TO ABIGAIL ADAMS
PHILADELPHIA, APRIL 14, 1776

. . . As to your extraordinary Code of Laws, I cannot but laugh. We have been told that our Struggle has loosened the bands of Government everywhere. That Children and Apprentices were disobedient—that schools and Colleges were grown turbulent—that Indians slighted their Guardians and Negroes grew insolent to their Masters. But your Letter was the first Intimation that another Tribe more numerous and powerful than all the rest were grown discontented.—This is rather too coarse a Compliment but you are so saucy, I won't blot it out.

Depend upon it., We know better than to repeal our Masculine systems. Although they are in full Force, you know they are little more than Theory. We dare not exert our Power in its full Latitude. We are obliged to go fair, and softly, and in Practice you know We are the subjects. We have only the Name of Masters, and rather than give up this, which would completely subject Us to the Despotism of the Petticoat, I hope General Washington and all our brave Heroes would fight. I am sure every good Politician would plot, as long as he would against Despotism, empire, Monarchy, Aristocracy, Oligarchy, or Ochlocracy,—A fine Story indeed. I begin to think the Ministry as deep as they are wicked. After stirring up Tories, Landjobbers, Trimmers, Bigots, Canadians, Indians, Negroes, Hanoverians, Hessians, Russians, Irish Roman Catholics, Scotch Renegades, at last they have stimulated the ladies to demand new Privileges and threaten to rebel.[9]

ABIGAIL ADAMS TO JOHN ADAMS, BRAINTREE, MAY 7, 1776

I can not say that I think you very generous to the Ladies, for while you are proclaiming peace and good will to Men, Emancipating all Nations, you insist upon retaining an absolute power over Wives. But you must remember that Arbitrary power is like most other things which are very hard, very liable to be broken—and notwithstanding all your wise Laws and Maxims we have it in our power not only to free ourselves but to subdue our Masters, and without violence throw both your natural and legal authority at our feet—

"Charm by accepting, by submitting sway
    Yet have our Humor most when we obey."[10]

JOHN ADAMS TO ABIGAIL ADAMS PHILADELPHIA, JULY 3, 1776

...The Hopes of Reconciliation, which were fondly entertained by Multitudes of honest and well meaning though weak and mistaken People, have been gradually and at last totally extinguished.... The Second of July 1776, will be the most memorable Epoch, in the History of America.—I am apt to believe that it will be celebrated, by succeeding Generations, as the great anniversary Festival. It ought to be commemorated, as the Day of Deliverance by solemn Acts of Devotion to God Almighty. It ought to be solemnized with Pomp and Parade, with Shows, Games, Sports, Guns, Bells, Bonfires and Illuminations from one End of this Continent to the other from this Time forward forever more.

You will think me transported with Enthusiasm but I am not.—I am well aware of the Toil and Blood and Treasure, that it will cost Us to maintain this Declaration, and support and defend these States.—yet through all the Gloom I can see the Rays of ravishing Light and Glory. I can see that the End is more than worth all the Means. And that Posterity will triumph in that Day's Transaction, even although We should rue it, which I trust in God We shall not.[11]

12. THE DECLARATION OF INDEPENDENCE

TEXT APPROVED BY CONGRESS, JULY 4, 1776. THE UNANIMOUS DECLARATION OF THE THIRTEEN UNITED STATES OF AMERICA

When, in the course of human events, it becomes necessary for one people to dissolve the political bands which have connected them with another, and to assume, among the powers of the earth, the separate and equal station to which the laws of nature and of nature's God entitle them, a decent respect to the opinions of mankind requires that they should declare the causes which impel them to the separation.

We hold these truths to be self-evident: That all men are created equal; that they are endowed by their Creator with certain unalienable rights; that among these are life, liberty, and the pursuit of happiness. That, to secure these rights, governments are instituted among men, deriving their just powers from the consent of the governed; that whenever any form of government becomes destructive of these ends, it is the right of the people to alter or to abolish it, and to institute new government, laying its foundation on such principles, and organizing its powers in such form, as to them shall seem most likely to effect their safety and happiness. Prudence, indeed, will dictate that governments long established should not be changed for light and transient causes; and accordingly all experience hath shown that mankind are more disposed to suffer, while evils are sufferable, than to right themselves by abolishing the forms to which they are accustomed. But when a long train of abuses and usurpations, pursuing invariably the same object, evinces a design to reduce them under absolute despotism, it is their right, it is their duty, to throw off such government, and to provide new guards for their future security. Such has been the patient sufferance of these colonies; and such is now the necessity which constrains them to alter their former systems of government. The history of the present King of Great Britain is a history of repeated injuries and usurpations, all having in direct object the establishment of an absolute tyranny over these states. To prove this, let facts be submitted to a candid world.

He has refused his assent to laws, the most wholesome and necessary for the public good.

He has forbidden his governors to pass laws of immediate and pressing importance, unless suspended in their operation till his assent should be obtained; and, when so suspended, he has utterly neglected to attend to them.

He has refused to pass other laws for the accommodation of large districts of people, unless those people would relinquish the right of representation in the legislature, a right inestimable to them, and formidable to tyrants only.

He has called together legislative bodies at places unusual, uncomfortable, and distant from the depository of their public records, for the sole purpose of fatiguing them into compliance with his measures.

He has dissolved representative houses repeatedly, for opposing, with manly firmness, his invasions on the rights of the people.

He has refused for a long time, after such dissolutions, to cause others to be elected; whereby the legislative powers, incapable of annihilation, have returned to the people at large for their exercise; the state remaining, in the mean time, exposed to all the dangers of invasions from without and convulsions within.

He has endeavored to prevent the population of these states; for that purpose obstructing the laws for naturalization of foreigners; refusing to pass others to encourage their migration hither, and raising the conditions of new appropriations of lands.

He has obstructed the administration of justice, by refusing his assent to laws for establishing judiciary powers.

He has made judges dependent on his will alone, for the tenure of their offices, and the amount and payment of their salaries.

He has erected a multitude of new offices, and sent hither swarms of officers to harass our people and eat out their substance.

He has kept among us, in times of peace, standing armies, without the consent of our legislatures.

He has affected to render the military independent of, and superior to, the civil power.

He has combined with others to subject us to a jurisdiction foreign to our constitution, and unacknowledged by our laws, giving his assent to their acts of pretended legislation:

For quartering large bodies of armed troops among us;

For protecting them, by a mock trial, from punishment for any murders which they should commit on the inhabitants of these states;

For cutting off our trade with all parts of the world;

For imposing taxes on us without our consent;

For depriving us, in many cases, of the benefits of trial by jury;

For transporting us beyond seas, to be tried for pretended offenses;

For abolishing the free system of English laws in a neighboring province, establishing therein an arbitrary government, and enlarging its boundaries, so as to render it at once an example and fit instrument for introducing the same absolute rule into these colonies;

For taking away our charters, abolishing our most valuable laws, and altering fundamentally the forms of our governments;

For suspending our own legislatures, and declaring themselves invested with power to legislate for us in all cases whatsoever.

He has abdicated government here, by declaring us out of his protection and waging war against us.

He has plundered our seas, ravaged our coasts, burned our towns, and destroyed the lives of our people.

He is at this time transporting large armies of foreign mercenaries to complete the works of death, desolation, and tyranny already begun with circumstances of cruelty and perfidy scarcely paralleled in the most barbarous ages, and totally unworthy the head of a civilized nation.

He has constrained our fellow-citizens, taken captive on the high seas, to bear arms against their country, to become the executioners of their friends and brethren, or to fall themselves by their hands.

He has excited domestic insurrection among us, and has endeavored to bring on the inhabitants of our frontiers the merciless Indian savages, whose known rule of warfare is an undistinguished destruction of all ages, sexes, and conditions.

In every stage of these oppressions we have petitioned for redress in the most humble terms; our repeated petitions have been answered only by repeated injury. A prince, whose character is thus marked by every act which may define a tyrant, is unfit to be the ruler of a free people.

Nor have we been wanting in attention to our British brethren. We have warned them, from time to time, of attempts by their legislature to extend an unwarrantable jurisdiction over us. We have reminded them of the circumstances of our emigration and settlement here. We have appealed to their native justice and magnanimity; and we have conjured them, by the ties of our common kindred, to disavow these usurpations, which would inevitably interrupt our connections and correspondence. They, too, have been deaf to the voice of justice and of consanguinity. We must, therefore, acquiesce in the necessity which denounces our separation, and hold them, as we hold the rest of mankind, enemies in war, in peace friends.

We, therefore, the representatives of the United States of America, in General Congress assembled, appealing to the Supreme Judge of the world for the rectitude of our intentions, do, in the name and by the authority of the good people of these colonies, solemnly publish and declare, that these United Colonies are, and of right ought to be, FREE AND INDEPENDENT STATES; that they are absolved from all allegiance to the British crown, and that all political connection between them and the state of Great Britain is, and ought to be, totally dissolved; and that, as free and independent states, they have full power to levy war, conclude peace, contract alliances, establish commerce, and to do all other acts and things which independent states may of right do. And for the support of this declaration, with a firm reliance on the protection of Divine Providence, we mutually pledge to each other our lives, our fortunes, and our sacred honor.

QUESTIONS

1. Consider that Galloway's "Plan of Union" was defeated by a single vote. Can you present arguments for and against the plan? How might its adoption have affected American history?

2. Both Paine and Wesley insist that they are the guardians of reason and liberty, yet they come to completely different conclusions about independence. How does each define the concepts of liberty and reason? What does Wesley mean by "true" liberty?

3. Compare the ideas in Paine's Common Sense with Jefferson's Declaration of Independence. For each author, what are the sources of knowledge, of wisdom? Are Paine's concerns addressed in the Declaration?

4. Both Seabury and Paine cast their enemies as tyrants. Do they understand tyranny and liberty in the same way?

5. Every year on July 4th there are public readings of the Declaration of Independence. Why do you think the document remains so important?

6. If the Loyalists rather than the Revolutionaries had won this bitterly fought contest, how do you think we would remember this era?

ADDITIONAL READING

Two of the better introductions to this period are Peter D. G. Thomas, *Tea Party to Independence: The Third Phase of the American Revolution, 1773–1776* (1991), and Benson Bobrick, *Angel in the Whirlwind: The Triumph of the American Revolution* (1997). An interesting account of the drafting of the Declaration of Independence is Pauline Maier's *American Scripture: Making the Declaration of Independence* (1997). John C. Dann, ed., *The Revolution Remembered: Eyewitness Accounts of the War for Independence* (1980), includes an interesting sample of primary materials from the Revolutionary era. For a stirring account of Paine's struggles for political equality, see Eric Foner, *Tom Paine and Revolutionary America* (1975). Edmund Morgan's *American Slavery, American Freedom* (1975) offers an interpretation that links black slavery to white equality. Among the more provocative interpretations of the period are Bernard Bailyn, *The Ideological Origins of the American Revolution* (1967); Gordon Wood, *The Radicalism of the American Revolution* (1992); and Ronald Hoffman and Peter J. Albert, eds., *The Transforming Hand of Revolution: Reconsidering the American Revolution as a Social Movement* (1996). For a popular account of the revolution, see Thomas Fleming, *Liberty* (1997). Prominent in recent historical debates on the Revolution are Gary Nash, *The Unknown American Revolution* (2005); Gordon Wood, *Revolutionary Characters* (2006); and Harvey Kaye, *Thomas Paine and the Promise of America* (2005). For a new account of leadership in this era see Robert Middlekauff, *Washington's Revolution* (2015).

ENDNOTES

1. *Journals of the Continental Congress, 1774–1789.* Vol. 1 (Washington, D.C.: Government Printing Office, 1904), pp. 49–51.
2. "An Alarm to the Legislature of the Province of New-York, Occasioned by the Present Political Disturbances in North America" (New York, 1775).
3. Benjamin Franklin to Joseph Galloway, February 25, 1775. American Philosophical Society.
4. Thomas Paine, *Common Sense: Addressed to the Inhabitants of America* (Philadelphia, 1776).
5. John Wesley, "A Sermon Preached at St. Matthew's, Bethnal Green, on Sunday, Nov. 12, 1775. For the Benefit of the Widows and Orphans of the Soldiers Who Lately Fell, Near Boston, in New-England" (Boston, 1775).
6. *Virginia Gazette*, November 25, 1775, reproduced in Frank Moore, *The Diary of the Revolution: A Centennial Volume Embracing the Current* (Hartford: The J.B. Burr Publishing Company, 1876), pp. 164–165.
7. *The History of Virginia*, v.IV (Petersburg, VA: Printed by M.W. Dunnavant, 1816), pp. 95–96.
8. Abigail Adams to John Adams, March 31, 1776, Adams Family Papers, Massachusetts Historical Society.
9. *Letters of John Adams, Addressed to His Wife. Edited by His Grandson, Charles Francis Adams.* Vol. 1 (Boston: Charles C. Little and James Brown, 1841), p. 97.
10. *Letters of Mrs. Adams: The Wife of John Adams, Vol. 1* (Boston: Charles C. Little and James Brown, 1840), p. 98.
11. *Letters of John Adams, Addressed to His Wife*, p. 123.

CHAPTER 5

FORMING A MORE PERFECT UNION: THE CONSTITUTION AND THE BILL OF RIGHTS

HISTORICAL CONTEXT

In five of our nation's presidential elections, the winner of the electoral college has actually lost the popular vote. Such outcomes have drawn criticism and confused many Americans who wonder whether we live in a democracy. Part of the confusion stems from public misconceptions about our electoral system, established by the Constitution of 1787. Historians have suggested that the Constitution is among the best-known and least-understood documents in American history. It was the product of remarkable debate about law and governance that involved complex issues such as slavery, representation, and individual rights. This chapter lets you explore part of that great debate.

The Constitution of 1787 was not the first constitution of the United States. During and immediately after the American Revolution, the supreme law of the land was known as the Articles of Confederation. Drafted in 1777 by the same body that produced the Declaration of Independence, the Articles established a "league of friendship" among the thirteen former English colonies. Under this constitution, each state retained its sovereignty, but sent representatives to a unicameral national Congress that had powers to conduct foreign affairs, declare war, maintain an army and navy, create a post office, and arbitrate disputes between states. However, Congress under the Articles did not have the power to collect taxes or regulate interstate trade. Moreover, at this time the United States had neither an independent executive branch nor a national court.

Could the Articles of Confederation succeed? Could government under them meet the needs of the people? All agreed that this was a difficult time economically. Some Americans, however, especially those who later would be known as Anti-Federalists, insisted that the hard times were understandable and temporary. They noted that for more than a century almost all of the clients with whom the American colonials had conducted business were British subjects. Since independence from England severed these connections, it was not surprising that the American people would suffer through a period of economic hardship until other commercial relationships could be established. To these Anti-Federalists, however, the worst times had passed and the future of the infant nation under the Articles appeared bright.

Other Americans, including those who later would support the new constitution, were less optimistic about the ability of the republic to recover from the economic quagmire of the 1780s. Their concerns multiplied in 1786 when an armed rebellion against governmental authorities broke out in western Massachusetts. Led by the Revolutionary War veteran Captain Daniel Shays, a band of 1,500 discontented and indebted rebels stormed the jails in order to liberate imprisoned debtors, and Shays's men used physical force to prevent the courts from foreclosing on mortgages. These acts of resistance persuaded many that strong measures were needed to restore the social order. Frustrated at the lingering depression and fearful of the spread of mob violence, increasing numbers of Americans advocated strengthening the authority of the central government so that it would be able to deal with future crises.

In September of 1786, a group of concerned Americans from five states gathered in Annapolis, Maryland, to discuss ways to resolve the troubles. From this convention came a call for each of the states to send delegates to a new, larger convention that would meet in Philadelphia the following May. The purpose of the Philadelphia meeting was to "take into consideration the situation . . . [and] to devise such further provisions as shall appear to [the delegates] necessary to render the constitution of the federal government adequate to the exigencies of the Union." Congress tacitly accepted the Annapolis proposal and asked the states to send representatives to Philadelphia. According to the instructions of Congress, however, this convention was being called "for the sole and express purpose of revising the Articles of Confederation." To legally amend the Articles, all thirteen states would have to accept the proposed changes. Twelve states responded to the call of Congress and sent delegates to Philadelphia. The state of Rhode Island, however, refused to participate.

Between May 25 and September 17, 1787—almost four months—the fifty-five delegates who arrived in Philadelphia presented several plans of governance, debated the merits of each plan, negotiated compromises, and drafted a new constitution that they announced would take effect when ratified by nine states. After nearly seventeen weeks of work, these "Founding Fathers" ultimately settled on a document that was both modest in size and ambitious in scope. Excluding the names of the signers, the Constitution of 1787 contained about 4,400 words. More than one-half of these words were included in Article I, the part that detailed the composition and powers of Congress. Article II, the next largest section, with about 1,000 words, specified the selection process and powers of the President. The remainder of the Constitution, Articles III, IV, V, VI, and VII, together contained barely another thousand words. In these sections, the founders defined the powers of the judiciary, discussed the relationships between the national and the state governments, outlined the amendment and ratification processes, and established other miscellaneous guidelines for citizens and officeholders.

INTRODUCTION TO DOCUMENTS 1 AND 2

We begin with the individuals who argued against the proposed Constitution. Between 1787 and 1789, the critics of the new government, known as "Anti-Federalists," waged a vigorous campaign. Documents 1 and 2 include selections from two outspoken foes of the new Constitution, Patrick Henry and Mercy Otis Warren. Both Henry and Warren had impeccable credentials as revolutionary patriots. Renowned for his flamboyant oratory, Henry had served Virginia as a member of the Continental Congress and later as governor. The excerpts printed in the following section are taken from the speeches he delivered on June 4 and 5, 1788, at the Virginia State Ratifying Convention. Document 2 contains excerpts from Warren's political pamphlet entitled "Observations on the New Constitution and on the Federal and State Conventions by a Columbian Patriot." (Note that "Columbian" referred to the thirteen colonies, a name taken from Christopher Columbus.) Like Henry, during the revolution, Warren was a strong and vocal patriot who used her literary skills to lampoon the British and undermine Loyalist sentiment. Later in life, she would write *History of the Rise, Progress and Termination of the American Revolution* (1805), an account that included some critical comments about President John Adams and provoked his retort: "History is not the province of the ladies." According to Henry and Warren, what were the major problems with the Constitution of 1787? Do they share the same concerns?

1. THE SPEECHES OF PATRICK HENRY IN THE VIRGINIA STATE RATIFYING CONVENTION (1788)

Mr. Chairman.—The public mind, as well as my own, is extremely uneasy at the proposed change of Government. . . . A year ago the minds of our citizens were at perfect repose. Before the meeting of the late Federal Convention at Philadelphia, a general peace, and an universal tranquillity prevailed in this country;—but since that period [the people] are exceedingly uneasy and disquieted. . . . This proposal of altering our Federal Government is of a most alarming nature: . . . you ought to be extremely cautious, watchful, jealous of your liberty; for instead of securing your rights you may lose them forever. . . .

I would make this enquiry of those worthy characters who composed a part of the late Federal Convention. I am sure they were fully impressed with the necessity of forming a great consolidated Government, instead of a confederation. That this is a consolidated Government is demonstrably clear, and the danger of such a Government, is, to my mind, very striking. I have the highest veneration of those Gentlemen,—but, Sir, give me leave to demand, what right had they to say, We, the People. My political curiosity, exclusive of my anxious solicitude for the public welfare, leads me to ask who authorised them to speak the language of, We, the People, instead of We, the States? . . . That they exceeded their power is perfectly clear. . . . The Federal Convention ought to have amended the old system—for this purpose they were solely delegated: The object of their mission extended to no other consideration. You must therefore forgive the solicitation of one unworthy member, to know what danger could have arisen under the present confederation, and what are the causes of this proposal to change our Government. . . .

Is it necessary for your liberty, that you should abandon those great rights by the adoption of this system? Is the relinquishment of the trial by jury, and the liberty of the press, necessary for your liberty? Will the abandonment of your most sacred rights tend to the security of your liberty? Liberty [is] the greatest of all earthly blessings—give us that precious jewel, and you may take everything else. . . .

In some parts of the plan before you, the great rights of freemen are endangered, in other parts absolutely taken away. How does your trial by jury stand? In civil cases gone—not sufficiently secured in criminal—this best privilege is gone: But we are told that we need not fear, because those in power being our Representatives, will not abuse the powers we put in their hands: I am not well versed in history, but I will submit to your recollection, whether liberty has been destroyed most often by the licentiousness of the people, or by the tyranny of rulers. . . . My great objection to this Government is, that it does not leave us the means of defending our rights; or, of waging war against tyrants: It is urged by some Gentlemen, that this new plan will bring us an acquisition of strength, an army, and the militia of the States: This is an idea extremely ridiculous: Gentlemen cannot be in earnest. This acquisition will trample on your fallen liberty: Let my beloved Americans guard against that fatal lethargy that has pervaded the universe: Have we the means of resisting disciplined armies? when our only defense, the militia is put into the hands of Congress? The Honorable Gentleman said, that great danger would ensue if the Convention rose without adopting this system: I ask, where is that danger? I see none: Other Gentlemen have told us within these walls, that the Union is gone—or, that the Union will be gone: Is not this trifling with the judgement of their fellow citizens? Till they tell us the ground of their fears, I will consider them as imaginary: I rose to make enquiry where those dangers were; they could make no answer: I believe I never shall have that answer: Is there a disposition in the people of this country to revolt against the dominion of laws? Has there been a single tumult in Virginia? . . .

To encourage us to adopt it, they tell us, that there is a plain easy way of getting amendments: When I come to contemplate this part, I suppose that I am mad, or, that my countrymen are so: The way to amendment, is, in my conception, shut. . . . For four of the smallest States, that do not collectively contain one-tenth part of the population of the United States, may obstruct the most salutary and necessary amendments: Nay, in these four States, six-tenths of the people may reject these amendments; and suppose, that amendments shall be opposed to amendments (which is highly probable) is it possible, that three-fourths can ever agree to the same amendments? A bare majority in these four small States may hinder the adoption of amendments; so that we may fairly and justly conclude, that one-twentieth part of the American people, may prevent the removal of the most grievous inconveniences and oppression, by refusing to accede to amendments. A trifling minority may reject the most salutary amendments. Is this an easy mode of securing the public liberty? It is, Sir, a most fearful situation, when the most contemptible minority can prevent the alteration of the most oppressive Government; for it may in many respects prove to be such: Is this the spirit of republicanism? . . .

If we admit this Consolidated Government it will be because we like a great splendid one. Some way or other we must be a great and mighty empire; we must have an army, and a navy, and a number of things: When the American spirit was in its youth, the language of America was different. Liberty, Sir, was then the primary object. We are descended from a people whose Government was founded on liberty. . . . But now, Sir, the American spirit, assisted by the ropes and chains of consolidation, is about to convert this country to a powerful and mighty empire: If you make the citizens of this country agree to become the subjects of one great consolidated empire of America, your Government will not have sufficient energy to keep them together: Such a Government is incompatible with the genius of republicanism: There will be no checks, no real balances, in this Government. . . . This Constitution is said to have beautiful features; but when I come to examine these features, Sir, they appear to me horridly frightful: Among other deformities, it has an awful squinting; it squints towards monarchy; And does not this raise indignation in the breast of every American? Your President may easily become King: Your Senate is so imperfectly constructed that your dearest rights may be sacrificed by what may be a small minority; and a very small minority may continue forever unchangeably this Government, although horridly defective: Where are your checks in this Government?[1]

2. OBSERVATIONS ON THE NEW CONSTITUTION AND ON THE FEDERAL AND STATE CONVENTIONS BY A COLUMBIAN PATRIOT (1788)

MERCY OTIS WARREN

. . . All writers on government agree, and the feelings of the human mind witness the truth of these political axioms, that man is born free and possessed of certain unalienable rights—that government is instituted for the protection, safety, and happiness of the people, and not for the profit, honor, or private interest of any man, family, or class of men—That the origin of all power is in the people, and that they have an incontestable right to check the creatures of their own creation, vested with certain powers to guard the life, liberty and property of the community. . . . [Warren then gives her specific objections to the new constitution.]

1. [A]nnual election is the basis of responsibility.— Man is not immediately corrupted, but power without limitation, or amenability, may endanger the brightest virtue—whereas a frequent return to the bar of their Constituents is the strongest check against the corruptions to which men are liable. . . .

2. There is no security in the [new] system, either for the rights of conscience, or the liberty of the Press. . . .

3. There are no well defined limits of the Judiciary Powers, they seem to be left as a boundless ocean. . . .

4. The Executive and the Legislative are so dangerously blended as to give just cause of alarm. . . .

5. The abolition of trial by jury in civil cases. . . .

6. . . . Standing armies have been the nursery of vice and the bane of liberty from the Roman legions . . . to the planting of the British cohorts in the capitals of America.

7. Notwithstanding the delusory promise to guarantee a Republican form of government to every State in the Union. . . . Every source of revenue is in the monopoly of Congress, and if the several legislatures in their enfeebled state, should against their own feelings be necessitated to attempt a dry tax for the payment of their debts, and the support

of internal police, even this may be required for the purposes of the general government.

8. As the new Congress are empowered to determine their own salaries, the requisitions for this purpose may not be very moderate, and the drain for public moneys will probably rise past all calculation. . . .

9. There is no provision for a rotation, nor any thing to prevent the perpetuity of office in the same hands for life; which by a little well timed bribery, will probably be done, to the exclusion of men of the best abilities from their share in the offices of government. . . .

10. The inhabitants of the United States, are liable to be dragged from the vicinity of their own county, or state, to answer to the litigious or unjust suit of an adversary, on the most distant borders of the Continent: in short the appellate jurisdiction of the Supreme Federal Court, includes an unwarrantable stretch of power over the liberty, life, and property of the subject, through the wide Continent of America.

11. One Representative to thirty thousand inhabitants is a very inadequate representation. . . .

12. If the sovereignty of America is designed to be elective, the circumscribing the votes to only ten electors in this State, and the same proportion in all the others, is nearly tantamount to the exclusion of the voice of the people in the choice of their first magistrate. It is vesting the choice solely in an aristocratic junto. . . .

13. A Senate chosen for six years will, in most instances, be an appointment for life, as the influence of such a body over the minds of the people will be coequal to the extensive powers with which they are vested, and they will not only forget, but be forgotten by their constituents— a branch of the Supreme Legislature thus set

beyond all responsibility is totally repugnant to every principle of a free government.

14. There is no provision by a bill of rights to guard against the dangerous encroachments of power in too many instances to be named. . . .

15. The difficulty, if not impracticability, of exercising the equal and equitable powers of government by a single legislature over an extent of territory that reaches from the Mississippi to the Western lakes, and from them to the Atlantic ocean, is an insuperable objection to the adoption of the new system. . . .

16. It is an undisputed fact, that not one legislature in the United States had the most distant idea when they first appointed members for a convention, entirely commercial, or when they afterwards authorized them to consider on some amendments of the Federal union, that they would without any warrant from their constituents, presume on so bold and daring a stride, as ultimately to destroy the state governments. . . .

17. The first appearance of the article which declares the ratification of nine states sufficient for the establishment of the new system, wears the face of dissension, is a subversion of the union of the Confederated States, and tends to the introduction of anarchy and civil convulsions, and may be a means of involving the whole country in blood.

18. The mode in which this constitution is recommended to the people to judge without either the advice of Congress, or the legislatures of the several states, is very reprehensible—it is an attempt to force it upon them before it could be thoroughly understood, and may leave us in that situation, that in the first moments of slavery the minds of the people agitated by the remembrance of their lost liberties, will be like the sea in a tempest, that sweeps down every mound of security.

. . . [I]t is to be feared we shall soon see this country rushing into the extremes of confusion and violence, in consequence of the proceedings of a set of gentlemen, who disregarding the purposes of their appointment, have assumed powers unauthorized by any commission, have unnecessarily rejected the confederation of the United States, and annihilated the sovereignty and independence of the individual governments. . . .

It has been observed by a zealous advocate for the new system, that most governments are the result of fraud or violence, and this with design to recommend its acceptance—but has not almost every step towards its fabrication been fraudulent in the extreme? Did not the prohibition strictly enjoined by the general Convention, that no member should make any communication to his Constituents, or to gentlemen of consideration and abilities in the other States, bear evident marks of fraudulent designs? . . . And the hurry with which it has been urged to the acceptance of the people, without giving time, by adjournments, for better information, and more unanimity has a deceptive appearance. . . .

[I]f after all, on a dispassionate and fair discussion, the people generally give their voice for a voluntary dereliction of their privileges, let every individual who chooses the active scenes of life, strive to support the peace and unanimity of his country, though every other blessing may expire—And while the statesman is plodding for power, and the courtier practicing arts of dissimulation without check— while the rapacious are growing rich by oppression, and fortune throwing her gifts into the lap of fools, let the sublimer characters, the philosophic lovers of freedom who have wept over her exit, retire to the calm shades of contemplation, there they may look down with pity on the inconsistency of human nature, the revolutions of states, the rise of kingdoms, and the fall of empires.[2]

INTRODUCTION TO DOCUMENTS 3, 4, AND 5

The supporters of the new constitution responded to the Anti-Federalists volley for volley. The following documents contain some of the arguments offered by three well-known delegates who attended the Philadelphia convention. Document 3 includes the views of George Washington, the most respected man in the country due to his military leadership in the Revolutionary War. The government's inability to properly pay the soldiers after the war demonstrated to Washington the fundamental weakness of the Articles of Confederation, prompting him to lobby for ratification through his personal correspondence. According to these letters, why was Washington more optimistic than Henry and Warren about this new constitution? Do you think his letters would have allayed their concerns as Anti-Federalists?

Documents 4 and 5 include selections from *The Federalist Papers,* a collection of eighty-five essays that were published in New York City newspapers under the pseudonym "Publius." The strategy of *The Federalist Papers* was to persuade citizens that the Constitution was the best possible compromise, given the divisions that beset Americans. The following selections from *The Federalist Papers* were written by James Madison and Alexander Hamilton. Why does Madison go to such lengths in Federalist No. 39 to characterize the new central government as federal rather than national? In Federalist No. 84, why did Hamilton consider a Bill of Rights unnecessary?

3. FROM THE LETTERS OF GEORGE WASHINGTON

GEORGE WASHINGTON TO HENRY KNOX
MOUNT VERNON, OCTOBER 15, 1787

My dear Sir . . .

The Constitution is now before the judgement seat. It has, as was expected, its adversaries, and its supporters; which will preponderate is yet to be decided. The former, it is probable, will be most active because the Major part of them it is to be feared, will be governed by sinister and self important considerations on which no arguments will work conviction— the opposition from another class of them (if they are men of reflection, information and candor) may perhaps subside in the solution of the following plain, but important questions. 1. Is the Constitution which is submitted by the Convention preferable to the government (if it can be called one) under which we now live? 2. Is it probable that more confidence will, at this time, be placed in another Convention (should the experiment be tried) than was given to the last? and is it likely that there would be a better agreement in it? Is there not a Constitutional door open for alterations and amendments, & is it not probable that real defects will be as readily discovered after, as before, trial? and will not posterity be as ready to

apply the remedy as ourselves, if there is occasion for it, when the mode is provided? To think otherwise will, in my judgement, be ascribing more of the amor patria—more wisdom—and more foresight to ourselves, than I conceive.
Go: Washington[3]

GEORGE WASHINGTON TO THE
MARQUIS DE LAFAYETTE
MOUNT VERNON, FEBRUARY 7, 1788

My dear Marqs,

. . . With regard to the two great points (the pivots on which the whole machine must move) my Creed is simply: 1. That the general Government is not invested with more Powers than are indispensably necessary to perform [the] functions of a good Government; and, consequently, that no objection ought to be made against the quantity of Power delegated to it. 2. That these Powers (as the appointment of all Rulers will forever arise from, and, at short stated intervals, recur to the free suffrage of the People) are so distributed among the Legislative, Executive, and Judicial Branches, into which the general Government is arranged, that it can never be in danger of degenerating into a monarchy, an Oligarchy, an Aristocracy, or any other despotic or oppressive form; so long as there shall remain any virtue in the body of the People. . . .

We are not to expect perfection in this world: but mankind, in modern times, have apparently made some progress in the science of Government. Should that which is now offered to the People of America, be found an experiment less perfect than it can be made—a Constitutional door is left open for its amelioration. . . . So many . . . contradictory, and, in my opinion, unfounded objections have been urged against the System in contemplation; many of which would operate equally against every efficient Government that might be proposed. I will only add, as a farther opinion founded on the maturest deliberation, that there is no alternative—no hope of alteration—no intermediate resting place—between the adoption of this and a recurrence to an unqualified state of Anarchy, with all its deplorable consequences. . . .
Go. Washington[4]

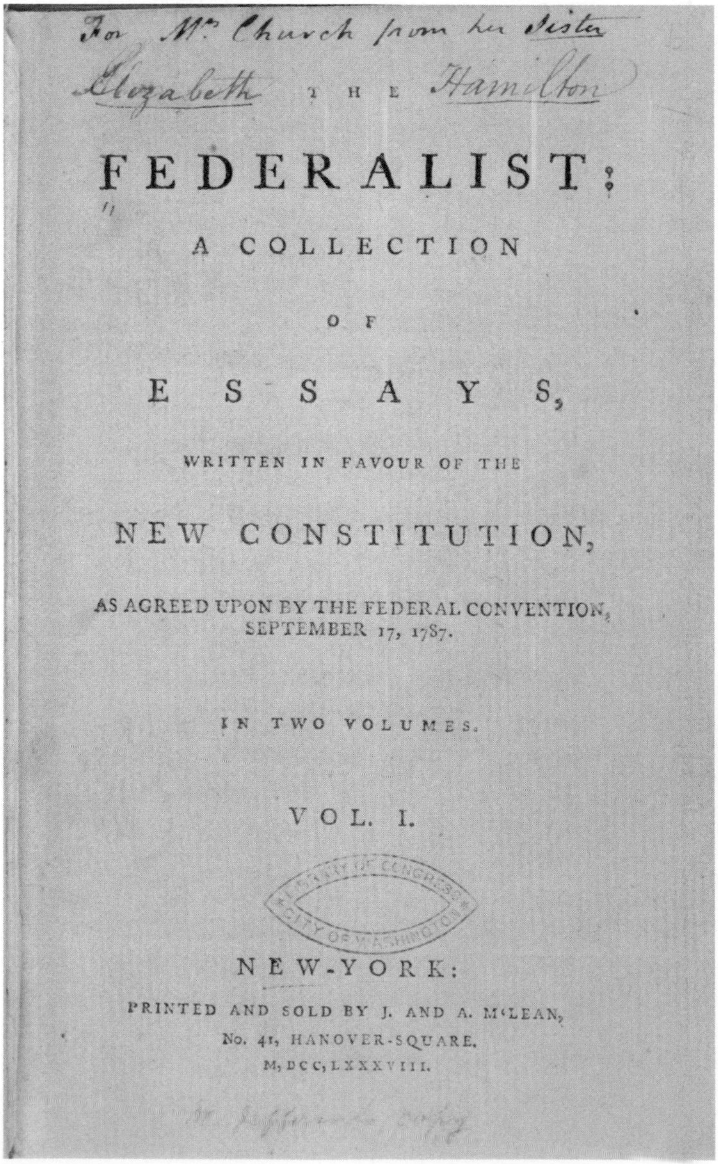

For Mrs Church from her Sister Elizabeth Hamilton

THE

FEDERALIST:

A COLLECTION

OF

ESSAYS,

WRITTEN IN FAVOUR OF THE

NEW CONSTITUTION,

AS AGREED UPON BY THE FEDERAL CONVENTION, SEPTEMBER 17, 1787.

IN TWO VOLUMES.

VOL. I.

NEW-YORK:

PRINTED AND SOLD BY J. AND A. M'LEAN, No. 41, HANOVER-SQUARE.

M,DCC,LXXXVIII.

Image 5.1 Title Page from the Federalist Papers, 1788

The Federalist Papers were immediately published and widely distributed, engaging the arguments of the anti-Federalists and their skepticism about the need to replace the Articles of Confederation.

Source: Library of Congress.

4. FROM *THE FEDERALIST PAPERS,* NUMBER 39 (1788)

JAMES MADISON

The House of Representatives, like that of one branch at least of all the State legislatures, is elected immediately by the great body of the people. The Senate, like the present Congress, and the Senate of Maryland, derives its appointment indirectly from the people. The President is indirectly derived from the choice of the people, according to the example in most of the States. Even the judges, with all other officers of the Union, will, as in the several States, be the choice, though a remote choice, of the people themselves, the duration of the appointments is equally conformable to the republican standard, and to the model of State constitutions. The House of Representatives is periodically elective, as in all the States; and for the period of two years, as in the State of South Carolina. The Senate is elective, for the period of six years; which is but one year more than the period of the Senate of Maryland, and but two more than that of the Senates of New York and Virginia. The President is to continue in office for the period of four years; as in New York and Delaware, the chief magistrate is elected for three years, and in South Carolina for two years. In the other States the election is annual. In several of the States, however, no constitutional provision is made for the impeachment of the chief magistrate. And in Delaware and Virginia he is not impeachable till out of office. The President of the United States is impeachable at any time during his continuance in office. The tenure by which the judges are to hold their places, is, as it unquestionably ought to be, that of good behavior. The tenure of the ministerial offices generally, will be a subject of legal regulation, conformably to the reason of the case and the example of the State constitutions. . . .

The House of Representatives will derive its powers from the people of America; and the people will be represented in the same proportion, and on the same principle, as they are in the legislature of a particular State. So far the government is NATIONAL, not FEDERAL. The Senate, on the other hand, will derive its powers from the States, as political and coequal societies; and these will be represented on the principle of equality in the Senate, as they now are in the existing Congress. So far the government is FEDERAL, not NATIONAL. The executive power will be derived from a very compound source. The immediate election of the President is to be made by the States in their political characters. The votes allotted to them are in a compound ratio, which considers them partly as distinct and coequal societies, partly as unequal members of the same society. The eventual election, again, is to be made by that branch of the legislature which consists of the national representatives; but in this particular act they are to be thrown into the form of individual delegations, from so many distinct and coequal bodies politic. From this aspect of the government it appears to be of a mixed character, presenting at least as many FEDERAL as NATIONAL features. . . .

The proposed Constitution, therefore, is, in strictness, neither a national nor a federal Constitution, but a composition of both. In its foundation it is federal, not national; in the sources from which the ordinary powers of the government are drawn, it is partly federal and partly national; in the operation of these powers, it is national, not federal; in the extent of them, again, it is federal, not national; and, finally, in the authoritative mode of introducing amendments, it is neither wholly federal nor wholly national.[5]

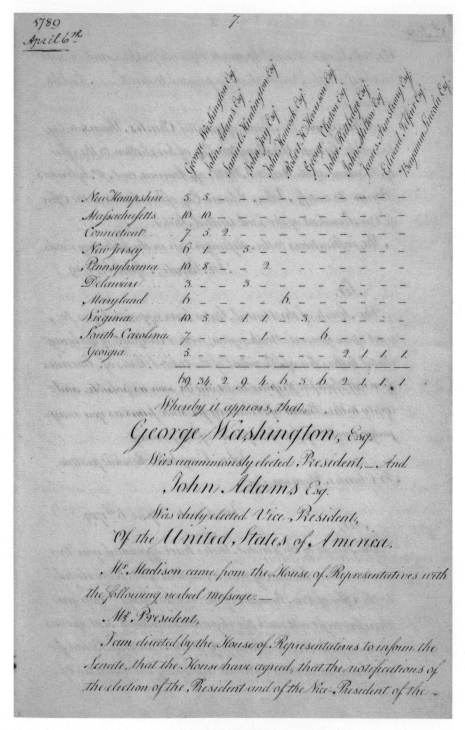

Image 5.2 Record of George Washington's election as the nation's first president

The April 1789 election of George Washington by the U.S. Congress was unanimous. All sixty-nine electors casting one of their two votes for the hero of the Revolutionary War, who had presided over the Constitutional Convention.

Source: Senate Journal of the First Congress; May 14, 1789; Records of the U.S. Senate, Record Group 46, National Archives.

5. FROM *THE FEDERALIST PAPERS,* NUMBER 84 (1788)

ALEXANDER HAMILTON

It has been several times truly remarked that bills of rights are, in their origin, stipulations between kings and their subjects, abridgements of prerogative in favor of privilege, reservations of rights not surrendered to the prince. Such was MAGNA CHARTA, obtained by the barons, sword in hand, from King John. Such were the subsequent confirmations of that charter by succeeding princes. Such was the PETITION OF RIGHT assented to by Charles the First in the beginning of his reign. Such, also, was the Declaration of Right presented by the Lords and Commons to the Prince of Orange in 1688, and afterwards thrown into the form of an act of parliament called the Bill of Rights. It is evident, therefore, that, according to their primitive signification, they have no application to constitutions professedly founded upon the power of the people, and executed by their immediate representatives and servants. Here, in strictness, the people surrender nothing; and as they retain every thing they have no need of particular reservations. "WE, THE PEOPLE of the United States, to secure the blessings of liberty to ourselves and our posterity, do ORDAIN and ESTABLISH this Constitution for the United States of America." Here is a better recognition of popular rights, than volumes of those aphorisms which make the principal figure in several of our State bills of rights, and which would sound much better in a treatise of ethics than in a constitution of government. . . .

I go further, and affirm that bills of rights, in the sense and to the extent in which they are contended for, are not only unnecessary in the proposed Constitution, but would even be dangerous. They would contain various exceptions to powers not granted; and, on this very account, would afford a colorable pretext to claim more than were granted. For why declare that things shall not be done which there is no power to do? Why, for instance, should it be said that the liberty of the press shall not be restrained, when no power is given by which restrictions may be imposed? . . .

On the subject of the liberty of the press, as much as has been said, I cannot forbear adding a remark or two: in the first place, I observe, that there is not a syllable concerning it in the constitution of this State; in the next, I contend, that whatever has been said about it in that of any other State, amounts to nothing. What signifies a declaration, that "the liberty of the press shall be inviolably preserved"? What is the liberty of the press? Who can give it any definition which would not leave the utmost latitude for evasion? I hold it to be impracticable; and from this I infer, that its security, whatever fine declarations may be inserted in any constitution respecting it, must altogether depend on public opinion, and on the general spirit of the people and of the government.[6]

INTRODUCTION TO DOCUMENT 6

Hamilton's argument against a Bill of Rights notwithstanding, the Anti-Federalist opposition forced some concessions from the Federalists. After the new government was formed, Congress sent to the states a proposal to add ten amendments to the original constitution, which are included in Document 6. In 1791, this liberty-protecting Bill of Rights was ratified. Note especially the language of the preamble, which acknowledges the fears of the Anti-Federalists about centralized state power. The fight for basic freedoms—of speech, worship, the press, and so forth—highlights the key issue for those attempting to create a new government: how to have both liberty and stability. Put another way, who could be trusted to govern and who needed governing?

6. THE BILL OF RIGHTS, DECEMBER 15, 1791

PREAMBLE

Congress of the United States begun and held at the City of New York, on Wednesday, the Fourth of March, one thousand seven hundred and eighty nine.

The Conventions of a number of the States having at the time of their adopting the Constitution, expressed a desire, in order to prevent misconstruction or abuse of its powers, that further declaratory and restrictive clauses should be added: And as extending the ground of public confidence in the Government, will best insure the beneficent ends of its institution.

RESOLVED by the Senate and House of Representatives of the United States of America, in Congress assembled, two thirds of both Houses concurring, that the following Articles be proposed to the Legislatures of the several States, as Amendments to the Constitution of the United States, all or any of which Articles, when ratified by three fourths of the said Legislatures, to be valid to all intents and purposes, as part of the said Constitution; viz: ARTICLES in addition to, and Amendment of the Constitution of the United States of America, proposed by Congress, and ratified by the Legislatures of the several States, pursuant to the fifth Article of the original Constitution.

AMENDMENTS

Amendment I: Congress shall make no law respecting an establishment of religion, or prohibiting the free exercise thereof; or abridging the freedom of speech, or of the press; or the right of the people peaceably to assemble, and to petition the Government for a redress of grievances.

Amendment II: A well regulated Militia, being necessary to the security of a free State, the right of the people to keep and bear Arms, shall not be infringed.

Amendment III: No Soldier shall, in time of peace be quartered in any house, without the consent of the Owner, nor in time of war, but in a manner to be prescribed by law.

Amendment IV: The right of the people to be secure in their persons, houses, papers, and effects, against unreasonable searches and seizures, shall not be violated, and no Warrants shall issue, but upon probable cause, supported by Oath or affirmation, and particularly describing the place to be searched, and the persons or things to be seized.

Amendment V: No person shall be held to answer for a capital, or otherwise infamous crime, unless on a presentment or indictment of a Grand Jury, except in cases arising in the land or naval forces, or in the Militia, when in actual service in time of War or public danger; nor shall any person be subject for the same offence to be twice put in jeopardy of life or limb; nor shall be compelled in any criminal case to be a witness against himself, nor be deprived of life, liberty, or property, without due process of law; nor shall private property be taken for public use, without just compensation.

Amendment VI: In all criminal prosecutions, the accused shall enjoy the right to a speedy and public trial, by an impartial jury of the State and district wherein the crime shall have been committed, which district shall have been previously ascertained by law, and to be informed of the nature and cause of the accusation; to be confronted with the witnesses against him; to have compulsory process for obtaining witnesses in his favor, and to have the Assistance of Counsel for his defence.

Amendment VII: In suits at common law, where the value in controversy shall exceed twenty dollars, the right of trial by jury shall be preserved, and no fact tried by a jury, shall be otherwise reexamined in any Court of the United States, than according to the rules of the common law.

Amendment VIII: Excessive bail shall not be required, nor excessive fines imposed, nor cruel and unusual punishments inflicted.

Amendment IX: The enumeration in the Constitution, of certain rights, shall not be construed to deny or disparage others retained by the people.

Amendment X: The powers not delegated to the United States by the Constitution, nor prohibited by it to the States, are reserved to the States respectively, or to the people.

INTRODUCTION TO DOCUMENTS 7 AND 8

The Constitution and Bill of Rights were not designed to protect the freedoms of all persons living in the United States equally. Women were denied the rights of citizenship, including voting. Property-less white men, too, were disenfranchised. The founders also maneuvered around the problem of slavery. They avoided the very word, preferring euphemisms like "persons held to service." Wishing to treat slaves neither as full citizens nor as nonentities, the framers devised the famous "three-fifths" compromise—each slave would be counted as three-fifths of one person for purposes of taxation and representation. Slaveowners did the voting for their chattels. The issue of slavery was extremely volatile, and the ongoing importation of new slaves from Africa was especially contentious.

The founders compromised on the slave trade by declaring there could be no attempt to outlaw it for twenty years. This was not good enough for those who had begun to believe that holding slaves was sinful. Organizations formed on both sides of the Atlantic, including the Providence Society for Abolishing the Slave-Trade. The Rhode Island men, many of them Quakers (also referred to as "The Friends"), declared slavery inimical to the new constitution, supported only by fraud and violence. Document 7 is an excerpt from their report. This new organization elected a slate of officers, including, as secretary, Moses Brown, a wealthy Providence merchant who had freed his own slaves years before. Brown and his brother John helped endow the College of Rhode Island, which became Brown University. John, however, not only owned slaves, he continued to outfit ships and send them to Africa to bring back more for sale in the West Indies. He argued with those who would abolish the trade, including his brother, in an open letter to the newspaper, provided in Document 8. How do the two brothers differ in their assumptions? What are their justifications for freedom? For enslavement?

7. REPORT OF THE PROVIDENCE SOCIETY FOR ABOLISHING THE SLAVE-TRADE (FEBRUARY 1789)

It having pleased the Creator of mankind to make of one blood all nations of men, and having by the diffusion of his light, manifested that, however diversified by colour, situation, religion, or different states of society, it becomes them to promote each other's happiness, as members of one great family. It is therefore the duty of those who profess to maintain their own rights, and especially those who acknowledge the obligations of Christianity, to extend, by the use of such means as are or may be in their power, the blessings of freedom to the whole human race; and in a more particular manner to such of their fellow-creatures as by the laws and constitutions of the United States are entitled to their freedom, and who by fraud or violence are or may be detained in bondage. And as, by the African slave-trade, a system of slavery, replete with human misery, is erected and carried on, it is incumbent on them to endeavour the suppression of that unrighteous commerce; to excite a due observance of such good and wholesome laws as are or may be enacted for the abolition of slavery, and for the support of the rights of those who are entitled to freedom by the laws of the country in which they live; and to afford such relief as we may enable to those unhappy fellow-citizens, who, like the sons of Africa, falling into the hands of unmerciful men, may be carried into slavery at Algiers or elsewhere.[7]

8. TO THE CITIZENS OF THE STATE OF RHODE ISLAND (FEBRUARY 1789)

JOHN BROWN

. . . [I hope] that the time and abilities of the society may be principally employed in pointing out a better method of peopling the West-Indies; for the produce of these islands is so highly esteemed by all ranks of people, that it cannot be expected that the cultivation of that part of the world will cease, even should the carrying of the blacks to those parts be totally stopt. . . . Would they [the Quakers] not shew their goodness to their neighbours in a more conspicuous light, if they would allow them equal liberty of conscience with themselves, till the *grand question* is determined in Europe on the slave trade? Will there be one the less brought from the coast of Guinea by this State's stopping, if all the Europeans continue the trade?

For my part, I wish the whole race of mankind, of every colour, all the happiness that was designed them in their creation; yet none will pretend to say, but that there ever have been and ever will be distinctions among men; some strong and robust, some weak and effeminate, some industrious and some indolent; of course, some rich and some poor. In short, every one seems to have been designed for some purpose or other for which he is fitted; and as it is, I believe, universally agreed, that the agriculture of the West-India islands must have an annual supply of labourers, over and above their natural increase, the deaths of the labourers there exceeding the births on an average for any given time, how are the islands to be supplied? Will it be a satisfaction to the Friends to have the Negroes put to death by their conquerors, in the wars of Africa? This is always the case, where there are no purchasers, and of course the deficiency of the labourers of the West-India islands must be made up of white people; but from what country, the Friends will do well to point out.

—*A Citizen*[8]

INTRODUCTION TO DOCUMENT 9

Historians have long noted the contradiction of the framers' championing liberty while they practiced slavery. The northern colonies had fewer slaves and therefore less at stake; as states they assumed that slavery would die out. But in the South, the ideal of equality contrasted most sharply with slavery. The historian Edmund S. Morgan has argued that the two were dependent on each other during the Revolutionary era:

> Aristocrats could more safely preach equality in a slave society than in a free one. Slaves did not become leveling mobs, because their owners would see to it that they had no chance to. The apostrophes to equality were not addressed to them. And because Virginia's labor force was composed mainly of slaves, who had been isolated by race and removed from the political equation, the remaining free laborers and tenant farmers were too few in number to constitute a serious threat to the superiority of the men who assured

them of their equality. . . . Virginia's small farmers could perceive a common identity with the large. . . . Neither was a slave. And both were equal in not being slaves.[9]

The revolutionary idea that human beings were equal by natural right allowed the colonists to ridicule a king and reject the rule of Parliament. But their devotion to equality had severe limits. In 1787, Thomas Jefferson published his *Notes on the State of Virginia*. He lamented the fact that whites had not yet taken the opportunity to view blacks and Indians as "subjects of natural history." In Document 9, he offers observations on those of African lineage. Can you reconcile Jefferson's views here with the ideas he put forth in the Declaration in Chapter 4?

9. FROM *NOTES ON THE STATE OF VIRGINIA* (1787)

THOMAS JEFFERSON

. . . The first difference which strikes us is that of colour. Whether the black of the negro resides in the reticular membrane between the skin and scarf-skin, or in the scarf-skin itself; whether it proceeds from the colour of the blood, the colour of the bile, or from that of some other secretion, the difference is fixed in nature, and is as real as if its seat and cause were better known to us. And is this difference of no importance? Is it not the foundation of a greater or less share of beauty in the two races? Are not the fine mixtures of red and white, the expressions of every passion by greater or less suffusions of colour in the one, preferable to that eternal monotony, which reigns in the countenances, that immoveable veil of black which covers all the emotions of the other race? Add to these, flowing hair, a more elegant symmetry of form, their own judgement in favour of the whites, declared by their preference of them, as uniformly as is the preference of the Oran-ootan [orangutan] for the black women over those of his own species. The circumstance of superior beauty, is thought worthy of attention in the propagation of our horses, dogs, and other domestic animals; why not in that of man? Besides those of colour, figure, and hair, there are other physical distinctions proving a difference of race. They have less hair on the face and body. They secrete less by the kidneys, and more by the glands of the skin, which gives them a very strong and disagreeable odour. This greater degree of transpiration renders them more tolerant of heat, and less so of cold, than the whites. . . . A black, after hard labour through the day, will be induced by the slightest amusements to sit up till midnight, or later, though knowing he must be out with the first dawn of the morning. They are at least as brave, and more adventuresome. But this may perhaps proceed from a want of forethought, which prevents their seeing a danger till it be present. When present, they do not go through it with more coolness or steadiness than the whites. They are more ardent after their female: but love seems with them to be more an eager desire, than a tender delicate mixture of sentiment and sensation. Their griefs are transient. Those numberless afflictions, which render it doubtful whether heaven has given life to us in mercy or in wrath, are less felt, and sooner forgotten with them. In general, their existence appears to participate more of sensation than reflection. To this must be ascribed their disposition to sleep when abstracted from their diversions, and unemployed in labour. An animal whose body is at rest, and who does not reflect, must be disposed to sleep of course. Comparing them by their faculties of memory, reason, and imagination, it appears to me, that in memory they are equal to the whites; in reason much inferior, as I think one could scarcely be found capable of tracing and comprehending the investigations of Euclid; and that in imagination they are dull, tasteless, and anomalous. . . . Some have been liberally educated, and all have lived in countries where the arts and sciences are cultivated to a considerable degree, and have had before their eyes samples of the best works from abroad. The Indians, with no advantages of this kind, will often carve figures on their pipes not destitute of design and merit. They will crayon out an animal, a plant, or a country, so as to prove the existence of a germ in their minds which only wants cultivation. They astonish you with strokes of the most sublime oratory; such as prove their reason and sentiment strong, their imagination glowing and elevated. But never yet could I find that a black had uttered a thought above the level of plain narration; never see even an elementary trait of painting or sculpture. In music they are more generally gifted than the whites with accurate ears for tune and time, and they have been found capable of imagining a small catch. Whether they will be equal to the composition of a more extensive run of melody, or of complicated harmony, is yet to be proved. Misery is often the parent of the most affecting touches in poetry.—Among the blacks is misery enough, God knows, but no poetry. . . .

. . . I advance it therefore as a suspicion only, that the blacks, whether originally a distinct race, or made distinct by time and circumstances, are inferior to the whites in the endowments both of body and mind. It is not against experience to suppose, that different species of the same genus, or varieties of the same species, may possess different qualifications. Will not a lover of natural history then, one who views the gradations in all the races of animals with the eye of philosophy, excuse an effort to keep those in the department of man as distinct as nature has formed them? This unfortunate difference of colour, and perhaps of faculty, is a powerful obstacle to the emancipation of these people. Many of their advocates, while they wish to vindicate the liberty of human nature, are anxious also to preserve its dignity and beauty. . . .[10]

INTRODUCTION TO DOCUMENTS 10 AND 11

Benjamin Banneker was a free black living in Maryland. Although his early education was minimal, as an adult he taught himself trigonometry and calculus. In 1791, he served as assistant surveyor in laying out the boundaries for the newly created District of Columbia. That same year, he used his mathematical abilities to do the calculations for an astronomical almanac (people relied on such works to learn the timing of natural phenomena, such as tides, seasons, and lengths of days). Banneker's almanac went through twenty-nine editions and sold in cities throughout the Middle Atlantic states. Having read the *Notes on the State of Virginia*, Banneker sent a copy of his almanac to then-Secretary of State Thomas Jefferson, along with a letter, provided as Document 10. Banneker uses the revolutionary generation's rhetoric of slavery and freedom from England to politely question Jefferson's characterization of African Americans. Document 11 is Jefferson's reply to Banneker.

10. LETTER FROM BENJAMIN BANNEKER TO THOMAS JEFFERSON

MARYLAND, BALTIMORE COUNTY, NEAR ELLICOTT'S LOWER MILLS, AUGUST 19TH 1791. THOMAS JEFFERSON SECRETARY OF STATE.

Sir, I am fully sensible of the greatness of that freedom which I take with you on the present occasion; a liberty which Seemed to me Scarcely allowable, when I reflected on that distinguished, and dignifyed station in which you Stand; and the almost general prejudice and prepossession which is so previlent in the world against those of my complexion. . . .

Sir I freely and Chearfully acknowledge, that I am of the African race, and, in that colour which is natural to them of the deepest dye,* and it is under a Sense of the most profound gratitude to the Supreme Ruler of the universe, that I now confess to you, that I am not under that State of tyrannical thraldom, and inhuman captivity, to which too many of my brethren are doomed; but that I have abundantly tasted of the fruition of those blessings which proceed from that free and unequalled liberty with which you are favoured and which I hope you will willingly allow you have received from the immediate Hand of that Being from whom proceedeth every good and perfect gift.

Sir, Suffer me to recall to your mind that time in which the Arms and tyranny of the British Crown were exerted with every powerful effort, in order to reduce you to a State of Servitude; look back I intreat you on the variety of dangers to which you were exposed, reflect on that time in which every human aid appeared unavailable, and in which even hope and fortitude wore the aspect of inability to the Conflict, and you cannot but be led to a Serious and grateful Sense of your miraculous and providential preservation; You cannot but acknowledge, that the present freedom and tranquillity which you enjoy you have mercifully received, and that it is the peculiar blessing of Heaven.

This, Sir, was a time in which you clearly saw into the injustice of a State of Slavery, and in which you had Just apprehensions of the horrors of its condition, it was now Sir, that your abhorrence thereof was so excited, that you publickly held forth this true and invaluable doctrine, which is worthy to be recorded and remembered in all Succeeding ages. "We hold these truths to be Self evident, that all men are created equal, and that they are endowed by their creator with certain inalienable rights, that amongst these are life, liberty, and the persuit of happiness."

Here, Sir, was a time in which your tender feelings for your selves engaged you thus to declare, you were then impressed with proper ideas of the great valuation of liberty, and the free possession of those blessings to which you were entitled by nature; but Sir how pitiable is it to reflect, that altho you were so fully convinced of the benevolence of the Father of mankind, and of his equal and impartial distribution of those rights and privileges which he had conferred upon them, that you should at the Same time counteract his mercies, in detaining by fraud and violence so numerous a part of my brethren under groaning captivity and cruel oppression, that you should at the Same time be found guilty of that most criminal act, which you professedly detested in others, with respect to yourselves.

Sir, I suppose that your knowledge of the situation of my brethren is too extensive to need a recital

---

* My Father was brought here a Slave from Africa.

here; neither shall I presume to prescribe methods by which they may be relieved, otherwise than by recommending to you, and all others, to wean yourselves from those narrow prejudices which you have imbibed with respect to them, and as Job proposed to his friends "Put your Souls in their Souls' stead," thus shall your hearts be enlarged with kindness and benevolence towards them, and thus shall you need neither the direction of myself or others in what manner to proceed herein.

And now, Sir, altho my Sympathy and affection for my brethren hath caused my enlargement thus far, I ardently hope that your candour and generosity will plead with you in my behalf, when I make known to you, that it was not originally my design; but that having taken up my pen in order to direct to you as a present, a copy of an Almanack which I have calculated for the Succeeding year, I was unexpectedly and unavoidably led thereto. . . .

And now Sir, I . . . Shall conclude and Subscribe my Self with the most profound respect,

Your most Obedient humble Servant
Benjamin Banneker.[11]

11. THOMAS JEFFERSON'S REPLY TO BENJAMIN BANNEKER

PHILADELPHIA, AUG. 30. 1791

SIR, I Thank you sincerely for your letter of the 19th instant and for the Almanac it contained. No body wishes more than I do to see such proofs as you exhibit, that nature has given to our black brethren, talents equal to those of the other colors of men, and that the appearance of a want of them is owing merely to the degraded condition of their existence, both in Africa & America. I can add with truth, that no body wishes more ardently to see a good system commenced for raising the condition both of their body & mind to what it ought to be, as fast as the imbecility of their present existence, and other circumstances which cannot be neglected, will admit.

I have taken the liberty of sending your Almanac to Monsieur de Condorcet, Secretary of the Academy of Sciences at Paris, and member of the Philanthropic society, because I considered it as a document to which your whole colour had a right for their justification against the doubts which have been entertained of them.

I am with great esteem, Sir your most obed[t] humble serv[t]

Thomas Jefferson.[12]

QUESTIONS

1. Why did Patrick Henry believe that the new Constitution would erode individual liberties? What did he mean when he wrote that the Constitution "squints toward monarchy?"
2. Did James Madison and Alexander Hamilton speak directly to the concerns of the anti-Federalists?
3. Why did some say a Bill of Rights was needed, while others believed it was unnecessary? In what sense was the Bill of Rights a victory for the Anti-Federalists?
4. If you were a delegate to a state ratifying convention, would you have voted for or against the Constitution of 1787? Explain the reasons for your vote.
5. What was the fundamental conflict over slavery between brothers Moses and John Brown of Providence, Rhode Island?

6. Jefferson famously wrote in the Declaration of Independence, "We hold these truths to be self-evident: That all men are created equal." Does his *Notes on the State of Virginia* clarify or muddle what he seemed to mean in that sentence?

ADDITIONAL READING

Much has been written on the Philadelphia convention and the new Constitution. A classic piece that has had a great impact on twentieth-century American historiography is Charles Beard, *An Economic Interpretation of the Constitution of the United States* (1913). Other, more recent publications of importance include Christopher Collier and James Collier, *Decision in Philadelphia* (1987); Forest McDonald, *Novus Ordo Seclorum: The Intellectual Origins of the Constitution* (1985); Roger H. Brown, *Redeeming the Republic: Federalists, Taxation and the Origins of the Constitution* (1993); Calvin Jillson, *Congressional Dynamics* (1994); and Richard Beeman et al., eds., *Beyond Confederation: Origins of the Constitution* (1987). For the arguments of the Anti-Federalists, see Jackson Turner Main, *The Antifederalists: Critics of the Constitution* (1961). There has been renewed interest in the making of the Constitution of late: see, for example, Cass R. Sunstein, *The Declaration of Independence and the Constitution of the United States of America* (2004), Jack Rakove, *Original Meanings: Politics and Ideas in the Making of the Constitution* (1996); Richard Beeman, *Plain, Honest Men: The Making of the American Constitution* (2010); and Joseph Ellis, *The Quartet: Orchestrating the Second American Revolution, 1783–1789* (2015).

ENDNOTES

1. *Debates and Other Proceedings of the Convention of Virginia . . .* (Petersburg, VA: Hunter & Prentis, 1788), pp. 35–37.
2. Mercy Otis Warren, *Observations on the New Constitution* (Boston, 1788).
3. "From George Washington to Henry Knox, 15 October 1787," *Founders Online*, National Archives.
4. "From George Washington to Lafayette, 7 February 1788," *Founders Online*, National Archives.
5. James Madison, "The Conformity of the Plan to Republican Principles," *The Independent Journal*, January 16, 1788.
6. Alexander Hamilton, "Certain General and Miscellaneous Objections to the Constitution Considered and Answered," *McLean's Edition*, May 28, 1788.
7. *Providence Gazette*, February 26, 1789. Courtesy of the Rhode Island Historical Society.
8. *Providence Gazette*, February 14, 1789. Courtesy of the Rhode Island Historical Society.
9. Edmund S. Morgan, *American Slavery, American Freedom: The Ordeal of Colonial Virginia* (New York: Norton, 1975), pp. 280–281.
10. Thomas Jefferson, *Notes on the State of Virginia* (Philadelphia: Pritchard and Hall, 1788).
11. "To Thomas Jefferson from Benjamin Banneker, 19 August 1791," *Founders Online*, National Archives.
12. "From Thomas Jefferson to Benjamin Banneker, 30 August 1791," *Founders Online*, National Archives.

CHAPTER 6

RELIGIOUS REVIVALS AND SOCIAL REFORM IN THE EARLY REPUBLIC

HISTORICAL CONTEXT

Debating the appropriate boundary between government and religion has been an American pastime for more than two centuries. Shortly after the ratification of the Constitution of 1787, Congress considered a number of potential amendments designed to satisfy those who believed the new Constitution did not adequately protect individual liberties. To address a concern related to religion, Congressman James Madison of Virginia suggested the following amendment:

> The civil rights of none shall be abridged on account of religious belief or worship, nor shall any national religion be established, nor shall the full and equal rights of conscience be in any manner, or any pretext, infringed.

Agreeing with the idea, but rejecting the language, other members of Congress suggested their own phrasing. One by one, Congress considered and then rejected several versions. After weeks of sober reflection and debate, Congress sent to the states for ratification these words: "Congress shall make no law respecting an establishment of religion, or prohibiting a free exercise thereof. . . ." Twenty-seven months later, after three-fourths of the states ratified these words along with other liberty-protecting amendments, the "establishment" and "free exercise" clauses became memorialized as the opening lines in the Bill of Rights.

Inserting these protections into the Constitution did not settle the argument about the appropriate role of government in religious affairs, but it did narrow the debate. Originally, the clauses applied only to the federal government, as states were free to tax citizens to support a given church. Connecticut officially recognized the Congregational Church as the "established" state church. Massachusetts, while insisting that "no subject shall be hurt . . . for worshipping GOD in the manner and season most agreeable to the dictates of his own conscience," also required local communities to provide suitable provisions for houses of worship and for the support of "Protestant teachers of piety, religion and morality," requirements that essentially resulted in state support for Congregational churches. Although neither Connecticut nor Massachusetts initially ratified the Bill of Rights (each did so only in 1939) and each maintained state support for churches until 1818 and 1833, respectively, public sentiment during the early national era was clearly moving in the direction of separating religious institutions from state support.

These developments frightened a dwindling remnant of Protestant churchgoers who viewed the events of their generation with alarm. For several decades, politics rather than religion had dominated the thoughts of most Americans. Normal church activities, interrupted during the years of the revolution, continued to be undermined after the war by the incessant geographical mobility of the people. Meanwhile, Christian leaders—appalled that the Constitution of 1787 made no reference to God and that the recently added establishment clause of the First Amendment seemed to distance the nation even further from its religious underpinnings—complained about the growing secularization of society and the religious apathy of the American people.

Statistically, at least, some of their complaints were justified. While about four in ten Americans during the 1790s attended religious worship intermittently, fewer than one in ten was an official church member. Moreover, in almost every community, the most active churchgoers were women—the least influential members of society. To many Christian ministers, early national churches appeared to be weak, feminine institutions, a far cry from the once powerful and prestigious churches of colonial times. As the nation entered a new age characterized by religious voluntarism without state support, the low membership rates and the growing gender disparities in churches troubled clergymen who recognized that it was primarily adult men who paid the bills and brought authority to their congregations.

All these concerns notwithstanding, religious disestablishment allowed innovations that would bring renewal to a wide variety of sects and institutions. To survive in an age of voluntarism, churches had to compete with each other for members and for financial support. This struggle encouraged them to implement new strategies designed to win souls and bring more contributors into their congregations. Churches turned to aggressive styles of evangelism, including camp meetings, street preaching, town revivals, the creation of Sunday schools, and the establishment of Bible and religious tract societies. Not all sects embraced these new methods of recruitment, but those that did tended to grow while those that did not generally lost shares in the deregulated religious "marketplace."

By emphasizing the personal and emotional dimension of faith and the role of the individual, evangelical religion also laid the groundwork for a sustained wave of reform. By the 1820s, religious leaders such as Lyman Beecher directed public attention to a range of social reforms, and the most influential of these was the movement to control the consumption of alcohol. Temperance was one of the earliest and most ambitious efforts at social reform in American history, for alcohol infused nearly every male activity in contemporary life. By using existing church networks and organizational techniques learned through the revivals, preachers and other reformers were able to communicate their message to a wide range of Americans. Though temperance societies reached back to the very early nineteenth century, it was only with the energy brought by religious revivals that the movement's influence peaked in the 1830s and 1840s.

The American Temperance Society was founded in 1826, and by 1834 there were over 5,000 local and regional branches of the society throughout the nation. The movement influenced young Abraham Lincoln in the 1840s, and by 1855 most states had passed legislation limiting the production of alcohol. Using both persuasion and legislation, temperance reformers substantially reduced alcohol consumption between 1830 and 1850. Their success inspired the growth of other reform movements, especially antislavery.

The documents in this chapter explore the separation of church and state, religious revivals, and social reform. As you examine these texts, try to identify the major arguments both for and against religious disestablishment and the ensuing religious innovations during this era of evangelical enthusiasm. Why did people passionately support or oppose these innovations? What factors—class, gender, region, or denominational affiliation—influenced their responses? How did religious leaders channel this religious enthusiasm into social reform?

INTRODUCTION TO DOCUMENTS 1, 2, AND 3

Our first set of documents explores the relationship between government and religion. John Leland was a Massachusetts Baptist preacher who spent fifteen years, between 1776 and 1791, serving churches in Virginia before his opposition to slavery prompted his return to New England. Leland strongly supported James Madison's work to establish religious freedom, enshrined in the First Amendment, as reflected in Document 1. A few years later, an association of Baptists in Danbury, Connecticut, wrote to President Jefferson to protest what they viewed as that state's insufficient protection of religion in their newly adopted state constitution. Jefferson's response of New Year's Day of 1802 is Document 2. His key phrase of a "wall of separation between Church and State" became central to Supreme Court discussion of religion in the modern era. The third document contains the Reverend Lyman Beecher's reflections on the decision of Connecticut to eliminate state support for the Congregational Church. Young Beecher was a leading antidisestablishmentarian (which simply refers to someone in favor of maintaining an established state church). Yet, looking back decades later, Beecher wrote in his diary how much his views had changed and why.

1. "THE EXCESS OF CIVIL POWER EXPLODED"

JOHN LELAND

The principle that civil rulers have nothing to do with religion in their official capacities is . . . much interwoven in the Baptist plan. . . . The legitimate powers of government extend only to punish men for working ill to their neighbors, and no way affect the rights of conscience. The nation of Israel received their civil and religious laws from Jehovah, which were binding on them and no other; and with the extirpation of that nation, were abolished. For a Christian commonwealth to be established upon the same claim is very presumptuous, without they have the same charter from Heaven. Because the nation of Israel had a divine grant of the land of Canaan, and orders to enslave the heathen, some suppose Christians have an equal right to take away the land of the Indians, and make slaves of the negroes. Wretched religion that pleads for cruelty and injustice. . . . The very tendency of religious establishments by human law is to make some hypocrites and the rest fools; they are calculated to destroy those very virtues that religion is designed to build up; to encourage fraud and violence over the earth. It is error alone, that stands in need of government to support it; truth can and will do better without: so ignorance calls in anger in a debate, good sense scorns it. Religion, in its purest ages, made its way in the world, not only without the aid of the law, but against all the laws of haughty monarchs, and all the maxims of the schools. . . .

Government should protect every man in thinking and speaking freely, and see that one does not abuse another. The liberty I contend for is more than toleration. The very idea of toleration, is despicable; it supposes that some have a pre-eminence about the rest, to grant indulgence; whereas, all should be equally free, Jews, Turks, Pagans and Christians. Test oaths, and established creeds, should be avoided as the worst of evils. A general assessment, (forcing all to pay some preacher,) amounts to an establishment; if government says I must pay somebody, it must next describe that somebody, his doctrine and place of abode. That moment a minister is so fixed as to receive a stipend by legal force, that moment he ceases to be a gospel ambassador, and becomes a minister of the state. This emolution is a temptation too great for avaricious men to withstand. This doctrine turns the gospel into merchandise, and sinks religion upon a level with other things.

As it is not the province of civil government to establish forms of religion, and force a maintenance for the preachers, so it does not belong to that power to establish fixed holy days for divine worship. That the Jewish seventh-day Sabbath was of divine appointment, is unquestionable; but that the Christian first-day Sabbath is of equal injunction, is more doubtful. If Jesus appointed the day to be observed, he did it as the head of the church, and not as the king of nations; or if the apostles enjoined it, they did it in the capacity of Christian teachers, and not as human legislators. As the appointment of such days is not part of human legislation, so the breach of the Sabbath (so called) is no part of civil jurisdiction. I am not an enemy of holy days (the duties of religion cannot be performed without fixed times,) but these times should be fixed by the mutual agreement of religious societies, according to the word of God, and not by civil author. I see no clause in the federal constitution, or the constitution of Virginia, to empower either the federal or Virginia legislature to make any sabbatical laws.[1]

2. JEFFERSON'S LETTER TO THE DANBURY BAPTISTS (1802)

To messers. Nehemiah Dodge, Ephraim Robbins, & Stephen S. Nelson, a committee of the Danbury Baptist association in the state of Connecticut.
Gentlemen

The affectionate sentiments of esteem and approbation which you are so good as to express towards me, on behalf of the Danbury Baptist association, give me the highest satisfaction. . . .

Believing with you that religion is a matter which lies solely between Man & his God, that he owes account to none other for his faith or his worship, that the legitimate powers of government reach actions only, & not opinions, I contemplate with sovereign reverence that act of the whole American people which declared that their legislature should "make no law respecting an establishment of religion, or prohibiting the free exercise thereof," thus building a wall of separation between Church & State. Adhering to this expression of the supreme will of the nation in behalf of the rights of conscience, I shall see with sincere satisfaction the progress of those sentiments which tend to restore to man all his natural rights, convinced he has no natural right in opposition to his social duties.

I reciprocate your kind prayers for the protection & blessing of the common Father and creator of man, and tender you for yourselves & your religious association, assurances of my high respect & esteem.

Th Jefferson Jan. 1. 1802.[2]

3. "THE BEST THING THAT EVER HAPPENED TO THE STATE OF CONNECTICUT"

LYMAN BEECHER

It was a time of great depression and suffering. . . . I worked as hard as mortal man could, and at the same time preached for revivals with all my might, and with success, till at last, what with domestic afflictions and all, my health and spirits began to fail. It was as dark a day as ever I saw. The odium thrown upon the ministry was inconceivable. The injury done to the cause of Christ, as we then supposed, was irreparable. For several days I suffered what no tongue can tell *for the best thing that ever happened to the State of Connecticut.* It cut the churches loose from dependence on state support. It threw them wholly on their own resources and on God. They say ministers have lost their influence; the fact is, they have gained. By voluntary efforts, societies, missions, and revivals, they exert a deeper influence than ever they could by queues, and shoe-buckles, and cocked hats, and goldheaded canes. . . .

For years we of the standing order had been the scoff and by-word of politicians, sectarians, and infidels, and had held our tongues; but now the Lord began to pour out his Spirit. . . . Revivals now began to pervade the state. The ministers were united, and had been consulting and praying.

Political revolution had cut them off from former sources of support, and caused them to look to God. Then there came such a time of revival as never before in the state. I remember how we all used to feel before the revolution happened. Our people thought they should be destroyed if the law should be taken away from under them. . . . And the fact is, we all felt that our children would scatter like partridges if the tax law was lost. . . . When the storm burst upon us, indeed, we thought we were dead for a while. But we found we were not dead. Our fears had magnified the danger. We were thrown on God and on ourselves, and this created that moral coercion which makes men work. Before we had been standing on what our fathers had done, but now we were obliged to develop all our energy. On the other hand, the other denominations lost all the advantage they had had before, so that the very thing in which the enemy said, "Raze it raze it to the foundations," laid the corner-stone of our prosperity to all generations. The law compelling every man to pay somewhere was repealed. The consequence unexpectedly was, first, that the occasion of animosity between us and the minor sects was removed, and infidels could no more make capital with them against us, and they then began themselves to feel the dangers of infidelity, and to react against it, and this laid the basis of co-operation and union of spirit. And, besides, that tax law had for more than twenty years really worked to weaken us and strengthen them. All the stones that shelled off and rolled down from our eminence lodged in their swamp. Whenever a man grew disaffected, he went off and paid his rates with the minor sects; but on the repeal of the law there was no such temptation. Take this revolution through, it was one of the most desperate battles ever fought in the United States. It was the last struggle of the separation of Church and State.[3]

INTRODUCTION TO DOCUMENTS 4–8

The documents in this set describe what Americans thought about one of the innovative methods of church recruitment of the early national era, the religious camp meeting. The first camp meeting erupted spontaneously during the summer of 1800 when a Presbyterian minister named James McGready invited nearby Protestants to a four-day gathering near his church in Gasper River, Kentucky. News of the success of this outdoor meeting spread rapidly across the frontier, and the following summer a number of Protestants held an outdoor revival at Cane Ridge, Kentucky, a site closer to the population center of the region. The Cane Ridge revival, perhaps the largest and wildest of the early camp meetings, attracted some 25,000 participants, an incredible crowd considering that the population of Lexington, the state's largest city, barely exceeded 2,000.

As rumors of the events at Cane Ridge circulated around the nation, evangelicals back East adopted the camp meeting model. Recall that in Document 3, for instance, Beecher welcomed the revivals to Connecticut in the early 1820s. By that time, camp meetings were as commonplace within a day's journey of the great eastern cities as they were on the western frontier. Document 4 is an 1803 letter from a woman named Fanny Lewis to her father describing a camp meeting near Baltimore. Document 5 is an image that captures a religious revival in the late 1820s, three decades after the first outpourings in Kentucky.

The next two documents express clerical opinions of the camp meeting experiences. Document 6 was written by Martin J. Spalding, a Kentucky-born Catholic priest who was very critical of the emotional outpourings that characterized these revivals (Spalding, incidentally, eventually became the archbishop of Baltimore). Similarly, Document 7, which is taken from the Methodist Protestant periodical *Wesleyan Repository* (published in Philadelphia in 1820), attempts to discredit camp meetings by associating them with popular secular events such as fairs and horse races that most evangelicals readily denounced as sinful. Document 8 is a brief defense of religious revivals by the most powerful evangelist of the era, Charles Grandison Finney. Here Finney argues—quite contrary to Spalding—that emotion and passion were central to authentic religious experience.

In examining these documents, attempt to identify the underlying values held by the authors. What, for instance, were their attitudes toward the place of emotion in religion, toward work and leisure? Why might Spalding have doubted the authenticity of these revivals, while Lewis and Finney so enthusiastically embraced them? Why does Scrutator, for instance, so vehemently object to camp meetings, given that they were successful means of spreading the Gospel? And what does Finney mean by "worldly excitements that agitate Christendom" and are "unfriendly to religion?"

4. FANNY LEWIS, LETTER TO HER FATHER

BALTIMORE, OCTOBER 1803

I hasten to give you some account of our glorious camp-meeting; but alas! all description fails. It would take an Addison or a Pope to give you even an idea of the lovely grove, particularly in the night, when the moon glimmered through the trees, and all was love and harmony. The stand was placed at the bottom of several small hills, on which our tents and wagons were placed. The meeting began on Saturday; and was very lively.

On Sunday morning Mr. S——— called his family to prayer-meeting. At ten o'clock public preaching began, and great was the power of God. There was scarce any intermission day or night. It looked awful and solemn to see a number of fires burning before the tents, and the trees with lanterns and candles suspended to them. No sound was heard, except Glory to God in the highest! or mercy! mercy! Such was a night, my father, I never saw or felt before. Many souls were converted, and many witnessed that God was able to cleanse from all sin.

On Monday morning there was such a gust of the power of God, that it appeared to me, the very gates of hell would give way. All the people were filled with wonder, love, and praise. Mr. S——— came and threw himself in our tent, crying "Glory! glory! this is the happiest day I ever saw." He says he never knew such a continual power and increase of the love of God for three days and nights. We call it "the happy Monday." Yes, it was a happy, happy Monday! a day long to be remembered, and a night never to be forgotten. O! how I longed for you, that you might share in the happiness of your unworthy child. Nor was our parting less glorious than our meeting; for several received perfect love after the congregation broke up. They were under the necessity of dismissing the people for want of preachers; all that were present were worn out. Truly the harvest was great, but the labourers were few.

Those who were absent, know not what they have lost; nor can they form any idea of what we enjoyed. It was none other than the gate of heaven.

Where! O! where shall we begin to praise redeeming love, for the peace and comfort and assurance our souls felt in realizing the promises of an unchangeable Jehovah. Camp-meeting! why the very name thrills through my every nerve! and almost makes me think I am in the charming woods. Every foot of ground seemed to me sacred. I saw nothing, heard nothing to molest my peace: Not one jarring string. Everything seemed to combine together to promote the glory of God, and his gospel.

Such indeed, my dear father, was our meetings; and I can but lament my inability to give you an account of it; but it was better felt than expressed. Sometimes you would see more than one hundred hands raised in triumphant praise with united voices, giving glory to God, for more than one hour together, with every mark of unfeigned humility and reverence.

The time between services was not taken up with "what shall we eat, or what shall we drink," but in weeping with those that wept, and rejoicing with those that rejoiced, and that had found their pearl of great price.

The preachers all seemed as men filled with new wine. Some standing crying, others prostrate on the ground, as insensible to every earthly object; while the Master of assemblies was speaking to the hearts of poor sinners, who stood trembling under a sense of the power and presence of a sin-avenging God. They seemed unwilling to move from the spot where they stood, with their eyes fixed on them that were rejoicing in God their Saviour.

After all was over, I walked over the ground by moon-light—the scene was solemn and delightful. When I left the place, I cannot describe the emotion I felt. It was something like parting with all that was dear to me. My foolish heart kept saying, adieu ye sacred grove, adieu—never, never shall I see you more.

I am your dutiful
And affectionate daughter,
Fanny Lewis[4]

5. CAMP MEETING PORTRAIT (c. 1829)

CAMP-MEETING
[Copyright secured]

Image 6.1 Portrait of Camp Meeting

This lithograph captures the energy and emotion of contemporary revivals. Note the passionate congregation, the egalitarian arrangement of the assembly, and the skepticism exhibited by those at the left and right.

Source: "Camp Meeting," A. Rider *pinxit*; drawn on stone by H. Bridport, Kenney & Lucas Lithography, c. 1829. Library of Congress.

6. "A FANATICISM AS ABSURD AS IT WAS BLASPHEMOUS" (1844)

MARTIN J. SPALDING

To understand more fully how very "precious and astonishing" this great revival was, we must further reflect: 1st, that it produced, not a mere momentary excitement, but one that lasted for several successive years. 2ndly, that it was not confined to one particular denomination, but, to a greater or less extent, pervaded all. 3rdly, that men of sense and good judgement in other matters were often carried away by the same fanaticism which swayed the mob. 4thly, that this fanaticism was as widespread as it was permanent—not being confined to Kentucky, but pervading most of the adjoining states and territories. And 5thly, that though some were found who had good sense enough to detect the impostor, yet they were comparatively few in number, and wholly unable to stay the rushing torrent of fanaticism, even if they had had the moral courage to attempt it.

Such are some of the leading features of a movement in religion (!) which is perhaps one of the most extraordinary recorded in history, and to which we know of but few parallels, except in some of the fanatical doings of the Anabaptists in Germany during the first years of their history. The whole matter furnishes one more conclusive evidence of the weakness of the human mind when left to itself; and one more sad commentary on the Protestant rule of faith.

Here we see whole masses of population, spread over a vast territory, boasting too of their enlightenment and Bible-learning, swayed for years by a fanaticism as absurd as it was blasphemous; and yet believing all this to be the work of the Holy Spirit! Let Protestants after this talk about Catholic ignorance and superstition! Had Catholics ever played the "fantastic tricks" which were played off by Protestants during these years, we would perhaps never hear the end of it. . . .

Besides the "exercises" [referred to earlier] there was also the jumping exercise. Spasmodic convulsions, which lasted sometimes for hours, were the usual sequel to the falling exercise. Then there were the "exercises" of screaming and shouting and crying. A camp meeting during that day exhibited the strangest bodily feats, accompanied with the most Babel-like sounds. An eyewitness of undoubted veracity stated to us that, in passing one of the campgrounds, he noticed a man in the "barking exercise," clasping a tree with his arms, and dashing his head against it until it was all besmeared with blood, shouting all the time that he had "treed his Saviour"! Another eyewitness stated that in casually passing by a camp in the night, while the exercises were at the highest, he witnessed scenes of too revolting a character even to be alluded to here.

One of the most remarkable features, perhaps, of these "exercises" is the apparently well-authenticated fact that many fell into them by a kind of sympathy, almost in spite of themselves, and some even positively against their own will! Some who visited the meetings to laugh at the proceedings, sometimes caught the contagion themselves. There seems to have then existed in Kentucky a kind of mental and moral epidemic—a sort of contagious frenzy—which spread rapidly from one to another.[5]

7. CAMP-MEETINGS AND AGRICULTURAL FAIRS (1820)

WESLEYAN REPOSITORY, PHILADELPHIA

It has been for a long time a question of serious concern to many sober and considerate members of our Society, whether Camp Meetings did not involve such attendant evils *near large cities* and in *populous countries*, as to counterbalance much of their intended good. On this subject, too, we may have been too partial to our own doings, to have duly attended to the voices or opinions of others; but we have now a chance to open our eyes to *facts* resulting from the *acts of others*, which bear sufficient analogy, in my opinion, to some of our Camp Meetings—and may, therefore, present us with a fair occasion, if we will consider it, of examining the reality of the alleged many evils, consequent on long continued night assemblages of indiscriminate masses of people. I allude to the recent "Agricultural Exhibitions and Fairs", [that] assemblage of riot, revel, and general vice, which lately assembled in the vicinity of Philadelphia for several continuous days and nights. . . .

Probably several may feel prompt to condemn the Fairs, (who see the vices of large promiscuous crowds) who, notwithstanding, will suppress or stifle their conviction of their obvious similarity to the ungovernable crowds which have surrounded some camp-meetings. Why camp-meetings alone should be exempt from the general objection, of being worse than useless, when and where they incidentally involve as much or more evil than good, is not made out a clear case to my mind. . . .

To impute, as we generally do, all the conversions which ensue to the special influence of the camp-meeting,

is not, I think, conclusive reasoning, because the fact is, that almost all of such are composed of those who came with previous design and awakening, and determined to find their rest there. And who could say, that the same time and prayerfulness employed at some regular church, and for the same objects, would not produce an equal or greater proportion of good? . . .

If woods-meetings, in places where churches abound, do indeed far surpass in productive good the churches, why should we not, like the Druids, hold all our meetings in the open air, and give the value of our buildings in charities?

It may be questioned, too, whether the habit of leaving the ordinary churches to seek encampments in the woods, does not, in many cases, tend to draw us off unwarily from our principal design of worship, and engage our affections to the novelties of the scenes, the greetings of new faces, the hospitalities of reciprocal visits, the exemption from the usual labors and cares, the reports of the doings within and without the camp: All these things may give pleasing agitations to the mind; but are they certainly holy? And is it not possible that those who thus frequent them from choice, and not of necessity, (having left their churches to attend them) may and do acquire undue disrelish to the ordinary worship of the year to which they must however return. Take away the worship, and there would remain sufficient gratifications to allure the most of young people, and thousands if equally fed and freed from labor, would follow them perpetually. . . .

[As] to the loss of time, money and labor resulting to the general weal, from the assemblage of such crowds for sinister purposes, it might not be deemed irrelevant here to glance at the same facts attendant on large and protracted camp-meetings. If "time is money," and "labor is the wealth of the community," as is granted by all, it must be admitted that camp-meetings, in countries where churches for the ordinary congregation exist, is one of the most expensive measures to the community where they prevail, that could be devised. It could be easily demonstrated, that at any given camp-meeting, where the totality of persons, at any given time, was equal to 5,000 persons, with the horses and carriages, night and day, for one week, it is attended, at a moderate computation, with a loss of productive labor and expense for diet, drink, &c of 25,000 dollars— exclusive of cost of tents, furniture, congregation benches, and pulpits, and the time employed in preparation of camp, and for return. Whether we will heed

it or not, it is nevertheless true, that as surely as a militia training, or horserace, near a great city, puts in requisition and motion, the idle and the profligate for ten to fifteen miles surrounding the centre of attraction, so true it also is, that the roads, inns and booths of the country which environ a camp-meeting, witness the same followers, with their revellings, profanity and idleness, and further departure from all that is good. These may be very unpopular sentiments to appear in your paper; but if some Methodists can and do entertain such sentiments, should you not thus expose their obliquity, that due measures may be taken to subdue such objections, and to save those who are thus out of the way? Let the evil be known, lest the remedy might not appear to be necessary to be applied.

Scrutator[6]

8. "RELIGION MUST BE MAINLY PROMOTED BY MEANS OF REVIVALS" (1835)

CHARLES GRANDISON FINNEY

Almost all the religion in the world has been produced by revivals. God has found it necessary to take advantage of the excitability there is in mankind, to produce powerful excitements among them, before he can lead them to obey. Men are so spiritually sluggish, there are so many things to lead their minds off from religion, and to oppose the influence of the Gospel, that it is necessary to raise an excitement among them, till the tide rises so high as to sweep away the opposing obstacles. They must be so excited that they will break over these counteracting influences, before they will obey God. Not that excited feeling is religion, for it is not; but it is excited desire, appetite and feeling that prevents religion. The

will is, in a sense, enslaved by the carnal and worldly desires. Hence it is necessary to awaken men to a sense of guilt and danger, and thus produce an excitement of counter feeling and desire which will break the power of carnal and worldly desire and leave the will free to obey God.

Look back at the history of the Jews, and you will see that God used to maintain religion among *them* by special occasions, when there would be a great excitement, and people would turn to the Lord. And after they had been thus revived, it would be but a short time before there would be so many counteracting influences brought to bear upon them, that religion would decline, and keep on declining, till God could have time—so to speak—to convict them of sin by his Spirit and rebuke them by his providence, and thus so gain the attention of the masses to the great subject of salvation, as to produce a widespread awakening of religious interest, and consequently a revival of religion.

. . . The state of the world is still such, and probably will be till the millennium is fully come, that religion must be mainly promoted by means of revivals . . . the state of the Christian world is such, that to expect to promote religion without excitements is unphilosophical and absurd. The great political, and other worldly excitements that agitate Christendom, are all unfriendly to religion, and divert the mind from the interests of the soul. Now these excitements can only be counteracted by *religious* excitements. And until there is religious principle in the world to put down irreligious excitements, it is vain to try to promote religion, except by counteracting excitements. . . .

It is altogether improbable that religion will ever make progress among *heathen* nations except through the influence of revivals. The attempt is now making to do it by education, and other cautious and gradual improvements. But so long as the laws of mind remain what they are, it cannot be done in this way. There must be excitement sufficient to wake up the dormant moral powers, and roll back the tide of degradation and sin.[7]

INTRODUCTION TO DOCUMENTS 9–12

Camp meetings helped spread the word and bring new converts into the Christian fold. While there was competition between congregations and denominations to attract new members, all evangelical religion aimed to make Americans more observant and also to improve their daily conduct. It was men like William Otter, an itinerant plasterer, whom these evangelicals hoped to reform. Otter was one of the few workingmen of the era who left us a memoir of his times. He worked hard at his trade, but above all, he was a "jolly fellow." The phrase described men for whom the life of drinking, fighting, gambling, and playing cruel jokes (especially against African Americans, the Irish, or invalids) brought the greatest satisfactions. Taverns were their churches, and well-liquored "sprees" of storytelling, card-playing, and brawling, their services. Theirs was an old form of male behavior, familiar for centuries to men in Europe. Document 9 is a passage from Otter's memoir, describing an 1806 Christmas riot between Irish and native-born American gangs in front of a New York City Catholic church.

By the 1820s, the rough ways of the jolly fellows came under assault from Christians and the middle class, for whom sobriety and steady habits paved the way to prosperity, solid family life, and Godliness. Documents 10–12 show evidence of the growing number of temperance activists who sought to reform men like Otter. Document 10, an excerpt from Lyman Beecher's 1825 sermons, invokes the moral, social, and economic costs of drink. After describing the evils of drunkenness, Beecher turned to the remedies. His campaign spawned innumerable local temperance societies, including the Cold Water Temperance Group for children. Document 11 is one of their songs, followed by a lithograph of the "Drunkard's Progress," depicting the inevitable path from moderation to utter self-destruction, in Document 12. While examining these documents, ask yourself whether William Otter would have been persuaded by temperance reformers to change his ways. Who might have been converted to the cause of temperance, and, more generally, why do you think this movement was so successful in the antebellum era?

9. TALES OF A "JOLLY FELLOW"

WILLIAM OTTER

. . . On Christmas eve we went to amuse ourselves at a dance; it being very common to make merry on holidays; while there and in the act of dancing we heard of a riot that had been raised at the Catholic Church near the park; Lane and myself left the house and went to the church. . . . [It] was surrounded with a motley crew of Irish and sailors, we inquired what was the matter, we were informed that the Irish had killed a sailor. The Irish and the sailors were engaged in deadly conflict, and without farther ceremony we entered the list of combatants and espoused the cause of the sailors, and the mob fought from the door of the church to Irish town, being the distance of about one fourth of a mile, and kept on fighting all that night, Lane and myself, in company with three or four more who came with Lane and myself from the dance, went into a grogshop in Irish town and asked the keeper of the shop for a half pint of rum; he told us to clear out for a set of rascals; without farther ceremony upon any account, we fell to and waled the grogshop keeper and two more hands who seemed to espouse his cause, most elegantly; his wife went into the cellar and we shut her down in the cellar, and took possession of the shop; having by this time cleared out all hands, we fell to and drank as much as we pleased, and while we were refreshing ourselves the mob came in and began to break bottles, glasses, pitchers, barrels, and all and every thing they could find in the shop; and fought on till day light throughout Irishtown; laying all Irishtown waste; . . . It was sometime in the afternoon on Christmas day before I got home. . . .

[*A year later, Otter was working in the Eastern Pennsylvania town of Columbus, when he decided to attend church services with a friend, a local innkeeper and a true jolly fellow.*]

On Sunday evening, Mr. C. was caught in one of his sprees, he and myself went to a Methodist meeting, when we had been there a few minutes a preacher mounted the pulpit and began to preach, and raised his voice to an excessive pitch. Mr. C. he asked me, what I thought of him, (meaning the preacher,) I told him I thought he was a tarnel fool in my judgement, he wanted to display by force of voice what he should have done in eloquence. In the middle of his sermon Mr. C. got up and interrupted the man of the gospel, and in terms not to be misunderstood; he refuted the preacher, and in conclusion told him he was a damned liar; which remark, acted in the meeting-house among the zealous members as would a firebrand in a magazine of powder; they began a general fight, some were for putting Mr. C. out of the meeting-house; by some friendly interference on our part, we got Mr. C. home to his house, he became so outrageous, that he began to break all his bar furniture; he played hokey among the bottles, decanters, tumblers and glasses; smashed everything that came in his way, not even content with that, he threw the kegs out into the bargain. His wife, for such gross misdemeanor, as she held all the property in the house, and the house itself by virtue of her former marriage, had Mr. C. committed to jail. . . ."[8]

10. "THE NATIONAL REMEDY FOR INTEMPERANCE" (1828)

LYMAN BEECHER

What then is this universal, natural, and national remedy for intemperance?

It Is The Banishment Of Ardent Spirits From The List Of Lawful Articles Of Commerce, By A Correct And Efficient Public Sentiment; Such As Has Turned Slavery Out Of Half Our Land, And Will Yet Expel It From The World.

Nothing should now be said, by way of crimination for the past, for verily we have all been guilty in this thing; so that there are few in the land, whose brother's blood may not cry out against them from the ground, on account of the bad influence which has been lent in some way to the work of destruction.

We are not therefore to come down in wrath upon the distillers, and importers, and venders of ardent spirits. None of us are enough without sin to cast the first stone. For who would have imported, or distilled, or vended, if all the nominally temperate in the land had refused to drink? It is the buyers who have created the demand for ardent spirits, and made distillation and importation a gainful traffick. And it is the custom of the temperate too, which inundates the land with the occasion of so much and such unmanageable temptation. Let the temperate cease to buy—and the demand for ardent spirits will fall in the market three fourths, and ultimately will fail wholly, as the generation of drunkards shall hasten out of time.

... Let us all rather confess the sins which are past, and leave the things which are behind, and press forward in one harmonious attempt to reform the land, and perpetuate our invaluable blessings.

This however cannot be done effectually so long as the traffick in ardent spirits is regarded as lawful, and is patronized by men of reputation and moral worth in every part of the land. Like slavery, it must be regarded as sinful, impolitic, and dishonorable. That no measures will avail short of rendering ardent spirits a contraband of trade, is nearly self-evident.

... Could all the forms of evil produced in the land by intemperance, come upon us in one horrid array—it would appal [sic] the nation, and put an end to the traffick in ardent spirits. If in every dwelling built by blood, the stone from the wall should utter all the cries which the bloody traffick extorts—and the beam out of the timber should echo them back—who would build such a house?—and who would dwell in it? What if in every part of the dwelling, from the cellar upward, through all the halls and chambers—babblings, and contentions, and voices, and groans, and shrieks, and wailings, were heard day and night! What if the cold blood oozed out, and stood in drops upon the walls; and, by preternatural art, all the ghastly skulls and bones of the victims destroyed by intemperance, should stand upon the walls, in horrid sculpture within and without the building!—who would rear such a building?

Oh! Were the sky over our heads one great whispering gallery, bringing down about us all the lamentation and woe which intemperance creates, and the firm earth one sonorous medium of sound, bringing up around us from beneath the wailings of the damned, whom the commerce in ardent spirits had sent thither;—these tremendous realities, assailing our sense, would invigorate our conscience, and give decision to our purpose of reformation.

... No great melioration of the human condition was ever achieved without the concurrent effort of numbers, and no extended, well-directed application of moral influence, was ever made in vain. Let the temperate part of the nation awake, and reform, and concentrate their influence in a course of systematic action, and success is not merely probable, but absolutely certain.... The language of Heaven to our happy nation is "be it unto thee even as thou wilt," and there is no despondency more fatal, or more wicked, than that which refuses to hope, and to act, from the apprehension that nothing can be done.[9]

11. THE COLD WATER ARMY PLEDGE FOR CHILDREN OF CONNECTICUT (c. 1845)

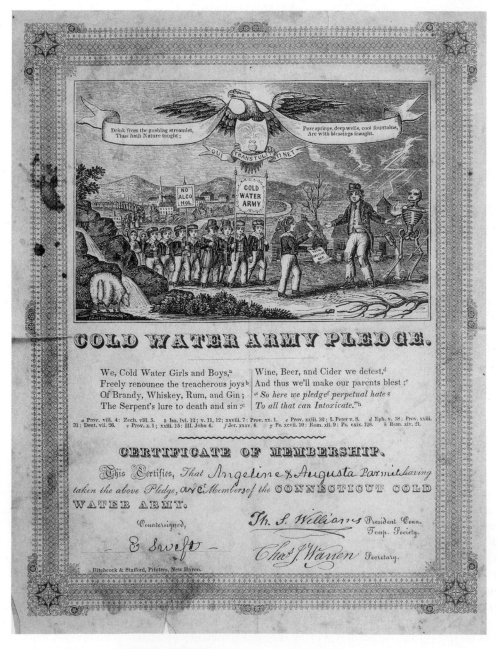

Image 6.2 Certificate of the Cold Water Army Pledge

The temperance movement spawned countless local societies, even enlisting the membership of children. Note the use of Biblical verse and stark imagery to convey the evils of drink to youth.

Source: American Antiquarian Society.

12. THE DRUNKARD'S PROGRESS (c. 1846)

Image 6.3 The Drunkard's Progress: from the first glass to the grave (c. 1846)

This lithograph, one of many popular prints made to generate support for temperance, claimed that even modest alcohol consumption led to a life of sin, crime, and ultimately death.

Source: (New York: N. Currier, c. 1846). Library of Congress.

INTRODUCTION TO DOCUMENTS 13 AND 14

The fight against alcohol consumption may have been the most widely adopted evangelical reform of the antebellum era, but it was certainly not the only one. Evangelicals, convinced of the perfectibility of society, brought their zeal to many areas of antebellum life, including prison reform, Sabbatarianism ("blue laws" prohibiting work or raucous play on the Sabbath), and the fight against slavery. The organized antislavery movement gained momentum after January 1, 1831, when William Lloyd Garrison began to publish *The Liberator*, his uncompromising abolitionist newspaper. The revivalist movement of earlier decades convinced many that slavery was not merely unjust, but a sin that demanded repentance. These evangelicals infused a measure of passion and urgency into the fight against slavery, demanding immediate emancipation. The documents quoted here convey that urgency. Document 13 was written by Mary Livermore, a female preacher whose success brought her wide audiences and even repeated invitations to preach to Congress. By the 1830s, she firmly believed in the imminent return of Christ, a conviction that put her at odds with most evangelicals at the time. Her letter to former president James Madison was most likely prompted by his recent appointment as a representative to the convention in Richmond to discuss proposed revisions to the Virginia state constitution's rules on white male voting rights. The convention did not act on slavery, but ironically, just two years later, the revolt of the slave Nat Turner prompted a debate over slavery in the Virginia legislature. As you read Livermore's letter, consider how she connects her faith to social action, and why she is so convinced that slavery is not just unjust but an affront to God's will.

By 1834, the antislavery crusade had become national in scope. Evangelicals, however, were somewhat divided about their commitments to opposing slavery. Both Lyman Beecher and Charles Finney worried that the demands for immediate emancipation would roil Protestant churches, perhaps along sectional lines. Finney had evangelized thousands in the 1830s, including Theodore Dwight Weld, who enrolled at Lane Theological Seminary in 1833, and by the next year insisted—along with many of his fellow students—on the adoption of abolitionism as a test of one's religious commitments. By 1836, Weld was a leader of the antislavery movement, and expressed concern that Finney was insufficiently committed to the cause. Finney's response—which urged caution and predicted a grave split in the churches and the country at large—is Document 14. As you read his letter to Weld, ask how Finney understands the relationship between faith and social action, and why he has such serious concerns about Weld's approach to the latter. What differentiates his understanding of religious identity and moral obligation from that of Livermore?

13. HARRIET LIVERMORE, LETTER TO JAMES MADISON

CHARLESTON IN SOUTH CAROLINA, OCTOBER 22. AD. 1829

Sir

A female, quite unknown to you, who has nothing commendatory in herself, but an alliance to that sex, which is called "the weaker vessel", very respectfully solicits your attention a few moments, to the subject of a *petition* she has to lay to at your feet. An impression that your time is very closely occupied, leads me to believe you will give a preference to brevity rather than be detained by a long preface of apology, for this seeming temerity in a woman, & stranger—Therefore I will hasten to my disclosure of the point to which my heart is drawn; and first.

I am a daughter of the happy part of our favored country called New Engd. and of course an advocate for liberty. I profess a belief in the gospel of Jesus Christ, & am consequently opposed to the Article of SLAVERY—I love my native country, therefore I am jealous of her laws, desiring they may be all equal, that no disproportion may offend the eye of Heaven, and draw divine judgements on a flourishing, enterprising, & (in some respects) happy Continent. I feel myself in duty to my Saviour, Master, & lawgiver, which is Christ Jesus, obligated to love my neighbor, especially to love the souls of men, women and children, for his Name sake, in whom there is all fulness of redemption, alike for Greek or Jew, barbarian Pythian bond or free, Glory, honor and praise for ever to his *Great* Name!

You now, sir, have the subject that relates to my petition in the abstract; and (on account of the present movements in *"old V[irginia]"*) you may possibly anticipate my petition also. I have abhorred slavery, from the first dawn of *moral* intellect, by which I intend my advent on a religious life; for to my infantile apprehension of the word morality, its meaning is inseparable with gospel purity, & I believe in no other foundation than *Christ's* exposition of the law of *GOD*, on which to raise a superstructure that will answer our purpose, when summoned to appear before him as the Judge of quick and dead—[this amounts] to supreme & undivided love to God, followed by equal charity to our fellow beings, who are *all* members of his intelligent creation below the sun. To view the subject (slavery) in abstract is sufficient for a feeble daughter of the North. She understands her weakness too well to attempt its analyzation. Its abolition she apprehends desirable to the full extent of desire for reformation in ultimo; but extremely difficult, while love of luxury, & lust for gold enslave the nobler part of man, the *mind*—but *amelioration* appears attainable and gradual emancipation may be so conducted, as to elicit a hope that succeding generations, will experience such degrees of benefit, as to excite feelings of veneration & gratitude toward the memory of statesmen & legislators of the present age. Hearing of your state [convention], even now in session, I am induced to offer my simple entreaty that you sir, will even become an enthusiast, (excuse this expression) in your exertions to *hold* the door *open* in ancient Va, through which *celestial* born freedom may finally pass; & thus a complete espousal one day be witnessed between the Northern, Western Eastern and southern states of N America—a *door* sir which instrumentally you aided to unfold in Ohio—for which you have the esteem & blessing of thousands.

Perhaps Sir, an enquiry arises in your mind concerning me, *who I am*? I answer I am a kind of *nobody*, a small, insignificant being in the world's estimate—I am a single woman, forty one years of age—the most that I can say for myself is, that I fear *GOD*; & love *Jesus*—you may also enquire, why so lonely a mortal with views as above, shd wander so far from home, & into a slave country? I reply, that I am a chronic invalid, & unable to endure my native winter winds. For two years past have pined under the assaults of pain turned Rheumatic, & extreme debility called nervous—Physicians, parent, & [friends] in [Massachusetts] advised this change of climate. *Charleston* was my *own* choice—I am mostly a prisoner to my chamber. I may or may not recover—It is as *God* pleases—

Since my arrival here, I have conversed with persons of both sexes, (who have called on the pilgrim stranger,) on the subject of slavery—& I may say, from *respectable* authority, that a large proportion of this community, are very desirous that Va may prosper in every essay toward emancipating her bond slaves; & that there is in S. Carolina, thousands of white people who are distressed & burdened on the account of slavery.

I must inevitably close—have indulged my rambling pen already too far; & deem an apology now necessary—please sir, to forgive me—I shall add only, in union with a respectful adieu, my delight in believing that your name is already on the hon[ore]d list, with Fox & Pitt, & to express my best wishes for your present & eternal peace—That yr last days may be the best of your life, & your latest moments expire in divine peace, is Sir, the prayer of
Harriet Livermore,
The Pilgrim Stranger

"O sons of freedom, equalize your laws,
Be all consistent plead the negro's cause
That every nation in your code may see
Columbia's negro like Columbia free."[10]

14. CHARLES G. FINNEY, LETTER TO THEODORE DWIGHT WELD

OBERLIN [OHIO] 21ST JULY, 1836

Dr. Br. Weld.

. . . My particular object in writing to you at the present time is to talk with you a little about the present state of the church, our country, abolition, etc. Br. Weld is it not true, at last do you not fear it is, that we are in our present course going fast into a civil war? Will not our present movements in abolition result in that? Shall we not ere long be obliged to take refuge in a military despotism? Have you no fear of this? If not, why have you not? Nothing is more manifest to me than that the present movements will result in this, unless your mode of abolitionizing the country be greatly modified. To suggest to some minds what I have here said would be evidence either of a pro slavery spirit, or of cowardice. But D[ea]r Weld you *think*, and certainly you can not but discern the signs of the times. Now what is to be done? How can we save our country and affect the speedy abolition of slavery? This is my answer. What say you to it? The subject is now before the publick mind. It is upon the conscience of every man, so that now every new convert will be an abolitionist of course. Now if abolition can be made an append[a]ge of a general revival of religion all is well. I fear no other form of carrying this question will save our country or the liberty or soul of the slave. One most alarming fact is that the absorbing abolitionism has drunk up the spirit of some of the most efficient moral men and is fast doing so [to] the rest, and many of our abolition brethren seem satisfied with nothing less than this. This I have been trying to resi[s]t from the beginning as I have all along foreseen that should that take place, the church and world, ecclesiastical and state leaders, will become embroiled in one common infernal squabble that will roll a wave of blood over the land. The causes now operating are in my view as certain to lead to this result as a cause is to produce an effect, unless the publick mind can be engrossed with the subject of salvation and make abolition an appendage, just as we made temperance an appendage of the revival in Rochester. Nor w'd this in my judgement retard the work at all. I was then almost

alone in the field as an Evangelist. Then 10,0000 were converted in one year, every one of which was a temperance man. The same w'd now be the case in abolition. We can now, with you and my theological class, bring enough laborers into the field to, under God, move the whole land in 2 years. If you will all turn in I will get dismissed from my charge in N. York if need be, and lay out what strength I have in promoting the work. When I am unable to preach I will counsel and pray and, the Lord willing, we will make thorough work of it. I believe we are united in the opinion here that abolition can be carried with more dispatch and with infinitely more safety in this indirect than in any other way. Now if you are not of this opinion, and if you are, I think by all means that you should come out here and let us consult immediately. The fact is, D[ea]r W[eld], our leading abolitionists are good men, but there are but few of them *wise* men. Some of them are reckless. Others are so denunciatory as to kill all prayer about it. There is very little confidence and concert among many of our abolitionists. It is high time that we understood each other.

. . . Suffice it to say that unless we can come to a better understanding among ourselves, act more harmoniously and wisely and piously, I fear that all the evils and horrors of civil war will be the consequence. Last year I tried to get you to N. York. It would have done infinite good. But you w'd not go. Will you now come here and let us fast and pray over this subject to see what God will say to us in this matter? Now don't fail to come soon. . . . I tell you again that unless we can have such an extensive Revival of religion as to soften the church and alarm the world we are all among the breakers. C. G. Finney[11]

POSTSCRIPT

Both temperance and abolition—as well as a host of other reform movements—were fueled by the evangelical fervor of the Second Great Awakening. But while temperance gained widespread acceptance, antislavery agitation remained relatively marginal within northern politics until mid-century. It was the prospect of slavery expanding into the western territories, rather than moral scruples against the South's "peculiar institution," that turned northern public opinion against bondage. Ultimately, of course, a horrific civil war, not moral suasion, destroyed slavery.

QUESTIONS

1. What, if anything, does the conflict over wording in the First Amendment reveal about contemporary attitudes toward religion?

2. How do you explain the outpouring of religious enthusiasm in this era? Can you imagine William Otter at a revival? Why or why not?
3. Why do you think temperance reform was so successful and appealing in this era?
4. Do you see connections between the success of temperance reform and the character of religious revivals? How did Lyman Beecher frame the relationship between religious belief and reform?
5. Mary Livermore and Charles G. Finney were both proudly evangelical and opposed to slavery; however, while Livermore insisted that her beliefs obligated her to support immediate emancipation, Finney had serious misgivings about the same. In light of their shared faith, why did they come to such different conclusions?

ADDITIONAL READING

Many historians view this era as crucial in reshaping American religious institutions. Two important authors making this case are Nathan Hatch, *Democratization of American Christianity* (1989), and Jon Butler, *Awash in a Sea of Faith* (1990). Amanda Porterfield directly engages these arguments in *Conceived in Doubt: Religion and Politics in the New American Nation* (2012). A classic overview of the revivals in upstate New York is Whitney Cross, *The Burned Over District* (1950). On camp meetings, see Charles Johnson, *The Frontier Camp Meeting* (1955), and Terry Bilhartz, *Urban Religion and the Second Great Awakening* (1986). On the complexity of revivals and reform, see Paul Johnson, *A Shopkeeper's Millennium: Society and Revivals in Rochester, New York, 1815–1837* (1979). For a close look at southern developments in this time, see Christine Lee Heyrman, *Southern Cross: The Beginnings of the Bible Belt* (1997), and Al Raboteau, *Slave Religion: The "Invisible Institution" in the American South* (2004). Richard Stott explores the world of men like William Otter in *Jolly Fellows: Male Milieus in Nineteenth-Century America* (2008).

ENDNOTES

1. *The Virginia Chronicle*, in *Writings of the Late Elder John Leland* (New York, 1845), p. 119.
2. *Thomas Jefferson to Danbury, Connecticut, Baptist Association, January 1, 1802*. Thomas Jefferson Papers, Library of Congress, Series I, Microfilm Reel 025.
3. *Autobiography, correspondence, etc., of Lyman Beecher, D.D.* (New York: Harper and Brothers, 1864), v.1, pp. 344, 452–453.
4. *Extracts of Letters Containing Some Account of the Work of God Since 1800* (New York: Totten for Cooper & Wilson, 1805), pp. 88–91.
5. *Martin J. Spalding, Sketches of the Early Catholic Missions of Kentucky* (Louisville: B. J. Webb, 1844), pp. 104–105.
6. *Wesleyan Repository* (Philadelphia: William Smith Stockton, 1820), pp. 138–143.
7. Charles G. Finney, *Lectures on Revivals of Religion* (Oberlin, OH: E. J. Goodrich, 1868), pp. 9–11.
8. William Otter, *History of My Own Times; or, the Life and Adventures of William Otter, comprising a series of events, and musical incidents altogether original* (Emmitsburg, MD: 1835), pp. 82–83 and 173–174.
9. Lyman Beecher, from *Six Sermons on the Nature, Occasions, Signs, Evils, and Remedy of Intemperance* (Boston: T. R. Marvin, 1828), pp. 64–66, 81–82, 86–87.
10. Harriet Livermore to James Madison, October 22, 1829, James Madison Papers, Manuscript Division, Series 1, General Correspondence, Microfilm Reel 22. Library of Congress.
11. Finney to Weld, July 21, 1836, Weld-Grimke Family Papers, William L. Clements Library, University of Michigan.

CHAPTER 7

THE AMBITIONS AND LIMITATIONS OF JACKSONIAN DEMOCRACY

HISTORICAL CONTEXT

Patriots of the early national era proudly proclaimed "all men are created equal" and extolled the principles of shared governance. Yet, during the nation's first half-century, the United States was ruled overwhelmingly by a class of well-educated East Coast gentlemen. Then, in 1828, Americans elected General Andrew Jackson, a different type of president. Nicknamed "Old Hickory" from his "tough as hickory" reputation. Jackson was not like his presidential predecessors.

Born in 1767 in the backwoods of North Carolina and raised without a father, Jackson lost his two brothers in the revolution. At age fourteen, he became an orphan when his mother died of typhus while tending American soldiers in that war. An acquaintance of the young Jackson wrote, "Andrew Jackson was the most roaring, rollicking, game-cocking, horse-racing, card-playing, mischievous fellow that ever lived." Crude and self-reliant, Jackson had a firebrand personality, boldly challenging adversaries to duels, and once he killed a man to protect the honor of his wife. Jackson achieved national fame as a military general, self-made man, and champion of the underdog.

General Jackson's popularity earned him a place on the ballot in the 1824 presidential election, and he actually won a plurality of the popular votes. Yet he lost to John Quincy Adams in the House of Representatives when the Speaker of the House, Henry Clay, threw his support behind Adams. When president-elect Adams announced that Clay would be his Secretary of State, Jackson and his outraged supporters insisted the election had been stolen from the American people. Together they spent the next four years organizing for political revenge, in the process coalescing into the new Democratic Party.

According to the custom of the times, candidates for president did not campaign for the office, but let others do the politicking for them. In 1828, however, Jackson's campaign manager, Martin Van Buren, put him on public display, turning public parades and community events into Democratic Party rallies. At every opportunity, the Democrats reminded the public that Jackson was at once a war hero and a common man. Adams's supporters turned this around, lambasting Jackson for his lack of education and civility. They also questioned his honor by asserting that he had married his wife, Rachel, before her divorce had been finalized. Unaware that the divorce was still pending, the Jacksons "remarried" to correct the clerical error. Nevertheless, Adams's supporters called Jackson a bigamist and Rachel an adulteress. The slurs got uglier: "General Jackson's mother was a COMMON PROSTITUTE, brought to this country by the British soldiers. She afterwards married a Mulatto Man, with whom she had several children, of which GENERAL JACKSON IS ONE!!"[1]

Jackson's supporters countered with mudslinging of their own, claiming that Adams was corrupt, immoral, aristocratic, and elitist. And this negative approach seemed to produce results, for a staggering 300 percent more voters turned out in 1828 than in 1824. Most of these new voters preferred the crude Jackson to the cultured Adams. Jackson won the election by a solid margin, securing 56 percent of the popular vote and 68 percent of the electoral vote. The growing turnout was also a result of changes in voting laws. Because most of the original states limited suffrage to male property owners or taxpayers in the early years of the republic, only about one-half of white males were eligible to vote. Later states, including Vermont, Kentucky, Tennessee, Alabama, Ohio, Indiana, Illinois, and Missouri, either opened suffrage to all white males over the age of twenty-one or lowered the taxpayer qualifications to levels that allowed almost all white adult males in these states to vote. New Jersey, Maryland, and New York followed suit, eliminating property qualifications for voters in the early nineteenth century.

Unfortunately, this movement toward universal white manhood suffrage stymied or reversed the fortunes of free blacks and propertied women, citizens who had enjoyed voting privileges in some of the original states before "white manhood" replaced property as the determining suffrage qualification. By 1840, more than 90 percent of the adult white men in the United States could vote. In anticipation of Jackson's presidency, National Republican Daniel Webster nervously reflected: "When he comes he will bring a breeze with him. Which way it will blow, I cannot tell. . . . My fear is stronger than my hope."

To Webster, transferring political clout from men of culture and property to the "grimy masses" carried great dangers. His fears were compounded on Inauguration Day, March 4, 1829, when 20,000 visitors (a number that approximated the normal population of the city) converged on the nation's capital. Roaring with Jackson's familiar campaign shout, "Huzza! Huzza! Huzza!" Old Hickory's supporters swarmed to the White House for an inaugural party. Skeptics described a scene in which the well-wishers scrambled for the free food and drink, orange punch spiked with liquor spilled onto the floor, expensive china plates were smashed, muddy boots stained the carpets and filthy clothes dirtied the furniture. Pressed into a corner by the crowd seeking to shake his hand, Jackson escaped out an open window. Journalist Amos Kendall, a friend to the president, wrote, "It was a proud day for the people. . . . General Jackson is their own president." Supreme Court justice Joseph Story described the day differently: "The reign of King 'Mob' seemed triumphant."

For the next twelve years, Jackson, Van Buren, and the Democrats controlled both the White House and Congress. A century ago, historians emphasizing the egalitarian and democratic tendencies of the era labeled it "the Age of Jacksonian Democracy." Since then, many historians have asserted that the age was not democratic at all but instead was a period when the gap between the rich and the poor widened and when the greatest rewards went not to the laboring masses but to those who kept slaves on plantations and forced Indians from their homes or killed Mexicans in order to secure more land (Jackson himself owned a thousand-acre plantation and dozens of slaves). Others view the period more favorably as a romantic age of individualism when social mobility and economic opportunity dissolved traditional family and church ties and forced Americans to become more self-reliant.

Just as historians have offered different interpretations of the Age of Jackson, so, too, have biographers. Some portray Jackson as a champion of frugality and limited government, while others describe him as a demagogue who exploited the masses. Most scholars agree that he was a visible symbol of a more democratic and egalitarian future where authority came to be shared more equitably among the classes and throughout the regions. If he was not the agent of the sorts of reforms that characterized his era—outlined in Chapter 6—Jackson still personified the shift from a republic governed by educated elites into a patriarchal democracy that reached out to white men—even poor white men—but not to women and minorities. This irony of expanding freedom and democratic rights for some but not others is examined first through assessments of Jackson as a political leader, and then through his Indian policies.

INTRODUCTION TO DOCUMENTS 1, 2, AND 3

The first two documents are taken from the campaign of 1828. Document 1 is a portion of a powerful anti-Jackson broadside accusing him of authorizing the "unjust military execution" of six soldiers in 1815. These handbills were created by John Binns, a pro-Adams publisher in Philadelphia. Binns and other supporters of Adams designed these "coffin handbills" to detail what they believed to be Jackson's unscrupulous and vicious actions, in the process directly undercutting his heroic military reputation. As you read the coffin inscription, note the language used by Binns and the Jackson opposition, and ask whom they hoped to persuade. Others hammered Jackson for his "bold" and open pursuit of the presidency, an unseemly display of ambition for the early nineteenth century.

Document 2 is a political cartoon that directly satirizes Binns's use of these coffin handbills. In the image we see Binns straining under a large load of coffins with Henry Clay on the left and President Adams on the right. Binns remarks that he is sinking under the weight of the "coffins" he created, while Adams clings to the presidential chair "in spite of the wishes of the people." This pro-Jackson cartoon skewers the old guard as ineffectively fighting Jackson's democratic appeal.

Document 3 is an editorial from a newspaper published shortly after Jackson took office, warning the Democrats not to become complacent. How does the author define the Jacksonian vision and what it means to be a Democrat? Why might he have raised the danger of political "slavery" in the second paragraph?

1. A COFFIN HANDBILL (1828)

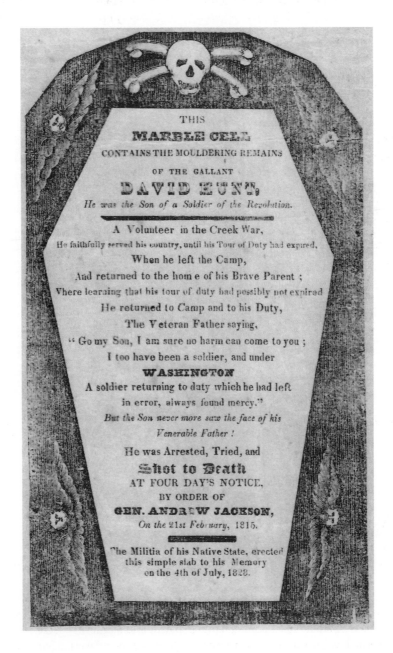

Image 7.1 Monumental Inscriptions!

This is a portion of an anti-Jackson poster that accused the candidate of authorizing the execution of innocent soldiers several decades earlier. What type of language was used to describe that act?

Source: John Binns, "Monumental Inscriptions!" (Philadelphia, 1828). Courtesy of Boston Rare Maps.

2. SATIRIZING THE COFFIN HANDBILLS (1828)

Image 7.2 "The Pedlar and his Pack or the Desperate Effort, an Over Balance" (1828)

Artist James Akin took aim at the many anti-Jackson coffin handbills issued to support incumbent President John Quincy Adams. Akin portrays Binns as groaning under the weight of the propaganda he created, while Henry Clay at left and President Adams at right do anything to maintain their grip on political power.

Source: James Akin (Philadelphia? 1828), Courtesy Library of Congress.

3. FROM *THE DEMOCRATIC REPUBLICAN* (1829)

The causes which have produced so great an excitement among the freemen of these United States, during the late political conflict, have ceased, and genuine Republicanism has once more triumphed. Andrew Jackson has taken the chair of State, and his enemies and calumniators are humbled at his feet. In reflecting upon these important facts, and while we feel rejoiced at so signal a victory over the remnant of Aristocracy, there is imminent danger, that all this excitement and all this joy will be succeeded by apathy, and a criminal, fatal neglect of the important duties, which always devolve upon freemen. But, Heaven forbid, that the advantages which have been gained, and the pure principles, which have been so firmly established, by the recent victory, should be forgotten or neglected. Every man, we repeat it, every man has political duties devolving upon him, of a nature calculated to awaken attention and call forth his best energies. And, in this country of freedom, it would seem most astonishing, that any individual should be indifferent to the important concerns of the nation. It is indeed not sufficient, that we appear at the ballot boxes and cast our suffrages for our rulers—it is not sufficient, that we attach ourselves to a particular party and perform the ordinary duties of freemen—we must improve every opportunity of increasing our political knowledge and unite heart and hand in promoting the cause of liberty. . . .

We feel secure on account of our recent success, and this feeling of security may prove our ruin. And, while we are sluggish and inactive, our enemies are vigilant, and no arts or devices will be left untried by them. The enemies of Jackson have nothing to lose; and they are desperate to a degree of madness never before exhibited in this country. Our venerated Chief Magistrate has been the object of their bitterest and most abhorred assaults for the last four years, and now that he is exalted by the free suffrages of his fellow citizens to the highest and most enviable station on earth, their tongues have become envenomed and their hearts hardened. . . . And they in their rage have not been satisfied with hurling their poisoned shafts upon Jackson alone—the partner of his bosom, while living was their jest and sport; and the grave affords no security against their slander. Yes, not only have the very portals of the tomb been broken, by the hands of these worse than barbarians; but our Hero, whose heart was filled with anguish for his loss, has been himself the object of renewed attack. And what must we not expect from those men, who deride the finer feelings of humanity, and to the overwhelming sorrows of the afflicted, add their most malignant poison? We must expect that such men, destitute of the common feelings of our nature, will exercise the grossest and most detested passions, in all their doings. It is not a matter of wonder, that they object to every step, which President Jackson takes, be it good, bad, or indifferent. It is not surprising, that at this early hour, they should use every means to embarrass his measures, and endeavor to cheat the public into a belief that "all is wrong." These things they unblushingly do; and nothing can defeat their malicious designs, but the determination of his friends, honestly to defend him; and, to make a sure defense, one and all must awake to duty, and rest assured that although the "battle's fought and victory's won," "the danger is not over."[2]

INTRODUCTION TO DOCUMENTS 4–9

One of President Jackson's most controversial measures related to the Bank of the United States, which had been established in 1791 by Congress. The bank's initial charter expired in 1811, and five years later, Congress created the Second Bank with another twenty-year term. But by the 1830s, the bank had become the target of heated criticism. Supporters, who coalesced around the new Whig Party in the 1830s, argued that the bank facilitated the financing of internal improvements that would bind the country together and enhance commerce. But many decried the bank, particularly Americans who had moved into the trans-Appalachian west and who saw it as unfairly controlling their credit. These and other critics caricatured the bank as run by elites, a monster crushing the people, controlled by foreign interests. Jackson opposed the bank, and vetoed the congressional bill renewing its charter in 1832. His message explaining the veto is Document 4, followed by Senator Daniel Webster's response the next day (Document 5), an equally passionate defense of the bank and criticism of Jackson's veto. Note the way both Jackson and Webster describe their opponents as abusing power and violating the rights of the American people.

The "bank war" became integral to the 1832 presidential campaign and heightened the stakes in an already contentious and partisan election. In Document 6, the anti-Jackson forces argue that the president has become a monarch, criticizing him along the lines that Webster had advanced in July. Document 7 is a campaign advertisement sympathetically listing Jackson's first-term accomplishments. Document 8 is from the *Salem Gazette*, an editorial outlining Jackson's record as president.

Webster, Henry Clay, and their allies were unable to override Jackson's veto, and when the latter won reelection in November, he continued to assault the idea of a national bank. He ordered the Secretary of the Treasury to stop federal deposits to the bank, and when the Secretary refused, Jackson removed him from office. Jackson's old foe, Clay, responded by introducing a congressional resolution to censure the president, the first time such an act had been taken. Yet in many ways Jackson had prevailed, ending the Bank of the United States. In Document 9, Jackson assesses the bank and the economy toward the end of his eight-year presidency in 1837. What can these highly partisan sources reveal about political life in this era? Who would be likely to support Jackson's reelection bid?

4. PRESIDENT JACKSON VETOES THE BANK

PRESIDENT ANDREW JACKSON

JULY 10, 1832

The bill "to modify and continue" the act entitled "An act to incorporate the subscribers to the Bank of the United States" was presented to me on the 4th July instant. Having considered it with that solemn regard to the principles of the Constitution which the day was calculated to inspire, and come to the conclusion that it ought not to become a law, I herewith return it to the Senate, in which it originated, with my objections.

A bank of the United States is in many respects convenient for the Government and useful to the people. Entertaining this opinion, and deeply impressed with the belief that some of the powers and privileges possessed by the existing bank are unauthorized by the Constitution, subversive of the rights of the States, and dangerous to the liberties of the people, I felt it my duty at an early period of my Administration to call the attention of Congress to the practicability of organizing an institution combining all its advantages and obviating these objections. I sincerely regret that in the act before me I can perceive none of those modifications of the bank charter which are necessary, in my opinion, to make it

compatible with justice, with sound policy, or with the Constitution of our country.

. . . [The Bank] enjoys an exclusive privilege of banking under the authority of the General Government, a monopoly of its favor and support, and, as a necessary consequence, almost a monopoly of the foreign and domestic exchange. The powers, privileges, and favors bestowed upon it in the original charter, by increasing the value of the stock far above its par value, operated as a gratuity of many millions to the stockholders.

. . . Every monopoly and all exclusive privileges are granted at the expense of the public, which ought to receive a fair equivalent. The many millions which this act proposes to bestow on the stockholders of the existing bank must come directly or indirectly out of the earnings of the American people.

. . . It is not conceivable how the present stockholders can have any claim to the special favor of the Government.

. . . Of the twenty-five directors of this bank five are chosen by the Government and twenty by the citizen stockholders. From all voice in these elections the foreign stockholders are excluded by the charter. In proportion, therefore, as the stock is transferred to foreign holders the extent of suffrage in the choice of directors is curtailed. . . . The entire control of the institution would necessarily fall into the hands of a few citizen stockholders. . . . There is danger that a president and directors would then be able to elect themselves from year to year, and without responsibility or control manage the whole

concerns of the bank during the existence of its charter. It is easy to conceive that great evils to our country and its institutions might flow from such a concentration of power in the hands of a few men irresponsible to the people.

Is there no danger to our liberty and independence in a bank that in its nature has so little to bind it to our country?[3]

5. RESPONSE TO THE PRESIDENT'S VETO

SENATOR DANIEL WEBSTER

JULY 11, 1832

. . . Before proceeding to the Constitutional question, there are some other topics, treated in [Jackson's] message, which ought to be noticed. It commences by an inflamed statement of what it calls the "favor" bestowed upon the original Bank, by the Government, or indeed, as it is phrased, the "monopoly of its favor and support," and through the whole message all possible changes are rung on the "gratuity," the "exclusive privileges," and "monopoly," of the bank charter. Now, Sir, the truth is, that the powers conferred on the Bank, are such, and no others, as are usually conferred on similar institutions. They constitute no monopoly, although some of them are of necessity and with propriety exclusive privileges. . . .

There is a larger, and a much more just view of the subject. The bill was not passed for the purpose of benefiting the present stockholders. Their benefit, if any, is incidental, and collateral. . . . Congress passed the bill, not as a bounty or a favor to the present stockholders, nor to comply with any demand of right, on their part; but to promote great public interests, for great public objects. Every bank must have some stockholders, unless it be such a bank as the President has recommended, and in regard to which he seems not likely to find much concurrence of other men's opinions; and if the stockholders, whoever they may be, conduct the affairs of the bank prudently, the expectation is, always of course, that they will make it profitable to themselves, as well as useful to the

public. If a bank charter is not to be granted, because it may be profitable, either in a small or great degree, to the stockholders, no charter can be granted. The objection [of Jackson] lies against all banks.

. . . From the commencement of the Government it has been thought desirable to invite, rather than to repel, the introduction of foreign capital. . . . It is easy to say that there is danger to liberty, danger to independence, in a bank open to foreign stockholders—because it is easy to say any thing. But neither reason nor experience proves any such danger. The foreign stockholder cannot be a director. He has no voice even in the choice of directors. His money is placed entirely in the management of the directors appointed by the President and Senate, and by the American stockholders. . . . Our liberties, indeed, must stand upon very frail foundations, if the government cannot, without endangering them, avail itself of those common facilities, in the collection of its revenues, and the management of its finances, which all other governments, in commercial countries, find useful and necessary.

. . . I now proceed, sir, to a few remarks upon the President's constitutional objections to the Bank. . . . He denies that the constitutionality of the Bank is a settled question . . . [yet] for thirty-six years, out of the forty-three, during which the Government has been in being, a BANK has existed, such as is now proposed to be continued. . . . Every President, except the present, has considered it a settled question. . . . If the president thinks lightly of the authority of Congress, in construing the constitution, he thinks still more lightly of the authority of the Supreme Court. He asserts a right of individual judgement, on constitutional questions, which is totally inconsistent with any proper administration of the government, or any regular execution of the laws. Social disorder, entire uncertainty in regard to individual rights and individual duties, the cessation of legal authority, confusion, the dissolution of free government!—all these, are the inevitable consequences of the principles adopted by the message, whenever they shall be carried to their full extent. Hitherto, it has been thought that the *final decision* of constitutional questions belonged to the supreme judicial tribunal . . . when a law has been passed by Congress, and approved by the President, it is now no longer in the power, either of the same President, or his successors, to say whether the law is constitutional or not. . . .

The President is as much bound by the law as any private citizen. . . . That which is now claimed for the President, is, in truth, nothing less, and nothing else, than the old *dispensing power* asserted by the kings of England. . . . Such an universal power, as is now claimed for him . . . is nothing else than pure despotism. If conceded to him, it makes him, at once, what Louis the Fourteenth proclaimed himself to be, when he said, "I AM THE STATE."[4]

6. "KING ANDREW" (1832)

Image 7.3 "King Andrew" (1832 or 1833)

This caricature of Jackson underscored his unilateral approach to governance. The language beneath the image included a series of accusations that Jackson had placed himself above the law, concluding, "Shall he reign over us, Or shall the PEOPLE RULE?" Given that Jackson portrayed himself as a man of the people, why was he pictured here as a monarch?

Source: Anonymous, New York? Courtesy of Library of Congress.

7. "TEN REASONS FOR ADVOCATING THE RE-ELECTION OF GENERAL JACKSON" (1832)

UTICA OBSERVER

1. Because our country was never more prosperous than under General Jackson's administration.
2. Because by a majority of the votes of his countrymen, he has twice been declared to be the choice of the people.
3. Because he will be the last President from the number of Revolutionary heroes whom the people may honor with their suffrages.
4. Because of his firmness in opposing the "great monied aristocracy" which seeks to master our government, and threatens to overthrow our free institutions.
5. Because of his wise and humane policy with regard to the Indian tribes.
6. Because of his efforts to suppress "the undue exertion of federal power" and his endeavors to maintain the rights of the States.
7. Because of his wise policy as respects foreign nations, of whom he "asks nothing that is not clearly right, and submits to nothing that is wrong."
8. Because he has settled difficulties with foreign nations which have baffled the diplomacy of previous administrations.
9. Because he has ever shown himself anxious to cherish and perpetuate the liberties of the people.
10. Because in the discharge of his duties he has invariably taken a straight forward course, proving himself to be the disinterested patriot, the upright statesman, and the honest man.

8. WHY, WHAT EVIL HATH HE WROUGHT (1832)

SALEM GAZETTE

General Jackson, since his election, has broken every promise, forfeited every pledge, and departed from every principle, which, before his election he professed to hold as sacred or regard as important.—He has gone upon the avowed principle of "rewarding his friends and punishing his enemies"; of turning out those who had voted against him, and putting in those who had voted for him.—He has compelled all who enjoy office, as a compensation for their appointments, and under the penalty of instant ejection, to support his measures, whether right or wrong, and to submit to exactions upon their salaries for the support of new presses and extra publications, and hired election minions.—He has re-appointed men to office whom the Senate have twice rejected, thereby entirely destroying the share of the Senate in the appointing power, and the weight which the constitution gives it as a body of advice and of restraint upon the executive.

He has cruelly and wantonly refused to execute treaties made with Indian nations, which have been ratified by the Senate, approved by every President, and adjudged valid by the Supreme Court.—He has claimed and exercised supreme power over the people, Congress and courts of the United States in his late veto message, and advanced doctrines subversive of the foundations of the government, connected with the disgraceful and dishonest appeals of a demagogue, for the purpose of prejudicing the different parts of the community against each other.—He has made frequent and illegal use of the veto power, without any reference to principle in its use; for he has applied it in some cases, and not in others which were of a precisely similar character. He has applied it in capricious and wanton attempts to ruin the internal improvements of the country, to break down industry and destroy its profits, to introduce an unsettled currency, and depreciate to a great amount the value of property. . . .

He has enacted in time of peace greater taxes for the people than any previous President, and squandered them on profligate favorites, for idle and totally useless purposes. He has threatened to beat Senators, and rejoiced because Representatives were cudgeled for the free expression of their opinions. He has threatened to shoot fellow citizens while in the peaceable pursuit of their business; invited ministers of the gospel to his house under the pretence of cordial intercourse, and then driven them into corners and bullied them; approved of schemes to cheat the public treasury of its funds, and appropriated those funds to a great extent in bribery and corruption.

Will any of our fellow-citizens, after a proper consideration of these charges, every one of which has been substantiated by irrefutable proof, bestow their suffrages to continue the elevation of a man, whose character is thus "marked by every act which may define a tyrant?"[5]

9. THE CAUSE OF FREEDOM WILL CONTINUE TO TRIUMPH OVER ALL ITS ENEMIES (1837)

ANDREW JACKSON

The planter, the farmer, the mechanic, and the laborer all know that their success depends upon their own industry and economy and that they must not expect to become suddenly rich by the fruits of their toil. Yet these classes of society form the great body of the people of the United States; they are the bone and sinew of the country; men who love liberty and desire nothing but equal rights and equal laws and who, moreover, hold the great mass of our national wealth, although it is distributed in moderate amounts among the millions of freemen who possess it. But, with overwhelming numbers and wealth on their side, they are in constant danger of losing their fair influence in the government, and with difficulty maintain their just rights against the incessant efforts daily made to encroach upon them.

The mischief springs from the power which the moneyed interest derives from a paper currency which they are able to control; from the multitude of corporations with exclusive privileges which they have succeeded in obtaining in the different states and which are employed altogether for their benefit; and unless you become more watchful in your states and check this spirit of monopoly and thirst for exclusive privileges, you will, in the end, find that the most important powers of government have been given or bartered away, and the control over your dearest interests has passed into the hands of these corporations.

The paper money system and its natural associates, monopoly and exclusive privileges, have already struck their roots deep in the soil; and it will require all your efforts to check its further growth and to eradicate the evil. The men who profit by the abuses and desire to perpetuate them will continue to besiege the halls of legislation in the general government as well as in the states and will seek, by every artifice, to mislead and deceive the public servants. It is to yourselves that you must look for safety and the means of guarding and perpetuating your free institutions. . . .

In presenting to you, my fellow citizens, these parting counsels, I have brought before you the leading principles upon which I endeavored to administer the government in the high office with which you twice honored me. Knowing that the path of freedom is continually beset by enemies who often assume the disguise of friends, I have devoted the last hours of my public life to warn you of the danger.

The progress of the United States under our free and happy institutions has surpassed the most sanguine hopes of the founders of the republic. Our growth has been rapid beyond all former example—in numbers, in wealth, in knowledge, and all the useful arts which contribute to the comforts and convenience of man; and from the earliest ages of history to the present day, there never have been 13 million people associated together in one political body who enjoyed so much freedom and happiness as the people of these United States. You have no longer any cause to fear danger from abroad; your strength and power are well known throughout the civilized world, as well as the high and gallant bearing of your sons.

It is from within, among yourselves, from cupidity, from corruption, from disappointed ambition and inordinate thirst for power, that factions will be formed and liberty endangered. It is against such designs, whatever disguise the actors may assume, that you have especially to guard yourselves. You have the highest of human trusts committed to your care. Providence has showered on this favored land blessings without number and has chosen you as the guardians of freedom to preserve it for the benefit of the human race. May He who holds in His hands the destinies of nations make you worthy of the favors He has bestowed and enable you, with pure hearts and pure hands and sleepless vigilance, to guard and defend to the end of time the great charge He has committed to your keeping.[6]

INTRODUCTION TO DOCUMENTS 10, 11, AND 12

The next five documents explore Jackson's Indian policies relative to the Cherokee Nation during his presidency, which resulted in the forcible removal of 16,000 Native Americans from the southeastern states to new territories west of the Mississippi River by 1838. Jackson's predecessor, John Quincy Adams, had found the idea of native relocation immoral and opposed the growing pressure from the southern states to eject the 60,000 native Americans still living on their ancestral lands east of the Appalachian Mountains. These five "Civilized Tribes" included the Cherokee, Chickasaw, Creek, Seminole, and Chocktaw. In Georgia, many whites envied the large territories controlled by the Cherokee, a tribe that had established its own courts, constitution, and system of education. In part this institutional strength had come through the leadership of the Cherokee's elected principal chief, John Ross. Ross worked hard to strengthen treaties that protected the Cherokee's sovereignty, but those federal promises proved no match for the growing hunger for land among Georgians. The governor and legislature began to extend state law onto Cherokee land, so by the time Jackson was inaugurated in 1829, a crisis existed, which he addressed by sending an Indian Removal Bill to Congress, calling for the tribes to voluntarily emigrate to new lands west of the Mississippi.

While the Cherokee resisted relocation and pursued recourse through the courts, the other major tribes responded to federal pressure and began to cede their lands and move west of the Mississippi. Jackson called on the Cherokee to join them. Documents 10 through 12 are taken from the debate around the legislation for removal. Document 10 is from the leaders of the Cherokee Nation, asking federal officials to uphold tribal territorial sovereignty in the face of Georgia's encroachment. In Document 11, a group of women in Steubenville, Ohio, express their support for the tribe and opposition to the Indian Removal Bill. In Document 12. President Jackson articulates the reasons for the Indian Removal Act. Note how questions of freedom, security, and sovereignty are addressed in Documents 10 and 11 and how Jackson responds to such issues in Document 12.

10. MEMORIAL OF THE CHEROKEE NATION (DECEMBER 1829)

To the honorable the senate and house of representatives of the United States of America, in congress assembled:

The undersigned memorialists, humbly make known to your honorable bodies, that they are free citizens of the Cherokee Nation. Circumstances of late occurrence have troubled our hearts, and induced us at this time to appeal to you, knowing that you are generous and just. . . .

Brothers—we address you according to usage adopted by our forefathers, and the great and good men who have successfully directed the councils of the nation you represent—we now make known to you our grievances. We are troubled by some of your own people. Our neighbor, the state of Georgia, is pressing hard upon us, and urging us to relinquish our possessions for her benefit. We are told, if we do not leave the country, which we dearly love, and betake ourselves to the western wilds, the laws of the state will be extended over us, and the time, 1st of June, 1830, is appointed for the execution of the edict. When we first heard of this we were grieved and appealed to our father, the president, and begged that protection might be extended over us. But we were doubly grieved when we understood, from a letter of the secretary of war to our delegation, dated March of the present year [1829], that our father the president had refused us protection, and that he had decided in favor of the extension of the laws of the state over us.—This decision induces us to appeal to the immediate representatives of the American people. We love, we dearly love our country, and it is due to your

honorable bodies, as well as to us, to make known why we think the country is ours, and why we wish to remain in peace where we are.

The land on which we stand, we have received as an inheritance from our fathers, who possessed it from time immemorial, as a gift from our common father in heaven. We have already said, that when the white man came to the shores of America, our ancestors were found in peaceable possession of this very land. They bequeathed it to us as their children, and we have sacredly kept it as containing the remains of our beloved men. This right of inheritance we have *never ceded*, nor ever *forfeited*. Permit us to ask, what better right can a people have to a country, than the right of *inheritance and immemorial peaceable possession?* We know it is said of late by the state of Georgia, and by the executive of the United States, that we have forfeited this right—but we think this is said gratuitously. At what time have we made the forfeit? What crime have we committed, whereby we must forever be divested of our country and rights? Was it when we were hostile to the United States, and took part with the king of Great Britain, during the struggle for independence? If so, why was not this forfeiture declared in the first treaty of peace between the United States and our beloved men? . . .

In addition to that first of all rights, the right of inheritance and peaceable possession, we have the faith and pledge of the U. States, repeated over and over again, in treaties made at various times. By these treaties our rights as a separate people are distinctly acknowledged, and guarantees given that they shall be secured and protected. So we have always understood the treaties. The conduct of the government towards us, from this organization until very lately, the talks given to our beloved men by the presidents of the United States, and the speeches of the agents and commissioners, all concur to show that we are not mistaken in our interpretation.

In view of the strong ground upon which their rights are founded, your memorialists solemnly protest against being considered as tenants at will, or as mere occupants of the soil, without possessing the sovereignty. We have already stated to your honorable bodies, that our forefathers were found in possession of this soil in full sovereignty, by the first European settlers; and as we have never ceded nor forfeited the occupancy of the soil and the sovereignty over it, we do solemnly protest against being forced to leave it, either [by] direct or by indirect measures. To the land of which we are now in possession we are attached — it is our father's gift—it contains their ashes—it is the land of our nativity, and the land of our intellectual birth. We cannot consent to abandon it, for another *far inferior,* and which holds out to us no inducements. . . . To deliver and protect them from all these and every encroachment upon their rights, the undersigned memorialists do most earnestly pray your honorable bodies. Their existence and future happiness are at stake—divest them of their liberty and country, and you sink them in degradation, and put a check, if not a final stop, to their present progress in the arts of civilized life, and in the knowledge of the Christian religion. Your memorialists humbly conceive, that such an act would be in the highest degree oppressive. From the people of these United States, who perhaps, of all men under heaven, are the most religious and free, it cannot be expected.—Your memorialists, therefore, cannot anticipate such a result. You represent a virtuous, intelligent and Christian nation. To you they willingly submit their cause for your righteous decision. *Cherokee nation, Dec. 1829.*[7]

11. MEMORIAL FROM THE LADIES OF STUEBENVILLE, OHIO, FEBRUARY 15, 1830

To the Honorable the Senate and House of Representatives of the United States: The Memorial of the Undersigned Residents of the State of Ohio and Town of Steubenville, Respectfully Sheweth:

. . . [T]he present crisis in the affairs of the Indian nations, calls loudly on *all* who can feel the woes of humanity . . . , to bestow on this subject, involving as it does the prosperity and happiness of more than fifty thousand of our fellow Christians; the immediate consideration, demanded by its interesting nature and pressing importance.

It is readily acknowledged, that the wise and venerated founders of our country's free institutions, have committed the powers of government to those whom nature and reason declare the best fitted to exercise them; and your memorialists would sincerely deprecate any presumptuous interference on the part of their own sex, with the ordinary political affairs of the country, as wholly unbecoming the character of American Females. Even in private life we may not presume to direct the general conduct, or control the acts of those who stand in the near and guardian relations of husbands and brothers yet all admit that *there are times* when duty and affection call on us to *advise* and *persuade,* as well as to cheer or to console. And if we approach the public representatives of our husbands and brothers, only in the humble character of suppliants in the cause of mercy and humanity, may we not hope that even the small voice of *female* sympathy will be heard?

. . . When, therefore, injury and oppression threaten to crush a hapless people within our borders, we, the feeblest of the feeble, appeal with confidence to those who should be the representatives of national virtues as they are the depositories of national powers, and implore them to succor the weak & unfortunate.—In despite of the *undoubted natural right*, which the Indians have, to the land of their forefathers, and in the face of solemn treaties, pledging the faith of the nation for their secure possession of those lands, it is intended, we are told, to force them from their native soil, and to compel them to seek new homes in a distant and dreary wilderness. To you then, as the constitutional protectors of the Indians within our territory and as the peculiar guardians of our national character, and our country's welfare, we solemnly and earnestly appeal to save this remnant of a much injured people from annihilation, to shield our country from the curses denounced on the cruel and ungrateful, and to shelter the American character from lasting dishonor.

And your petitioners will ever pray. [The petition was signed by 63 women.][8]

12. MESSAGE TO CONGRESS (1830)

ANDREW JACKSON

President's Message to Congress

. . . It gives me pleasure to announce to Congress that the benevolent policy of the Government, steadily pursued for nearly thirty years, in relation to the removal of the Indians beyond the white settlements, is approaching to a happy consummation. Two important tribes have accepted the provision made for their removal at the last session of Congress; and it is believed that their example will induce the remaining tribes, also, to seek the same obvious advantages.

The consequences of a speedy removal will be important to the United States, to individual States, and to the Indians themselves. The pecuniary advantages which it promises to the Government are the least of its recommendations. It puts an end to all possible danger of collision between the authorities of the General and State Governments, on account of the Indians. It will place a dense and civilized population in large tracts of country now occupied by a few savage hunters. By opening the whole territory between Tennessee on the north, and Louisiana on the south, to the settlement of the whites, it will incalculably strengthen the southwestern frontier, and render the adjacent States strong enough to repel future invasion without remote aid. It will relieve the whole State of Mississippi, and the western part of Alabama, of Indian occupancy, and enable those States to advance rapidly in population, wealth, and power. It will separate the Indians from immediate contact with the settlements of whites; free them from the power of the States; enable them to pursue happiness in their own way, and under their own rude institutions; will retard the progress of decay, which is lessening their numbers; and perhaps cause them gradually, under the protection of the Government, and through the influence of good counsels, to cast off their savage habits, and become an interesting, civilized, and Christian community. . . .

Toward the aborigines of the country no one can indulge a more friendly feeling than myself, or would go further in attempting to reclaim them from their wandering habits, and make them a happy and prosperous people. I have endeavored to impress upon them my own solemn convictions of the duties and powers of the General Government in relation to the State authorities. For the justice of the laws passed by the States within the scope of their reserved powers, they are not responsible to this Government. As individuals, we may entertain and express our opinions of their acts; but, as a Government, we have as little right to control them as we have to prescribe laws to foreign nations.

. . . Philanthropy could not wish to see this continent restored to the condition in which it was found by our forefathers. What good man would prefer a country covered with forests, and ranged by a few thousand savages, to our extensive republic, studded with cities, towns, and prosperous farms; embellished with all the improvements which art can devise, or industry execute; occupied by more than twelve millions of happy people, and filled with all the blessings of liberty, civilization, and religion!

The present policy of the Government is but a continuation of the same progressive change, by a milder process. The tribes which occupied the countries now constituting the Eastern States were annihilated, or have melted away, to make room for the whites. The waves of population and civilization are rolling to the Westward; and we now propose to acquire the countries occupied by the red men of the South and West, by a fair exchange, and, at the expense of the U. States, to send them to a land where their existence may be prolonged, and perhaps made perpetual. Doubtless it will be painful to leave the graves of their fathers; but what do they more than our ancestors did, or than our children are now doing? To better their condition in an unknown land, our forefathers left all that was dear in earthly objects. Our children, by thousands, yearly leave the land of their birth, to seek new homes in distant regions. Does humanity weep at these painful separations from every thing, animate and inanimate, with which the young heart has become entwined? Far from it. It is rather a source of joy that our country affords scope where our young population may range unconstrained in body or in mind, developing the power and faculties of man in their highest perfection. . . . How many thousands of our own people would gladly embrace the opportunity of removing to the west on such conditions! If the offers made to the Indians were extended to them, they would be hailed with gratitude and joy.

Rightly considered, the policy of the General Government towards the red man is not only liberal but generous. . . . It is, therefore, a duty which this Government owes to the new States, to extinguish, as soon as possible, the Indian title to all lands which Congress themselves have included within their limits. When this is done, the duties of the General Government in relation to the States and Indians within their limits are at an end.[9]

INTRODUCTION TO DOCUMENTS 13, 14, AND 15

The passage of the Indian Removal Act led to division among the Cherokee about how to respond. Federal pressure led many to voluntarily move, even though most remained opposed to removal. Meanwhile, the Georgia legislature continued to pass a series of laws that placed Cherokee land under state control. In 1831, the legislature called for a lottery to distribute that land in the fall of 1832. To prepare for that land lottery, the state began to survey and map the Cherokee lands. Document 13 is a detail from one of those maps, printed well *before* the Cherokee had "agreed" to cede the entirety of this territory. Note the subtitle for the map, which describes the land as having great potential for development.

The Cherokee Nation continued to resist such encroachments, and John Ross challenged Georgia's actions in a case that went to the Supreme Court. In 1832, the Court sided with the Cherokee, arguing in *Worcester v. Georgia* that the state of Georgia had no jurisdiction over sovereign Cherokee lands. Yet President Jackson rejected the Court's decision—a deeply controversial move—and continued to press the Cherokee to abandon their lands and accept the federal government's offer of new territories in what would become Oklahoma.

While negotiations between the Cherokee Nation and the U.S. government stalled, a federal representative traveled to New Echota to conclude an agreement paying the Cherokee $5 million for all their lands east of the Mississippi River, in exchange for removal to the west within two years. Document 14 is Jackson's forceful and aggressive statement to the Cherokee people at the height of those tense negotiations in March 1835. After the Treaty of New Echota was signed, Ross spent two years trying to reverse it. His response to Jackson's pressure on the Cherokee to move is found in Document 15. While some like Ross continued to resist, in May 1838, the U.S. military began to forcibly move 16,000 Cherokee into camps to prepare for the long trek west of the Mississippi. Conditions in the camps fostered disease, violence, and death. The first groups moved in the heat and drought of summer, while others perished in a brutal winter that followed. In the forced relocation that became known as the "Trail of Tears," over 4,000 Cherokee perished.

13. CARTOUCHE FROM A MAP OF CHEROKEE LANDS (1831)

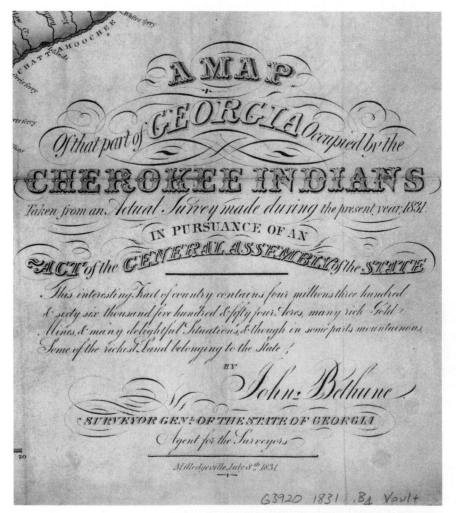

Image 7.4 Detail from map of the Cherokee lands

The state of Georgia began to survey and distribute land owned by the Cherokee tribe before they had been forcibly removed West. This map was made pursuant to the General Assembly's instructions. It describes the country as having "rich gold mines and many delightful situations . . . some of the richest land belonging to the state."

Source: John Bethune, "A Map of that Part of Georgia Occupied by the Cherokee Indians" (Milledgeville, 1831), Courtesy of Library of Congress.

14. ANDREW JACKSON'S MESSAGE TO THE CHEROKEE TRIBE OF INDIANS (1835)

My Friends: I have long viewed your condition with great interest. For many years I have been acquainted with your people, and under all variety of circumstances, in peace and war. Your fathers were well known to me, and the regard which I cherished for them has caused me to feel great solicitude for your situation. To those feelings, growing out of former recollections, have been added the sanction of official duty, and the relation in which, by the constitution and laws, I am placed towards you. Listen to me, therefore, as your fathers have listened, while I communicate to you my sentiments on the critical state of your affairs.

You are now placed in the midst of a white population. Your peculiar customs, which regulated your intercourse with one another, have been abrogated by the great political community among which you live; and you are now subject to the same laws which govern the other citizens of Georgia and Alabama. You are liable to prosecutions for offences, and to civil actions for a breach of any of your contracts. Most of your people are uneducated, and are liable to be brought into collision at all times with their white neighbors. Your young men are acquiring habits of intoxication. With strong passions, and without those habits of restraint which our laws inculcate and render necessary, they are frequently driven to excesses which must eventually terminate in their ruin. The game has disappeared among you, and you must depend upon agriculture and the mechanic arts for support. And, yet, a large portion of your people have acquired little or no property in the soil itself, or in any article of personal property which can be useful to them. How, under these circumstances can you live in the country you now occupy? Your condition must become worse and worse, and you will ultimately disappear, as so many tribes have done before you.

Of all this I warned your people, when I met them in council eighteen years ago. I then advised them to sell out their possessions east of the Mississippi, and to remove to the country west of that river. This advice I have continued to give you, at various times, from that period down to the present day; and can you now look back and doubt the wisdom of this counsel? Had you then removed, you would have gone with all the means necessary to establish yourselves in a fertile country, sufficiently extensive for your subsistence, and beyond the reach of the moral evils which are now hastening your destruction. Instead of being a divided people as you now are, arrayed into parties bitterly opposed to each other, you would have been a prosperous and a united community. Your farms would have been opened and cultivated, comfortable houses would have been erected, the means of subsistence abundant, and you would have been governed by your own customs and laws, and removed from the effects of a white population. Where you now are, you are encompassed by evils, moral and physical, and these are fearfully increasing.

. . . I have no motive, my friends, to deceive you. I am sincerely desirous to promote your welfare. Listen to me, therefore, while I tell you that you cannot remain where you now are. Circumstances that cannot be controlled, and which are beyond the reach of human laws, render it impossible that you can flourish in the midst of a civilized community. You have but one remedy within your reach; and that is, to remove to the West and join your countrymen, who are already established there. And the sooner you do this, the sooner you will commence your career of improvement and prosperity.

. . . The choice is now before you. May the Great Spirit teach you how to choose. The fate of your women and children, the fate of your people, to the remotest generation, depend upon the issue. Deceive yourselves no longer. Do not cherish the belief that you can ever resume your former political situation, while you continue in your present residence. As certain as the sun shines to guide you in your path, so certain is that you cannot drive back the laws of Georgia from among you. Every year will increase your difficulties. Look at the condition of the Creeks. See the collisions which are taking place with them. See how their young men are committing depredations upon the property of our citizens, and are shedding their blood. This cannot and will not be allowed. Punishment will follow, and all who are engaged in these offences must suffer. Your young men will commit the same acts, and the same consequences must ensue.

Think, then, of all these things. Shut your ears to bad counsels. Look at your condition as it now is, and then consider what it will be if you follow the advice I give you. Your friend,

Andrew Jackson
Washington, March 16, 1835[10]

15. CHIEF JOHN ROSS, TO THE SENATE AND HOUSE OF REPRESENTATIVE (1836)

After the departure of [our real tribal delegation from Washington,] a contract was made by the Rev. John F. Schermerhorn, and certain individual Cherokees, purporting to be a "treaty, concluded at New Echota, in the State of Georgia, on the 29th day of December, 1835, by General William Carroll and John F. Schermerhorn, commissioners on the part of the United States, and the chiefs, headmen, and people of the Cherokee tribes of Indians." A spurious Delegation, in violation of a special injunction of the general council of the nation, proceeded to Washington City with this pretended treaty, and by false and fraudulent representations supplanted in the favor of the Government the legal and accredited Delegation of the Cherokee people, and obtained for this instrument, after making important alterations in its provisions, the recognition of the United States Government. And now it is presented to us as a treaty, ratified by the Senate, and approved by the President, and our acquiescence in its requirements demanded, under the sanction of the displeasure of the United States, and the threat of summary compulsion, in case of refusal. It comes to us, not through our legitimate authorities, the known and usual medium of communication between the Government of the United States and our nation, but through the agency of a complication of powers, civil and military.

By the stipulations of this instrument, we are despoiled of our private possessions, the indefeasible property of individuals. We are stripped of every attribute of freedom and eligibility for legal self-defence. Our property may be plundered before our eyes; violence may be committed on our persons; even our lives may be taken away, and there is none to regard our complaints. We are denationalized; we are disfranchised. We are deprived of membership in the human family! We have neither land nor home, nor resting place that can be called our own. And this is effected by the provisions of a compact which assumes the venerated, the sacred appellation of treaty.

We are overwhelmed! Our hearts are sickened, our utterance is paralized, when we reflect on the condition in which we are placed, by the audacious practices of unprincipled men, who have managed their stratagems with so much dexterity as to impose on the Government of the United States, in the face of our earnest, solemn, and reiterated protestations.

The instrument in question is not the act of our Nation; we are not parties to its covenants; it has not received the sanction of our people. The makers of it sustain no office nor appointment in our Nation, under the designation of Chiefs, Head men, or any other title, by which they hold, or could acquire, authority to assume the reins of Government, and to make bargain and sale of our rights, our possessions, and our common country. And we are constrained solemnly to declare, that we cannot but contemplate the enforcement of the stipulations of this instrument on us, against our consent, as an act of injustice and oppression, which, we are well persuaded, can never knowingly be countenanced by the Government and people of the United States; nor can we believe it to be the design of these honorable and highminded individuals, who stand at the head of the Govt., to bind a whole Nation, by the acts of a few unauthorized individuals. And, therefore, we, the parties to be affected by the result, appeal with confidence to the justice, the magnanimity, the compassion, of your honorable bodies, against the enforcement, on us, of the provisions of a compact, in the formation of which we have had no agency.[11]

QUESTIONS

1. What accounts for Jackson's polarizing effect on the electorate in 1828 and 1832? What types of voters gravitated toward him, and who were driven away? How was he portrayed by foes and allies?
2. Modern campaigns are often criticized for embracing attack ads, scandal-mongering, and excessive focus on image rather than substance. To what degree did the elections of Jackson include these elements?
3. Why was Indian removal the most logical policy in the minds of Georgians and President Jackson? How did they argue that it was in the best interests of the Cherokee to move west? How did the Cherokee respond?
4. The expansion of democracy in the Jacksonian era led to the abridgement of rights for Native Americans. How do you explain this apparent paradox?
5. In the debate over the Second Bank of the United States, both Jackson and Webster accused the other side of violating the rights and acting unconstitutionally. On what grounds did each make these claims?
6. In your view did Jackson's position against the bank align with the more general outlook of the Jacksonian Democrats? Why did Jackson respond so strongly to the bank?

ADDITIONAL READING

For an entertaining introduction to Andrew Jackson, see Robert Remini, *The Life of Andrew Jackson* (2001), and H. W. Brands, *Andrew Jackson: His Life and Times* (2005). For the politics of the era, see Daniel Feller's *The Jacksonian Promise: America, 1815–1840* (1995); Lawrence Frederick Kohl's *The Politics of Individualism: Parties and the American Character in the Jacksonian Era* (1989); Sean Wilentz, *The Rise of American Democracy: From Jefferson to Lincoln* (2005); and Joel Silbey, *Martin Van Buren and the Emergence of American Popular Politics* (2005). Serious students of the period should consult Arthur Schlesinger Jr.'s 1946 Pulitzer Prize–winning *The Age of Jackson* (2005). Also of interest is Charles Seller's provocative study on the impact of capitalism, entitled *The Market Revolution: Jacksonian America, 1815–1846* (1991). Robert Remini ably covers the bank war in *Andrew Jackson and the Bank War: A Study in the Growth of Presidential Power* (1967). For a dramatic account of the fight over Indian removal, see Steve Inskeep, *Jacksonland: President Andrew Jackson, Cherokee Chief John Ross, and a Great American Land Grab* (2015).

ENDNOTES

1. *Daily National Journal,* September 3, 1828.
2. From the *Democratic Republican,* reprinted in the New Hampshire *Patriot and State Gazette* (published as *New-Hampshire Patriot and State Gazette*), May 11, 1829, Concord, NH: Readex/New Hampshire Historical Society.
3. Andrew Jackson, "Message from the President of the United States, Returning the Bank Bill, with His Objections," July 10, 1832, 22nd Congress, 1st Session, Senate Document 180.
4. "Speech of the Hon. Daniel Webster, in the Senate of the United States," July 11, 1832 (Boston: J. E. Hinckley and Co., 1832), pp. 9–11, 14–21.
5. *Salem Gazette,* November 30, 1832, v.10, n.87, p. 2.
6. Farewell Address of Andrew Jackson to the People of the United States, in Francis Newton Thorpe, *The Statesmanship of Andrew Jackson* (New York: Tandy-Thomas Company, 1909), pp. 493-516.
7. Memorial of the Cherokee Nation, December 1829, from *Cherokee Phoenix,* January 20, 1830, p. 1. University of Georgia Library.
8. Memorial from the Ladies of Steubenville, Ohio, February 15, 1830, Record Group 233, U.S. House of Representatives, National Archives, ARC identifier 306633.
9. Andrew Jackson, President's Message, 21st Congress, 2nd Session, in Appendix to *Gales & Seaton's Register,* Library of Congress, pp. ix–x.
10. Andrew Jackson, March 16, 1835, in document n. 286, 24th Congress, 1st Session, pp. 40–43.
11. John Ross, letter to Congress, in "Report from the Secretary of War," Serial Set Vol. No. 315, Session Vol. No. 2, 25th Congress, 2nd Session, Senate Document 120, pp. 799–802.

CHAPTER 8

THE UPHEAVAL OF WESTWARD EXPANSION

HISTORICAL CONTEXT

The story is a simple one. On March 6, 1836, 183 men, eight of them Mexican and the rest American, were killed trying to defend the fortress Alamo in San Antonio de Béjar, Texas. They were overwhelmed shortly after dawn by hundreds of Mexican troops under General Antonio López de Santa Anna. The victors paid a high price. Scaling the walls and taking the fortress cost the attacking army almost four times as many men as died defending it. The last half dozen or so Americans surrendered; they were immediately executed by order of Santa Anna.

But no good story is ever truly simple.

Seven-day-old Juan Nepomuceno Seguín was baptized in the parish church of San Antonio de Béjar on November 3, 1806. Seguín's father and grandfather were baptized in the very same church in this outpost of the Spanish Empire. Indeed, Seguín's great-great-grandfather had been a soldier and then a rancher and local leader in the region, and over the decades, the family had prospered and helped make the settlement of Spanish Texas permanent. Seguín's father, José Erasmo Seguín, controlled over 15,000 acres of land, and Juan, too, became part of the local elite.

The 1820s and 1830s, the years of Juan's young adulthood, were turbulent times. Early in the nineteenth century, Spain held more territory west of the Mississippi River than did the United States. Although a big chunk of the trans–Mississippi West had been acquired through the Louisiana Purchase of 1803, Spanish land still stretched from Louisiana and the Gulf Coast to the Pacific Ocean, and from the northern border of present-day California east to the Rocky Mountains and south through Mexico and beyond.

Yet the Spanish Empire fell apart rapidly. The contagion of colonial rebellion spread from North America, and soon new nations in the southern hemisphere defied and liberated themselves from Spanish rule. Independence came to Mexico in 1821, and that new nation claimed all of the land in the northernmost parts of the old Spanish Empire, from the Yucatán Peninsula north past Santa Fe and Yerba Buena (later San Francisco).

The northeastern portion of the new Mexican nation was in a precarious position. These borderlands were quite underpopulated, and *Norteamericanos* alternately offered to buy or threatened to take them. The Mexican government decided that a stable population would help secure the region, so for a small amount of money and vague pledges to become Roman Catholics and Mexican citizens, immigrants from the United States were allowed to settle. Men such as Stephen F. Austin, who became a close friend of the Seguín family, made money leading hundreds of families into Texas. By 1835, nearly 30,000 white Americans had settled in the area, vastly outnumbering the Mexican population. The majority of these whites were southerners; many brought slaves with them to Texas, where they hoped to grow rich on fresh land that was perfect for growing cotton.

But serious problems plagued the area. Under a new constitution, the Mexican government merged the provinces of Texas and Coahuila in 1824. Many Americans as well as Tejanos (Mexicans living in Texas) felt that the arrangement would not work, that they would be governed from afar and taxed for others' support. Additional issues arose. Would there really be an established church? Certainly, white Protestants had been free to practice their religion up until now, but Catholicism was Mexico's official religion. Another question was whether slavery would continue. Some in the Mexican congress were strongly opposed to servitude, and the Mexican government outlawed slavery in 1829, though enforcement of the law was all but nonexistent. With open migration from the United States, would that continue? As many of the immigrants grew wary of their hosts (there was even an abortive uprising in 1826, which some Anglos fomented, but which others helped to put down), Mexico declared the border closed in 1830, although Americans continued to come in illegally.

Thereafter, the U.S. government became increasingly belligerent toward Mexico, and southerners aggressively sought new lands to farm with their slaves. In addition, Mexico's new leader, General Antonio López de Santa Anna, seemed determined to rule in a manner that the Americans—and many Mexicans—considered autocratic. In March 1836, a group of Texans declared their separation from Mexico; This sparked a brief war— beginning with the battle at the Alamo—that produced an independent Texas Republic that would last for nine years before Texas became a state. Many Americans began to think of territorial expansion as not just appealing but inevitable, and a new strain of racism made many Anglos intolerant of their Mexican neighbors.

The American decision to annex Texas worsened the already tense relations with Mexico. The ensuing war began on the disputed southern border of Texas, but quickly the American military set its sights on the far west, wresting California from Mexico's weak control. The Mexican–American War remains one of the most controversial conflicts in our nation's history. Many questioned the justification for war and suspected that the motives really lay more in the desire to acquire new territory than in national defense. When the Treaty of Guadalupe Hidalgo was signed in early 1848, the United States had enlarged its territory by one-third but had created tremendous internal discord over the future of slavery in those western territories. The documents below explore complexities of westward expansion by focusing on the Texas rebellion, the controversy over annexation, and the war with Mexico.

INTRODUCTION TO DOCUMENTS 1 AND 2

The following documents give a sense of the tensions in the borderlands that long predated the Texas Revolution. Note how each side characterized the other. What sort of differences did the authors seem to emphasize? Who was each author's intended audience, and how did it affect the claims each author made? Document 1 includes observations made in 1828 and 1829 by General Manuel Mier y Terán, a hero of Mexico's War for Independence who headed a special commission to investigate the boundary between Mexico and the United States. By 1835, the situation had so deteriorated that citizens of San Augustine petitioned for independence (Document 2). Copying the pattern set by American cities like Boston in the 1770s, Anglos in these towns formed Committees of Safety and Correspondence. Note the petition's assertion that Anglos and Mexicans are both culturally and politically incompatible.

1. A MEXICAN GENERAL DESCRIBES THE BORDERLANDS, 1828 AND 1829

MANUEL MIER Y TERÁN

. . . As one covers the distance from Béjar to this town [Nacogdoches] he will note that Mexican influence is proportionately diminished until on arriving in this place he will see that it is almost nothing. And indeed, whence could such influence come? Hardly from superior numbers in population, since the ratio of Mexicans to foreigners is one to ten; certainly not from the superior character of the Mexican population, for exactly the opposite is true, the Mexicans of this town comprising what in all countries is called the lowest class—the very poor and very ignorant. The naturalized North Americans in the town maintain an English school, and send their children north for further education; the poor Mexicans not only do not have sufficient means to establish schools, but they are not of the type that take any thought for the improvement of its public institutions or the betterment of its degraded condition. . . . Thus, I tell myself that it could not be otherwise than that from such a state of affairs should arise an antagonism between the Mexicans and foreigners, which is not the least of the smoldering fires which I have discovered. Therefore, I am warning you to take timely measures. Texas could throw the whole nation into revolution.

The colonists murmur against the political disorganization of the frontier, and the Mexicans complain of the superiority and better education of the colonists; the colonists find it unendurable that they must go three hundred leagues to lodge a complaint against the petty pickpocketing that they suffer from a venal and ignorant *alcalde* [magistrate]. . . . Meanwhile, the incoming stream of new settlers is unceasing. . . .

[One year later, Mier y Terán wrote the following to Mexico's Minister of War.] . . .The North Americans have conquered whatever territory adjoins them. In less than half a century, they have become masters of extensive colonies which formerly belonged to Spain and France, and of even more spacious territories from which have disappeared the former owners, the Indian tribes. There is no Power like that to the north, which by silent means, has made conquests of momentous importance. Such dexterity, such constancy in their designs, such uniformity of means of execution which always are completely successful, arouses admiration. Instead of armies, battles, or invasions, which make a great noise and for the most part are unsuccessful, these men lay hands on means, which, if considered one by one, would be rejected as slow, ineffective, and at times palpably absurd. They begin by assuming rights, as in Texas, which it is impossible to sustain in a serious discussion, making ridiculous pretensions based on historical incidents which no one admits—such as the voyage of La Salle, which was an absurd fiasco, but serves as a basis for their claim to Texas. Such extravagant claims as these are now being presented for the first time to the public by dissembling writers. . . .

In the meantime, the territory against which these machinations are directed, and which has usually remained unsettled, begins to be visited by adventurers and *empresarios;* some of these take up their residence in the country. . . . They incite uprisings in the territory in question and usually manifest a deep concern for the rights of the inhabitants.[1]

2. PETITION FROM THE COMMITTEE OF VIGILANCE AND PUBLIC SAFETY FOR THE MUNICIPALITY OF SAN AUGUSTINE (1835)

. . . In the year of eighteen hundred and twenty-one, Texas was an uninhabited wilderness, infested by hostile Indians, from the Sabine river to San Antonio; not excepting Nacogdoches itself. Encouraged by the invitation of the colonization laws, the settlement of the wilderness was commenced, and continued by individual enterprises, entirely unaided by succors of any kind from the government; the settlement of the country has not cost the government one cent. The emigrants dared to settle an unreclaimed wilderness, the haunt of wild beasts, and the home of the daring and hostile savages; and in so doing, poured out their blood like water. . . .

The Anglo-Americans and the Mexicans, if not primitively a different people, habit, education and religion, have made them essentially so. The two people cannot mingle together. The strong prejudices that existed at the first emigrations . . . [have] increased many fold. And as long as the people of Texas belong to the Mexican nation, their interests will be jeopardised, and their prosperity cramped. And they will always be more or less affected by the excitements of that revolutionary people.

Of all the times for Texas to declare herself independent, the present is perhaps the most exquisitely appropriate. The causes will fully justify the act before the enlightened world, and win its approbation. . . . Then, fellow-citizens, let us instruct our delegates to the next convention to pass a *Declaration of Independence* with one loud and unanimous voice. . . .[2]

INTRODUCTION TO DOCUMENTS 3–7

While some settlers—like those in Saint Augustine—sought independence, others aimed to restore freedoms that had been curtailed by the Mexican government. Their grievances spilled over into hostilities in the fall of 1835. This conflict climaxed in early 1836, when General Santa Anna defeated the Texans at the Battle of the Alamo. Just after that defeat, the Texans declared their independence, and prevailed against Mexico in a victory at the Battle of San Jacinto, after which Santa Anna retreated. Mexicans, however, disputed the legitimacy of independence, and many blamed the United States for the loss of Texas, given that so many volunteers were Americans who migrated after the onset of hostilities. Documents 3 and 4 convey the passionate mindset of some of those migrants and their reasons for supporting the separation of Texas from Mexico. Document 5 is an urgent call for Americans to migrate to Texas and support its fight for independence. Conversely, the images in Documents 6 and 7 capture the equally passionate opposition to American involvement in Texas, which was considered by many a brazen violation of Mexican sovereignty and laws against slavery.

3. TEXAS DECLARATION OF INDEPENDENCE (MARCH 2, 1836)

... The Mexican government, by its colonization laws, invited and induced the Anglo American population of Texas to colonize its wilderness under the pledged faith of a written constitution, that they should continue to enjoy that constitutional liberty and republican government to which they had been habituated in the land of their birth, the United States of America.

In this expectation they have been cruelly disappointed, inasmuch as the Mexican nation has acquiesced to the late changes made in the government by General Antonio Lopez de Santa Anna, who, having overturned the constitution of his country, now offers, as the cruel alternative, either to abandon our homes, acquired by so many privations, or submit to the most intolerable of all tyranny, the combined despotism of the sword and the priesthood. ...

It has failed and refused to secure, on a firm basis, the right of trial by jury. ...

It has failed to establish any public system of education. ...

It has made piratical attacks upon our commerce, by commissioning foreign desperadoes, and authorizing them to seize our vessels, and convey the property of our citizens to far distant ports for confiscation.

It denies us the right of worshipping the Almighty according to the dictates of our own conscience, by the support of a national religion, calculated to promote the temporal interest of its human functionaries, rather than the glory of the true and living God.

It has demanded us to deliver up our arms, which are essential to our defence—the rightful property of freemen—and formidable only to tyrannical governments.

It has invaded our country both by sea and by land, with the intent to lay waste our territory, and drive us from our homes: and has now a large mercenary army advancing to carry on against us a war of extermination.

It has through its emissaries, incited the merciless savage, with the tomahawk and scalping knife, to massacre the inhabitants of our defenseless frontiers.

It has been, during the whole time of our connection with it, the contemptible sport and victim of successive military revolutions, and hath continually exhibited every characteristic of a weak, corrupt, and tyrannical government. ...

The necessity of self-preservation, therefore, now decrees our eternal political separation.

We, therefore, the delegates, with plenary powers, of the people of Texas, in solemn convention assembled, appealing to a candid world for the necessities of our condition, do hereby resolve and declare, that our political connection with the Mexican nation has forever ended, and that the people of Texas do now constitute a free, sovereign, and independent republic, and are fully invested with all the rights and attributes which properly belong to independent nations; and, conscious of the rectitude of our intentions, we fearlessly and confidently commit the issue to the supreme Arbiter of the destinies of nations.[3]

4. PUBLIC MEETING IN NASHVILLE, TENNESSEE (MAY 11, 1836)

In pursuance of public notice previously given, by a call signed by a large number of highly respectable citizens of Nashville and Davidson county, a numerously attended public meeting of the citizens of this city and county convened at the court-house in Nashville, on Saturday, the 11th instant. . . .

Every man in the Union has the undoubted right to emigrate to Texas if he chooses. This is lawful. Our citizens may vest a hundred millions in Texas cotton and sugar lands—far superior to any other on this continent. Who, or what is to prevent them? To do so is lawful. That is not all. There are cases where laws and treaties are as cobwebs in the way of the torrent of popular passion and will. Such a case the Mexican Government had the wickedness to present by the cold-blooded and inhuman slaughter of the defenders of the Alamo. . . .

With a restless and migratory population of young men, whose physical prowess and romantic and chivalrous daring have even excelled the trained Indian warrior, when tested hand-to-hand, of whom the valley of the Mississippi can furnish, perhaps, one hundred thousand, ready to embark in any enterprise promising to be fraught with stirring adventures, what but peace is to prevent an army from Texas marching on Mexico—a city which is now, more than in a former age, possessed of those fatal charms that once tempted the Spaniard to her ruin?

The project has in it more of romantic attractions to daring ambition than any presented since the days of Pizarro and Cortes. Who fears successful resistance? The European Spaniards have been cut off or driven from the country by the Mexican revolution. The Mexican native never could fight, nor has he a motive: he of the mixed blood is no soldier, and the creole a most indifferent one. Before an army made up of the *material* supposed, Mexico would fall without a struggle. This it is the business of the United States to prevent; and it can only be prevented by recognizing the claim of Texas to be severed from Mexico, and an interference to end the war. . . .

1. *Resolved, therefore,* That, in the opinion of this meeting, the Republic of Texas is severed from Mexico; that she has a Government, in fact, in successful operation, republican in its character, and which she has abundant means to maintain; that no good reason exists why the Congress and Executive Government of the United States should not immediately recognise the independence of the Republic of Texas.

2. *Resolved,* That, in the opinion of this meeting, the present session of Congress should not be permitted to close until the independence of Texas is fully recognised, and every arrangement made with the new government consistent with the best interests of the United States. And this meeting hereby petitions the Executive and the Congress of the United States to give effect to these our wishes; and especially in recognising, in the most unequivocal terms, Texas as severed from Mexico, and that she is a free, sovereign, and independent state.

3. *Resolved,* That the Executive of the United States, and our Senators and Representatives in Congress from the State of Tennessee, are most respectfully requested to use their best exertions to give effect to our petition and wishes as expressed in these proceedings. . . .[4]

5. TEXAS FOREVER!! (1836)

TEXAS FOREVER!!

The usurper of the South has failed in his efforts to enslave the freemen of Texas.

The wives and daughters of Texas will be saved from the brutality of Mexican soldiers.

Now is the time to emigrate to the Garden of America.

A free passage, and all found, is offered at New Orleans to all applicants. Every settler receives a location of

EIGHT HUNDRED ACRES OF LAND.

On the 23d of February, a force of 1000 Mexicans came in sight of San Antonio, and on the 25th Gen. St. Anna arrived at that place with 2500 more men, and demanded a surrender of the fort held by 150 Texians, and on the refusal, he attempted to storm the fort, twice, with his whole force, but was repelled with the loss of 500 men, and the Americans lost none. Many of his troops, the liberals of Zacatecas, are brought on to Texas in irons and are urged forward with the promise of the women and plunder of Texas.

The Texian forces were marching to relieve St. Antonio, March the 2d. The Government of Texas is supplied with plenty of arms, ammunition, provisions, &c. &c.

Image 8.1 Texas Forever!!

An 1836 poster, recruiting Americans to settle in Texas, "the garden of America," and to help defend it against Santa Anna's soldiers in exchange for land.

Source: Broadside Collection, BC_0248, The Dolph Briscoe Center for American History, The University of Texas at Austin.

6. THE EAGLE OF LIBERTY (*c.* 1836)

Image 8.2 American opposition to the Texas Revolution.

This image, first published about 1836 and repeatedly reprinted, framed the rebellion in Texas—and the support for American annexation—as driven by slavery and an affront to Mexican sovereignty. Note here that the "eagle of liberty" is associated with Mexico, not the United States.

Source: Benjamin Lundy, "The Legion of Liberty" (New York: American Anti-Slavery Society, 1843). 2007/001-19-45, Courtesy of Texas State Library and Archives Commission.

7. MORAL MAP OF THE U.S. (1837)

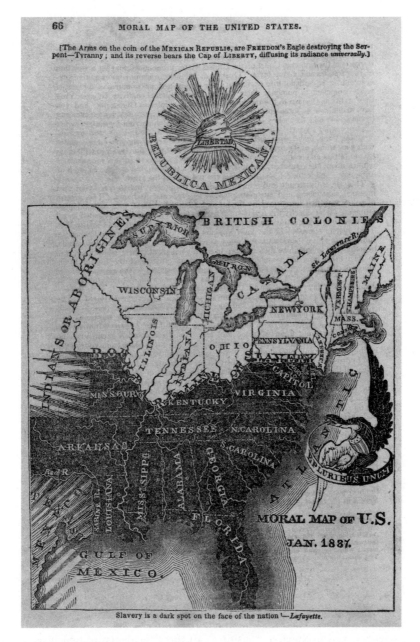

Image 8.3 Moral Map of the U.S." (1837)

As early as 1836, many Americans relentlessly opposed to the annexation of Texas. This "Moral Map" argued that the settlement of Texas was undertaken to extend slavery into a region where it had been outlawed by Mexico.

Source: Julius Rubens Ames and the American Anti-Slavery Society, "Liberty" (1837). Courtesy of P. J. Mode Collection, Cornell University.

Texas independence immediately led to the possibility of annexation by the United States. Yet though the prospect of American territorial expansion into the southwest appealed to many, the legality of slavery made annexation a highly charged and divisive issue, politically and morally. As a result, Texas remained an independent republic for nine years. Throughout that period, thoughts of Manifest Destiny—the idea that Americans were divinely ordained to expand their national domain into the West—expanded, laying the groundwork for the openly annexationist presidential candidate, James K. Polk. When Polk won in 1844, outgoing president John Tyler quickly annexed Texas but in doing so renewed the sectional strife that had waxed and waned for years. He had also renewed tensions with Mexico, which considered the Texas annexation an illegal act against its national sovereignty. These next documents trace the debate over territorial growth.

In Document 8, the Mexican Secretary of War assesses the terrible impact of Texas independence on his nation's future. What accounts for his predictions that Mexico would lose so much of its northern territory? In Document 9 newspaper editor John O'Sullivan articulates a vision of American exceptionalism that is predicated on westward expansion. In 1845, just after the nation had annexed Texas and handed the expansionist Polk a presidential victory, O'Sullivan again returned to this theme in his second essay. In Document 11, President Polk forcefully prepares Americans for the possibility of war with Mexico and advocates the acquisition of additional new lands in the west and northwest. Proponents of Manifest Destiny sparked equally forceful opponents, particularly those who believed that territorial expansion would inevitably lead to the growth of the nation's most polarizing institution, slavery. On what grounds does O'Sullivan argue for the nation's geographical expansion? Does Polk share his assumptions?

8. MEXICAN SECRETARY OF WAR JOSE MARIA TORNEL Y MENDIVIL ON THE LOSS OF TEXAS (1837)

Everywhere meetings have been held, presided over, as in New York, by public officials of the government, to collect money, buy ships, enlist men, and fan that spirit of animosity that characterizes all the acts of the United States with regard to Mexico. . . . Our character, our customs, our very rights have been painted in the darkest hues, while the crimes of the Texans have been applauded in the house of the President, in the halls of the capitol, in the marts of trade, in public meetings, in small towns, and even in the fields. The President of the Mexican republic was publicly executed in effigy in Philadelphia in an insulting and shameful burlesque. The world has witnessed all these incidents, of which we have become aware through the shameful accounts in the newspapers of the United States. Could greater insults, outrages, or indignities be offered us by an open declaration of war? Let national indignation answer the question.

. . . The loss of Texas will inevitably result in the loss of New Mexico and the Californias. Little by little our territory will be absorbed, until only an insignificant part is left to us. Our destiny will be similar to the sad lot of Poland. Our national existence, acquired at the cost of so much blood, recognized after so many difficulties, would end like those weak meteors which, from time to time, shine fitfully in the firmament and disappear. . . .

. . . Five thousand infantry and 500 cavalry would be enough, more than enough, to put an end to the high hopes of the Texans, to drive them to the banks of the Sabine, and to reconquer the favors of destiny. The superiority of the Mexican soldier over the mountaineers of Kentucky and the hunters of Missouri are [sic] well known. He knows how to endure all privations with serene calmness, and how to overcome hunger and conquer death herself. Veterans, seasoned by twenty years of wars, cannot be intimidated by the presence of an enemy, ignorant of the art of war, incapable of discipline, and renowned for insubordination. . . .

The fear that we will find ourselves involved in a war against the United States if we refuse to subscribe to the terms demanded is not without foundation. If their diplomacy has been dictated by a preconceived plan,—and this cannot be doubted by those who have observed the skill with which the cabinet in Washington directs its affairs—it is obvious that their aim has been to acquire possession of the disputed territory by force if necessary. This will involve us in more serious difficulties than even those presented by the Texas question itself. War with the United States, however, need not be feared, for our final salvation may depend upon it.[5]

9. THE GREAT NATION OF FUTURITY (1839)

JOHN L. O'SULLIVAN

The American people having derived their origin from many other nations, and the Declaration of National Independence being entirely based on the great principle of human equality, these facts demonstrate at once our disconnected position as regards any other nation; that we have, in reality, but little connection with the past history of any of them, and still less with all antiquity, its glories, or its crimes. On the contrary, our national birth was the beginning of a new history, the formation and progress of an untried political system, which separates us from the past and connects us with the future only; and so far as regards the entire development of the natural rights of man, in moral, political, and national life, we may confidently assume that our country is destined to be *the great nation* of futurity.

It is so destined, because the principle upon which a nation is organized fixes its destiny, and that of equality is perfect, is universal. It presides in all the operations of the physical world, and it is also the conscious law of the soul—the self-evident dictate of morality, which accurately defines the duty of man to man, and consequently man's rights as man. Besides, the truthful annals of any nation furnish abundant evidence, that its happiness, its greatness, its duration, were always proportionate to the democratic equality in its system of government.

. . . What friend of human liberty, civilization, and refinement, can cast his view over the past history of the monarchies and aristocracies of antiquity, and not deplore that they ever existed? What philanthropist can contemplate the oppressions, the cruelties, and injustice inflicted by them on the masses of mankind, and not turn with moral horror from the retrospect?

America is destined for better deeds. It is our unparalleled glory that we have no reminiscences of battle fields, but in defence of humanity, of the oppressed of all nations, of the rights of conscience, the rights of personal enfranchisement. Our annals describe no scenes of horrid carnage, where men were led on by hundreds of thousands to slay one another, dupes and victims to emperors, kings, nobles, demons in the human form called heroes. We have had patriots to defend our homes, our liberties, but no aspirants to crowns or thrones; nor have the American people ever suffered themselves to be led on by wicked ambition to depopulate the land, to spread desolation far and wide, that a human being might be placed on a seat of supremacy.

We have no interest in the scenes of antiquity, only as lessons of avoidance of nearly all their examples. The expansive future is our arena, and for our history. We are entering on its untrodden space, with the truths of God in our minds, beneficent objects in our hearts, and with a clear conscience unsullied by the past. We are the nation of human progress, and who will, what can, set limits to our onward march?[6]

10. ANNEXATION (1845)

JOHN L. O'SULLIVAN

It is now time for the opposition to the Annexation of Texas to cease. . . . It is time for the common duty of Patriotism to the Country to succeed;—or if this claim will not be recognized, it is at least time for common sense to acquiesce with decent grace in the inevitable and the irrevocable. . . . Texas is now ours. . . . Her star and her stripe may already be said to have taken their place in the glorious blazon of our common nationality; and the sweep of our eagle's wing already includes within its circuit the wide extent of her fair and fertile land. . . .

Nor is there any just foundation for the charge that Annexation is a great pro-slavery measure—calculated to increase and perpetuate that institution. Slavery had nothing to do with it. Opinions were and are greatly divided, both at the North and South, as to the influence to be exerted by it on Slavery and the Slave States. That it will tend to facilitate and hasten the disappearance of Slavery from all the northern tier of the present Slave States, cannot surely admit of serious question. The greater value in Texas of the slave labor now employed in those States, must soon produce the effect of draining off that labor southwardly, by the same unvarying law that bids water descend the slope that invites it. Every new Slave State in Texas will make at least one Free State from among those in which that institution now exists—to say nothing of those portions of Texas on which slavery cannot

spring and grow—to say nothing of the far more rapid growth of new States in the free West and Northwest, as these fine regions are overspread by the emigration fast flowing over them from Europe, as well as from the Northern and Eastern States of the Union as it exists. On the other hand, it is undeniably much gained for the cause of the eventual voluntary abolition of slavery, that it should have been thus drained off towards the only outlet which appeared to furnish much probability of the ultimate disappearance of the negro race from our borders. The Spanish-Indian-American-populations of Mexico, Central America and South America afford the only receptacle capable of absorbing that race whenever we shall be prepared to slough it off—to emancipate it from slavery, and (simultaneously necessary) to remove it from the midst of our own. Themselves already of mixed and confused blood, and free from the "prejudices" which among us so insuperably forbid the social amalgamation which can alone elevate the Negro race out of a virtually servile degradation even though legally free, the regions occupied by those populations must strongly attract the black race in that direction; and as soon as the destined hour of emancipation shall arrive, will relieve the question of one of its worst difficulties, if not absolutely the greatest.

. . . California will, probably, next fall away from the loose adhesion which, in such a country as Mexico, holds a remote province in a slight equivocal kind of dependence on the metropolis. . . . the Anglo-Saxon foot is already on its borders. Already the advance guard of the irresistible army of Anglo-Saxon emigration has begun to pour down upon it, armed with the plough and the rifle, and marking its trail with schools and colleges, courts and representative halls, mills and meeting houses. A population will soon be in actual occupation of California, over which it will be idle for Mexico to dream of dominion.[7]

11. FIRST ANNUAL MESSAGE

PRESIDENT JAMES POLK

DECEMBER 2, 1845

Fellow-Citizens of the Senate and the House of Representatives:

In performing for the first time the duty imposed on me by the Constitution of giving to you information of the state of the Union . . . I am happy that I can congratulate you on the continued prosperity of our country. Under the blessings of Divine Providence and the benign influence of our free institutions, it stands before the world a spectacle of national happiness.

. . . In pursuance of the joint resolution of Congress "for annexing Texas to the United States," my predecessor, on the 3d day of March, 1845, elected to submit the first and second sections of that resolution to the Republic of Texas as an overture on the part of the United States for her admission as a State into our Union. . . . This accession to our territory has been a bloodless achievement. No arm of force has been raised to produce the result. The sword has had no part in the victory. We have not sought to extend our territorial possessions by conquest, or our republican institutions over a reluctant people. It was the deliberate homage of each people to the great principle of our federative union. If we consider the extent of territory involved in the annexation, its prospective influence on America, the means by which it has been accomplished, springing purely from the choice of the people themselves to share the blessings of our union, the history of the world may be challenged to furnish a parallel.

. . . I regret to inform you that our relations with Mexico since your last session have not been of the amicable character which it is our desire to cultivate with all foreign nations. On the 6th day of March last the Mexican envoy extraordinary and minister plenipotentiary to the United States made a formal protest in the name of his Government against the joint resolution passed by Congress "for the annexation of Texas to the United States," which he chose to regard as a violation of the rights of Mexico, and in consequence of it he demanded his passports. He was informed that the Government of the United States did not consider this joint resolution as a violation of any of the rights of Mexico, or that it afforded any just cause of offense to his Government; that the Republic of Texas was an independent power, owing no allegiance to Mexico and constituting no part of her territory or rightful sovereignty and jurisdiction . . . all diplomatic intercourse between the two countries was suspended.

. . . Since that time Mexico has until recently occupied an attitude of hostility toward the United States— has been marshaling and organizing armies, issuing proclamations, and avowing the intention to make war on the United States, either by an open declaration or by invading Texas. Both the Congress and convention of the people of Texas invited this Government to send an army into that territory to protect and defend them against the menaced attack. The moment the terms of annexation offered by the United States were accepted by Texas the latter became so far a part of our own country as to make it our duty to afford such protection and defense. I therefore deemed it proper, as a precautionary measure, to order a strong squadron to the coasts of Mexico and to concentrate an efficient military force on the western frontier of Texas.

. . . Beyond all question the protection of our laws and our jurisdiction, civil and criminal, ought to be immediately extended over our citizens in Oregon. They have had just cause to complain of our long neglect in this particular, and have in consequence been compelled for their own security and protection to establish a provisional government for themselves. Strong in their allegiance and ardent in their attachment to the United States, they have been thus cast upon their own resources. They are anxious that our laws should be extended over them, and I recommend that this be done by Congress with as little delay as possible

. . . For the protection of emigrants whilst on their way to Oregon against the attacks of the Indian tribes occupying the country through which they pass, I recommend that a suitable number of stockades and blockhouse forts be erected along the usual route between our frontier settlements on the Missouri and the Rocky Mountains, and that an adequate force of mounted riflemen be raised to guard and protect them on their journey.

. . . Oregon is a part of the North American continent, to which, it is confidently affirmed, the title of the United States is the best now in existence. . . .

The rapid extension of our settlements over our territories heretofore unoccupied, the addition of new States to our Confederacy, the expansion of free principles, and our rising greatness as a nation are attracting the attention of the powers of Europe, and lately the doctrine has been broached in some of them of a "balance of power" on this continent to check our advancement. The United States, sincerely desirous of preserving relations of good understanding with all nations, can not in silence permit any European interference on the North American continent, and should any such interference be attempted will be ready to resist it at any and all hazards.[8]

INTRODUCTION TO DOCUMENTS 12–15

The outbreak of war between the United States and Mexico was seen by many Americans as a war over slavery, for any new lands gained in the West would immediately be subject to questions about labor. To this end, Democratic congressman David Wilmot proposed a simple amendment stating that any lands gained from a victory over Mexico would be closed to slavery (remember, Texas had been annexed *before* the war with Mexico). The defeat of this "Wilmot Proviso" highlighted the issues at stake, even though Wilmot was not opposed to slavery in the southern states. His speech defending this proviso is Document 12. Wilmot's amendment opened the floodgates of controversy among the states themselves, many of which passed resolutions regarding the character of slavery in a war that was still underway. Document 13 is one such resolution, passed by the antislavery legislature in Massachusetts. Texas and Virginia were just two southern states that responded in kind, assertively defending the legitimacy of the war and of slavery in the West. Those resolutions are Documents 14 and 15. Do these opponents of war share any of the values or reasoning of those advocating expansion in Documents 9, 10, and 11?

12. THE WILMOT PROVISO (1847)

PENNSYLVANIA CONGRESSMAN DAVID WILMOT, SPEECH IN CONGRESS

. . . Slavery should be forever excluded from any territory that might be subsequently acquired by the United States from the Republic of Mexico.

. . . We ask that this Government protect the integrity of free territory against the aggressions of slavery—against its wrongful usurpations. Sir, I was in favor of the annexation of Texas. I supported it with the whole influence which I possessed, and I was willing to take Texas in as she was. I sought not to change the character of her institutions. Texas was a slave country. . . . We voted for the annexation of Texas. The Democracy of the North was for it, to a man. We are for it now—firmly for it. Sir, we are fighting this war for Texas, and for the South. I affirm it; here is a matter well known to the Union. . . .

Now, sir, we are told that California is ours; and so it is. . . . And all we ask in the North is, that the character of its territory be preserved. It is free; and it is part of the established law of nations, and all public law, that when it shall come in to this Union, all laws there existing, not inconsistent with its new allegiance, will remain in force. This fundamental law, which prohibits slavery in California, will be in force; this fundamental law, which prohibits slavery in New Mexico, will be in force. Shall the South invade it? Shall the South make this Government an instrument for the violation of its neutrality, and for the establishment of slavery in these territories, in defiance of law? That is the question. There is no question of abolition here, sir. It is a question whether the South shall be permitted , by aggression, by invasion of right, by subduing free territory and planting slavery upon it, to wrest this territory to the accomplishment of its own sectional purposes and schemes? That is the question. And shall we of the North submit to it? Must we yield this? It is not, sir, in the spirit of the compact; it is not, sir, in the Constitution. . . .

When territory presents itself for annexation with slavery already established, I stand ready to take it, if national considerations require it, as they did in the case of Texas. I will not change its institutions, then. I make no war upon the South. I have no squeamish sensitiveness on the subject of slavery—no morbid sympathy for the slave. But I stand for the integrity of the territory. It shall remain free, so far as my voice and vote can aid in the preservation of its free character.[9]

13. THE LEGISLATURE OF MASSACHUSETTS, CONCERNING SLAVERY

MARCH 3, 1847

Resolves concerning the existence and extension of slavery within the jurisdiction of the United States.

Resolved, unanimously, That the legislature of Massachusetts views the existence of human slavery, within the limits of the United States, as a great calamity—an immense moral and political evil, which ought to be abolished as soon as that end can be properly and constitutionally attained; and that its extension should be uniformly and earnestly opposed by all good and patriotic men throughout the Union.

Resolved, unanimously, That the people of Massachusetts will strenuously resist the annexation of any new territory to this Union, in which the institution of slavery is to be tolerated or established: and the legislature, in behalf of the people of this commonwealth, do hereby solemnly protest against the acquisition of any additional territory, without an express provision, by Congress, that there shall be neither slavery nor involuntary servitude in such territory, otherwise than for the punishment of crime.[10]

14. VIRGINIA OPPOSES THE WILMOT PROVISO

VIRGINIA GENERAL ASSEMBLY, MARCH 8, 1847

[T]his general assembly [deems] this proviso to be destructive of the compromises of the constitution of the United States, and an attack on the dearest rights of the south, as well as a dangerous and alarming usurpation by the federal government: Therefore;

1. *Be it resolved unanimously by the general assembly of Virginia,* That the government of the United States has no control, directly or indirectly, mediately or immediately, over the institution of slavery, and that in taking any such control, it transcends the limits of its legitimate functions by destroying the internal organization of the sovereignties who created it.

2. *Resolved unanimously,* That all territory which may be acquired by the arms of the United States, or yielded by treaty with any foreign power, belongs to the several states of this union, as their joint and common property, in which each and all have equal rights, and that the enactment by the federal government of any law which should directly or by its effects prevent the citizens of any state from emigrating with their property of whatever description into such territory would make a discrimination unwarranted by and in violation of the constitution and the rights of the states from which such citizens emigrated, and in derogation of that perfect equality that belongs to the several states as members of this Union, and would tend directly to subvert the Union itself. . . .

5. *Resolved unanimously,* That the passage of the above-mentioned proviso makes it the duty of every slaveholding state, and of all the citizens thereof, as they value their dearest privileges, their sovereignty, their independence, their rights of property, to take firm, united and concerted action in this emergency.[11]

15. THE TEXAS LEGISLATURE DEFENDS SLAVERY AND THE WAR AGAINST MEXICO

JOINT RESOLUTION ON THE "PROVISO," SLAVERY, THE TARIFF, AND THE WAR AGAINST MEXICO, MARCH 18, 1848

SECTION 1.

Be it resolved by the Legislature of the State of Texas, That any attempt on the part of the Congress of the United States to interfere with the domestic and internal policy of the States or Territories, is unwarranted by the Constitution of the United States, and in violation of the rights of the States. The "Proviso," if submitted to, would prevent the slaveholding States from enjoying the full benefits of any territory which may be hereafter acquired, by the United States. The Constitution of the United States recognizes slavery, as one of our domestic institutions, and we acknowledge no right to abolish it, but that which belongs to the slaveholding States themselves. We will not submit to any law, which prohibits the citizens of the Southern States, from taking their property to any territory which may be acquired from Mexico.

. . . *Resolved further*, That we consider the war with Mexico, as necessary to the vindication of our national honor, as a war which was brought on by Mexico, by making an attack upon the army of the United States, at a time when the Mexican government expected to destroy that gallant band—who have added fresh lustre to the American name. After the bad faith, which has characterized the Mexicans, we have nothing to hope for, but that justice which we must compel them to grant by force of arms. We recommend, therefore, a vigorous prosecution of the war, until we obtain full indemnity for the wrongs and injuries done us. If it be necessary to appropriate some of the most valuable portions of Mexican Territory, we recommend that it be done. We should never give up California. We should secure a communication between the Atlantic and Pacific oceans, across the Isthmus, for all time to come. We should take possession of the Mexican ports, collect her revenues, and levy a tax upon all the property of the nation, to support our armies.

. . . Approved, March 18, 1848[12]

INTRODUCTION TO DOCUMENTS 16–17

The Treaty of Guadalupe Hidalgo (Document 16) brought an end to the war between the United States and Mexico. It was signed in February 1848, just weeks after the discovery of gold at Sutter's Mill in central California. For $15 million, Mexico would cede the vast territory of the far West, the later states of California, Arizona, New Mexico, Utah, and Colorado as well as portions of west Texas. This enlarged the United States by one-third and stretched its western border to the Pacific Ocean (soon thereafter extending northwest with the acquisition of Oregon Territory from the British). The Treaty of Guadalupe Hidalgo transferred not just land but also people, thousands of Mexicans who had lived in the Southwest for generations. Several articles in the treaty directly addressed citizenship and property rights for Mexicans, who overnight became Americans. Yet Article 10 of the treaty, which guaranteed the persistence of Mexican land grants, was expressly removed, anticipating the difficulty that many Mexican Americans would later have in defending their property—as well as their citizenship rights—in a nation that was increasingly suspicious of nonwhites within its population. Article eleven was very important to Mexico, providing some redress for Indian raids. But it was difficult to enforce, and was annulled within a few years.

Document 17 is a map typical of American history textbooks from the mid-nineteenth century down to our own day. Note the way that the expansion of the United States is framed as an orderly series of events, where conflict and conquest are minimized.

16. SELECTED ARTICLES FROM THE *TREATY OF GUADALUPE HIDALGO* (1848)

TREATY OF PEACE, FRIENDSHIP, LIMITS, AND SETTLEMENT WITH THE REPUBLIC OF MEXICO, FEBRUARY 2, 1848

In the name of Almighty God:

The United States of America and the United Mexican States, animated by a sincere desire to put an end to the calamities of the war which unhappily exists between the two republics, and to establish upon a solid basis relations of peace and friendship . . . have for that purpose appointed their respective plenipotentiaries . . . who, after a reciprocal communication of their respective full powers, have, under the protection of Almighty God, the author of peace, arranged, agreed upon, and signed the following *Treaty*. . . .

ARTICLE VIII

Mexicans now established in territories previously belonging to Mexico, and which remain for the future within the limits of the United States . . . shall be free to continue where they now reside, or to remove at any time to the Mexican republic, retaining the property which they possess in the said territories, or disposing thereof. . . .

. . . Those who shall prefer to remain in the said territories, may either retain the title and rights of Mexican citizens, or acquire those of citizens of the United States.

. . . In the said territories, property of every kind, now belonging to Mexicans not established there, shall be inviolably respected. The present owners, the heirs of these, and all Mexicans who may hereafter acquire said property by contract, shall enjoy with respect to it guarantees equally ample as if the same belonged to citizens of the United States.

ARTICLE X [STRICKEN FROM SIGNED TREATY]

All grants of land made by the Mexican government or by the competent authorities, in territories previously appertaining to Mexico, and remaining for the future within the limits of the United States, shall be respected as valid, to the same extent that the same grants would be valid, to the said territories had remained within the limits of Mexico. [This article was stricken out upon ratification by the Senate, but the principles protecting Mexican land grants in the United States were affirmed in the Protocol of Queretaro a few months later.]

ARTICLE XI

Considering that a great part of the territories which, by the present treaty, are to be comprehended for the future within the limits of the United States, is now occupied by savage tribes, who will hereafter be under the exclusive control of the government of the United States, and whose incursions within the territory of Mexico would be prejudicial in the extreme, it is solemnly agreed that all such incursions shall be forcibly restrained by the government of the United States whensoever this may be necessary; and that when they cannot be prevented, they shall be punished by the said government, and satisfaction for the same shall be exacted—all in the same way, and with equal diligence and energy, as if the same incursions were meditated or committed within its own territory, against its own citizens.

17. MAP OF UNITED STATES HISTORY (1853)

EMMA WILLARD

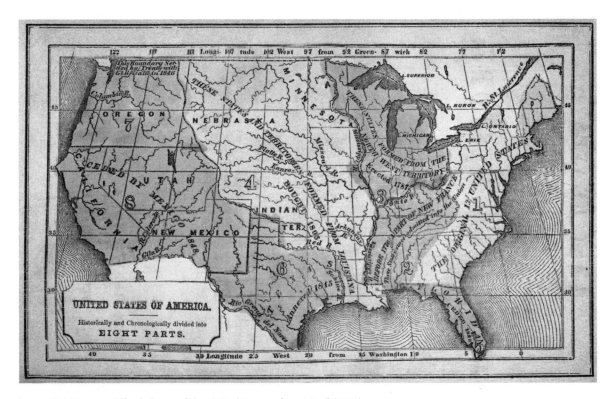

Image 8.4 Emma Willard, "Map of the United States of America" (1853)

Emma Willard, one of the most influential educators of the pre–Civil War era, ardently supported the nation's expansion to the Pacific. This map served as the opening image in her history of the war, written immediately after its conclusion.

Source: Emma Willard, *Last Leaves of American History* (New York: A. S. Barnes, 1853). Courtesy of University of Missouri Library, Kansas City.

POSTSCRIPT

The end of the war with Mexico not only brought extensive new lands for the United States but also questions regarding slavery that dominated the election of 1848. These tensions were settled to some degree by the Compromise of 1850, a series of congressional measures that closed California to slavery but guaranteed the return of slaves who fled their masters, known as "fugitives." A young congressman from Illinois, Abraham Lincoln, had opposed the Mexican war on the House floor. While the it raged on, he alluded to the issue of slavery's extension and the violence of the conflict and said of President Polk, "[[H]e feels the blood of this war, like the blood of Abel, is crying to Heaven against him." Though settled for a time, the issue of slavery in the territories arose again and again throughout the 1850s. Just as consequential for the future of the West was the discovery of gold in California only a few weeks after the signing of the Treaty of Guadalupe Hidalgo. The gold rush brought enormous migration to California and quickly resulted in the creation of a new state.

QUESTIONS

1. What sorts of tensions can you find between Anglo immigrants and Mexicans before the actual fighting began and immediately afterward?
2. On what grounds did Anglos justify their actions on the Mexican borderlands? How did the Mexicans respond? Can you imagine that Texas would have remained part of Mexico?
3. Do you think the Texas revolution was a freedom struggle? A land grab? An ethnic conflict?
4. How did Americans characterize Mexicans and Mexico in these tense decades of conflict? Why were migration and annexation so controversial?
5. Why did the war with Mexico become so divisive in the United States? What was at stake?
6. Do the events in this chapter change the way you think about immigration in our own day?

ADDITIONAL READING

For the story of the defense of the Alamo and how it has been remembered, see Randy Roberts and James S. Olson, *A Line in the Sand: The Alamo in Blood and Memory* (2001); also see Paul D. Lack, *The Texas Revolutionary Experience* (1992). The classic study of American expansion during this era is Frederick Merk, *Manifest Destiny and Mission in American History* (1963); also well respected is Reginald Horsman, *Race and Manifest Destiny: the Origins of American Racial Anglo-Saxonism* (1981). For a fine collection of primary sources on Texas, some of them from Mexican archives, see John H. Jenkins's ten-volume work, *Papers of the Texas Revolution, 1835–1836* (1973). On the U.S. Mexico War see Amy S. Greenberg, *A Wicked War: Polk, Clay, Lincoln, and the 1846 U.S. Invasion of Mexico* (2012); Robert W. Merry, *A Country of Vast Designs: James K. Polk, the Mexican War and the Conquest of the American Continent* (2010); and Robert Johanssen, *The Mexican War in the American Imagination* (1985). On the era during which Mexico controlled these lands, see David J. Weber, *The Mexican Frontier, 1821–1846* (1982). For iconography, see Susan Prendergast Schoelwer, *Alamo Images: Changing Perceptions of a Texas Experience* (1985).

ENDNOTES

1. Excerpted from "Mier y Teran to Guadeloupe Victoria, Nacogdoches, June 30, 1828." In Alaine Howren, "Causes and Origins of the Decree of April 6, 1830," *Southwestern Historical Quarterly*, v.16 n.4 (April 1913), pp. 395–398. Also excerpted from "Mier y Teran to Minister of War, Pueblo Viejo, November 13, 1829, in Ohland Morton, *Teran and Texas: A Chapter in Texas-Mexican Relations* (Austin, 1948), pp. 99–101. Reprinted by permission of the Texas State Historical Association.
2. *The Telegraph and Texas Register* (San Felipe de Austin), January 23, 1836, pp. 102–103.
3. Constitution of the Republic of Texas. To Which Is Prefixed the Declaration of Independence, Made in Convention, March 2, 1836 (Washington, D.C.: Printed by Gales and Seaton, 1836), pp. 3–7.

4. "Proceedings of a Meeting of the Citizens of Nashville, Tenn., in favor of Recognising the Independence of Texas. June 27, 1836." *Public Documents Printed by Order of the Senate of the United States. First Session of the Twenty-Fourth Congress* (Washington, D.C.: Printed by Gales & Seaton, 1836), Volume 9, document 418.

5. Excerpted from David J. Weber, ed., *Foreigners in Their Native Land* (Albuquerque: University of New Mexico Press, 1973), pp. 114–116.

6. "The Great Nation of Futurity," *United States Democratic Review,* v 6, i.23 (November 1839), pp. 426–430, quotes pp. 426–427.

7. "Annexation," *United States Democratic Review,* v.17, i.85 (July–August 1845), pp. 5–10.

8. Edwin Williams, *Statesman's Manual. Presidents' Messages, Inaugural, Annual and Special, from 1789 to 1846.* v.2 (New York: Edward Walker, 1847), pp. 1447–1458.

9. The *Congressional Globe,* 29th Congress, 2d session (Washington, D.C.: Blair & Ives, 1847), pp. 352–354.

10. "Resolves of the Legislature of Massachusetts, Concerning Slavery." March 3, 1847. In Records of the Senate, 29th Congress, 2nd Session. S. Doc. 219.

11. *Acts of Virginia,* 1846–1847, p. 236.

12. *Laws passed by the Second Legislature of the State of Texas,* volume 2 (Houston: Printed at the Telegraph Office, 1848), pp. 132–134.

CHAPTER 9

IDEALS AND REALITIES FOR ANTEBELLUM WOMEN

HISTORICAL CONTEXT

Looking back over her girlhood in New England in the 1840s, Lucy Larcom declared,

> It was seldom said to little girls, as it always has been said to boys, that they ought to have some definite plan while they were children, what to be and do when they were grown up. There was usually but one path open before them, to become good wives and housekeepers. And the ambition of most girls was to follow their mothers' footsteps in this direction; a natural and laudable ambition.[1]

By the early nineteenth century, the role of the wife and housekeeper was indeed being upheld as the ideal one for middle-class women. Yet ideals and realities are not the same things. Larcom's mother ran a boardinghouse for young women who worked in textile mills, so Lucy knew firsthand many women who did not live within the domestic ideal.

Equally important, Larcom questioned the desirability of what some have called the "cult of true womanhood"—that cluster of beliefs that placed a woman in the home not only for domestic duties but also as the moral center and spiritual font of family values. Larcom recalled that she had sometimes been encouraged to develop her talents and learn to be a useful citizen: "Girls, as well as boys must often have been conscious of their own peculiar capabilities—must have desired to cultivate and make use of their individual powers."

Larcom's thoughts on her own girlhood addressed problems that many American women experienced. The nineteenth century was an era of changing identities, and the "proper" roles of men and women were not always clear. Gender identity—how we define what it means to be a man or a woman—was very much influenced by the economy. By the 1830s and 1840s, many farms in the soil-poor Northeast failed, as new markets for agricultural goods opened up and as the vast lands of the South and the Midwest produced unprecedented quantities of staple crops. Moreover, in the eastern cities, the old artisanal method of manufacture—a household-based economy that gave a productive role to women and children—was being replaced. The increased division of labor under capitalism brought new factories and the wage-labor system. While farms and artisanal shops were highly patriarchal (i.e., men were given the dominant role as authority figures and decision makers), they also made labor a family-centered activity. The new, more specialized system that gradually replaced the old tended to disperse family members: children at school, men at the job, and women in the home. Production became divorced from the household. In other words, the old economic function of the family declined, and the middle-class family became more the center for fulfilling domestic and emotional needs, such as cooking, education, spiritual uplift, and religious instruction

This new division of roles within the family presented dilemmas for the middle-class American woman. She could simply accept the domestic tasks of homemaker, mother, and spiritual guide. Certainly, it was flattering to be told that homemaking was the godliest of occupations, the most elevating for humankind. Ironically, the women who wrote in this vein, women like writer-reformer Catherine Beecher, were themselves stepping out of the private household to enter the public world of work and commerce. After all, it was fine to argue that raising good children and providing a haven for one's husband were the noblest of tasks, but money, power, and status were all to be found outside the home.

POPPING THE QUESTION.

Image 9.1 A picture of love, courtship, and marriage.

Popular lithographs such as these (Images 9.1 and 9.2) sentimentalized the female experience. Do you see any similarities with modern popular depictions of love, marriage and motherhood?

Source: "Popping the Question" (Sarony & Major, lithographers, c. 1846), Courtesy of Library of Congress.

For other women, however, the cult of domesticity was a luxury. Some continued to work on farms, where the sheer labor of milking, harvesting, preserving, churning, and sewing, not to mention daily cooking, cleaning, and nursing, left little time for pure moral uplift. Other women— young, unmarried, widowed, immigrant, some abandoned by their husbands, some with elderly parents—needed to earn a living, and many of these worked either as domestic servants in others' homes or as operatives in new factories like the Lowell textile mills in Massachusetts. Perhaps some of these women would have enjoyed the luxury of staying home as a wife and mother, but many clearly welcomed the chance to go out into the world. Nevertheless, domestic labor was demeaning, and work in the mills required long hours at low pay. Both were subject to the vagaries of the marketplace, including wage

Image 9.2 The ideal of motherhood.

Source: "The Happy Mother" (Sarony and Major, lithographers, c. 1846). Courtesy of the Library of Congress.

cuts and unemployment, and both quickly became stigmatized as lower-class occupations. The domestic ideal could be suffocating, but as a middle-class role, it promised higher social status than that afforded to working-class women.

Other middle-class women, a small but articulate group, rejected the domestic ideal outright. Some of them went so far as to draw parallels between their own situation and that of slaves. Sarah and Angelina Grimké, for example, sisters from South Carolina, noted that neither women nor slaves could vote or hold property; both had a limited public voice, and were restricted from positions of power and prestige. For white women like Lucy Larcom, who were given at least a rudimentary education and who were encouraged to lead useful lives, the cult of domesticity could be a trap. But at the most extreme, African-American women experienced how the oppression of both slavery and gender reinforced each other.

Many American women hated the lack of occupational outlets for their talents and loathed appearing submissive to men in public; home, the moral center of the universe, stifled them. But the alleged moral superiority of women—an idea supported by the spread of evangelical religion documented in Chapter 6—cut two ways, becoming a bulwark of activism. Women's spirituality could be expressed not just at home or in church but also in organizations that went out into the world to change it and spread benevolence. Thus, in the powerful reform movements of the antebellum era—antislavery, temperance, missionary work, education, and others—women founded organizations, proselytized, and assumed active public roles.

During these years, middle-class women gained a bit more control of their lives in two other ways. First, after about 1800, educational opportunities for girls expanded significantly, a function of mothers' desire to raise educated children to support the new republic. The proliferation of female schools—from small home-based classrooms to large and enduring seminaries—exposed young women to a range of topics, including not only traditional skills of needlework but also new subjects such as geography and botany. Second, throughout the nineteenth century, the birthrate declined, and it is clear that, by the 1840s, this decline was due in part to the deliberate practice of birth control. Smaller families gave women some freedom from the drudgery of daily home life. This was also an era that saw the decline of arranged marriages (in which parents worked out nuptial agreements for their children, often for economic motives) and the growing presence of the idea of romantic love, of choosing one's mate solely on the basis of personal attraction and emotional compatibility. Once again, this new way of arranging marriages gave women far more control of their lives than they had had under the older, more purely patriarchal ways.

The following documents capture much of the variety in women's identities around the middle of the nineteenth century, ranging from ringing endorsements of the cult of true womanhood to a feminist declaration of independence. However, it is probably best not to think of antebellum women as fitting into a single category, such as worker, mother, or activist. There was considerable ambivalence and overlap in roles and ideals. Some young mill workers probably longed for a cottage and a family as far from factories as possible; overburdened mothers fantasized about leaving home to seek their independence; promoters of the domestic ideal sought public acclaim; and feminists sometimes made demands for women's empowerment based on a highly gendered notion of inherent female moral superiority. This was an era of new possibilities, old expectations, and confusing goals and ideals.

INTRODUCTION TO DOCUMENTS 1, 2, AND 3

The antebellum decades witnessed a new awareness of women's place in American society, reflected in a growing literature written by and for women about their proper roles as wives and mothers. There was no shortage of advice about how women ought to act throughout their lives, which of course continues today. Lydia Maria Child, a highly educated reformer and activist who became a bestselling author at the age of twenty-two, wrote one such treatise, *The Mother's Book* (1831), while she was in her late twenties. Though she never became a parent, her book gave detailed advice on marriage and child rearing. Document 1 is a passage from *The Mother's Book* in which she focuses on adolescence and marriage. Document 2 is taken from A J. Graves's *Women in America* (1843), which argued from scripture that a woman's place was in the home. Compare Graves's understanding of women's "natural" place with that of the ladies of Steubenville in Chapter 7, who believed that female qualities obliged them to protect the weak in the era of Indian Removal.

Like Child, Catharine Beecher belonged to the first generation of formally schooled women in America. Her advice book, *Treatise on Domestic Economy for Young Ladies at Home and at School* (1847), argued for the domestic ideal, declaring that woman's subordination to man in the world of politics and work sheltered her and enabled her to perform the task of moral uplift. Document 3, "The Peculiar Responsibilities of American Women," is taken from Chapter 1. Beecher was a member of one of the most illustrious families of the nineteenth century, which included her father, the Reverend Lyman Beecher; her brother, the Reverend Henry Ward Beecher; and her sister, Harriet Beecher (Stowe), author of *Uncle Tom's Cabin*. As you read, ask how these women conceived of relations between the sexes. Beecher, for instance, argues that in America, women are equal to men, yet also insists on a degree of subordination. How, then, does she define "equality?"

---

1. ON THE DANGERS OF ADOLESCENCE: *THE MOTHER'S BOOK* (1831)

LYDIA MARIA CHILD

. . . The period from twelve to sixteen years of age is extremely critical in the formation of character, particularly with regard to daughters. The imagination is then all alive, and the affections are in full vigor, while the judgement is unstrengthened by observation, and enthusiasm has never learned moderation of experience. During this important period, a mother cannot be too watchful. As much as possible, she should keep a daughter *under her own eye*; and, above all things, she should encourage *entire confidence towards herself.* This can be done by a ready sympathy with youthful feelings, and by avoiding all unnecessary restraint and harshness.

. . . There is one subject, on which I am very anxious to say a great deal; but on which, for obvious reasons, I can say very little. Judging by my own observation, I believe it to be the greatest evil now existing in education. I mean the want of confidence between mothers and daughters on delicate subjects. Children, from books, and from their own observation, soon have their curiosity excited on such subjects; this is perfectly natural and innocent,

and if frankly met by a mother, it would never do harm. But on these occasions it is customary either to put young people off with lies, or still further to excite their curiosity by mystery and embarrassment. Information being refused them at the only proper source, they immediately have recourse to domestics, or immodest school-companions; and very often their young minds are polluted with filthy anecdotes of vice and vulgarity. This ought not to be. Mothers are the only proper persons to convey such knowledge to a child's mind. . . . A girl who receives her first ideas on these subjects from the shameless stories and indecent jokes of vulgar associates, has in fact prostituted her mind by familiarity with vice. . . . It is a bad plan for young girls to sleep with nursery maids, unless you have the utmost confidence in the good principles and modesty of your domestics. There is a strong love among vulgar people of telling secrets, and talking on forbidden subjects.

. . . There is no subject connected with education which has so important a bearing on human happiness as the views young people are taught to entertain with regard to matrimonial connexions. The dreams of silly romance, half vanity, and half passion, on the one hand, and selfish calculation on the other, leave but precious little of just thinking and right feeling on the subject. The greatest and most prevailing error in education consists in making lovers a subject of such engrossing and disproportionate interest in the minds of young girls. As soon as they can walk along, they are called "little sweet-heart," and "little wife"; as they grow older, the boyish liking of a neighbor, or school-mate, becomes a favorite jest; they often hear it said how lucky such and such people are, because they "*married off*" all their family so young; and when a pretty, attractive girl is mentioned, they are in the habit of hearing it observed, "She will be married young. She is too handsome and too interesting to live single long." But heedless vanity and silly romance, though a prolific source of unhappy marriages, are not so disastrous in their effects as worldly ambition, and selfish calculation. I never knew a marriage expressly for money, that did not end unhappily.[2]

2. WOMEN IN AMERICA (1843)

A. J. GRAVES

Our chief aim throughout these pages is to prove that [women's] domestic duties have a paramount claim over everything else upon her attention—that *home* is her appropriate sphere of action; and that whenever she neglects these duties, or goes out of this sphere of action to mingle in any of the great public movements of the day, she is deserting the station which God and nature have assigned to her. She can operate far more efficiently in promoting the great interests of humanity by supervising her own household than in any other way. Home, if we may so speak, is the cradle of the human race; and it is here the human character is fashioned either for good or for evil. It is the "nursery of the future man and of the undying spirit"; and woman is the nurse and the educator. Over infancy she has almost unlimited sway; and in maturer years she may powerfully counteract the evil influences of the world by the talisman of her strong, enduring love, by her devotedness to those intrusted to her charge, and by those lessons of virtue and of wisdom which are not of the world. . . .

That woman should regard home as her appropriate domain is not only the dictate of religion, but of enlightened human reason. Well-ordered families are the chief security for the permanent peace and prosperity of the state, and such families must be trained up by enlightened female influence acting within its legitimate sphere. . . .

Let man, then, retain his proud supremacy in the world's dominion; let him inscribe his name upon its high places, and be the leader of the congregated masses of his fellow-men, with all their excitements, their agitations, and their powerful concentration of effort; but these things belong not to woman. She best consults her happiness, best maintains her dignity, and best fulfils the great object of her being, by keeping alive the sacred flame of piety, patriotism, and universal love to man, upon the domestic altar; and by drawing worshippers around it, to send them forth from thence better citizens, and purer and holier men. . . .

. . . Then, when our husbands and our sons go forth into the busy and turbulent world, we may feel secure that they will walk unhurt amid its snares and temptations. Their hearts will be at home, where their treasure is; and they will rejoice to return to its sanctuary of rest, there to refresh their wearied spirits, and renew their strength for the toils and conflicts of life.[3]

3. FROM *TREATISE ON DOMESTIC ECONOMY FOR YOUNG LADIES* (1847)

CATHARINE BEECHER

. . . There must be the magistrate and the subject, one of whom is the superior, and the other the inferior. There must be the relations of husband and wife, parent and child, teacher and pupil, employer and employed, each involving the relative duties of subordination. The superior, in certain particulars, is to direct, and the inferior is to yield obedience. Society could never go forward, harmoniously, nor could any craft or profession be successfully pursued, unless these superior and subordinate relations be instituted and sustained.

But who shall take the higher, and who the subordinate, stations in social and civil life? This matter, in the case of parents and children, is decided by the Creator. He has given children to the control of parents, as their superiors, and to them they remain subordinate, to a certain age, or so long as they are members of their household. And parents can delegate such a portion of their authority to teachers and employers, as the interests of their children require.

In most other cases, in a truly democratic state, each individual is allowed to choose for himself, who shall take the position of his superior. No woman is forced to obey any husband but the one she chooses for herself; nor is she obliged to take a husband, if she prefers to remain single. So every domestic, and every artisan or laborer, after passing from parental control, can choose the employer to whom he is to accord obedience, or, if he prefers to relinquish certain advantages, he can remain without taking a subordinate place to any employer.

And the various privileges that wealth secures, are equally open to all classes. Every man may aim at riches, unimpeded by any law or institution which secures peculiar privileges to a favored class, at the expense of another. Every law, and every institution,

is tested by examining whether it secures equal advantages to all; and, if the people become convinced that any regulation sacrifices the good of the majority to the interests of the smaller number, they have power to abolish it. . . .

It appears, then, that it is in America, alone, that women are raised to an equality with the other sex; and that, both in theory and practice, their interests are regarded as of equal value. They are made subordinate in station, only where a regard to their best interests demands it, while, as if in compensation for this, by custom and courtesy, they are always treated as superiors. Universally, in this Country, through every class of society, precedence is given to woman, in all the comforts, conveniences, and courtesies, of life.

In civil and political affairs, American women take no interest or concern, except so far as they sympathize with their family and personal friends; but in all cases, in which they do feel a concern, their opinions and feelings have a consideration, equal, or even superior, to that of the other sex.

In matters pertaining to the education of their children, in the selection and support of a clergyman, in all benevolent enterprises, and in all questions relating to morals or manners, they have a superior influence. In such concerns, it would be impossible to carry a point, contrary to their judgement and feelings; while an enterprise, sustained by them, will seldom fail of success.

If those who are bewailing themselves over the fancied wrongs and injuries of women in this Nation, could only see things as they are, they would know, that, whatever remnants of a barbarous or aristocratic age may remain in our civil institutions, in reference to the interests of women, it is only because they are ignorant of them, or do not use their influence to have them rectified; for it is very certain that there is nothing reasonable, which American women would unite in asking, that would not readily be bestowed. . . .

There is such a disproportion between those who wish to hire, and those who are willing to go to domestic service, that, in the non-slaveholding States were it not for the supply of poverty-stricken foreigners there would not be a domestic for each family who demands one. And this resort to foreigners, poor as it is, scarcely meets the demand . . . .

The difficulties and sufferings, which have accrued to American women, from this cause, are almost incalculable. There is nothing, which so much demands system and regularity, as the affairs of a housekeeper, made up, as they are, of ten thousand desultory and minute items; and yet, this perpetually fluctuating state of society seems forever to bar any such system and regularity. The anxieties, vexations, perplexities, and even hard labor, which come upon American women, from this state of domestic service, are endless; and many a woman has, in consequence, been disheartened, discouraged, and ruined in health. . . .[4]

Image 9.3 The Life and Age of Woman.

Vernacular renderings of male and female stages of life date back to the medieval era, and were quite popular by the 1830s. What does this image tell you about contemporary views of gender and aging?

Source: James S. Baille, c. 1848. Library of Congress.

INTRODUCTION TO DOCUMENT 4

Among middle-class women, the views of Child, Graves, and Beecher quickly gained adherents; indeed, such women expressed ideas that others had felt earlier, even if they did not fully articulate them. But there were powerful alternative views. Sarah Grimké was the daughter of a South Carolina slaveholder. Like Graves, she relied on the Bible as her authority, but she reached very different conclusions. For women, as for African slaves, the main question was one of freedom, according to Grimké. In this letter to her sister Angelina, she examined a range of issues, from unequal pay through the nature of housekeeping duties.

4. "THE BONDS OF WOMANHOOD"

SARAH M. GRIMKÉ

BROOKLINE, MA 1837

My Dear Sister,

During the early part of my life, my lot was cast among the butterflies of the *fashionable* world; and of this class of women, I am constrained to say, both from experience and observation, that their education is miserably deficient; that they are taught to regard marriage as the one thing needful, the only avenue to distinction; hence to attract the notice and win the attentions of men, by their external charms, is the chief business of fashionable girls. They seldom think that men will be allured by intellectual acquirements, because they find, that where any mental superiority exists, a woman is generally shunned and regarded as stepping out of her "appropriate sphere," which, in their view, is to dress, to dance, to set out to the best possible advantage her person, to read the novels which inundate the press, and which do more to destroy her character as a rational creature, then any thing else. Fashionable women regard themselves, and are regarded by men, as pretty toys or as mere instruments of pleasure; and the vacuity of mind, the heartlessness, the frivolity which is the necessary result of this false and debasing estimate of women, can only be fully understood by those who have mingled in the folly and wickedness of fashionable life; and who have been called from

such pursuits by the voice of the Lord Jesus, inviting their weary and heavy laden souls to come unto Him and learn of Him, that they may find something worthy of their immortal spirit, and their intellectual powers; that they may learn the high and holy purposes of their creation, and consecrate themselves unto the service of God; and not, as is now the case, to the pleasure of man.

. . . To be married is too often held up to the view of girls as the sine qua non of human happiness and human existence. For this purpose more than for any other, I verily believe the majority of girls are trained. This is demonstrated by the imperfect education which is bestowed upon them, and the little pains taken to cultivate their minds, after they leave school, by the little time allowed them for reading, and by the idea being constantly inculcated, that although all household concerns should be attended to with scrupulous punctuality at particular seasons, the improvement of their intellectual capacities is only a secondary consideration, and may serve as an occupation to fill up the odds and ends of time. In most families, it is considered a matter of far more consequence to call a girl off from making a pie, or a pudding, than to interrupt her whilst engaged in her studies. This mode of training necessarily exalts, in their view, the animal above the intellectual and spiritual nature, and teaches women to regard themselves as a kind of machinery, necessary to keep the domestic engine in order, but of little value as the *intelligent* companions of men.

Let no one think, from these remarks, that I regard a knowledge of housewifery as beneath the acquisition of women. Far from it: I believe that a complete knowledge of household affairs is an indispensable requisite in a woman's education,—that by the mistress of a family, whether married or single, doing her duty thoroughly and *understandingly*, the happiness of the family is increased to an incalculable degree, as well as a vast amount of time and money saved. All I complain of is, that our education consists so almost exclusively in culinary and other manual operations. I do long to see the time, when it will no longer be necessary for women to expend so many precious hours in furnishing "a well spread table," but that their husbands will forego some of their accustomed indulgences in this way, and encourage their wives to devote some portion of their time to mental cultivation, even at the expense of having to dine sometimes on baked potatoes, or bread and butter. . . .

There is another way in which the general opinion, that women are inferior to men, is manifested, that bears with tremendous effect on the laboring class, and indeed on almost all who are obliged to earn a subsistence, whether it be by mental or physical exertion—I allude to the disproportionate value set on the time and labor of men and of women. A man who is engaged in teaching, can always, I believe, command a higher price for tuition than a woman—even when he teaches the same branches, and is not in any respect superior to the women. This I know is the case in boarding and other schools with which I have been acquainted, and it is so in every occupation in which the sexes engage indiscriminately. As for example, in tailoring, a man has twice, or three times as much for making a waistcoat or pantaloons as a woman, although the work done by each may be equally good. In those employments which are peculiar to women, their time is estimated at only half the value of that of men. . . . All these things evince the low estimation in which woman is held. . . .

There is another class of women in this country, to whom I cannot refer, without feelings of the deepest shame and sorrow. I allude to our female slaves. Our southern cities are whelmed beneath a tide of pollution; the virtue of female slaves is wholly at the mercy of irresponsible tyrants, and women are bought and sold in our slave markets, to gratify the brutal lust of those who bear the name of Christians. In our slave States, if amid all her degradation and ignorance, a woman desires to preserve her virtue unsullied, she is either bribed or whipped into compliance, or if she dares resist her seducer, her life by the laws of some of the slave States may be, and has actually been sacrificed to the fury of disappointed passion. Where such laws do not exist, the power which is necessarily vested in the master over his property, leaves the defenceless slave entirely at his mercy, and the sufferings of some females on this account, both physical and mental, are intense. . . . In Christian America, the slave has no refuge from unbridled cruelty and lust.

. . . Nor does the colored woman suffer alone: the moral purity of the white woman is deeply contaminated. In the daily habit of seeing the virtue of her enslaved sister sacrificed without hesitancy or remorse, she looks upon the crimes of seduction and illicit intercourse without horror, and although not personally involved in the guilt, she loses that value for innocence in her own, as well as the other sex, which is one of the strongest safeguards to virtue. She lives in habitual intercourse with men, whom she knows to be polluted by licentiousness, and often is she compelled to witness in her own domestic circle, those disgusting and heart-sickening jealousies and strifes which disgraced and distracted the family of Abraham. In addition to all this, the female slaves suffer every species of degradation and cruelty, which the most wanton barbarity can inflict; they are indecently divested of their clothing, sometimes tied up and severely whipped, sometimes prostrated on the earth, while their naked bodies are torn by the scorpion lash. . . . Can any American woman look at these scenes of shocking licentiousness and cruelty, and fold her hands in apathy, and say, "I have nothing to do with slavery"? *She cannot and be guiltless.*

I cannot close this letter, without saying a few words on the benefits to be derived by men, as well as women, from the opinions I advocate relative to the equality of the sexes. Many women are now supported, in idleness and extravagance, by the industry of their husbands, fathers, or brothers, who are compelled to toil out their existence, at the counting house, or in the printing office, or some other laborious occupation, while the wife and daughters and sisters take no part in the support of the family, and appear to think that their sole business is to spend the hard bought earnings of their male friends. I deeply regret such a state of things, because I believe that if women felt their responsibility, for the support of themselves, or their families it would add strength and dignity to their characters, and teach them more true sympathy for their husbands, than is now generally manifested,—a sympathy which would be exhibited by actions as well as words. Our brethren may reject my doctrine, because it runs counter to common opinions, and because it wounds their pride; but I believe they would be "partakers of the benefit" resulting from the Equality of the Sexes, and would find that woman, as their equal, was unspeakably more valuable than woman as their inferior, both as a moral and an intellectual being.

Thine in the bonds of womanhood,
Sarah M. Grimké[5]

INTRODUCTION TO DOCUMENT 5

The following document was written by one of those whom Grimké worried most about, female slaves. Harriet Jacobs was born into slavery in Edenton, North Carolina, in 1813. The events described in this passage took place around 1830. Jacobs's life was filled with drama. Unrelenting sexual exploitation finally drove her into hiding. For seven years, a black family sheltered her in a tiny crawl space of their home until Harriet was able to escape to New York City in 1842. Finally, she was reunited with her two children. Though on the face of it Jacobs's life was radically different from those of middle-class white women printed here, do you see any common experiences and concerns? Note that Harriet Jacobs wrote under the pseudonym Linda Brent and that Lydia Maria Child helped edit the manuscript for publication.

5. FROM *INCIDENTS IN THE LIFE OF A SLAVE GIRL* (1861)

HARRIET JACOBS

. . . I now entered on my fifteenth year—a sad epoch in the life of a slave girl. My master began to whisper foul words in my ear. Young as I was, I could not remain ignorant of their import. I tried to treat them with indifference or contempt. The master's age, my extreme youth, and the fear that his conduct would be reported to my grandmother, made him bear this treatment for many months. He was a crafty man, and resorted to many means to accomplish his purposes. Sometimes he had stormy, terrific ways, that made his victims tremble; sometimes he assumed a gentleness that he thought must surely subdue. Of the two, I preferred his stormy moods, although they left me trembling. He tried his utmost to corrupt the pure principles my grandmother had instilled. He peopled my young mind with unclean images, such as only a vile monster could think of. I turned from him with disgust and hatred. But he was my master. I was compelled to live under the same roof with him—where I saw a man forty years my senior daily violating the most sacred commandments of nature. He told me I was his property; that I must be subject to his will in all things. My soul revolted against the mean tyranny. But where could I turn for protection? No matter whether the slave girl be as black as ebony or as fair as her mistress. In either case, there is no shadow of law to protect her from insult, from violence, or even from death; all these are inflicted by fiends who bear the shape of men. The mistress, who ought to protect the helpless victim, has no other feelings towards her but those of jealousy and rage. . . .

I had entered my sixteenth year, and every day it became more apparent that my presence was intolerable to Mrs. Flint [the wife of Harriet Jacobs's owner]. Angry words frequently passed between her and her husband. He had never punished me himself, and he would not allow anybody else to punish me. In that respect, she was never satisfied; but, in her angry moods, no terms were too vile for her to bestow upon me. Yet I, whom she detested so bitterly, had far more pity for her than he had, whose duty it was to make her life happy. I never wronged her, or wished to wrong her; and one word of kindness from her would have brought me to her feet.

After repeated quarrels between the doctor and his wife, he announced his intention to take his youngest daughter, then four years old, to sleep in his apartment. It was necessary that a servant should sleep in the same room, to be on hand if the child stirred. I was selected for that office, and informed for what purpose that arrangement had been made. By managing to keep within sight of people, as much as possible, during the day time, I had hitherto succeeded in eluding my master, though a razor was often held to my throat to force me to change this line of policy. At night I slept by the side of my great aunt, where I felt safe. He was too prudent to come into her room. She was an old woman, and had been in the family many years. Moreover, as a married man, and a professional man [a doctor], he deemed it necessary to save appearances in some degree. But he resolved to remove the obstacle in the way of his scheme; and he thought he had planned it so that he should evade suspicion. He was well aware how much I prized my refuge by the side of my old aunt, and he determined to dispossess me of it. The first night the doctor had the little child in his room alone. The next morning, I was ordered to take my station as nurse the following night. A kind Providence interposed in my favor. During the day Mrs. Flint heard of this new arrangement and a storm followed. I rejoiced to hear it rage. . . .

The secrets of slavery are concealed like those of the Inquisition. My master was, to my knowledge, the father of eleven slaves. But did the mothers dare to tell who was the father of their children? Did the other slaves dare to allude to it, except in whispers among themselves? No, indeed! They knew too well the terrible consequences. . . .

Dr. Flint contrived a new plan. He seemed to have an idea that my fear of my mistress was his greatest obstacle. In the blandest tones, he told me that he was going to build a small house for me, in a secluded place, four miles away from the town. . . . When my master said he was going to build a house for me, and that he could do it with little trouble and expense, I was in hopes something would happen to frustrate his scheme; but I soon heard that the house was actually begun. I vowed before my Maker that I would never enter it. I had rather toil on the plantation from dawn till dark; I had rather live and die in jail, than drag on, from day to day, through such a living death. I was determined that the master, whom I so hated and loathed, who had blighted the prospects of my youth, and made my life a desert, should not, after my long struggle with him, succeed at last in trampling his victim under his feet. I would do any thing, every thing, for the sake of defeating him. What *could* I do? I thought and thought, till I became desperate, and made a plunge into the abyss.

And now, reader, I come to a period in my unhappy life, which I would gladly forget if I could. The remembrance fills me with sorrow and shame. . . . The influences of slavery had had the same effect on me that they had on other young girls; they had made me prematurely knowing, concerning the evil ways of the world. I knew what I did, and I did it with deliberate calculation.

But, O, ye happy women, whose purity has been sheltered from childhood, who have been free to choose the objects of your affection, whose homes are protected by law, do not judge the poor desolate slave girl too severely! If slavery had been abolished, I also, could have married the man of my choice; I could have had a home shielded by the laws; and I should have been spared the painful task of confessing what I am now about to relate; but all my prospects had been blighted by slavery. I wanted to keep myself pure; and, under the most adverse circumstances, I tried hard to preserve my self-respect; but I was struggling alone in the powerful grasp of the demon Slavery; and the monster proved too strong for me. I felt as if I was forsaken by God and man; as if all my efforts must be frustrated; and I became reckless in my despair.

I have told you that Dr. Flint's persecutions and his wife's jealousy had given rise to some gossip in the neighborhood. Among others, it chanced that a white unmarried gentleman had obtained some knowledge of the circumstances in which I was placed. He knew my grandmother, and often spoke to me in the street. He became interested for me, and asked questions about my master, which I answered in part. He expressed a great deal of sympathy, and a wish to aid me. He constantly sought opportunities to see me, and wrote to me frequently. I was a poor slave girl, only fifteen years old.

So much attention from a superior person was, of course, flattering; for human nature is the same in all. I also felt grateful for his sympathy, and encouraged by his kind words. It seemed to me a great thing to have such a friend. By degrees, a more tender feeling crept into my heart. He was an educated and eloquent gentleman; too eloquent, alas, for the poor slave girl who trusted in him. Of course I saw whither all this was tending. I knew the impassable gulf between us; but to be an object of interest to a man who is not married, and who is not her master, is agreeable to the pride and feelings of a slave, if her miserable situation has left her any pride or sentiment. It seems less degrading to give one's self, than to submit to compulsion. There is something akin to freedom in having a lover who has no control over you, except that which he gains by kindness and attachment. A master may treat you as rudely as he pleases, and you dare not speak; moreover, the wrong does not seem so great with an unmarried man, as with one who has a wife to be made unhappy. There may be sophistry in all this; but the condition of a slave confuses all principles of morality, and, in fact, renders the practice of them impossible. . . .

As for Dr. Flint, I had a feeling of satisfaction and triumph in the thought of telling *him*. From time to time he told me of his intended arrangements, and I was silent. At last, he came and told me the cottage was completed, and ordered me to go to it. I told him I would never enter it. He said, "I have heard enough of such talk as that. You shall go, if you are carried by force; and you shall remain there."

I replied, "I will never go there. In a few months I shall be a mother."

He stood and looked at me in dumb amazement, and left the house without a word. I thought I should be happy in my triumph over him. But now that the truth was out, and my relatives would hear of it, I felt wretched. Humble as were their circumstances, they had pride in my good character. Now, how could I look them in the face? My self-respect was gone! I had resolved that I would be virtuous, though I was a slave. I had said, "Let the storm beat! I will brave it till I die." And now, how humiliated I felt![6]

INTRODUCTION TO DOCUMENT 6

In 1848, ten years after Sarah Grimké wrote her letter to her sister, almost twenty years after Harriet Jacobs's torment at the hands of Dr. Flint, several women and a few men met in Seneca Falls, New York, and drew up their "Declaration of Sentiments," a women's Declaration of Independence addressing a whole range of legal and customary inequalities that they wanted changed. Which of the authors in this chapter might have been sympathetic to such a statement?

6. DECLARATION OF SENTIMENTS (1848)

WOMAN'S RIGHTS CONVENTION, SENECA FALLS, NEW YORK, JULY 1848

When, in the course of human events, it becomes necessary for one portion of the family of man to assume among the people of the earth a position different from that which they have hitherto occupied, but one to which the laws of nature and of nature's God entitle them, a decent respect to the opinions of mankind requires that they should declare the causes that impel them to such a course.

We hold these truths to be self-evident: that all men and women are created equal; that they are endowed by their Creator with certain inalienable rights; that among these are life, liberty, and the pursuit of happiness; that to secure these rights governments are instituted, deriving their just powers from the consent of the governed. Whenever any form of government becomes destructive of these ends, it is the right of those who suffer from it to refuse allegiance to it, and to insist upon the institution of a new government, laying its foundation on such principles, and organizing its powers in such form, as to them shall seem most likely to effect their safety and happiness. Prudence, indeed, will dictate that governments long established should not be changed for light and transient causes; and accordingly all experience hath shown that mankind are more disposed to suffer, while evils are sufferable, than to right themselves by abolishing the forms to which they were accustomed. But when a long train of abuses and usurpations, pursuing invariably the same object evinces a design to reduce them under absolute despotism, it is their duty to throw off such government, and to provide new guards for their future security. Such has been the patient sufferance of the women under this government, and such is now the necessity which constrains them to demand the equal station to which they are entitled.

The history of mankind is a history of repeated injuries and usurpations on the part of man toward woman, having in direct object the establishment of an absolute tyranny over her. To prove this, let facts be submitted to a candid world.

He has never permitted her to exercise her inalienable right to the elective franchise.

He has compelled her to submit to laws, in the formation of which she had no voice.

He has withheld from her rights which are given to the most ignorant and degraded men –both natives and foreigners.

Having deprived her of this first right of a citizen, the elective franchise, thereby leaving her without representation in the halls of legislation, he has oppressed her on all sides.

He has made her, if married, in the eye of the law, civilly dead.

He has made her, morally, an irresponsible being, as she can commit many crimes with impunity, provided they be done in the presence of her husband. In the covenant of marriage, she is compelled to promise obedience to her husband, he becoming, to all intents and purposes, her master—the law giving him power to deprive her of her liberty, and to administer chastisement.

He has so framed the laws of divorce, as to what shall be the proper causes, and in case of separation, to whom the guardianship of the children shall be given, as to be wholly regardless of the happiness of women—the law, in all cases, going upon a false supposition of the supremacy of man, and giving all power into his hands.

After depriving her of all rights as a married woman, if single, and the owner of property, he has taxed her to support a government which recognizes her only when her property can be made profitable to it.

He has monopolized nearly all the profitable employments, and from those she is permitted to follow, she receives but a scanty remuneration. He closes against her all the avenues to wealth and distinction which he considers most honorable to himself. As a teacher of theology, medicine, or law, she is not known.

He has denied her the facilities for obtaining a thorough education, all colleges being closed against her.

He allows her in Church, as well as State, but a subordinate position, claiming Apostolic authority for her exclusion from the ministry, and, with some exceptions, from any public participation in the affairs of the Church.

He has created a false public sentiment by giving to the world a different code of morals for men and women, by which moral delinquencies which exclude women from society, are not only tolerated, but deemed of little account in man.

He has usurped the prerogative of Jehovah himself, claiming it as his right to assign for her a sphere of action, when that belongs to her conscience and to her God.

He has endeavored, in every way that he could, to destroy her confidence in her own powers, to lessen her self-respect, and to make her willing to lead a dependent and abject life.

Now, in view of this entire disfranchisement of one-half the people of this country, their social and religious degradation—in view of the unjust laws above mentioned, and because women do feel themselves aggrieved, oppressed, and fraudulently deprived of their most sacred rights, we insist that they have immediate admission to all the rights and privileges which belong to them as citizens of the United States.

In entering upon the great work before us, we anticipate no small amount of misconception, misrepresentation, and ridicule; but we shall use every instrumentality within our power to effect our object. We shall employ agents, circulate tracts, petition the State and National legislatures, and endeavor to enlist the pulpit and the press in our behalf. We hope this Convention will be followed by a series of Conventions embracing every part of the country.[7]

INTRODUCTION TO DOCUMENT 7

Lucy Larcom's life changed dramatically when her father passed away. Financial pressure caused her mother to open up a boardinghouse for "girls" (many were in their twenties and thirties) who worked in the textile mills. Young Lucy alternated between school and the mills, but her intelligence and curiosity made her long for something more, a longing that most working-class people rarely got the chance to fulfill. Document 7 is her description of going to work in the textile mills in 1835, at the age of eleven. Larcom wrote her memoir more than fifty years after the events she describes here.

7. A NEW ENGLAND GIRLHOOD

LUCY LARCOM

During my father's life, a few years before my birth, his thoughts had been turned towards the new manufacturing town growing up on the banks of the Merrimack. He had once taken a journey there, with the possibility in his mind of making the place his home, his limited income furnishing no adequate promise of a maintenance for his large family of daughters. From the beginning, Lowell had a high reputation for good order, morality, piety, and all that was dear to the old-fashioned New Englander's heart.

After his death, my mother's thoughts naturally followed the direction his had taken; and seeing no other opening for herself, she sold her small estate, and moved to Lowell, with the intention of taking a corporation-house for mill-girl boarders. Some of the family objected, for the Old World traditions about factory life were anything but attractive; and they were current in New England until the experiment at Lowell had shown that independent and intelligent workers invariably give their own character to their occupation. My mother had visited Lowell, and she was willing and glad, knowing all about the place, to make it our home.

The change involved a great deal of work. "Boarders" signified a large house, many beds, and an indefinite number of people. Such piles of sewing accumulated before us! A sewing-bee, volunteered by the neighbors, reduced the quantity a little, and our child-fingers had to take their part. But the seams of those sheets did look to me as if they were miles long! . . .

Our house was quickly filled with a large feminine family. As a child, the gulf between little girlhood and young womanhood had always looked to me very wide. I supposed we should get across it by some sudden jump, by and by. But among these new companions of all ages, from fifteen to thirty years, we slipped into womanhood without knowing when or how.

Most of my mother's boarders were from New Hampshire and Vermont, and there was a fresh, breezy sociability about them which made them seem almost like a different race of beings from any we children had hitherto known.

We helped a little about the housework, before and after school, making beds, trimming lamps, and washing dishes. The heaviest work was done by a strong Irish girl, my mother always attending to the cooking herself. She was, however, a better caterer than the circumstances required or permitted. She liked to make nice things for the table, and, having been accustomed to an abundant supply, could never learn to economize. At a dollar and a quarter a week for board (the price allowed for mill-girls by the corporations), great care in expenditure was necessary. It was not in my

mother's nature closely to calculate costs, and in this way there came to be a continually increasing leak in the family purse. The older members of the family did everything they could, but it was not enough. I heard it said one day, in a distressed tone, "The children will have to leave school and go into the mill."

There were many pros and cons between my mother and sisters before this was positively decided. The mill-agent did not want to take us two little girls, but consented on condition we should be sure to attend school the full number of months prescribed each year. I, the younger one, was then between eleven and twelve years old.

I listened to all that was said about it, very much fearing that I should not be permitted to do the coveted work. For the feeling had already frequently come to me, that I was the one too many in the over-crowded family nest. Once, before we left our old home, I had heard a neighbor condoling with my mother because there were so many of us, and her emphatic reply had been a great relief to my mind.—

"There isn't one more than I want. I could not spare a single one of my children."

But her difficulties were increasing, and I thought it would be a pleasure to feel that I was not a trouble or burden or expense to anybody. So I went to my first day's work in the mill with a light heart. The novelty of it made it seem easy, and it really was not hard, just to change the bobbins on the spinning-frames every three quarters of an hour or so, with half a dozen other little girls who were doing the same thing. When I came back at night, the family began to pity me for my long, tiresome day's work, but I laughed and said,—

"Why, it is nothing but fun. It is just like play."

And for a little while it was only a new amusement; I liked it better than going to school and "making believe" I was learning when I was not. And there was a great deal of play mixed with it. We were not occupied more than half the time. The intervals were spent frolicking around among the spinning-frames, teasing and talking to the older girls, or entertaining ourselves with games and stories in a corner, or exploring, with the overseer's permission, the mysteries of the carding-room, the dressing-room, and the weaving-room.

TIME TABLE OF THE LOWELL MILLS,

To take effect on and after Oct. 21st, 1851.

The Standard time being that of the meridian of Lowell, as shown by the regulator clock of JOSEPH RAYNES, 43 Central Street.

	From 1st to 10th inclusive.				From 11th to 20th inclusive.				From 21st to last day of month.			
	1st Bell	2d Bell	3d Bell	Eve. Bell	1st Bell	2d Bell	3d Bell	Eve. Bell	1st Bell	2d Bell	3d Bell	Eve. Bell
January,	5.00	6.00	6.50	*7.30	5.00	6 00	6.50	*7.30	5.00	6.00	6.50	*7.30
February,	4.30	5.30	6.40	*7.30	4.30	5.30	6.25	*7.30	4.30	5.30	6.15	*7.30
March,	5.40	6.00		*7.30	5.20	5.40		*7.30	5.05	5.25		6.35
April,	4.45	5.05		6.45	4.30	4.50		6.55	4.30	4.50		7.00
May,	4.30	4.50		7·00	4.30	4.50		7.00	4.30	4.50		7.00
June,	"	"		"	"	"		"	"	"		"
July,	"	"		"	"	"		"	"	"		"
August,	"	"		"	"	"		"	"	"		"
September,	4.40	5.00		6.45	4.50	5.10		6.30	5.00	5.20		*7.30
October,	5.10	5.30		*7.30	5.20	5.40		*7.30	5.35	5.55		*7.30
November,	4.30	5.30	6.10	*7.30	4.30	5.30	6.20	*7.30	5.00	6.00	6.35	*7.30
December,	5.00	6.00	6.45	*7.30	5.00	6.00	6.50	*7.30	5.00	6·00	6.50	*7.30

* Excepting on Saturdays from Sept. 21st to March 20th inclusive, when it is rung at 20 minutes after sunset.

YARD GATES,

Will be opened at ringing of last morning bell, of meal bells, and of evening bells; and kept open Ten minutes.

MILL GATES.

Commence hoisting Mill Gates, Two minutes before commencing work.

WORK COMMENCES;

At Ten minutes after last morning bell, and at Ten minutes after bell which "rings in" from Meals.

BREAKFAST BELLS.

During March "Ring out"........at....7.30 a. m.........."Ring in" at 8.05 a. m.
April 1st to Sept. 20th inclusive.....at....7 00 " " .... " " at 7.35 " "
Sept. 21st to Oct. 31st inclusive.....at....7.30 " " .... " " at 8.05 " "
Remainder of year work commences after Breakfast.

DINNER BELLS.

"Ring out"........................12.30 p. m........."Ring in".... 1.05 p. m.

In all cases, the *first* stroke of the bell is considered as marking the time.

B. H. Penhallow, Printer, 28 Merrimack Street.

Image 9.4 Timetable of the Lowell Mills, 1851

This timetable conveys the expectations placed on workers in the early industrial era. How would this emphasis on time discipline have affected them What does this table convey about life in the mills, and how does it compare with the images elsewhere in this chapter?

Source: Merrimack Valley Textile Museum [American Textile History Museum], Lowell, Mass.

I never cared much for machinery. The buzzing and hissing and whizzing of pulleys and rollers and spindles and flyers around me often grew tiresome. I could not see into their complications, or feel interested in them. But in a room below us we were sometimes allowed to peer in through a sort of blind door at the great water-wheel that carried the works of the whole mill. It was so huge that we could only watch a few of its spokes at a time, and part of its dripping rim, moving with a slow, measured strength through the darkness that shut it in. It impressed me with something of the awe which comes to us in thinking of the great Power which keeps the mechanism of the universe in motion.

There were compensations for being shut in to daily toil so early. The mill itself had its lessons for us. But it was not, and could not be, the right sort of life for a child, and we were happy in the knowledge that, at the longest, our employment was only to be temporary.

When I took my next three months at the grammar school, everything there was changed, and I too was changed. The teachers were kind, and thorough in their instruction; and my mind seemed to have been ploughed up during that year of work, so that knowledge took root in it easily. It was a great delight to me to study, and at the end of the three months the master told me that I was prepared for the high school.

But alas! I could not go. The little money I could earn—one dollar a week, besides the price of my board—was needed in the family, and I must return to the mill. It was a severe disappointment to me, though I did not say so at home. I did not at all accept the conclusion of a neighbor whom I heard talking about it with my mother. His daughter was going to the high school, and my mother was telling him how sorry she was that I could not.

"Oh," he said, in a soothing tone, "my girl hasn't got any such head-piece as yours has. Your girl doesn't need to go."

Of course I knew that whatever sort of a "head-piece" I had, I did need and want just that very opportunity to study. I think the resolution was then formed, inwardly, that I *would* go to school again, some time, whatever happened. I went back to my work, but now without enthusiasm. I had looked through an open door that I was not willing to see shut upon me.

I began to reflect upon life rather seriously for a girl of twelve or thirteen. What was I here for? What could I make of myself? Must I submit to be carried along with the current, and do just what everybody else did? No: I knew I should not do that, for there was a certain Myself who was always starting up with her own original plan or aspiration before me, and who was quite indifferent as to what people generally thought.

Well, I would find out what this Myself was good for, and that she should be![8]

INTRODUCTION TO DOCUMENT 8

The letters of Malenda Edwards to Sabrina Bennett and of Mary Paul to her father give us insight into the life and labor of American women. Mill workers usually worked from eleven to thirteen hours per day, beginning around sunrise; they received very short breaks for meals, and their pay was not only low but also unstable, as mills often cut wages in response to oversupply, slack demand, or a quest for greater profits. "Mill girl" letters reveal that many of them considered their labor temporary and that they expected to marry or return to their old farms or small towns. This sense of transiency blunted the efforts of workers to organize for better working conditions. Nevertheless, in 1845, hundreds of mill workers petitioned the Massachusetts legislature for a ten-hour day. They complained that poor sanitary conditions and long hours were destroying their health. Their request was not granted.

8. LETTERS FROM MALENDA EDWARDS AND MARY PAUL (1839–1848)

MALENDA EDWARDS

APRIL 4, 1839

Dear Sabrina,

. . . You have been informed I suppose that I am a factory girl and that I am at Nashua and I have wished you were here too but I suppose your mother would think it far beneith your dignity to be a factory girl. There are very many young Ladies at work in the factories that have given up milinary d[r]essmaking & s[c]hool keeping for to work in the mill. But I would not advise any one to do it for I was so sick of it at first I wished a factory had never been thought of. But the longer I stay the better I like and I think if nothing unforesene calls me away I shall stay here till fall. . . . If you should have any idea of working in the factory I will do the best I can to get you a place with us. We have an excelent boarding place. We board with a family with whome I was acquainted with when I lived at Haverhill. Pleas to write us soon and believe your affectionate Aunt

Bristol [N.H.] Aug 18, 1845
Dear Sabrina,

We received your letter sent by Mr Wells and I embrace the first opportunity to answer it and will now confess that I am a tremendous lazy corespondent at the best—and between my house work and da[i]ry spining weaving and raking hay I find but little time to write so I think I have appologised sifficiently for not writing you before this. I am very glad indeed you have been so kind to write us so often this summer for I am always glad to hear from absent friends if I cannot see them. I think it was a kind providence that directed my steps to Haverhill last winter for it is not likely that I shall visit you again so long as father and mother live if I should live for so long for they fail fast especially father. He has had quite a number of ill turns this summer and I have been physician and nurse too. Dont you think Sabrina it is well I have taken some lessons in the line of phisick? Mother is able to do but little this sumer [compared] to what she has been sumers

past. The warm wether overcomes her very much but we get a long first rate. I have got the most of my wool spun and two webs wove and at the mill and have been out and raked hay almost every afternoon whilst they were haying. Father did not have but two days extra help about his haying and we have not had a moments help in the House. Mother commenced spinning this summer with great speed and thought she should do wonders but she only spun 17 skeins and gave it up as a bad bargain. We received a letter from Brother and Sister Colby about 3 weeks ago. They are well and prospering nicely. They have a young son born in May last. Thay call his name Allen James for his two uncles. They bought a half lot of land and built them a house four good rooms on the ground and paid for it. Then they bought the other half lot with a good brick house on it and Mary says if we will just step in we may see Elias and Molly with thare two pretty babies in thare own brick house almost as grand as Lawyer Bryants folks. O Sabrina how my western fever rages. Were it not for my father and mother I would be in the far west ere this summer closes but I shall not leave them for friends nor foes! Mary and Elias say Liz dont get married for you must come out here. I shall take up with thare advice unles I can find some kind hearted youth that want a wife and mother, one that is good looking and can hold up his head up. Then when all that comes to pass I am off in a fit of matrimony like a broken jug handle but till I find such an one I glory in being an old maid, ha ha ha! . . .

MARY S. PAUL

Lowell Dec 21st 1845
Dear Father

I received your letter on Thursday the 14th with much pleasure. I am well which is one comfort. My life and health are spared while others are cut off. Last Thursday one girl fell down and broke her neck which caused instant death. She was coming in or coming out of the mill and slipped down it being very icy. The same day a man was killed by the cars. Another had nearly all of his ribs broken. Another was nearly killed by falling down and having a bale of cotton fall on him. Last Tuesday we were paid. In all I had six dollars and sixty cents paid $4.68 for board. With the rest I got me a pair of rubbers and a pair of 50.cts shoes. Next payment I am to have a dollar a week beside my board. . . . Perhaps you would like something about our regulations about going in and coming out of the mill. At 5 o'clock in the morning the bell rings for the folks to get up and get breakfast. At half past six it rings for the girls to get up and at seven they are called into the mill. At half past 12 we have dinner are called back again at one and stay till half past seven. I get along very well with my work. . . . I think that the factory is the best place for me and if any girl wants employment I advise them to come to Lowell. Tell Harriet that though she does not hear from me she is not forgotten. I have little time to devote to writing that I cannot write all I want to. There are half a dozen letters which I ought to write to day but I have not time. Tell Harriet I send my love to her and all of the girls. Give my love to Mrs. Clement. Tell Henry this will answer for him and you too for this time.

Lowell Nov 5th 1848
Dear Father

Doubtless you have been looking for a letter from me all the week past. I would have written but wished to find whether I should be able to stand it—to do the work that I am now doing. I was unable to get my old place in the cloth room on the Suffolk or on any other corporation. I next tried the dressrooms on the Lawrence Cor[poration], but did not succe[e]d in getting a place. I almost concluded to give up and go back to Claremont, but thought I would try once more. So I went to my old overseer on the Tremont Cor. I had no idea that he would want one, but he *did*, and I went to work last Tuesday—warping—the same work I used to do.

It is *very* hard indeed and sometimes I think I shall not be able to endure it. I never worked so hard in my life but perhaps I shall get used to it. I shall try hard to do so for there is no other work that I can do unless I spin and that I shall not undertake on any account. I presume you have heard before this that the wages are to be reduced on the 20th of this month. It is *true* and there seems to be a good deal of excitement on the subject but I can not tell what will be the consequence. The companies pretend they are losing immense sums every *day* and therefore they are obliged to lessen the wages, but this seems perfectly absurd to me for they are constantly making *repairs* and it seems to me that this would not be if there were really any danger of their being obliged to *stop* the mills.

It is very difficult for any one to get into the mill on any corporation. All seem to be very full of help. I expect to be paid about two dollars a week but it will be dearly earned. . . .

Write soon. Yours affectionately
Mary S. Paul[9]

QUESTIONS

1. Lydia Maria Child, Catharine Beecher, and A. J. Graves were just a few of many who wrote publicly and adamantly about the ideal role for women within the family. Why would women have sought such literature in the antebellum era?
2. What does the treatment of sexuality and family in these documents reveal about the circumstances of life in this era for middle class women? Working class women? Enslaved women?
3. Note that both Graves and Grimké invoke religious ideals but come to very different conclusions about women's rights and role. How do you explain this?
4. Do you see any shared assumptions about women's roles in Documents 1 to 5? Where do they converge, and what divides their vision of female virtue?
5. In specific terms, describe the daily lives of women in the mills. How did the work affect them physically and psychologically?

6. Lydia Maria Child was deeply engaged in the abolitionist movement. How do you think she would have responded to the Declaration of Sentiments?

7. Sarah Grimké compared the condition of women with that of black slaves. Was this an accurate or an inaccurate comparison?

ADDITIONAL READING

Katherine Kish Sklar's *Catharine Beecher: A Study in Domesticity* (1973) is a fine biography of that very influential woman. Nancy F. Cott, *The Bonds of Womanhood: Woman's Sphere in New England, 1780–1835* (1977) is an important discussion of women's culture during the era. Carol Smith Rosenberg, *Disorderly Conduct: Visions of Gender in Victorian America* (1985) provides brilliant interpretive essays on women's experiences. Christine Stansell, *City of Women: Sex and Class in New York, 1789–1869* (1986), and Thomas Dublin, *Transforming Women's Work: New England Lives in the Industrial Revolution* (1994), describe the lives of working-class women. Mary P. Ryan's *Cradle of the Middle Class* (1981) offers insight into the origins of women's roles in middle-class culture, as does Catherine E. Kelly, *In the New England Fashion: Reshaping Women's Lives in the 19th Century* (1999). On women and reform, see Julie Roy Jeffries, *The Great Silent Army of Abolitionism* (1998); Nancy Isenberg, *Sex and Citizenship in Antebellum America* (1998); and Lori Ginzburg, *Women and the Work of Benevolence: Morality, Politics, and Class in the Nineteenth-Century United States* (1990). Harriet A. Jacobs, *Incidents in the Life of a Slave Girl* is available in an edited version by Jean Fagan Yellin (1987). Jeanne Boydston, *Home and Work: Housework, Wages, and the Ideology of Labor in the Early Republic* (1990) offers insight into the relationship between work inside and outside the home.

ENDNOTES

1. Lucy Larcom, *A New England Girlhood, Outlined from Memory* (Boston: Houghton Mifflin, 1889), p. 157.

2. *The Mother's Book. By Mrs. Child* (Boston: Carter and Hendee, 1831), pp. 146, 153, 161, 164.

3. A. J. Graves, *Women in America: Being an Examination into the Moral and Intellectual Condition of American Female Society* (New York: Harper and Brothers, 1843), pp. 155–164.

4. Catharine Beecher, *Treatise on Domestic Economy for Young Ladies at Home and at School* (New York: Harper and Brothers, 1847), pp. 25–43.

5. From Sarah M. Grimké, *Letters on the Equality of the Sexes and the Condition of Women* (Boston: Isaac Knapp, 1838), pp. 46–55.

6. Harriet Jacobs, *Incidents in the Life of a Slave Girl* (Boston: published for the author, 1861), pp. 44–87.

7. Elizabeth Cady Stanton, Susan B. Anthony, and Matilda Joslyn Gage, eds., *History of Woman Suffrage*, v.1 (Rochester, NY: Charles Mann, 1889), pp. 70–71.

8. Lucy Larcom, *A New England Girlhood, Outlined from Memory* (Boston: Houghton Mifflin, 1889), pp. 145–148, 152–156.

9. Thomas Dublin, ed., *Farm to Factory: Women's Letters, 1830–1860* (New York: Columbia University Press, 1981), pp. 74, 85–86, 103–104, 106. Reprinted by permission of the author.

CHAPTER 10

IMMIGRATION AND NATIVISM IN THE ANTEBELLUM ERA

HISTORICAL CONTEXT

It is a cliché to say that America is a nation of immigrants, but that does not make it any less true. From the Pilgrims of the seventeenth century down to "undocumented" workers in our own day, immigration has played a central and often controversial role in American history. In the 1840s and 1850s, millions of immigrants arrived in the United States, particularly from Ireland and Germany. With America's growing demand for labor, and European populations in search of greater political freedom and economic opportunity, the circumstances were set for unprecedented levels of immigration. The newcomers were drawn primarily to the manufacturing jobs in the Northeast and agricultural opportunity in the Midwest. With the South's labor force dominated by slavery, immigrants found few opportunities and mostly avoided the region.

The agricultural blight that ruined the Irish potato crop gave the first big push to migrants out of the Old World. Starvation and disease killed hundreds of thousands, beginning in 1845 and lasting for a decade, forcing well over a million abroad to Canada, Australia, and primarily to the United States. Letters home detailed the difficulties faced by both the migrants and those they left behind, not least of which was the fragmentation of families. The desperate poverty in Ireland—compounded by English policies that severely restricted the distribution of aid—led to a crisis that fundamentally influenced Irish culture. Hundreds of folk ballads attest not only to the loss brought by this famine and exile but also the hope felt by the possibilities of survival in a new country. Before mid-century, the Irish had been coming to America for decades, so when the crisis hit, stories from kinfolk in America about plentiful jobs lured countless more. The "Famine Irish" settled primarily in the cities of the Northeast, especially Boston, New York, and Philadelphia, working on the railroads, docks, and in mines, and Irish women sought jobs in the mills of the Northeast and as domestic servants.

Similarly, the failure of political uprisings in Germany and the Austro-Hungarian Empire—known as the Revolutions of 1848—left many Germans longing for greater freedom. These "Forty-Eighters" and their fellow German immigrants tended to be better educated than their Irish counterparts, and many brought with them tremendous knowledge and skills that had a profound influence upon science and cultural development here in the United States. Many of the Forty-Eighters were young, middle-class, and liberal in political outlook; several became prominent in the coming fight against slavery. As the documents reflect, they spread across the northern states, particularly in the Middle West, in states like Ohio, Wisconsin, Illinois, and Missouri, in the process creating large German neighborhoods in towns such as Cincinnati, Milwaukee, and Chicago. By 1850, for example, one-third of the state of Wisconsin was foreign-born, mostly German. Wisconsin promoted foreign settlement, using pamphlets and advertisements in multiple languages to encourage migration to the distant reaches of the state. Though not as densely concentrated as in Wisconsin, German settlements reached north to the upper Great Lakes and all the way south to Texas.

Massive immigration led to a backlash. One can always find suspicion of immigrants, but organized opposition in the mid-nineteenth century was a movement strong enough to help destroy the old Whig political party. Some of this antiforeign "nativist" sentiment was religiously motivated, driven by a belief that American cultural institutions were under attack from excessive foreign—especially Catholic—influence. A mostly Protestant nation, many Americans feared not just the religious practices of Catholics but also the power of the Catholic hierarchy. The Catholic Church had, after all, a long history of war and persecution in Europe. Many Americans also believed wild accusations, that convents were really brothels or that the Pope hoped to rule America. Nativists fought back by trying to restrict immigration, by sponsoring harsh temperance laws (as a way to curb what they perceived as German and Irish drunkenness), by decrying Catholic schools, and by insisting that the political power of foreigners at the ballot box be curbed. Another potent argument against the foreigners—particularly the Irish—was that they took Americans' jobs and undercut their wages. The sheer poverty of the famine immigrants terrified Americans, who believed that poor neighborhoods where the Irish clustered were hotbeds of crime and immorality. All of this anti-immigrant sentiment coalesced into the short-lived American Party.

A coda to mid-century immigration came on the West Coast, where quite different circumstances led to the migration of Chinese workers to California. Many were drawn to the Gold Rush in the middle of the century. By the 1860s they were the main laborers building the transcontinental railroad in the west, and a decade later, Chinese men comprised nearly a quarter of California's work force. The backlash against the Irish and Germans in the East during the 1850s was felt by the Chinese most strongly in the years after the Civil War.

Documents in this chapter cluster around several themes. First, we examine evidence of the Irish migration of the 1840s and 1850s, through letters, songs, and other materials. We then compare this experience with the simultaneous mass migration of Germans to the United States, through emigrant guidebooks, imagery, and the recollections of the immigrants themselves. The third section of this chapter uses several different types of documents—songs, broadsides, newspaper accounts, and other materials—to investigate the political and cultural reaction to these new Americans.

INTRODUCTION TO DOCUMENTS 1–4

The mass migration of the Irish to the United States in the late 1840s and 1850s had its roots in earlier waves. Document 1 is a traditional Irish folk ballad that captures the homesickness of this diaspora. "Poor Pat" traces Irish history in song, the rising rents that drove the peasants off the land, the failure of the potato crops resulting in the deaths of tens of thousands, the longing for Ireland, and the new realities of hard labor in America.

Document 2 consists of three letters to John Curtis from his family in Ireland. Curtis left just before the famine, and his sister and uncle describe the scene back home, the potato crop failure and with it, growing fears for the future. Read the letters for clues to contemporary life—such as the way that both Curtis's sister and his uncle ask about the possibility of migrating to North America. What else can these letters tell us about Irish emigration?

Document 3 is a passage from Harriet Martineau's *Letters from Ireland* (1852), a series of observations made during, as the Irish called it, the Great Hunger. Here Martineau observes the "American Wake," an emotional and somber ritual, similar to a funeral, marking the departure of family and friends leaving Ireland, usually never to return. Note Martineau's patronizing remark that the Irish, mourning their departing loved ones, were childlike in their emotions and her hope that they might mature later on.

Finally, Document 4 is one of the most well-known Irish ballads of emigration, "Skibbereen," written as a dialogue between father and son about the failed Irish nationalist political uprising in 1848. The uprising was inspired by the many rebellions across Europe in that year, but we should take care not to overemphasize Irish resistance at this moment in history. Most refugees during the Great Hunger fled their home country because of famine, not politics.

1. "POOR PAT MUST EMIGRATE"

IRISH FOLK BALLAD

. . . The devil a word I would say at all, although our wages are but small,
If they left us in our cabins, where our fathers drew their breath,
When they call upon rent-day, and the devil a cent you have to pay.
They will drive you from your house and home, to beg and starve to death
What kind of treatment, boys, is that, to give an honest Irish Pat?
To drive his family to the road to beg or starve for meat;

But I stood up with heart and hand, and sold my little spot of land;
That is the reason why I left and had to emigrate.

Such sights as that I've often seen, but I saw worse in Skibbareen,
In forty-eight (that time is no more) when famine it was great,
I saw fathers, boys, and girls with rosy cheeks and silken curls
All a-missing and starving for a mouthful of food to eat.

When they died in Skibbareen, no shroud or
  coffins were to be seen;
But patiently reconciling themselves to their
  horrid fate,
They were thrown in graves by wholesale which
  cause many an Irish heart to wail
And caused many a boy and girl to be most glad
  to emigrate.

Where is the nation or the land that reared such
  men as Paddy's land?
Where is the man more noble than he they call
  poor Irish Pat?
We have fought for England's Queen and beat
  her foes wherever seen;
We have taken the town of Delhi—if you please
  come tell me that,
We have pursued the Indian chief, and Nenah
  Sahib, that cursed thief,
Who skivered babes and mothers, and left them
  in their gore.

But why should we be so oppressed in the land
  of St. Patrick blessed.
The land from which we have the best, poor
  Paddy must emigrate. . . .

With spirits bright and purses light, my boys we
  can no longer stay,
For the shamrock is immediately bound for
  America,
For there is bread and work, which I cannot get
  in Donegal,
I told the truth, by great St. Ruth, believe me
  what I say,
Good-night my boys, with hand and heart, all
  you who take Ireland's part,
I can no longer stay at home, for fear of being
  too late,
If ever again I see this land, I hope it will be with
  a Fenian band;
So God be with old Ireland, poor Pat must
  emigrate.[1]

2. LETTERS FROM THE CURTIS FAMILY TO JOHN CURTIS IN PHILADELPHIA

HANNAH CURTIS, TO HER BROTHER

1845 Mountmellick November the 24
Dear brother John

I received your letter on the 14th of Nov which gave us great pleasure to hear from you that you are so well since you left home I was often suprisd you did not write to me before now, we are all quite well ever since you left us we are after moving up Street to live in Knaggs house next door to Mr. Timothy Dunnes it is him we have the house from we pay £12 a year for it we hold the other house in posesion yet Williams father and mother are still in it we intend to keep it and to keep the men lodging in it by that means we think it wont come heavy on us to keep the too houses for my part I am happy to be separated from the old pair it was very hard for one to live with them for they were always making mischief between William and I[.] Dear brother it is most dreadful the state the potatoes are in in Ireland and all over the world they are all tainted in the ground with every on it is the opinion of every one there will be no potatoes with every one in very short we are greatly afraid there will be a famine this year if the Lord does not do something for the people they are not aware of everything rates very high at present William can employ 10 men and has work for 3 or 4 more only for the way the potatoes has turned out.

WILLIAM DUNNE, TO HIS NEPHEW

1846 Friendly St Belfast November the 16
Dear John,

I now take the opertunity of sending you these few lines hoping that they will find you in good healthy and all friends as they have and me and family in the present thank you for all his blessings to us I was and am very glad to here how well you have got on in America I think it was A good job that your father Mother and family went the time they did for there is nothing here but hardship and starvation our potatoe crop is all . . . over Ireland this year but I suppose you have herd of it there was not one steme of potatoes in my house this three months it is very seldome that there does one come to market at all and what comes in not worth buying they cant be eat they, sell at 8 or 9 shillings per hundred[.] Everything else is very dear also and bad Everyday went for the poor and bad wages the people are starving in the west of Ireland and turning out for something to eat we think that there will be a rebellion if there is not something done your sister Hannah has wrote to me prety regular wince all her friends left her she did not know what it is to be alone and til now she lets me know . . . let me know if you think a person of my kind could make out A living I could have done pretty well some time Ago but Ireland is gone to the bad there is nothing but hardship and poverty in it nor no sign of anything Else at the present. . . . I hope you are saving Money you will let me know if you have Ever seen your uncle Thomothy or if you know where he lives or how he is getting on I often herd he was well of and had a good far you will let me know if you Ever see your grand Mother or how she is and all particulars about all friends Hannah says you talk of comeing to Ireland if you would think of it I would expect you to come by Belfast as it is generaly the shortest passage

HANNAH CURTIS, TO HER BROTHER

Mountmellick April 21, 1847
My Dear Brother John

I had heard a letter come on the morning of this day from John Cullen to his Mother and money in it for her it was Mrs Mulhall came to tell me about it[.] My uncle William Dunne write to me saying he had a letter from you I think the latter end of February saying you would let me have one from you in March I was every day expecting it but all in vain. . . . I related to you the state of the Country in that letter therefore I need not go over it any more only the distress that was amongst the people at that time was nothing to what it is at present the people are in a starving state the poor house is crowded with people and they are dying as fast as they can from 10 to 20 a day out of it there is some kind of a strange fever in it and it is the opinion of the Doctor it will spread over town and country when the weather grows warm no person can be sure of their lives one moment the times are so sudden you would scarcely see as many people with a funeral as would take it to the grave in fact I would not describe the aweful state of Ireland at present you all may think the people are not so bad on account of all the provision that is coming into it but only for it the country could be a great deal worse of but there is no trade of any kind doing nor no money in the country went is gone to America from every one that can go to America is going this year as there is no prospect of any think here but poverty and distress the Revd Father Healy is after getting I think above 50 letters and mony in them all they were sent to his care by people in America to their friends at home to take them out to them the post office here is ful of letters every day every one without mony dear John. . . .[2]

3. *LETTERS FROM IRELAND* (1852)

HARRIET MARTINEAU

The population of Castlebar was, if we were correctly informed, 6000 before the famine; and it is now between 3000 and 4000. Many have gone to the grave; but more have removed to other countries. Large sums are arriving by post, to carry away many more. We were yesterday travelling by the public car, when, at the distance of a few miles from Castlebar, on approaching a cluster of houses, we were startled—to say the truth, our blood ran cold—at the loud cry of a young girl who ran across the road, with a petticoat over her head, which did not conceal the tears on her convulsed face. A crowd of poor people came from—we know not where —most of them in tears, some weeping quietly, others with unbearable cries. A man, his wife, and three young children were going to America. They were well dressed, all shod, and the little girls bonneted. . . . All eyes were fixed on the neighbours who were going away for ever. The last embraces were terrible to see; but worse were the kissings and the claspings of the hands during the long minutes that remained after the woman and children had taken their seats. When we saw the wringing of hands and heard the wailings, we became aware, for the first time perhaps, of the full dignity of that civilization which induces control over the expression of emotions. All the while that this lamentation was giving a headache to all who looked on, there could not but be a feeling that these people, thus giving a free vent to their instincts, were as children, and would command

themselves better when they were wiser. Still, there it was, the pain and the passion: and the shrill united cry, when the car moved on, rings in our ears, and long will ring when we hear of emigration. . . .

There were no signs of affliction in them. It is denied here that the people are eager to go, as the newspapers assert. They go, we are told, because they must. Our own impression is that the greater number go without knowing much about it, because others have gone, or because they are sent for, or because they have a general idea that it is a fine thing for them. Many, of course, are more fully aware what they are about; but we do not see reason to suppose that political discontent has anything to do with it. . . . If any ill-feeling towards the English has come under our notice at all (amidst much good-will towards British settlers), it is merely in connection with Protestant proselytism—and of that there is likely to be plenty more if the Protestant zealots go on doing as some of them are doing now.[3]

4. "OLD SKIBBEREEN" (*c.* 1850)

YOUNG AMERICA AND HIS IRISH FATHER

O! Father, dear, I've often heard you speak of
  Erin's Isle—
Its scenes how bright and beautiful, how 'rich
  and rare' they smile;
You say it is a lovely land in which a Prince
  might dwell,
Then why did you abandon it, the reason to me
  tell?

My Son, I've loved my native land with fervor
  and with pride—
Her peaceful groves, her mountains rude, her
  valleys green and wide,
And there I've roamed in manhood's prime, and
  sported when a boy,
My shamrock and shillelagh sure my constant
  boast and joy.

But lo! A blight came o'er my crops, my sheep
  and cattle died,
The rack-rent too, alas! Was due, I could not
  have supplied;
The landlord drove me from the cot where born
  I had been,
And that, my boy's the reason why I left old
  Skibbereen.

O! what a dreadful sight it was that dark
  November day;
The Sheriff and the Peelers came to send us all
  away;
They set the roof a-blazing with a demon smile
  of spleen,
And when it fell, the crash was heard all over
  Skibbereen.

Your Mother dear, God rest her, fell upon
the snowy ground,
She fainted in her anguish at the desolation
round;—
She never rose, but passed away from life's
tumultuous scene,
And found a quiet grave of rest in poor old
Skibbereen.

Ah! Sadly I recall that year of gloomy '48;
I rose in vengeance with 'the boys' to battle
against fate:
We were hundred thro' the mountains wild, as
traitors to the Queen,—
And that, my boy's the reason why I left old
Skibbereen.

You then were only two years old, and feeble was
your frame
I would not leave you with my friends—you bore
my father's name!—
I wrapped you in my '*Cathamore*' at dead of night
unseen,
Then heav'd a sigh and bade good-by to poor old
Skibbereen.

O! Father, Father, when the day for vengeance
we will call,—
When Irishmen o'er field and fen shall rally one
and all,—
I'll be the man to lead the van beneath the flag
of green,
While loud on high we'll raise the cry—Revenge
for Skibbereen![4]

INTRODUCTION TO DOCUMENTS 5, 6, AND 7

In many ways, German migration to the United States paralleled that of the Irish, with political oppression and the hope for better opportunity. Yet the fact that most German migrants of this era were educated and skilled men gave them more latitude to make decisions about settlement. Besides, they were not facing starvation and plague. The next several documents profile that migration. Document 5 is taken from one of the dozens of advice manuals and guidebooks published for German immigrants in the 1840s and 1850s. This particular passage was written by a German-American minister in Boston, Frederick Bogen. Note the type of advice he passes on to his fellow migrants, and the way he integrates aspirational rhetoric with very practical instructions on how to assimilate into this new land. Bogen advises his countrymen not to retain their old language and customs, yet German culture held on tenaciously for generations, especially in cities and towns where large numbers of immigrants clustered. Bogen's advice manual included a copy of the U.S. Constitution and biographical sketches of George Washington and Benjamin Franklin.

Document 6 is a map published just two years later in Germany, advising prospective immigrants about the most common destinations in the United States and the modes of transportation and distances between them. The scale alone of the new country dwarfed Germany. Immigrants worked hard to recreate the kinship and communal networks of their home villages, towns, and regions. These "chain migrations"—where bonds of family and friendship caused people to settle together in a given place—established significant and enduring German-American communities in the American upper Midwest, as indicated on the map.

Document 7 is a reminiscence by Carl Schurz, one of the most notable German Americans who left his native country after the failed revolutions of 1848. By 1854 he had settled in Wisconsin, and in 1861 he joined the Union Army to fight in the Civil War. His public career included a term as U.S. senator as well as other high-ranking political positions, and a stint as editor of the *New York Evening Post*. Here he recalls his arrival in Wisconsin and the influence of German migrants on that state. Note his exceedingly positive appraisal of the emigrant's situation and opportunities.

5. ADVICE FOR GERMAN IMMIGRANTS (1851)

FREDERICK BOGEN

However different may be the reasons which induce Germans to leave their fatherland and come to America, yet they all agree in one wish—to live here free and happy. And indeed perhaps no country in the world offers such various opportunities to facilitate the accomplishment of this purpose as the *United States of America*.

A great blessing meets the German emigrant the moment he steps upon these shores: He comes into a free country; free from the oppression of despotism, free from privileged orders and monopolies, free from the pressure of intolerable taxes and imposts, free from constraint in matters of belief and conscience.

Every one can travel, free and untrammeled, whither he will, and settle where he pleases. No passport is demanded, no police mingles in his affairs and hinders his movements. Before him lies the country, exhaustless in its resources, with its fruitful soil, its productive mines, its immense products, both of the vegetable and animal kingdom, a portion of which he has never before seen; its countless cities and villages, where flourish industry, commerce, and wealth.

As numerous, however, as are the resources which this country affords, and as great as are the facilities with which it offers a ready support, yet numerous are the illusions and disappointed hopes, of which so many immigrants are the victims.

How many honest and good principled immigrants dream, before they leave the country of their fathers, that they shall find in the New World happiness which reality never furnishes; how many visions of glory during the voyage fill their anxious hearts that they never realize; how many a one on his arrival here, undertakes things which he soon repents of, and which remind him of the failure of his attempts. Frequently we see immigrants, after a shorter or longer sojourn, sometimes even during the first days after their arrival, disappointed, discouraged, full of lamentation and complaints, homesick and longing to return again to the "fleshpots of Europe."

. . . Above all, the immigrant must renounce the pernicious idea, that he is to gain his livelihood, perform his duty, and promote his happiness, by an obstinate reliance on his *German habits and customs*, by an inflexible indifference to the language, the spirit, and the social and political character of this country.

In the first place, as it concerns our means of living, we must, above and beyond all, *rely upon a knowledge of the English language*, and the progress that we make therein has the most important and propitious influence upon our welfare. It is well known, that the English language is by far the widest-spread, and, in the political and judicial life, the only usual language in this country. Whoever does not understand nor speak English, can make no use of his knowledge and abilities, or at the most, a very limited one.

It is of the highest importance for every immigrant, and the very means of his livelihood, going hand and hand with the study of the English language, that he finds, as soon as possible, an occupation adapted to his powers and abilities. Labor is a principal condition of his happiness, but it is not always possible for him to adhere to his former occupation, especially for those who were numbered in Germany among the more educated classes. What now must all these do?

. . . "Help yourself," is the American proverb, and God will help you.

But the mistake of many an immigrant is, that he waits for days, even weeks, spending in the mean while his precious money and his still more precious time, quietly waiting until some favorable accident comes to his relief. . . .

. . . The first duty of a citizen is to *labor;* and this brings honor and reward. It is a source of domestic happiness and political welfare, the main pillar in the temple of the Republic, especially if the virtues of frugality and temperance are coupled with it. Where there is no labor, morals, as well as the means of living, suffer and decay. . . . whoever is *able to work,* should labor and do good. . . . Fidelity and merit are the only sources of honor here. The rich stand on the same footing as the poor; the scholar is not above the humblest mechanic; and, therefore, no German ought to be ashamed to follow any occupation which, in a land where the prejudices of rank are so strong might be, perhaps, less esteemed. . . .

Let us be temperate, industrious, and frugal; let us remember our obligations to our Maker and our fellow-men, let us build up in our hearts a temple, wherein the rational farseeing spirit of American liberty, may live and flourish, and thus we may become *good, happy and free American citizens.*[5]

6. MAIN ROUTES FOR IMMIGRANTS IN NORTH AMERICA (1853)

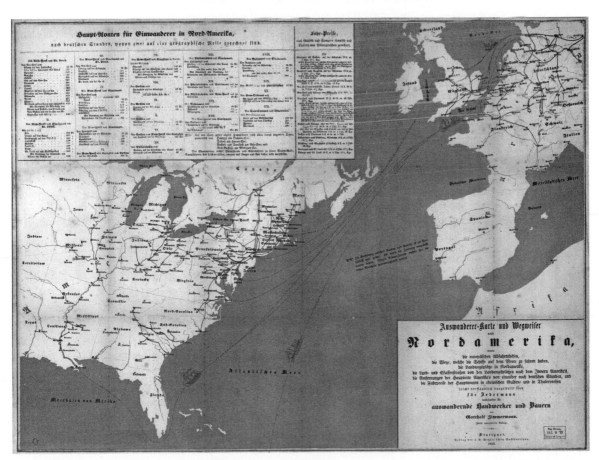

Image 10.1 Main Routes for Immigrants in North America (1853)

This map was designed for prospective German immigrants to the United States. Note the extensive networks in the northern and Midwestern states relative to those of the slave states. For Germans migrating to America, opportunity would be found primarily in the agricultural and industrial regions of the North.

Source: Gotthelf Zimmerman, *Auswanderer-karte und Wegweiser nach Nordamerica* (Stuttgart, 1853), Library of Congress.

7. REMINISCENCES OF A GERMAN IMMIGRANT TO WISCONSIN (1854)

CARL SCHURZ

From Chicago I went to Wisconsin, and there I found an atmosphere eminently congenial. Milwaukee, with a population much smaller than that of Chicago, had received rather more than its proportional share of the German immigration of 1848. The city had possessed a strong German element before,—good-natured, quiet, law-abiding, order-loving, and industrious citizens, with persons of marked ability among them, who contributed much to the growth of the community and enjoyed themselves in their simple and cheery way. But the "Forty-Eighters" brought something like a wave of spring sunshine into that life. They were mostly high-spirited young people, inspired by fresh ideals which they had failed to realize in the old world, but hoped to realize here; ready to enter upon any activity they might be capable of; and eager not only to make that activity profitable but also to render life merry and beautiful; and, withal, full of enthusiasm for the great American Republic which was to be their home and the home of their children. Some had brought money with them; others had not. Some had been educated at German universities for leaned professions, some were artists, some literary men, some merchants. Others had grown up in more humble walks of life, but, a very few drones excepted, all went to work with a cheerful purpose to make the best of everything.

. . . So far as I know, nowhere did [the Forty-Eighters'] influence so quickly impress itself upon the whole social atmosphere as in the German Athens of America, as Milwaukee was called at the Time. It is also true that, in a few instances, the vivacity of this spirit ran into attempts to realize questionable or extravagant theories. But, on the whole, the inspiration proved itself exhilaratingly healthy, not only in social, but soon in the political sense.

From Milwaukee I went to Watertown, a little city about 45 miles further west. . . . The population of Watertown was also preponderantly German—not indeed so much impregnated with the Forty-eight spirit as were the Milwaukeeans, although in Watertown,

too, I found a former university student whom in September, 1848, I had met as a fellow-member of the Students' Congress at Eisenach, Mr. Emil Rothe, and several other men who had taken part in the revolutionary movements of the time. . . . There were some Irish people, too, and some native Americans from New England or New York State, who owned farms, or ran the bank and a manufacturing shop or two, and two or three law offices. But these different elements of the population were all on a footing of substantial equality—neither rich nor poor, ready to work and enjoy life together, and tolerant of one another's peculiarities. Of culture and social refinement there was, of course, very little. Society was no longer in the pioneer stage, the backwoods condition. But it had the characteristic qualities of newness. . . . In Wisconsin the immigrant became a voter after one year's residence, no matter whether he had acquired his citizenship of the United States, or not: it was only required that he should have regularly abjured his allegiance to any foreign state or prince, and declared his intention to become a citizen of the United States. And of such early voters there were a good many.

. . . On the whole, the things that I saw and heard made the West exceedingly attractive to me. This was something of the America that I had seen in my dreams; a new country, a new society almost entirely unhampered by any traditions of the past; a new people produced by the free intermingling of the vigorous elements of all nations, with not old England alone, but the world for its motherland; with almost limitless opportunities open to all, and with equal rights secured by free institutions of government. Life in the West, especially away from the larger towns, lacked, indeed, the finer enjoyments of civilization to a degree hard to bear to those who had been accustomed to them. . . . But it offers, more than any other country, that compensation which consists in a joyous appreciation not only of that which is, but of that which is to be—the growth we witness, the development of which we are a part.[6]

INTRODUCTION TO DOCUMENTS 8–11

Anti-immigrant sentiment in the United States grew sharply with the waves of German and Irish immigrants in the 1840s. Much of this sentiment was inflected with suspicion of the Catholic Church and its influence over these new immigrants. Document 8 is a piece of sheet music promoting nativism, written to commemorate Philadelphia's violent anti-Catholic riots of May 1844. The song was "respectfully dedicated to the American Republicans of the United States," a nascent party (unrelated to the Republican Party of the 1850s) that worked to restrict immigration and oppose the influence of the Catholic Church. The torn flag was a reference to the accusation that Irish men had attacked the flag during the riot in Philadelphia. This tattered flag came to represent the perceived threat to America by Catholic immigrants.

By the 1850s, the fear of immigrants had grown significantly, forming support for the short-lived but influential American Party. Document 9 is a series of questions to be put to candidates for membership in the Pennsylvania branch of this secret party. The group was also known as the "Know-Nothing Party," for when asked about its organization and mission members responded, "I know nothing." Members pledged to support only native-born Americans—but no Roman Catholics—for political office. What does this document reveal about the methods and beliefs of the American Party? Document 10 is an 1852 broadside, advertising a new nativist paper, the "American Patriot," with even more explicit attacks on Catholics.

Document 11 is one Irish American's direct response to nativism. Thomas Colley Grattan was a prolific journalist and writer, who sympathetically profiled the aspirations and hopes of the Irish immigrants. He placed much of the responsibility for the condition of the Irish at the feet of Americans themselves, who took advantage of immigrants for political and economic gain. Note Grattan's somewhat patronizing attitude toward working-class Irish, whom he sometimes characterized as unambitious, ignorant, and drunk. The Irish poor seemed to embarrass Grattan.

8. "SEE OUR TORN FLAG STILL WAVING" (1844)

JAMES W. PORTER

A new national song the words by a native . . . respectfully dedicated to the American Republicans of the United States

See our Torn Flag still waving.
Rally round it in your might
Each his position firmly holding
Heaven will aid those in the right.
From each rocky hill and valley
Rise against the invading band,
In the name of Freedom rally,
To defend your Native Land

Foe[s] now your soil are pressing
They, your laws and rights defy,
Ask from Heaven a father's blessing,

Then for Freedom dare to die.
What though ruthless foes assail you,
Who in bloody deeds take pride,
Let not hope or courage fail you,
Freedom's God is on your side.

Freemen, rise! Ye that inherit
From a line of noble sires,
Manly blood and manly spirit,
Rise to guard your household fires.
By the parents that have rear'd you,
By your wives and children dear,
Lest those loved ones should scorn you
Rise, without a thought of fear.

Image 10.2 "See Our Torn Flag Still Waving" (1844)

This song was written in the wake of the violent riots of 1844 against Irish Americans in Philadelphia. What might the songwriter have meant with the final lines of the song, calling for Americans to "in the name of Freedom rally to defend your Native Land?"

Source: James W. Porter, (Philadelphia: James Porter, 1844), Library of Congress

Come as comes the tempest rushing,
Bending forests in its path,
As the mountain torrent gushing,
As the billows in their wrath;

From each rocky hill and valley,
Sweep away the invading band,
In the name of Freedom rally
To defend your Native Land.[7]

9. THE EXAMINER'S DUTY (c. 1855)

Examiner to Candidate. Are you a candidate for membership to our Order? [I am]

You will place your right hand on this holy emblem.

Obligation. You do solemnly promise declare and swear upon that sacred and Holy emblem before Almighty God, and these witnesses, that you will not divulge or make known to any person *whatever,* the nature of the questions I may ask you here, the names of the persons you may see here or that you know that such an organization is going on *as such*, whether you become a member of our organization or not? [I do]

Will you promise me this? [I will]

And that you will true and faithful answers give to all the questions I may ask you (so help you God). Are you by religious faith a Roman Catholic? [I am not]

Were you born in this country? [I was]

Were either of your parents? Any of your grand parents? Were any of your ancestors in this country during the Revolutionary War? If so then:

Are you willing to use your influence to elect to all offices of *Honor, Profit*, or *Trust*, none but native born citizens of *America*, of this *Country?* To the exclusion of *all* foreigners, and to *all* Roman Catholics, *whether* they be of native or Foreign Birth, regardless of all party predilections *whatever?* [Answer I am][8]

10. AMERICAN CITIZENS! (1852)

Image 10.3 "American Citizens!"

This 1852 advertisement for a nativist newspaper, "The American Patriot," captures the intense fear of the German and especially Irish immigrants of the 1840s and 1850s. These fears drove support for the American or "Know-Nothing" Party in the early 1850s. Based on this broadside, what were those fears, and how were they conveyed in text and imagery?

Source: (Boston: J. E. Farwell and Co., 1852), Library of Congress.

11. *THE IRISH IN AMERICA* (1859)

THOMAS COLLEY GRATTAN

One of the subjects which most naturally attracted my attention was the position and prospects of my emigrant fellow-countrymen throughout the Union. I was soon satisfied that I saw them in a character altogether new, and infinitely improved in comparison with that which they show in their native island or in Great Britain. The poverty, suffering, and discontent of the masses in Ireland are no doubt modified when they cross the channel, and shift the scene of existence to the English shore. Their industry has more scope, their earnings are larger, their material interests bettered. Small advantages, however, are gained in a moral sense. Degraded by a feeling of inferiority and the overbearing manner of their new fellow-subjects, far from the associations of home, and aloof from the community at large—without anchorage ground or a congenial soil, like sea-beaten ships or trees uprooted by the wind—they are, in the true, but perhaps impolitic, words of a great living statesman, "aliens in race, language, and religion." Thus it is that the mass of Irishmen, the poor, ill-educated, lower classes are never seen in their real native character, in what is, logically and legally, the land of their allegiance, or the step-mother country to which they may have removed.

. . . It is, in fact, unquestionable, that the Irishman looks upon America as the refuge of his race, the home of his kindred, the heritage of his children and their children. The Atlantic is, to his mind, less a barrier of separation between land and land, than is St. George's Channel. The shores of England are farther off, in his heart's geography, than those of New York or Massachusetts. . . . He has no feeling towards America but that of love and loyalty. To live on her soil, to work for the public good, and die in the country's service, are genuine aspirations of the son of Erin, when he quits the place of his birth for that of his adoption.

. . . The expectations of the new comer, romantic rather than reasonable, are too often cruelly checked in the first moments of his arrival. He gives his hand,—and an Irishman's hand almost always has his heart in it,—to the designing persons by whom, from various motives, he is watched for and caught up; but the cordiality of his grasp meets a cold return. He speaks in the fullness of sincerity; but no voice responds in the same key. His uncouth air, his coarse raiment, his blunders, and his brogue are certainly unattractive or ludicrous, to those who consider him only as a machine for doing the rough work of the State, or as an object of political speculation.

. . . By a rapid transition, on finding himself slighted and despised, he assumes the offensive, becomes violent, throws himself into the open arms of faction; drinks, swears, joins in riots; and, fancying that the hostile outpourings, by which a "party" assails him, speak the sense of the nation at large, he withdraws his proffered sympathy; and, seeing that he is stigmatized as an alien,—for he has learned the meaning of the word,—he falls into the circle of his fellow-countrymen, becomes one of the mass of ignorance and intemperance which disgraces the Atlantic cities, and is soon, in fact, little better than a colonist, in the land which he sought with that kind of reverence that propels a repentant sinner into the comforting bosom of the Church.

. . . Looking at what has been already done by the aid of foreign labour, the great public works of these cities, the canals, railroads, and indeed every enterprize of physical power, and seeing what yet remains to be accomplished before the continent can have fulfilled its destiny, the interruption of immigration would be an actual decree against improvement,— a ban on civilization,—a fiat for the perpetual existence of the wilderness, and for the everlasting establishment of savage life. But not more impossible was it for the despot king of old to stem the rising sea than it is for any combination now to stop the living tide of emigration that rolls from the shores of the Old World, following the course which nature itself points out, across that ocean over which the wanderers are piloted by the joint instincts of self-preservation and love of happiness. Statistical details are not easily procured to give, with any approach to accuracy, a statement of the increase of emigration from Europe. It has, however, been officially ascertained that hundreds of thousands of foreign passengers have arrived yearly for several years past, and the Irish population may now amount to four millions. That fact may startle even those whom it does not frighten. But let it act as it may on the hopes or fears of the naturalized or native population. . . .

But, it is nevertheless true that a powerful party has been organized and is in actual operation, with the avowed object of throwing back upon the Old World, if not the millions who have already arrived in the New, at least the hundreds of thousands who are standing expectant on the European shores, waiting for circumstances or a wind,— as the birds of passage whose instinct points out their congenial resting-place across the waste of waters. The avowed object of this short-sighted party, which has adopted the ambiguous but not quite inappropriate name of KNOW NOTHINGS, is the repeal of what they stigmatize as "the odious and destructive laws of naturalization now in existence." They say they are "determined to enter the lists with renewed energy and increased hope." . . .

One may ask if any "party" can really exist in America so forgetful of the past, so insensible to the present, so indifferent to the future, as to wish to confine any set of free men, in any country on earth, to the privilege which is conceded to the negro slave, ay, to the very beast of burthen, of lying down in idleness and repose, after the work of the day is done. . . .

. . . [I]t was not till the chance-presidency of Mr. Fillmore, and the formation of the KNOW-NOTHING party, with which he was identified, that avowedly hostile measures were taken to any extent against the Irish or other immigrants.

. . . It must be admitted that the Irish have to encounter considerable prejudices,—no matter from what causes arising,—in almost every section of the Union, though in different degrees. In some places they are openly and even violently expressed; in others, the feeling is slightly visible on the surface of common intercourse: but there is no observing Irishman, perhaps, who has not had, on some occasion or other, cause to notice the annoying fact. It must be remarked, that some of the different portions of the Union are much more congenial than others to the habits and feelings of Irishmen; and all seem to agree, that New England, taken on the whole, is the hardest soil for an Irishman to take root and flourish in. The settled habits of the people, the untainted English descent of the great majority, discrepancies of religious faith and forms, and a jealousy of foreign intermixture of any kind, all operate against those who would seek to engraft themselves on the Yankee stem, in the hope of a joint stock of interest or happiness. The bulk of Irish emigration to the Western States is comprised chiefly of agricultural labourers. Rigidly excluded in former times from improving by education his acknowledged quickness of intellect, the emigrant of this class has hitherto fitted only for the performance of offices requiring mere muscular exertion. Without any of those incentives to improvement possessed by the educated man, the beings we now speak of were doomed to a hopeless state of social inferiority. Their incapacity to perform any work requiring the application of intellectual power marked them out as hewers of wood and drawers of water. The high wages and good living, in comparison to what they had been accustomed to in Europe, ought to have given them more comforts, and raised them in the moral scale. But the pernicious addiction to whiskey-drinking, common to those poor people and the highly reprehensible habit of allowing it to them in large quantities, by the contractors for some of the public works, have, until lately, kept them in a state of mere brute enjoyment, so to call their degraded condition.[9]

INTRODUCTION TO DOCUMENTS 12, 13, AND 14

The tensions around nativism, particularly anti-Irish sentiment, reached a boiling point with the murder of Bill Poole, known as "Butcher Bill." Raised by English parents in New Jersey and New York, Poole was a butcher by trade, a renowned street fighter, and a leader of the infamous

Bowery Boys street gang. Men like Poole were politically connected, acting as enforcers on election day, assisting politicians in getting out the vote. In Poole's case, that meant work for the new anti-immigrant American Party. A shock wave rolled over New York City when he was shot to death in a saloon one night in February of 1855, after a dispute with a champion Irish prize fighter named John Morrissey. The two men exchanged words, Morrissey left the bar, and shortly thereafter members of his gang entered and murdered Poole. Thousands of mourners came out for Butcher Bill's funeral, and efforts to catch his killers kept the story in the newspapers for months.

Why did Poole's murder mean so much to so many New Yorkers? Consider that the city had approached a state of crisis by the mid-1850s. Since 1800, the population had increased tenfold—from 60,000 to 600,000—and nearly half of the city's residents had been born abroad, primarily in Ireland. Such a rapid influx of immigrants created overcrowding among an already impoverished population. Most of the famine immigrants were poor, and fatal diseases accompanied them across the Atlantic; New Yorkers were shocked at the squalor of their neighborhoods. They questioned the loyalty of the newcomers and reviled their Catholic faith. Finally, there was the abiding suspicion that the immigrants in their desperation took jobs from native-born Americans, and worked for fraction of their wages.

The result was an outpouring of public outrage at Butcher Bill's death, which was seen as a betrayal of American identity and ideals. Newspaper columns and pamphlets decried his murder as a symbol of the degradation of living standards and the destruction of jobs. While these shifts were primarily the result of industrialization and the growth of capitalist economy, many New Yorkers made sense of them by blaming immigrants.

The following three documents take you to a moment when nativism was at its height in New York City and show the meanings that contemporaries attached to Poole's death. Document 12 is an account of Poole's funeral, depicting his death as the slaughter of innocents at the hands of ruthless foreigners. Document 13 takes a much different view, skewering the political corruption that infested the city. Finally, Document 14 is excerpted from a deeply nativist tract that celebrated Poole's life and argued that a foreign conspiracy brought about his death. As you read, try to interpret the voices behind the documents to understand their fears. Who might have been sympathetic to Poole after his death, despite his violent life? Do you see other explanations for Poole's martyrdom in the press?

---

12. THE FUNERAL OF POOLE (MARCH 12, 1855)

THE NEW YORK DAILY TIMES

We have seen a great many very large popular demonstrations in this City at the funerals of great and distinguished men: but we remember none that exceeded in numbers that of WILLIAM POOLE, who was buried yesterday. The streets in the vicinity of his residence in Christopher-street,—the large open space directly in front of his house,—the windows, piazzas and roofs of the adjacent buildings, were crowded to suffocation. . . . A stranger, knowing nothing of the circumstances of the case, would deem it strange that the death of a man celebrated for nothing but his propensities and faculties for fighting, should call out a popular demonstration at least equal to that witnessed at the obsequies of JACKSON, CLAY, or WEBSTER. Persons familiar with this City and the peculiar features of this case, however, will have no difficulty in finding an explanation less discreditable to our people than the naked facts would imply. POOLE had a great many friends among the class to which he belonged,—comprising not only the fighting men and rowdies of the City, but the butchers, mechanics and working men at large. . . . the tragedy which ended his life was one of the most brutal and fearful ever known in our City It startled the public mind more than any similar event that has occurred for years. A gang of ruffians had laid a distinct and premeditated plot to murder him.

. . . But another element has had still greater influence in swelling the tide of public feeling. POOLE was an American, and had taken an active part in the crusade against foreigners which still enlists so much of public favor. This crusade, powerful as it is in religious and conservative circles, is still stronger and more determined and earnest in the class to which POOLE belonged. He and HYER [Tom Hyer, Bare-Knuckle Boxing Champion of America] were among the *fighting men* of the American order as against the bullies of foreign birth;—and this fact had very much to do with his death. It has been felt and believed everywhere that POOLE was murdered because he was active in the organized Native American interest,—because he was a very difficult man for the foreign rowdies to manage or to conquer. He has been regarded very generally as a *martyr* to the Native American cause;—and consequently the most conspicuous among the organizations that attended his funeral were the Chapters of the Order of United Americans, to which he belonged, and the *Protestant* associations which act in sympathy and in harmony with them.[10]

13. LESSONS FROM A MURDER (1855)

THE NEW YORK OBSERVER AND CHRONICLE

The murder of Bill Poole is no great calamity; on the contrary, the community would suffer no irreparable injury if the whole gang that were concerned in his death, of both parties, had shot each other, so that they had died in their blood. We have too many of just such men yet alive, and if the real murderers of Poole can be found, we hope that every one of them, principals and accessories, will be hung till they are dead. And may God have mercy on their souls.

But, in the midst of this city, on Broadway, and in its most frequented part, by a band of ruffians who make fighting their profession, and under circumstances of atrocity such as a civilized land ought not to exhibit, and would have startled us if the report had come from the rudest state of the society on the continent, a murder is perpetrated, and it scarcely produces a ripple on the surface of the public mind. Are we becoming familiar with crime and with blood? Has the sacredness of human life lost its power? . . . The murder of a man is a small matter compared with a general sapping of the public morals, the destruction of our social institutions, or such a perversion of our civil privileges, as places the avenues to offices of responsibility and trust, in the hands of such men as Bill Poole, Tom Hyer, Morrissey and their confederates. We are now informed that these monsters have for some years past been the managers of our political parties, trading with office seekers for the nomination and afterwards for the election, packing primary meetings, driving from the ballot boxes the lawful voter, and forcing in the votes of others, thwarting the will of the people, and making these men Aldermen, Justices, Mayors, and Legislators, whom they were paid to elect. . . .

Because our "city politics" have been in the hands of such bullies as these, it has come to pass that thousands of good men have turned away in disgust, and given up the matter as wholly beyond remedy and hope. . . .

One of the worst signs of the times is that many of our political papers, conducted by good citizens and thoughtful men, express no great apprehensions in view of this fearful state of things. They have been familiar with the facts for years, and perhaps, on that very account, are not astonished by any of the revelations which now fill others with such painful surprise. . . .

We know there are good men enough in this city to redeem our politics from the grasp of these mercenary troops of fighting men, whose stalls and shops are the markets in which offices and emoluments are disposed of as beef and poultry. We know that if the Roman Catholics were likely to get the ascendancy in our elections, thirty thousand and perhaps fifty thousand incorruptible Protestant voters would come

to the rescue. But we assure them that an enemy far more dangerous than the Pope or the Archbishop is among us, and has his hand on our throats. He may be as Bill Poole was, a member of a Native American Lodge, and a zealous hater of Irishmen, but he is only the more dangerous and deadly on that account. His name is *Corruption*. . . . It will not be in vain that this brawling and fighting politician has been shot down in the midst of his gang, if the tragedy opens the eyes of our good people to the necessity of taking the management of their public affairs into their own hands. Nay, the lives of a score of such men as Poole would be a paltry price to pay for the redemption of this city from the foul harpies now preying on its vitals.[11]

14. *THE LIFE OF WILLIAM POOLE* (1855)

The worst that can be said of William Poole, is, that he was a pugilist. . . . We do not mean by this to justify the pugilist, but we do insist upon it, that the man who braves the dangers of a single combat—knowing that only *two* must suffer in the conflict—is infinitely less criminal and incalculably braver, than is the king or emperor, who sends his *thousands* of fellow-beings to a bloody grave, to satisfy the cravings of a selfish and insatiable lust for power.

But, it is not our purpose now to speak of William Poole as a man, inasmuch as his merits and his faults have been freely discanted upon by a portion of the public press. . . . It is the *principle* involved in the affair, that now demands and justly merits the attention of the reader.

The Principle of Americanism . . . This principle, inherent in every *natural* human heart—was

the immediate cause of the martyrdom of William Poole. . . . *Another* martyr is added to the list, making in all, perhaps, some eighty or ninety who have been murdered for their love of country. At this rate, the Irish invasion will, eventually, prove more fatal than that of the British in the days of the Revolution.

. . . He was a true American, he lived and died "a true American," and the humiliating fact that he must die, in consequence of wounds inflicted by an ignoble hand, weighed heavily upon his heart. . . . Nearly his last words were these—"If I die, I die a true American; and what grieves me most is, thinking that I've been murdered by a set of Irish—by Morrissey in particular." . . . William Poole was murdered by a set of Irish ruffians who had resolved to perpetrate the crime, and who set about it calmly, coolly, and systematically.[12]

INTRODUCTION TO DOCUMENT 15

While the famine caused hundreds of thousands of Irish to flee to East Coast cities, and the failed uprisings of 1848 sent German immigrants across the Atlantic to the Midwest, the new West Coast state of California experienced its own wave of immigration. Going back to the late eighteenth century, trade between New England and the southern province of Guangzhou (Canton) in China had brought a trickle of Chinese merchants and sailors to America. Beginning in 1849, however, thousands of Chinese peasants sailed across the Pacific to participate in the California gold rush, numbering about 25,000 by 1852. Almost entirely men, they often came together from particular villages, sent money back to China, and intended to return after making enough to prosper back home. Early anti-Chinese nativism in this era grew into full-blown racist efforts to exclude them later in the century.

The gold rush also brought tens of thousands of migrants to California from back East. One man who came to make his fortune was Hinton Rowan Helper, from North Carolina. He did not succeed as a miner, and returned home in 1855. He wrote an embittered account of his time in California, *The Land of Gold, Reality versus Fiction,* including the following passage about the Chinese. What does Helper have to say about the Chinese, and how does he play immigrant groups off against each other? Two years after he returned from California, Helper wrote another book, a blockbuster, *The Impending Crisis of the South* (excerpted in chapter 11). In it he argued that the institution of slavery enriched plantation owners but impoverished the rest of the South, especially poor whites. Abolitionists distributed the book widely, for it was filled with charts, statistics, and invective against the plantation elite. Indeed, slaveholders feared that Helper's class-based argument would divide southerners, and he became *persona non grata* in his own state. After the war, Helper's racism deepened still further and he argued for wholesale deportation of the former slaves from the United States.

---

15. *THE CHINESE IN CALIFORNIA* (1855)

HINTON HELPER

According to reliable estimates, there are at the present time about forty thousand Chinese in California; and every vessel that arrives from the Celestial Empire brings additional immigrants. From a fourth to a fifth of these reside in San Francisco; the balance are scattered about over various parts of the State—mostly in the mines. A few females—say one to every twelve or fifteen males—are among the number; among these good morals are unknown, they have no regard whatever for chastity or virtue. You would be puzzled to distinguish the women from the men, so inconsiderable are the differences in dress and figure. . . .

. . . What the majority of them do for a livelihood is more than I can tell, as they have but few visible occupations. The laundry business affords those who live in San Francisco, and other cities, the most steady and lucrative employment. . . . So exalted an opinion have they of themselves that they think they are the most central, civilized, and enlightened people on earth, and

that they are the especial favorites of heaven—hence they are sometimes called "Celestials."

Is this Chinese immigration desirable? I think not; and, contrary to the expressed opinions of many of the public prints throughout the country, contend that it ought not to be encouraged. It is not desirable, because it is not useful; or, if useful at all, it is only to themselves—not to us. No reciprocal or mutual benefits are conferred. In what capacity do they contribute to the advancement of American interests? Are they engaged in any thing that adds to the general wealth and importance of the country? Will they discard their clannish prepossessions, assimilate with us, buy of us, and respect us? Are they not so full of duplicity, prevarication and pagan prejudices, and so enervated and lazy, that it is impossible for them to make true or estimable citizens? I wish their advocates would answer me these questions. . . .

Under the existing laws of our government, they, as well as all other foreigners, are permitted to work

2

the mines in California as long as they please, and as much as they please, without paying any thing for the privilege, except a small tax to the State. Even this has but recently been imposed, and half the time is either evaded or neglected. The general government, though it has sacrificed so much blood and treasure in acquiring California, is now so liberal that it refuses to enact a law imposing a tax upon foreign miners; and, as a matter of course, it receives no revenue whatever from this source. But the Chinese are more objectionable than other foreigners, because they refuse to have dealing or intercourse with us; consequently, there is no chance of making any thing of them, either in the way of trade or labor. They are ready to take all they can get from us, but are not willing to give anything in return. They did not aid in the acquisition or settlement of California, and they do not intend to make it their future home. They will not become permanent citizens, nor identify their lives and interests with the country. They neither build nor buy, nor invest capital in any way that conduces to the advantages of any one but themselves.

. . . Their places could and should be filled with worthier immigrants—Europeans, who would take the oath of allegiance to the country, work both for themselves and for the commonwealth, fraternize with us, and, finally, become part of us. All things considered, I cannot perceive what more right or business these semi-barbarians have in California than flocks of blackbirds have in a wheat field; for, as the birds carry off the wheat without leaving any thing of value behind, so do the Confucians gather the gold, and take it away with them to China, without compensation to us who opened the way to it.

. . . They have neither the strength of body nor the power of mind to cope with us in the common affairs of life; and as it seems to be a universal law that the stronger shall rule the weaker, it will be required of them, ere long, to do one of two things, namely—either to succumb, to serve us, or to quit the country. . . . No inferior race of men can exist in these United States without becoming subordinate to the will of the Anglo-Americans, or foregoing many of the necessaries and comforts of life. They must either be our equals or our dependents. It is so with the negroes in the South; it is so with the Irish in the North; it was so with the Indians in New England; and it will be so with the Chinese in California. . . . Our population was already too heterogeneous before the Chinese came; but now another adventitious ingredient has been added; and I should not wonder at all, if the copper of the Pacific yet becomes as great a subject of discord and dissension as the ebony of the Atlantic.[13]

QUESTIONS

1. Given that American immigration began long before the 1840s, how do you explain the outbreak of nativist hostilities in that decade? Why did American identity seem so besieged to those who identified as nativists?
2. In what respects were the German and Irish emigration experiences similar? Different? What about the Chinese?
3. To what degree was nativism a cultural, political, or social movement? Was it, in other words, motivated primarily by opposition to Catholicism? Alcohol? Ethnic identities? Competition for jobs? Racism?
4. Do the writings by Irish and German immigrants reveal optimism or pessimism about America?
5. Do today's controversies regarding immigration, ethnicity, and refugee status seem similar to or different from those in the mid-nineteenth century?

ADDITIONAL READING

The literature on American immigration in the mid nineteenth century is voluminous. The classic work on the political dimension of German migration is Carl Wittke, *Refugees of Revolution: The German Forty-Eighters in America* (1952), but see also Bruce Levine, *The Spirit of 1848* (1992) and Mischa Honeck, *We Are the Revolutionists: German-Speaking Immigrants and American Abolitionists after 1848* (2011). On the midwestern German experience, see Kathleen Conzen, *Immigrant Milwaukee, 1836–1860: Accommodation and Community in a Frontier City* (1976), and Hans Louis Trefousse, *Carl Schurz: A Biography* (1982). Irish immigration is explored in Hasia Diner, *Erin's Daughters: Irish Immigrant Women in the Nineteenth Century* (1983). J. Matthew Gallman has explored the influence of Irish in Philadelphia in *Receiving Erin's Children: Philadelphia, Liverpool, and the Irish Famine Migration, 1845–1855* (2000). Immigrant ballads are explored in Victor Greene, *A Singing Ambivalence: American Immigrants between Old World and New, 1830–1930* (2004). Some of the early examples of nativism and antiliquor laws are explored in Kyle Volk, *Moral Minorities and the Making of American Democracy* (2014). Classic works on nativism include Ray Allen Billington, *The Protestant Crusade, 1800–1860: A Study of the Origins of American Nativism* (1938), and John Higham, *Strangers in the Land: Patterns of American Nativism, 1860–1925* (1955). For more recent treatments, see Tyler Anbinder, *Nativism and Slavery: The Northern Know Nothings and the Politics of the 1850s* (1992).

ENDNOTES

1. A. W. Auner, Philadelphia, n.d.
2. Letters from Curtis Family Papers, #MSS072, Historical Society of Pennsylvania.
3. Harriet Martineau, *Letters from Ireland. Reprinted from the "Daily News"* (London: J. Chapman, 1852), pp. 139–141.
4. "Old Skibbereen," attributed to Patrick Carpenter. First printed in *The Wearing of the Green Song Book* (Boston: Patrick Donahoe, 1869), pp. 208–209.
5. F. W. Bogen, *The German in America, or Advice and Instruction for German Emigrants in the United States of America* (Boston, New York, and Philadelphia, 1851).
6. Carl Schurz, Frederic Bancroft, and William Archibald Dunning, *The Reminiscences of Carl Schurz: Illustrated with Portraits and Original Drawings, Vol. 2* (J. Murray, 1909).
7. James W. Porter, "See Our Torn Flag Still Waving," (Philadelphia: James Porter, 1844), Lot 10615–38, Prints and Photographs Division, Library of Congress.
8. Examiner's questions for admittance to the American (or Know-Nothing) Party, July 1854. American Party Collection, Manuscript Division, Library of Congress.
9. Thomas Colley Grattan, *Civilized America*. Vol. 2 (London: Bradbury and Evans, 1859), chapter 1.
10. "The Funeral of Poole," *New York Daily Times*, March 12, 1855, p. 4.
11. "Lessons from a Murder," *New York Observer and Chronicle*, March 15, 1855, v.33 i.11, p. 86.
12. *Life of William Poole, with a Full Account of the Terrible Affray in Which He Received His Death Wound* (New York: Clinton T. De Witt, Publisher, *c.* 1855), pp. 65–68.
13. Hinton Rowan Helper, *The Land of Gold: Reality Versus Fiction* (Baltimore: H. Taylor, 1855), chapter 7.

CHAPTER 11

A HOUSE DIVIDED:
FREE LABOR, SLAVE LABOR

HISTORICAL CONTEXT

The American Civil War was fought, in Abraham Lincoln's words, because the Union could no longer exist "half slave and half free." By 1860, 4 million Americans in the southern states were held in bondage. Many northerners believed that slave owners wanted to extend this system, while southerners felt that northerners were out to destroy the source of their wealth, their "peculiar institution" of black chattel slavery. The issues involved were not only about race; they were also about work.

As Americans, we long have taken it for granted that men and women should be free to learn the trade, craft, or profession they choose or to start a business making, buying, or selling goods. Whether or not individuals really do have an equal opportunity to succeed, most people in this country assume that individuals should be permitted to do the best they can for themselves and their families. By the middle of the nineteenth century, however, many Americans believed that southern slavery—the "Slave Power" they called it— threatened these assumptions.

The ideal of equality is often referred to as *liberalism*. For our purposes, we use the term to mean maximum civil liberty and economic opportunity for each individual. A liberal society is one where individuals seek their own betterment, unobstructed by inherited traits like race, gender, religion, or caste. Liberalism assumes that humans are born equal and that no one deserves more or less than another because of ascribed status (e.g., being born a prince or a peasant, a duke or a slave). Ideally, a liberal society enhances the freedom of each individual to maximize his or her economic opportunity and to compete against others on equal terms. To put it simply, the liberal ideal combines capitalism with civil liberties.

Liberalism in this sense is so essential to American ideology that it is hard to imagine alternatives. Yet when Adam Smith wrote his *Wealth of Nations* in 1776, his argument that unobstructed individual freedom to compete in open markets rendered the greatest good to both individuals and societies was quite new. Open markets meant that neither prices of goods nor wages for labor should be fixed by custom; one could sell one's muscle power, skills, ideas, inventions, and goods for as much as someone else was willing to pay. Before

Smith's time, various forms of servitude were the predominant forms of labor worldwide: Serfs and peasants were obligated to work particular lands for particular individuals, African and Indian slaves in the Americas were bought and sold, and even apprentices and indentured servants in the American colonies were not able to render their labor freely to the highest bidder but instead owed it to others for years at a time. The *ideal* of a liberal society grew increasingly compelling throughout Europe and North America during the nineteenth century, though the reality of true equal opportunity remained elusive.

In his classic study *Democracy in America*, published in the 1830s, the French traveler Alexis de Tocqueville marveled at how completely Americans accepted the ideology of equality. Unlike in his country, no tradition of respect for kings and aristocrats challenged this social ideal of maximum equality. Perhaps better than anyone else a generation after Tocqueville, Abraham Lincoln articulated the liberal creed. Indeed, he became a compelling political figure precisely because he was able to poetically express and defend this cherished belief when it was most threatened. On the eve of his race for the presidency against Steven A. Douglas, Lincoln declared:

> The prudent, penniless beginner in the world labors for wages awhile, saves a surplus with which to buy tools or land for himself, then labors on his own account another while, and at length hires another new beginner to help him. This, say its advocates, is free labor—the just, and generous, and prosperous system, which opens the way for all, gives hope to all, and energy, and progress, and improvement of condition to all.

Such a system, it was argued, gave wealth, happiness, and autonomy to the greatest number of people; each individual seeking his own good maximized benefits for society as a whole.

Lincoln added that a person who continued through life as a hired laborer did so, not because of any fault in the system, but "because of either a dependent nature which prefers it, or improvidence, folly, or singular misfortune." Even before the Civil War, this was an overly optimistic assessment of opportunity in America. The trend was toward consolidation, and while the numbers of small businesses did grow, an ever-increasing proportion of Americans were working as employees, and the great majority of these would be employees for life. The division of labor grew always finer, factories and shops grew ever larger, and, even in the country, farms became places where hired hands worked for others. Yet the ideals that Lincoln espoused were so attractive to Americans that they would continue to be taken as descriptions of reality long after a minority of citizens owned productive property (farms, businesses, factories, and so on) and the vast majority worked for them.

The very belief that employees had every expectation of someday becoming employers muted potential conflict between the two classes. After all, both shared the values of hard work, productivity, self-improvement, and autonomy, and both believed they were part of a system that could fulfill those values. The problem, of course, was that individuals who were free to acquire productive property also might try to take charge of more and more resources, monopolize markets, keep others out of the system, and control prices and wages. A truly open and egalitarian society is one that is easily threatened, because when wealth and power do accumulate, there are few institutions or individuals strong enough to check their influence.

Karl Marx viewed this problem as inherent in capitalist economies. Marx wrote his critique of liberal society during the middle of the nineteenth century. He argued that capitalism—whether in his native Germany, in England, where he was writing, or in America, which he studied—inevitably concentrated power and wealth in fewer and fewer hands and that, before long, a small number of individuals monopolized goods and services and exploited the masses for their own private benefit. For Marx, the fact that individuals were equal in the eyes of the law and free to enter economic markets was a cruel sham; power rested with the ownership of productive property, liberal ideology notwithstanding.

But one did not have to be a follower of Marx to be a critic of capitalism. In the following documents, we see how the central liberal ideal of autonomy—of individual independence from oppressive concentrations of power—seemed threatened on the eve of the Civil War.

INTRODUCTION TO DOCUMENT 1

Frederick Douglass was born a slave in Maryland, but as he reached his twenty-first year, he resolved to risk all and flee north. From then on, he dedicated himself to the abolitionist cause and, after the war, to the goal of freedmen's rights. Douglass was in no sense naïve about the racism that pervaded America nor about the difficult time that blacks had in the capitalist economy. In the following open letter to his former master, written on the tenth anniversary of his flight from bondage, Douglass described the breakup of his family and thereby invoked the sanctity of that institution to reveal slavery in terms deeply offensive to all that northerners held dear. Douglass's strategy was to paint slavery as antithetical to the most sacred American values.

---

1. OPEN LETTER TO THOMAS AULD

FREDERICK DOUGLASS

SEPTEMBER 3, 1848

Sir . . .

I have selected this day on which to address you, because it is the anniversary of my emancipation; and knowing of no better way, I am led to this as the best mode of celebrating that truly important event. . . .

I have often thought I should like to explain to you the grounds upon which I have justified myself in running away from you. . . . When yet but a child about six years old, I imbibed the determination to run away. The very first mental effort that I now remember on my part, was an attempt to solve the mystery, Why am I a slave? and with this question my youthful mind was troubled for many days, pressing upon me more heavily at times than others. When I saw the slave-driver whip a slave woman, cut the blood out of her neck, and heard her piteous cries, I went away into the corner of the fence, wept and pondered over the mystery. I had, through some medium, I know not what, got some idea of God, the Creator of all mankind, the black and the white, and that he had made the blacks to serve the whites as slaves. How he could do this and be *good*, I could not tell. I was not satisfied with this theory, which made God responsible for slavery, for it pained me greatly, and I have wept over it long and often. At one time, your first wife, Mrs. Lucretia, heard me singing and saw me shedding tears, and asked of me the matter, but I was afraid to tell her. I was puzzled with this question, till one night, while sitting in the kitchen, I heard some of the old slaves talking of their parents having been stolen from Africa by white men, and were sold here as slaves. The whole mystery was solved at once. Very soon after this my aunt Jinny and uncle Noah ran away, and the great noise made about it by your father-in-law, made me for the first time acquainted with the fact, that there were free States as well as slave States. From that time, I resolved that I would some day run away. The morality of the act, I dispose as follows: I am myself; you are yourself; we are two distinct persons, equal persons. What you are, I am. You are a man, and so am I. God created both, and made us separate beings. I am not by nature bound to you, or you to me. . . .

Since I left you, I have had a rich experience. I have occupied stations which I never dreamed of when a slave. Three out of the ten years since I left you, I spent as a common laborer on the wharves of New Bedford, Massachusetts. It was there I earned my first free dollar. It was mine. I could spend it as I pleased. I could buy hams or herring with it, without asking any odds of any body. That was a precious dollar to me. You remember when I used to make seven or eight, or even nine dollars a week in Baltimore, you would take every cent of it from me every Saturday night, saying that I belonged to you, and my earnings also. I never liked this conduct on your part—to say the best, I thought it a little mean. . . .

I married soon after leaving you: in fact, I was engaged to be married before I left you; and instead

of finding my companion a burden, she was truly a helpmeet. She went to live at service, and I to work on the wharf, and though we toiled hard the first winter, we never lived more happily. After remaining in New Bedford for three years, I met with Wm. Lloyd Garrison, a person of whom you have *possibly* heard, as he is pretty generally known among slaveholders. He put it into my head that I might make myself serviceable to the cause of the slave by devoting a portion of my time to telling my own sorrows, and those of other slaves which had come under my observation. This was the commencement of a higher state of existence than any to which I had ever aspired. I was thrown into society the most pure, enlightened and benevolent that the country affords. Among these I have never forgotten you, but have invariably made you the topic of conversation—thus giving you all the notoriety I could do. I need not tell you that the opinion formed of you in these circles, is far from being favorable. They have little respect for your honesty, and less for your religion.

. . . So far as my domestic affairs are concerned, I can boast of as comfortable a dwelling as your own. I have an industrious and neat companion and four dear children—the oldest a girl of nine years, and three fine boys, the oldest eight, the next six, and the youngest four years old. The three oldest are now going regularly to school—two can read and write, and the other can spell with tolerable correctness words of two syllables: Dear fellows! they are all in comfortable beds, and are sound asleep, perfectly secure under my own roof. There are no slaveholders here to rend my heart by snatching them from my arms, or blast a mother's dearest hopes by tearing them from her bosom. . . . Oh! sir, a slaveholder never appears to me so completely an agent of hell, as when I think of and look upon my dear children. It is then that my feelings rise above my control. I meant to have said more with respect to my own prosperity and happiness, but thoughts and feelings which this recital has quickened unfits me to proceed further in that direction. The grim horrors of slavery rise in all their ghastly terror before me, the wails of millions pierce my heart, and chill my blood. I remember the chain, the gag, the bloody whip, the death-like gloom overshadowing the broken spirit of the fettered bondman, the appalling liability of his being torn away from wife and children, and sold like a beast in the market. Say not that this is a picture of fancy. You well know that I wear stripes on my back inflicted by your direction; and that you, while we were brothers in the same church, caused this right hand, with which I am now penning this letter, to be closely tied to my left, and my person dragged at the pistol's mouth, fifteen miles, from the Bay side to Easton to be sold like a beast in the market, for the alleged crime of intending to escape from your possession. All this and more you remember, and know to be perfectly true, not only of yourself, but of nearly all of the slaveholders around you.

At this moment, you are probably the guilty holder of at least three of my own dear sisters, and my only brother in bondage. These you regard as your property. They are recorded on your ledger, or perhaps have been sold to human flesh mongers, with a view to filling your own ever-hungry purse. Sir, I desire to know how and where these dear sisters are. Have you sold them? or are they still in your possession? What has become of them? are they living or dead? And my dear old grand-mother, whom you turned out like an old horse, to die in the woods—is she still alive? Write and let me know all about them. If my grandmother be still alive, she is of no service to you, for by this time she must be nearly eighty years old—too old to be cared for by one to whom she has ceased to be of service, send her to me at Rochester, or bring her to Philadelphia, and it shall be the crowning happiness of my life to take care of her in her old age. . . . And my sisters, let me know all about them. I would write to them, and learn all I want to know of them, without disturbing you in any way, but that, through your unrighteous conduct, they have been entirely deprived of the power to read and write. You have kept them in utter ignorance, and have therefore robbed them of the sweet enjoyments of writing or receiving letters from absent friends and relatives. Your wickedness and cruelty committed in this respect on your fellow-creatures, are greater than all the stripes you have laid upon my back, or theirs. It is an outrage upon the soul—a war upon the immortal spirit, and one for which you must give account at the bar of our common Father and Creator.

. . . How, let me ask, would you look upon me, were I some dark night in company with a band of hardened villains, to enter the precincts of your elegant dwelling and seize the person of your own lovely daughter Amanda, and carry her off from your family, friends and all the loved ones of her youth—make her my slave—compel her to work, and I take her wages—place her name on my ledger as property—disregard her personal rights—fetter the powers of her immortal soul by denying her the right and privilege of learning to read and write—feed her coarsely—clothe her scantily, and whip her on the naked back occasionally; more and still more horrible, leave her unprotected—a degraded victim to the brutal lust of fiendish overseers, who would pollute, blight, and blast her fair soul—rob her of all dignity—destroy her virtue, and annihilate all in her person the graces that adorn the character of virtuous womanhood? I ask how would you regard me, if such were my conduct? Oh! the vocabulary of the damned would not afford a word sufficiently infernal, to express your idea of my God-provoking wickedness. Yet sir, your treatment of my beloved sisters is in all essential points, precisely like the case I have now supposed. Damning as would be such a deed on my part, it would be no more so than that which you have committed against me and my sisters.

I will now bring this letter to a close, you shall hear from me again unless you let me hear from you. I intend to make use of you as a weapon with which to assail the system of slavery—as a means of concentrating public attention on the system, and deepening their horror of trafficking in the souls and bodies of men. I shall make use of you as a means of exposing the character of the American church and clergy—and as a means of bringing this guilty nation with yourself to repentance. In doing this I entertain no malice towards you personally. There is no roof under which you would be more safe than mine, and there is nothing in my house which you might need for your comfort, which I would not readily grant. Indeed, I should esteem it a privilege, to set you an example as to how mankind ought to treat each other.
I am your fellow man, but not your slave,
Frederick Douglass[1]

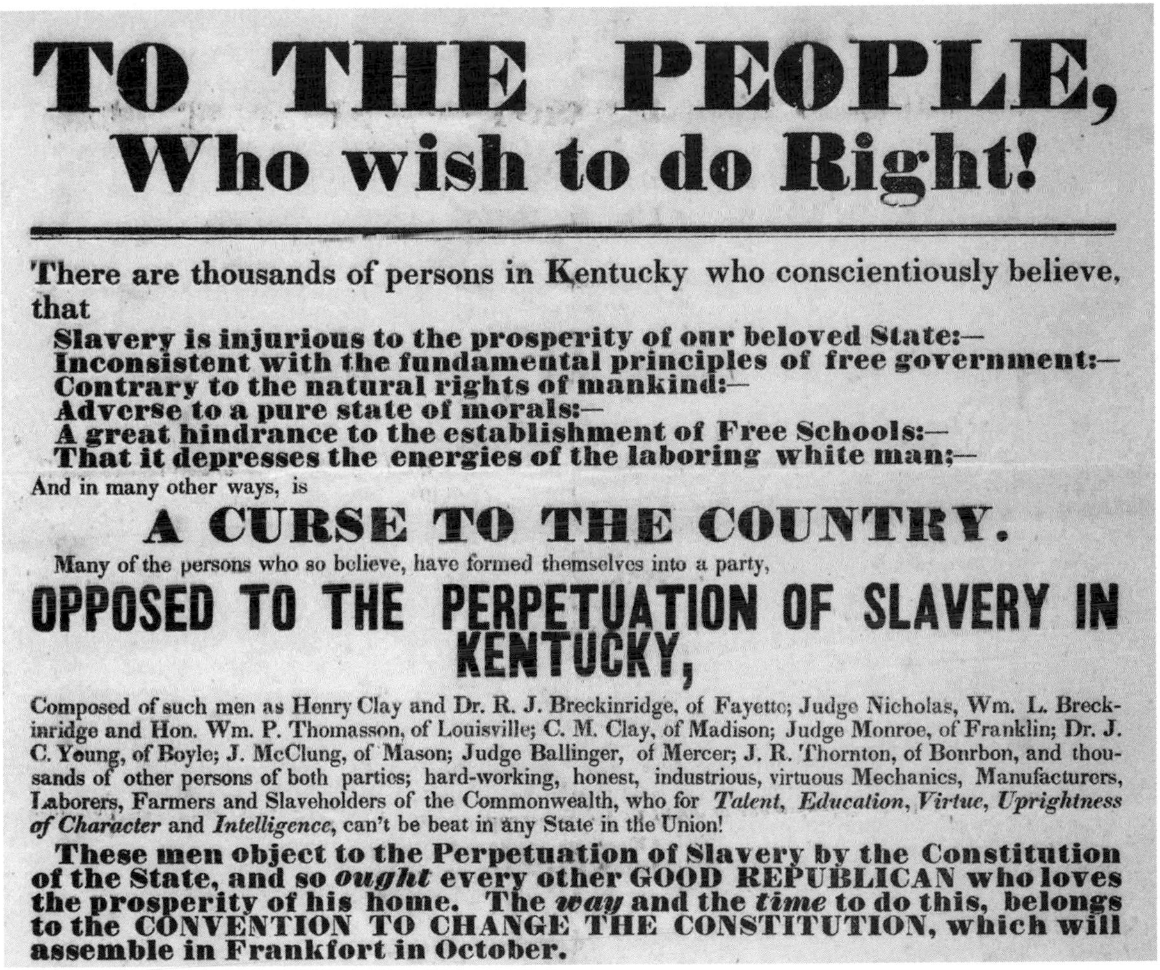

TO THE PEOPLE,
Who wish to do Right!

There are thousands of persons in Kentucky who conscientiously believe, that

Slavery is injurious to the prosperity of our beloved State:—
Inconsistent with the fundamental principles of free government:—
Contrary to the natural rights of mankind:—
Adverse to a pure state of morals:—
A great hindrance to the establishment of Free Schools:—
That it depresses the energies of the laboring white man;—

And in many other ways, is

A CURSE TO THE COUNTRY.

Many of the persons who so believe, have formed themselves into a party,

OPPOSED TO THE PERPETUATION OF SLAVERY IN KENTUCKY,

Composed of such men as Henry Clay and Dr. R. J. Breckinridge, of Fayette; Judge Nicholas, Wm. L. Breckinridge and Hon. Wm. P. Thomasson, of Louisville; C. M. Clay, of Madison; Judge Monroe, of Franklin; Dr. J. C. Young, of Boyle; J. McClung, of Mason; Judge Ballinger, of Mercer; J. R. Thornton, of Bourbon, and thousands of other persons of both parties; hard-working, honest, industrious, virtuous Mechanics, Manufacturers, Laborers, Farmers and Slaveholders of the Commonwealth, who for *Talent, Education, Virtue, Uprightness of Character* and *Intelligence*, can't be beat in any State in the Union!

These men object to the Perpetuation of Slavery by the Constitution of the State, and so *ought* every other GOOD REPUBLICAN who loves the prosperity of his home. The *way* and the *time* to do this, belongs to the CONVENTION TO CHANGE THE CONSTITUTION, which will assemble in Frankfort in October.

Image 11.1 To the People, Who Wish to Do Right! (1850)

This advertisement recruited Kentuckians into an anti-slavery party immediately after the Mexican War. The War's aftermath brought vast western territories into the Union and raised fears of an extended slaveholding empire. On what grounds do the southerners of this new party oppose slavery?

Source: Library of Congress.

INTRODUCTION TO DOCUMENTS 2–5

As the western territories were opened to the possibility of slavery, political opposition coalesced into the newly founded Republican Party. Central to their platform was the idea that Congress had not just the right but also the obligation to prohibit slavery from spreading into the west. In Document 2, Republicans framed this position not simply as opposition to slavery but also as a defense of free white labor. More, they charged the Democrats with plotting to effectively enslave white workers. Similarly, Document 3 alleged that the Democratic Party aligned its interests with the slaveholders, who were intent on expanding slavery into the western territories.

Document 4 reveals how Republican fears that judicial intervention would protect the expansion of slavery were realized with the Supreme Court's bombshell 1857 decision in *Dred Scott v. Sanford*. It is not an exaggeration to say that many northerners found the decision so threatening and immoral that antislavery ideas, previously seen as too radical, now were appealing. A clear path led from *Dred Scott* to the popularity of the new Republican Party, the election of Abraham Lincoln, and the secession of the southern states.

The case seemed like a simple one. Dred Scott, a slave, sued for freedom for himself and his family in his home state of Missouri in 1846. His master had taken him into territory declared free under the Missouri Compromise, and many slaves previously had been manumitted by judicial decision under similar circumstances. In 1850, a St. Louis court, not unexpectedly, decided in Scott's favor. Two years later, the Missouri Supreme Court overturned the lower court's decision, and finally the U.S. Supreme Court took up the case.

The majority opinion, written by Chief Justice Roger Taney of Maryland, took an extreme view. Legal scholars and historians consider it one of the most poorly conceived in the Court's history. The federal government, Taney wrote, had no right to limit slavery in the territories, which it had done with some success in the compromises of 1820, 1850, and 1854. The Missouri Compromise and all succeeding efforts to keep a lid on the volatile issue of slavery in the territories were now null and void. Taney went further, writing that the right to hold slaves was as absolute as the right to hold any property, which all states were bound to enforce. More, he ruled that blacks were granted neither rights nor protections under the Constitution; that from the founding, African Americans were viewed as "beings of an inferior order"; that they were "unfit to associate with the white race"; that they "possessed no rights which the white man was bound to respect"; and that they had been "justly and lawfully reduced to slavery."

There was, of course, abundant racism in the "free states," and most northerners were willing to let slavery exist. But they were not willing to accept what looked like an assault on their land and their ideals. Taney's decision opened the door to endless problems, not the least of which was the spectacle of southern slave hunters unrestrained in their invasion of northern cities as they searched for lost "property". It was not a long stretch from Justice McClean's dissent, excerpted in Document 5, to the feeling that an aggressive southern "Slave Power" now ran roughshod over northern law and custom.

---

2. THE DEFENSE OF FREE WHITE LABOR

THE NEW "DEMOCRATIC" DOCTRINE (1856) SLAVERY NOT TO BE CONFINED TO THE NEGRO RACE, BUT TO BE MADE THE UNIVERSAL CONDITION OF THE LABORING CLASSES OF SOCIETY.

The people of the Free States have so long yielded to the arrogant demands of the Slave Oligarchy in the South, that the latter has come to think it can carry any measure it sees fit, no matter how degrading it may be to the character of the free *white* men of the North.

Not many years ago the Southern slaveholders were contented to have their "human chattels protected in the States where they held them."

Next, they demanded and secured *five* Slave States from acquired territory, (La., Fla., Ark., Mo., and Texas,) while the Free States have only secured *two*—Iowa and California.

Next, the Slave power demanded all the territories, and broke down the Missouri Compromise, which secured a part of those territories to free labor.

Next, they demanded the right to come into the *free* States with their slaves whenever they choose, and stay as long as they please, and the United States' Courts seem about to yield to them, and grant this outrageous demand.

But the *last*, the *crowning*, the *diabolical* assumption is, that Slavery is not to be confined to the NEGRO RACE, but must be made to include *laboring* WHITE MEN, also. This doctrine, which is so monstrous and shocking as almost to seem incredible, is openly avowed and defended by the very many of the newspapers and of the public men of the South that support James Buchanan. The doctrine is also proclaimed by some Northern newspapers of the so-called Democratic party, but not generally with such boldness as in the South. . . .

JAMES BUCHANAN, the Presidential candidate of the men and the party who hold these odious views, advocated the doctrine in the United States Senate, of reducing the WAGES of AMERICAN OPERATIVES and LABORERS to the *European standard*, which is known to be about TEN CENTS A DAY. What a fit candidate Mr. Buchanan is for those who would make WHITE MEN Slaves!

JOHN C. FREMONT, the *true* Republican and true *Democrat*, who has worked his own way from poverty to greatness, pays . . . high tribute to the dignity of FREE LABOR.[2]

3. THE THREAT OF SLAVERY IN THE TERRITORIAL WEST (1856)

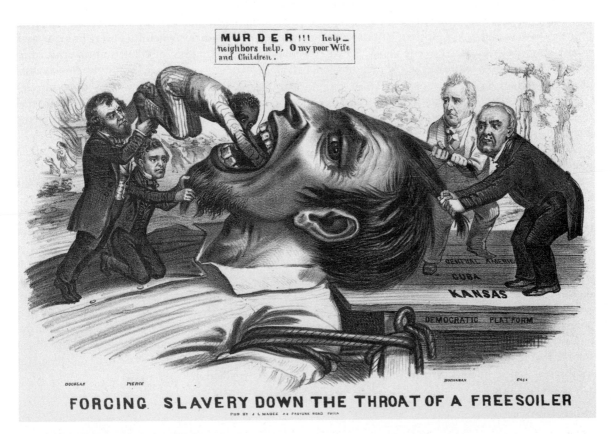

Image 11.2 An anti-slavery broadside

This satire of the 1856 Democratic Party Platform suggests that slaveholders could force the expansion of slavery into not just the American west, but into Central America and Cuba as well. Such fears fueled the birth and growth of the new Republican Party.

Source: J.L. Magee, Philadelphia (1856). Library of Congress.

4. MAJORITY OPINION, *DRED SCOTT* v. *JOHN SANDFORD* (MARCH 6, 1857)

CHIEF JUSTICE ROGER BROOKE TANEY

. . . The right of property in a slave is distinctly and expressly affirmed in the Constitution. The right to traffic in it, like an ordinary article of merchandise and property, was guaranteed to the citizens of the United States, every State that might desire it, for twenty years. And the Government in express terms is pledged to protect it in all future time, if the slave escapes from his owner. This is done in plain words— too plain to be misunderstood. And no word can be found in the Constitution which gives Congress a greater power over slave property, or which entitles property of that kind to less protection than property of any other description. The only power conferred is the power coupled with the duty of guarding and protecting the owner in his rights.

Upon these considerations, it is the opinion of the court that the act of Congress which prohibited a citizen from holding and owning property of this kind in the territory of the United States north of the line therein mentioned, is not warranted by the Constitution, and is therefore void; and that neither Dred Scott himself, nor any of his family, were made free by being carried into this territory; even if they had been carried there by the owner, with the intention of becoming a permanent resident.

We have so far examined the case as it stands under the Constitution of the United States and the powers thereby delegated to the Federal Government.

But there is another point in the case which depends on State power and State law. And it is contended, on the part of the plaintiff, that he is made free by being taken to Rock Island, in the State of Illinois, independently of his residence in the territory of the United States; and being so made free, he was not again reduced to a state of slavery by being brought back to Missouri.

Our notice of this part of the case will be very brief; for the principle on which it depends was decided in this court upon much consideration in the case of *Strader et al.* v. *Graham*. . . . In that case, the slaves had been taken from Kentucky to Ohio, with the consent of the owner, and afterwards brought back to Kentucky. And this court held that their status or condition, as free or slave, depended on the laws of Kentucky, when they were brought back into that State, and not of Ohio; and that this court had no jurisdiction to revise the judgement of a state court upon its own laws. This was the point directly before the court, and the decision that this court had no jurisdiction turned upon it, as will be seen by the report of the case.

So in this case. As Scott was a slave when taken into the state of Illinois by his owner, and was there held as such, and brought back in that character, his status as free or slave depended on the laws of Missouri, and not of Illinois. . . .

Upon the whole, therefore, it is the judgement of this court, that it appears by the record before us that the plaintiff in error is not a citizen of Missouri, in the sense in which the word is used in the Constitution; and that the Circuit Court of the United States, for that reason, had no jurisdiction in the case, and could give no judgement in it. Its judgement for the defendant must, consequently, be reversed, and a mandate issued, directing the suit to be dismissed for want of jurisdiction.[3]

5. DISSENTING OPINION, *DRED SCOTT* v. *JOHN SANDFORD* (MARCH 6, 1857)

JUSTICE JOHN MCCLEAN

. . . The sovereignty of the Federal Government extends to the entire limits of our territory. Should any foreign power invade our jurisdiction, it would be repelled. There is a law of Congress to punish our citizens for crimes committed in districts of [the] country where there is no organized Government. . . . If there be a right to acquire territory, there necessarily must be an implied power to govern it. . . .

The States of Missouri and Illinois are bounded by a common line. The one prohibits slavery, the other admits it. This has been done by the exercise of that sovereign power which appertains to each. We are bound to respect the institutions of each, as emanating from the voluntary action of people. Have the people of either any right to disturb the relations of the other? Each State rests upon the basis of its own sovereignty, protected by the Constitution. Our Union has been the foundation of our prosperity and national glory. Shall we not cherish and maintain it? This can only be done by respecting the legal rights of each State.

If a citizen of a State shall entice or enable a slave to escape from the service of his master, the law holds him responsible, not only for the loss of the slave, but he is liable to be indicted and fined for the misdemeanor. . . .

Let these facts be contrasted with the case now before the Court. Illinois has declared in the most solemn and impressive form that there shall be neither slavery nor involuntary servitude in that State, and that any slave brought into it, with a view of becoming a resident shall be emancipated. And effect has been given to this provision of the Constitution by the decision of the Supreme Court of that State. With a full knowledge of these facts, a slave is brought from Missouri to Rock Island, in the State of Illinois, and is retained there as a slave for two years, and then taken to Fort Snelling, where slavery is prohibited by the Missouri Compromise Act, and there he is detained two years longer in a state of slavery. Harriet, his wife, was also kept at the same place four years as a slave, having been purchased in Missouri. They were then removed to the State of Missouri, and sold as slaves, and in the action before us they are not only claimed as slaves, but a majority of my brethren have held that on their being returned to Missouri the status of slavery attached to them.

I am not able to reconcile this result with respect due to the State of Illinois. Having the same rights of sovereignty as the State of Missouri in adopting a Constitution, I can perceive no reason why the institutions of Illinois should not receive the same consideration as those of Missouri. Allowing to my brethren [the other Supreme Court Judges] the same right of judgement that I exercise myself, I must be permitted to say that it seems to me the principle laid down will enable the people of a slave State to introduce slavery into a free State, for a longer or shorter time, as may suit their convenience; and by returning the slave to the State whence he was brought, by force or otherwise, the status of slavery attaches, and protects the rights of the master, and defies the sovereignty of the free State. . . .[4]

INTRODUCTION TO DOCUMENTS 6 AND 7

Hinton Rowan Helper's *Impending Crisis of the South* and George Fitzhugh's *Cannibals All! or Slaves Without Masters* were extreme books in their day. Both were published in 1857, just as the fragile compromises that had kept the union together were coming apart. Helper went much further than most northerners in his vituperation against slaveholders. Similarly, Fitzhugh's argument that slavery should not be confined to blacks but was the appropriate condition for most people was an extremist stance that was rejected by fellow slaveholders. But by taking radical positions, each man sharpened the larger debate. Southerners suspected that most northerners secretly agreed with Helper but were unwilling to admit it; northerners feared that Fitzhugh actually spoke for a power-hungry conspiracy that wanted to enslave most free white men in the North as well as in the South.

Note that Helper's hatred of slavery did not arise from sympathy for African Americans. On the contrary, he believed they were, whether slave or free, an "undesirable population" and that, once emancipated, they should be colonized in Africa, though nearly all had been born and raised in America. Rather, it was the alleged contrast of what free labor did for the North and slave labor to the South that he dwelled on: "In the former, wealth, intelligence, power, progress, and prosperity are the prominent characteristics; In the latter, poverty, ignorance, imbecility, inertia, and extravagance, are the distinguishing features." Slavery's impact on poor whites most concerned Helper, for by concentrating wealth (land and slaves) in the hands of the few, he argued, the system degraded the majority, gave them no incentive for hard work and self-improvement.

George Fitzhugh, on the other hand, argued that so-called free society made cannibals of all and rendered humans selfish and heartless. The solution was not, as many northern reformers would have it, to tinker with society to make it more humane. "To secure true progress," Fitzhugh declared, "we must unfetter genius and chain down mediocrity. Liberty for the few—Slavery, in every form, for the mass." Or, even more pithily: "'Some were born with saddles on their backs, and others booted and spurred to ride them'—and the riding does them good."

Fitzhugh explicitly rejected race as the basis for enslavement; racism, he felt, hardened masters' hearts toward their slaves. He was a true conservative in the classical sense of the word. He argued that humans, white or black, were not born with equal inheritances of money or talent, so that for most, liberty meant merely the chance to be exploited by those more rich, powerful, or intelligent. Freedom, progress, equality of opportunity, and autonomous individualism were all pipe dreams. Human beings, Fitzhugh believed, were predators, and only systems of bondage recognized this fact, kept human beings from each other, and imposed mutual rights and obligations on masters and slaves. The ideology of equal opportunity and capitalism, he argued, was merely a ruse by which the strong exploited the weak. The world, he concluded, was too little governed; most people needed masters to tell them what to do.

If the following passages are extreme, they give a good sense of the clash of northern and southern assumptions, how the two sides viewed each other and the underlying values that would soon explode in civil war.

6. CANNIBALS ALL! (1857)

GEORGE FITZHUGH

We are all, North and South, engaged in the White Slave Trade, and he who succeeds best is esteemed most respectable. It is far more cruel than the Black Slave Trade, because it exacts more of its slaves, and neither protects nor governs them. We boast that it exacts more when we say, "that the *profits* made from employing free labor are greater than those from slave labor." The profits, made from free labor are the amount of the products of such labor, which the employer, by means of the command which capital or skill gives him, takes away, exacts, or "exploitates" from the free laborer. The profits of slave labor are that portion of the products of such labor which the power of the master enables him to appropriate. These profits are less, because the master allows the slave to retain a larger share of the results of his own labor than do the employers of free labor. But we not only boast that the White Slave Trade is more exacting and fraudulent (in fact, though not in intention) than Black Slavery; but we also boast that it is more cruel, in leaving the laborer to take care of himself and family out of the pittance which skill or capital have allowed him to retain. When the day's labor is ended, he is free, but is overburdened with the cares of family and household, which make his freedom an empty and delusive mockery. But his employer is really free, and may enjoy the profits made by others' labor, without a care, or a trouble, as to their well-being. The negro slave is free, too, when the labors of the day are over, and free in mind as well as body; for the master provides food, raiment, house, fuel, and everything else necessary to the physical well-being of himself and family. The master's labors commence just when the slave's end. No wonder men should prefer white slavery to capital, to negro slavery, since it is more profitable, and is free from all the cares and labors of black slave-holding. . . .

The negro slaves of the South are the happiest, and, in some sense, the freest people in the world. The children and the aged and infirm work not at all, and yet have all the comforts and necessaries of life provided for them. They enjoy liberty, because they are oppressed neither by care nor labor. The women do little hard work, and are protected from the despotism of their husbands by their masters. The negro men and stout boys work, on the average, in good weather, not more than nine hours a day. The balance of their time is spent in perfect abandon. Besides, they have their Sabbaths and holidays. White men, with so much of license and liberty, would die of ennui; but negroes luxuriate in corporeal and mental repose. With their faces upturned to the sun, they can sleep at any hour; and quiet sleep is the greatest of human enjoyments. "Blessed be the man who invented sleep." 'Tis happiness in itself—and results from contentment with the present, and confident assurance of the future. We do not know whether free laborers ever sleep. They are fools to do so; for, whilst they sleep, the wily and watchful capitalist is devising means to ensnare and exploitate them. The free laborer must work or starve. He is more of a slave than the negro, because he works longer and harder for less allowance than the slave, and has no holiday, because the cares of life with him begin when its labors end. He has no liberty, and not a single right. . . .

We agree with Mr. Jefferson that all men have natural and inalienable rights. To violate or disregard such rights, is to oppose the designs and plans of Providence, and cannot "come to good." The order and subordination observable in the physical, animal, and human world show that some are formed for higher, others for lower stations—the few to command, the many to obey. We conclude that about nineteen out of every twenty individuals have "a natural and inalienable right" to be taken care of and protected, to have guardians, trustees, husbands, or masters; in other words, they have a natural and inalienable right to be slaves. The one in twenty are as clearly born or educated or some way fitted for command and liberty. Not to make them rulers or masters is as great a violation of natural right as not to make slaves of the mass. A very little individuality is useful and necessary to society—much of it begets discord, chaos and anarchy. . . .

. . . What is falsely called Free Society is a very recent invention. It proposes to make the weak, ignorant, and poor, free, by turning them loose in a world owned exclusively by the few (whom nature and education have made strong, and whom property has made stronger) to get a living. In the fanciful state of nature, where property is unappropriated, the strong have no weapons but superior physical and mental power with which to oppress the weak. Their power of oppression is increased a thousand fold when they become the exclusive owners of the earth and all the things thereon. They are masters without the obligations of masters, and the poor are slaves without the rights of slaves.

It is generally conceded, even by abolitionists, that the serfs of Europe were liberated because the multitude of laborers and their competition as freemen to get employment, had rendered free labor cheaper than slave labor. But, strange to say, few seem to have seen that this is in fact asserting that they were less free after emancipation than before. Their obligation to labor was increased; for they were compelled to labor more than before to obtain a livelihood, else their free labor would not have been cheaper than their labor as slaves. They lost something in liberty, and everything in rights—for emancipation liberated or released the masters from all their burdens, cares, and liabilities, whilst it increased both the labors and the cares of the liberated serf. . . .

We do not agree with the authors of the Declaration of Independence, that governments "derive their just powers from the consent of the governed." The women, the children, the negroes, and but few of the non-property holders were consulted, or consented to the Revolution, or the governments that ensued from its success. As to these, the new governments were self-elected despotisms, and the governing class self-elected despots. Those governments originated in force, and have been continued by force. All governments must originate in force, and be continued by force. The very term, government, implies that it is carried on against the consent of the governed. Fathers do not derive their authority, as heads of families, from the consent of wife and children, nor do they govern their families by their consent. They never take the vote of the family as to the labors to be performed, the moneys to be expended, or as to anything else. Masters dare not take the vote of slaves as to their government. If they did, constant holiday, dissipation, and extravagance would be the result. Captains of ships are not appointed by the consent of the crew, and never take their vote, even in "doubling Cape Horn." If they did, the crew would generally vote to get drunk, and the ship would never weather the cape. Not even in the most democratic countries are soldiers governed by their consent, nor is their vote taken on the eve of battle. They have some how lost (or never had) the "inalienable rights of life, liberty, and the pursuit of happiness," and, whether Americans or Russians, are forced into battle without and often against their consent. Riots, mobs, strikes, and revolutions are daily occurring. The mass of mankind cannot be governed by Law. More of despotic discretion, and less of Law, is what the world wants. . . .

. . . The negro sees the driver's lash, becomes accustomed to obedient cheerful industry, and is not aware that the lash is the force that impels him. The free citizen fulfills *con amore*, his round of social, political, and domestic duties, and never dreams that the Law, with its fines and jails, penitentiaries and halters, or Public Opinion, with its ostracism, its mobs, and its tar and feathers, help to keep him revolving in his orbit. Yet, remove these physical forces, and how many good citizens would shoot, like fiery comets, from their spheres, and disturb society with their eccentricities and their crimes.[5]

7. THE IMPENDING CRISIS OF THE SOUTH (1857)

HINTON ROWAN HELPER

It is a fact well known to every intelligent Southerner that we are compelled to go to the North for almost every article of utility and adornment, from matches, shoepegs and paintings up to cotton-mills, steamships and statuary; that we have no foreign trade, no princely merchants, nor respectable artists; that, in comparison with the free states, we contribute nothing to the literature, polite arts and inventions of the age . . . that almost everything produced at the North meets with ready sale, while, at the same time, there is no demand, even among our own citizens, for the productions of Southern industry; that, owing to the absence of a proper system of business amongst us, the North becomes, in one way or another, the proprietor and dispenser of all our floating wealth, and that we are dependent on Northern capitalists for the means necessary to build our railroads, canals and other public improvements . . . and that nearly all the profits arising from the exchange of commodities, from insurance and shipping offices, and from the thousand and one industrial pursuits of the country, accrue to the North, and are there invested in the erection of those magnificent cities and stupendous works of art which dazzle the eyes of the South, and attest the superiority of free institutions! . . .

The causes which have impeded the progress and prosperity of the South, which have dwindled our commerce, and other similar pursuits, into the most contemptible insignificance; sunk a large majority of our people in galling poverty and ignorance, rendered a small minority conceited and tyrannical, and driven the rest away from their homes; entailed upon us a humiliating dependence on the Free States; disgraced us in the recesses of our own souls, and brought us under reproach in the eyes of all civilized and enlightened nations—may all be traced to one common source, and there find solution in the most hateful and horrible word, that was ever incorporated into the vocabulary of human economy—*Slavery!*

Reared amidst the institution of slavery, believing it to be wrong both in principle and in practice, and having seen and felt its evil influences upon individuals, communities and states, we deem it a duty, no less than a privilege, to enter our protest against it, and to use our most strenuous efforts to overturn and abolish it! Then we are an abolitionist? Yes! not merely a freesoiler, but an abolitionist, in the fullest sense of the term. We are not only in favor of keeping slavery out of the territories, but, carrying our opposition to the institution a step further, we here unhesitatingly declare ourself in favor of its immediate and unconditional abolition, in every state in this confederacy, where it now exists! Patriotism makes us a freesoiler; state pride makes us an emancipationist; a profound sense of duty to the South makes us an abolitionist; a reasonable degree of fellow feeling for the negro, makes us a colonizationist. . . .

In the South, unfortunately, no kind of labor is either free or respectable. Every white man who is under the necessity of earning his bread, by the sweat of his brow, or by manual labor, in any capacity, no matter how unassuming in deportment, or exemplary in morals, is treated as if he was a loathsome beast, and shunned with the utmost disdain. His soul may be the very seat of honor and integrity, yet without slaves—himself a slave—he is accounted as nobody. . . .

Non-slaveholders of the South! farmers, mechanics and workingmen, we take this occasion to assure you that the slaveholders, the arrogant demagogues whom you have elected to offices of honor and profit, have hoodwinked you, trifled with you, and used you as mere tools for the consummation of their wicked designs. They have purposely kept you in ignorance, and have, by moulding your passions and prejudices to suit themselves, induced you to act in direct opposition to your dearest rights and interests. . . .

Henceforth, let it be distinctly understood that ownership of slaves constitutes ineligibility—that it is a crime, as we verily believe it is, to vote for a slavocrat for any office whatever. Indeed, it is our honest conviction that all the proslavery slaveholders, who are alone responsible for the continuance of the baneful institution among us, deserve to be at once reduced to a parallel with the basest criminals that lie fettered within the cells of our public prisons. . . .

And, then, there is the Presidency of the United States, which office has been held *forty-eight* years by slaveholders from the South, and only *twenty* years by non-slaveholders from the North. Nor is this the full record of oligarchal obtrusion. On an average, the offices of Secretary of State, Secretary of the Treasury, Secretary of the Interior, Secretary of the Navy, Secretary of War, Postmaster-General and Attorney-General, have been under the control of slavedrivers nearly two-thirds of the time. The Chief Justices and the Associate Justices of the Supreme Court of the United States, the Presidents pro tem. of the Senate, and the Speakers of the House of Representatives,

have, in a large majority of instances, been slave-breeders from the Southern side of the Potomac. . . .

Some few years ago, when certain ethnographical oligarchs proved to their own satisfaction that the negro was an inferior "type of mankind," they chuckled wonderfully, and avowed, in substance, that it was right for the stronger race to kidnap and enslave the weaker—that because Nature had been pleased to do a trifle more for the Caucasian race than for the African, the former, by virtue of its superiority, was perfectly justifiable in holding the latter in absolute and perpetual bondage! No system of logic could be more antagonistic to the spirit of true democracy. It is probable that the world does not contain two persons who are exactly alike in all respects; yet "*all* men are endowed by their Creator with certain *inalienable* rights, among which are life, *liberty*, and the pursuit of happiness." . . . we do not believe in the unity of the races. This is a matter, however, which has little or nothing to do with the great question at issue. . . . slavery is a shame, a crime, and a curse—a great moral, social, civil, and political evil—an oppressive burden to the blacks, and an incalculable injury to the whites—a stumbling-block to the nation, an impediment to progress, a damper on all the nobler instincts, principles, aspirations and enterprises of man, and a dire enemy to every true interest.[6]

INTRODUCTION TO DOCUMENT 8

If Fitzhugh and Helper were extremists, Abraham Lincoln and Steven A. Douglas spoke for the great majority of moderate Americans. Yet their famous campaign debates for the U.S. Senate—stretching across Illinois through the summer and fall of 1858 and resulting in Douglas's reelection to the U.S. Senate—signaled just how intractable the issue of slavery had become.

For years, the territories—those lands that eventually would become states—had been a source of trouble. Not only did new states have the potential to tip the balance of power, North versus South, in the federal government, but the vast western lands also had great emotional significance. The West was a lightning rod for the ideals of rural self-sufficiency, republican virtue, democratic government, and equality of opportunity. Compromises had been reached, notably in 1820 and 1850, but the issue of slavery in the territories kept threatening to explode, and in the late 1850s, Stephen Douglas's support for popular sovereignty lit the fuse.

Douglas insisted that the West must be kept open for new white men to succeed and prosper, to create the local institutions that best served their interests. Lincoln countered that the western territories should become free states to confine slavery and put it on the road to eventual extinction.

Fitzhugh and Helper argued about slavery as a labor system; for both men, the key issues were how work was organized, how goods were distributed, and how power was exercised. Douglas, on the other hand, was much more explicit in arguing on grounds of race. He invoked white fears of black economic and even sexual predations. Lincoln defended himself against Douglas's attacks by making clear his belief in blacks' inferiority—intellectual, physical, and social—yet insisted that this must not stand in the way of their natural rights. Above all, he insisted that all men possessed a God-given claim to the fruits of their labor.

---

8. *THE LINCOLN–DOUGLAS DEBATES* (1858)

FIRST DEBATE, AUGUST 21
OTTAWA, ILLINOIS
STEPHEN DOUGLAS

. . . I ask you, are you in favor of conferring upon the negro the rights and privileges of citizenship? Do you desire to strike out of our State constitution that clause which keeps slaves and free negroes out of the State, and allow the free negroes to flow in, and cover your prairies with black settlements? Do you desire to turn this beautiful State into a free negro colony, in order that when Missouri abolishes slavery she can send one hundred thousand emancipated slaves into Illinois, to become citizens and voters, on an equality with yourselves? If you desire negro citizenship, if you desire to allow them to come into the State and settle with the white man, if you desire them to vote on an equality with yourselves, and to make them eligible to office, to serve on juries, and to adjudge your rights, then support Mr. Lincoln and the Black Republican party, who are in favor of the citizenship of the negro. For one, I am opposed to negro citizenship in any and every form. I believe this government was made on the white basis. I believe it was made by white men, for the benefit of white men and their posterity forever, and I am in favor of confining citizenship to white men, men of European birth and

descent, instead of conferring it upon negroes, Indians, and other inferior races. . . .

FIRST DEBATE,
ABRAHAM LINCOLN

. . . I have no purpose to introduce political and social equality between the white and the black races. There is a physical difference between the two, which, in my judgement, will probably forever forbid their living together upon the footing of perfect equality; and inasmuch as it becomes a necessity that there must be a difference, I, as well as Judge Douglas, am in favor of the race to which I belong having the superior position. I have never said anything to the contrary, but I hold that, notwithstanding all this, there is no reason in the world why the negro is not entitled to all the natural rights enumerated in the Declaration of Independence—the right to life, liberty, and the pursuit of happiness. I hold that he is as much entitled to these as the white man. I agree with Judge Douglas he is not my equal in many respects—certainly not in color, perhaps not in moral or intellectual endowment. But in the right to eat the bread, without the leave of anybody else, which his own hand earns, he is my equal and the equal of Judge Douglas, and the equal of every living man. . . .

SECOND DEBATE, AUGUST 27
FREEPORT, ILLINOIS
STEPHEN DOUGLAS

. . . The last time I came here to make a speech, while talking from the stand to you, people of Freeport, as I am doing today, I saw a carriage, and a magnificent one it was, drive up and take a position on the outside of the crowd; a beautiful young lady was sitting on the box-seat, whilst Fred[erick] Douglass and her mother reclined inside, and the owner of the carriage acted as driver. I saw this in your own town. . . . All I have to say of it is this, that if you Black Republicans think that the negro ought to be on a social equality with your wives and daughters, and ride in a carriage with your wife, whilst you drive the team, you have perfect right to do so. I am told that one of Fred Douglass's kinsmen, another rich black negro, is now traveling in this part of the State making speeches for his friend Lincoln as the champion of black men. . . . All I have to say on that subject is, that those of you who believe that the negro is your equal and ought to be on an equality with you socially, politically, and legally, have a right to entertain those opinions, and of course will vote for Mr. Lincoln.

FOURTH DEBATE, SEPTEMBER 18
CHARLESTON, ILLINOIS
ABRAHAM LINCOLN

. . . I am not, nor ever have been, in favor of making voters or jurors of negroes, nor of qualifying them to hold office, nor to intermarry with white people; and I will say in addition to this that there is a physical difference between the white and black races which I believe will forever forbid the two races living together on terms of social and political equality. And inasmuch as they cannot so live, while they do remain together there must be the position of superior and inferior, and I as much as any other man am in favor of having the superior position assigned to the white race. I say upon this occasion I do not perceive that because the white man is to have the superior position the negro should be denied everything. I do not understand that because I do not want a negro woman for a slave I must necessarily

want her for a wife. My understanding is that I can just let her alone. I am now in my fiftieth year, and I certainly never have had a black woman for either a slave or a wife. So it seems to me quite possible for us to get along without making either slaves or wives of negroes. . . . I have never had the least apprehension that I or my friends would marry negroes if there was no law to keep them from it; but as Judge Douglas and his friends seem to be in great apprehension that they might, if there was no law to keep them from it, I give him the most solemn pledge that I will to the very last stand by the law of this State, which forbids the marrying of white people with negroes. . . .

FIFTH DEBATE, OCTOBER 7
GALESBURG, ILLINOIS
STEPHEN DOUGLAS

. . . The signers of the Declaration of Independence never dreamed of the negro when they were writing that document. They referred to white men, to men of European birth and European descent, when they declared the equality of all men. I see a gentleman there in the crowd shaking his head. Let me remind him that when Thomas Jefferson wrote that document he was the owner, and so continued until his death, of a large number of slaves. Did he intend to say in that Declaration that his negro slaves, which he held and treated as property, were created his equals by divine law, and that he was violating the law of God every day of his life by holding them as slaves? It must be borne in mind that when that Declaration was put forth, every one of the thirteen colonies were slave-holding colonies, and every man who signed that instrument represented a slaveholding constituency. Recollect, also, that no one of them emancipated his slaves, much less put them on an equality with himself, after he signed the Declaration. On the contrary, they all continued to hold their negroes as slaves during the Revolutionary War. Now, do you believe—are you willing to have it said—that every man who signed the Declaration of Independence declared the negro his equal, and then was hypocrite enough to hold him as a slave, in violation of what he believed to be the divine law?

And yet when you say that the Declaration of Independence includes the negro, you charge the signers of it with hypocrisy.

I say to you frankly, that in my opinion this government was made by our fathers on the white basis. It was made by white men for the benefit of white men and their posterity forever, and was intended to be administered by white men in all time to come. But while I hold that under our Constitution and political system the negro is not a citizen, cannot be a citizen, and ought not to be a citizen, it does not follow by any means that he should be a slave. On the contrary, it does follow that the negro as an inferior race ought to possess every right, every privilege, every immunity which he can safely exercise consistent with the safety of the society in which he lives. Humanity requires, and Christianity commands, that you shall extend to every inferior being, and every dependent being, all the privileges, immunities, and advantages which can be granted to them consistent with the safety of society. If you ask me the nature and extent of these privileges, I answer that that is a question which the people of each State must decide for themselves. Illinois has decided that question for herself. We have said that in this State the negro shall not be a slave, nor shall he be a citizen. Kentucky holds a different doctrine. . . . In the compromise measures of 1850, Mr. Clay declared that this great principle ought to exist in the Territories as well as in the States, and I reasserted his doctrine in the Kansas and Nebraska bill in 1854. . . .

SEVENTH DEBATE, OCTOBER 15
ALTON, ILLINOIS
ABRAHAM LINCOLN

. . . The real issue in this controversy—the one pressing upon every mind—is the sentiment on the part of one class that looks upon the institution of slavery as a wrong, and of another class that does not look upon it as a wrong. The sentiment that contemplates the institution of slavery in this country as a wrong is the sentiment of the Republican party. It is the sentiment around which all their actions, all their arguments, circle; from which all their propositions radiate. They look upon it as being a moral, social, and political wrong. . . .

That is the real issue. That is the issue that will continue in this country when these poor tongues of Judge Douglas and myself shall be silent. It is the eternal struggle between these two principles—right and wrong—throughout the world. They are the two principles that have stood face to face from the beginning of time; and will ever continue to struggle. The one is the common right of humanity, and the other the divine right of kings. It is the same principle in whatever shape it develops itself. It is the same spirit that says, "You toil and work and earn bread, and I'll eat it." No matter in what shape it comes, whether from the mouth of a king who seeks to bestride the people of his own nation and live by the fruit of their labor, or from one race of men as an apology for enslaving another race, it is the same tyrannical principle. . . .

INTRODUCTION TO DOCUMENT 9

Harriet Beecher Stowe's *Uncle Tom's Cabin* was probably the best-known book in America during the nineteenth century, the Bible excepted. The work set off a firestorm of controversy when first published in 1851–1852. Stowe's story drew on the conventions of melodrama: exciting scenes of escape and rescue, of cruelty and forbearance, of suffering and redemption, and of pure good confronting the blackest evil. Stowe used this dramatic form to write an impassioned condemnation of slavery. The passage reprinted here is taken from the end of the book, where Stowe finished her narrative and now told the reader in the didactic style of the day how the curse of slavery might be ended. Note how her indictment of slavery brings together the themes of economic opportunity, virtuous hard work, sacred motherhood, and evangelical religion. Abraham Lincoln allegedly called Stowe "the little woman who started the big war." He exaggerated, of course, but the debate at the center of *Uncle Tom's Cabin* over slave labor versus free labor eventually consumed the nation.

---

9. FROM *UNCLE TOM'S CABIN; OR LIFE AMONG THE LOWLY* (1852)

HARRIET BEECHER STOWE

The writer has given only a faint shadow, a dim picture, of the anguish and despair that are, at this very moment, riving thousands of hearts, shattering thousands of families, and driving a helpless and sensitive race to frenzy and despair. There are those living who know the mothers whom this accursed traffic has driven to the murder of their children; and themselves seeking in death a shelter from woes more dreaded than death. Nothing of tragedy can be written, can be spoken, can be conceived, that equals the frightful reality of scenes daily and hourly acting on our shores, beneath the shadow of American law, and the shadow of the cross of Christ. . . .

But, what can any individual do? Of that, every individual can judge. There is one thing that every individual can do,—They can see to it that *they feel right.* An atmosphere of sympathetic influence encircles every human being; and the man or woman who *feels* strongly, healthily, and justly on the great interests of humanity, is a constant benefactor to the human race. See, then, to your sympathies in this matter! Are they in harmony with the sympathies of Christ? or are they swayed and perverted by the sophistries of worldly policy?

Christian men and women of the north! still further,—you have another power; you can *pray!* Do you believe in prayer? or has it become an indistinct apostolic tradition? You pray for the heathen abroad; pray also for the heathen at home. And pray for those distressed Christians whose whole chance of religious improvement is an accident of trade and sale: from whom any adherence to the morals of Christianity is, in many cases, an impossibility, unless they have given them, from above the courage and grace of martyrdom.

But, still more. On the shores of our free states are emerging the poor, shattered, broken remnants of families,—men and women, escaped, by miraculous providences, from the surges of slavery,—feeble in knowledge, and, in many cases, infirm in moral constitution, from a system which confounds and confuses every principle of Christianity and morality. They come to seek a refuge among you; they come to seek education, knowledge, Christianity. . . .

Do you say, "We don't want them here; let them go to Africa?"

That the providence of God has provided a refuge in Africa, is, indeed, a great and noticeable fact; but that is no reason why the Church of Christ should throw off that responsibility to this outcast race which her profession demands of her.

To fill up Liberia with an ignorant, inexperienced, half-barbarized race, just escaped from the chains of slavery, would be only to prolong, for ages, the period of struggle and conflict which attends the inception of new enterprises. Let the Church of the north receive these poor sufferers in the spirit of Christ; receive them to the educating advantages of Christian republican society and schools, until they have attained to somewhat of a moral and intellectual maturity, and then assist them in their passage to those shores, where they may put in practice the lessons they have learned in America. . . .

The first desire of the emancipated slave, generally, is for *education*. There is nothing that they are not willing to give or do to have their children instructed; and, so far as the writer has observed herself, or taken the testimony of teachers among them, they are remarkably intelligent and quick to learn. The results of schools, founded for them by benevolent individuals in Cincinnati, fully establish this.

The author gives the following statement of facts, on the authority of Professor C. E. Stowe, then of Lane Seminary, Ohio, with regard to emancipated slaves, now resident in Cincinnati; given to show the capability of the race, even without any very particular assistance or encouragement.

The initial letters alone are given. They are all residents of Cincinnati.

"B—. Furniture-maker; twenty years in the city; worth ten thousand dollars, all his own earnings; a Baptist.

"C—. Full black; stolen from Africa; sold in New Orleans; been free fifteen years; paid for himself six hundred dollars; a farmer; owns several farms in Indiana; Presbyterian; probably worth fifteen or twenty thousand dollars, all earned by himself.

"K—. Full black; dealer in real estate; worth thirty thousand dollars; about forty years old; free six years; paid eighteen hundred dollars for his family; member of the Baptist Church; received a legacy from his master, which he has taken good care of, and increased.

"G—. Full black; coal-dealer; about thirty years old; worth eighteen thousand dollars; paid for himself twice, being once defrauded to the amount of sixteen hundred dollars; made all his money by his own efforts,—much of it while a slave, hiring his time of his master, and doing business for himself; a fine, gentlemanly fellow. . . .

If this persecuted race, with every discouragement and disadvantage, have done thus much, how much more they might do if the Christian Church would act towards them in the spirit of her Lord! . . .[7]

INTRODUCTION TO DOCUMENTS 10 AND 11

The Republican Party, born out of the desire to protect free white labor, ran Abraham Lincoln as its candidate for president in 1860. Document 10 is a campaign poster from that election, touting the party's platform as "Free Speech, Free Homes, Free Territory," and "Protection to American Industry." Note the iconography in the poster, framing the issues of the moment in terms of labor. Yet advocates of slavery saw Lincoln's victory as a disastrous development that guaranteed bloodshed. In Document 11, that argument is explicitly made in a broadside that points blame not just at the Republican Party but at Hinton Rowan Helper. His 1857 tract, *The Impending Crisis of the South*, banned and outlawed in the South, grew in popularity among many northerners until it became a revered document for Republicans, who distributed tens of thousands of copies. Note the way each side of the slavery debate portrayed itself as the defender of freedom.

10. REPUBLICAN PARTY BROADSIDE (1860)

Image 11.3 Republican Campaign Broadside (1860)

The Republican Party's principle of free labor was profoundly meaningful in a society where slavery was seen as aggressively expansionist.

Source: W.H. Rease, Library of Congress

11. ANTI-HELPER BROADSIDE (1861)

**WHO ENDORSED THE HELPER BOOK!
WHO WERE THE INCITERS TO BLOODSHED?
READ! READ! READ!**

In the year 1857, an individual named Hinton Rowan Helper, who had been forced to leave his native State,

North Carolina, in disgrace, published a book, of which he was the reputed author, entitled "The Impending Crisis." The book recommended *direct* warfare on Southern society, "be the consequences what they might." It was so extravagant in tone, and so diabolical in its designs, that it was at first generally supposed to be the work of a fool or a madman. No one could believe that any sane or civilized person really entertained any such devilish purposes as it professed.— What, however, was the surprise of the public when the book was actually adopted by the Republican party as a campaign document, and its atrocious principles endorsed by sixty-eight Republican members of Congress and *all the influential members of the party! . . .*

We now ask, in all candor, whether these men, the leaders of the Republican party, who endorsed and circulated the above book, are not morally, before High Heaven, responsible for the revolution and bloodshed which has followed? If they *really* intended to carry out their cowardly designs, when they got into power, then every honorable man will justify the South in taking measures as she thought would ensure her safety. . . . Can the people be any longer deceived as to who are justly responsible, before God, for our present *horrible fratricidal*, and devastating negro equality, civil war?[8]

QUESTIONS

1. Why was the *Dred Scott* decision so powerful in galvanizing opposition to slavery among northerners?
2. What were Hinton Helper's and George Fitzhugh's views on race? Lincoln's and Douglas's?
3. What persuasive strategies did the different participants in the slavery debate use to make their points?
4. What were the fundamental conflicts of values, beliefs, and ideologies between the various individuals in this chapter?
5. In what sense was it true that the debate over slavery was not really about black people, but more about whites?
6. After reading this chapter, do you see the conflict over slavery as exclusively a regional battle between North and South, or were there other complicating factors?

ADDITIONAL READING

To understand the ideology of the North and the South, see Eric Foner, *Free Soil, Free Labor, Free Men: The Ideology of the Republican Party Before the Civil War* (1970); Foner, *Politics and Ideology in the Age of the Civil War* (1980); and Eugene Genovese, *The World the Slaveholders Made: Two Essays in Interpretation* (1969). On southern households, see Stephanie McCurry, *Masters of Small Worlds* (1997). For background on the sectional conflict, see David M. Potter, *The Impending Crisis: 1848–1861* (1971); C. Vann Woodward, *American Counterpoint: Slavery and Racism in the North–South Dialogue* (1964); and James M. McPherson, *Battle Cry of Freedom* (1988). On economics, see Richard H. Abbott, *Cotton and Capital* (1991); Walter Johnson, *River of Dark Dreams: Slavery and Empire in the Cotton Kingdom* (2013); Sven Beckert, *Empire of Cotton* (2015); and Edward Baptist, *The Half Has Never Been Told: Slavery and the Making of American Capitalism* (2014). For the ideological conflicts undergirding the era, see Bruce Levine, *Half Slave and Half Free* (1992), and Tyler Anbinder, *Nativism and Slavery: The Northern Know Nothings and the Politics of the 1850s* (1992). On the public discourse, see David Zarefsky, *Lincoln, Douglass, and Slavery: In the Crucible of Public Debate* (1990), and William Miller, *Arguing about Slavery* (1996). On slavery, see Ira Berlin, *Many Thousands Gone* (2000), and Walter Johnson, *Soul by Soul* (2001).

ENDNOTES

1. Frederick Douglass, *My Bondage and My Freedom* (London: Partridge and Oakey, 1855).
2. *New "Democratic" Doctrine.* (Washington, D.C., 1856), Library of Congress.
3. Chief Justice Robert Taney, Majority Opinion, *Dred Scott v. Sandford* (1857).

4. Justice John McLean, Dissenting Opinion, *Dred Scott v. Sandford* (1857).
5. George Fitzhugh, *Cannibals All! or, Slaves Without Masters* (Richmond, VA: A. Morris, 1857).
6. Hinton Rowan Helper, *The Impending Crisis of the South* (New York: Burdick Brothers, 1857).
7. Harriet Beecher Stowe, *Uncle Tom's Cabin, or Life Among the Lowly* (Boston: John P. Jewett & Co., 1852).
8. *Who Endorsed the Helper Book! Who Were the Inciters to Bloodshed?* (New York, 1861), Library of Congress.

CHAPTER 12

HOW DID AMERICAN
SLAVERY END?

HISTORICAL CONTEXT

Most Americans have a highly moral understanding of the American Civil War. It looms in our national imagination as a devastating but necessary conflict that redeemed the country from slavery. The narrative was central to Stephen Spielberg's successful film *Lincoln* (2012), which dramatized the president's struggle to secure passage of the Thirteenth Amendment in 1865. That story isn't wrong; it is just too simple. Such a moral narrative, however moving, can blind us to the complex origins and causes of the war. Ending slavery was at the heart of the conflict, yes, but there was nothing uncomplicated about American slavery.

Think of it this way: just because the war ended slavery does not mean the war was fought *to free the slaves*. While the sectional crisis was undoubtedly rooted in slavery, the victory of Abraham Lincoln as president in 1860 did not necessarily threaten that labor system. Indeed, the newly elected president had spent much of his campaign reassuring southerners that while he and the Republican Party objected to the *expansion* of slavery, they had no intention—and no power—to attack the institution where it legally existed. The Republicans went so far as to offer a constitutional amendment to protect slavery on the eve of Lincoln's inauguration. Yet by leaving the Union, southern secessionists sparked a war that eventually forced the Lincoln administration to use any means at its disposal to subdue the rebellion. President Lincoln, then, went from promising not to touch slavery in 1861, to attacking it by 1863, and finally amending the Constitution to destroy it completely in 1865.

As Chapter 11 demonstrated, the prospect of expanding slavery westward in the 1850s shocked and disturbed many northerners and drove them to join the new Republican Party. The Party had dedicated itself to preventing the extension of slavery into new territories, but was dealt a blow when the 1857 *Dred Scott* v. *Sanford* decision made it clear that rights of property extended to slave owners moving west. This, however, inadvertently advanced the popularity of the Republicans and gave the relatively unknown Abraham Lincoln a clear issue on which to stand. Perhaps the most remarkable thing about the 1858 Lincoln–Douglas debates was that they hinged not on the issues internal to Illinois, but on the legality of slavery in the territories. Though Lincoln lost that Senate race, he became a major force in the party, with national name recognition and a clear commitment to the Republican position of respecting slavery where it existed while objecting to its growth into the territories.

In 1860, Lincoln and Douglas faced each other for the presidency, but this time two other candidates split the southern vote. The race reflected deepening sectional tensions, with southerners and northerners increasingly suspicious of each other's motives. Despite the four-way race, Lincoln managed to win more electoral votes than the other three candidates combined, a reflection of the growing population of the northern states. Lincoln's victory led to an astonishing series of events that shocked Americans in both the North and South. First, leaders in South Carolina moved ahead with their plans to leave the Union once Lincoln was elected, and by Christmas had declared themselves independent of the United States. In the ensuing weeks, six other states followed, seceding from the Union and banding together to form the Confederate States of America on February 1.

Historians have debated whether it was possible to de-escalate the secession crisis in the winter of 1861. There was certainly no shortage of efforts to stave off disunion. Kentucky Senator John Crittenden advanced a compromise that permitted slavery to extend into the American Southwest, while clearly limiting it in the northern territories. President-elect Lincoln rejected Crittenden's plan as a violation of the Republican Party platform of limiting the growth of slavery, though he remained open to other possible options and compromises that might stem the secession crisis. Perhaps the most revealing is an amendment proposed by Thomas Corwin, Republican Congressman from Ohio. Corwin, like many in his party, believed that the federal government had no power to end slavery where it existed. He hoped that a clear statement of this fact might reassure southern slaveholders and so proposed a Constitutional amendment to that effect. Protect slavery where it existed, Corwin reasoned, and you potentially avert secession and war.

Corwin was joined in his effort by several antislavery activists, including Thaddeus Stevens and Owen Lovejoy. Republicans and other antislavery members of Congress understood the limits of their power to eradicate slavery and acknowledged that any changes to that effect would have to be undertaken by the slave states themselves. Corwin's amendment—which would have been the Constitution's thirteenth—passed both houses of Congress. In his inaugural address, Lincoln repeatedly vowed to leave slavery untouched in the southern states and acknowledged the Corwin amendment. In the ensuing weeks, several states ratified the amendment, though it was ultimately rendered moot by the onset of war. This turn of events demonstrates that even those who hated slavery were willing to *protect* the institution in an effort to end the secession crisis. This original Thirteenth Amendment reminds us that for many Americans, emancipation was not worth the risk of war.

Yet South Carolina had already seceded, followed by Mississippi, Florida, Alabama, Georgia, Louisiana, and Texas. Just a month after his inauguration, Lincoln faced the question of whether to protect Fort Sumter, situated just off the coast of Charleston. South Carolinians considered Lincoln's decision to resupply the fort an act of aggression and, on April 12, opened fire. In response, Lincoln called up 75,000 volunteers from state militias to suppress the rebellion. This act spurred Virginia to secede, followed by North Carolina, Arkansas, and Tennessee. The momentum toward war seemed irreversible, even welcome after decades of crises over slavery. One of the great ironies, of course, is that by leaving the union slaveholders finally destroyed the very thing they hoped to protect. When a new Thirteenth Amendment to the Constitution finally passed, it abolished slavery for good.

The following letters, speeches, and images enable you to explore the complex history of emancipation during the Civil War. As you examine the documents, ask yourself how this history unfolded and whether alternative outcomes were possible. What options were available to Lincoln, and how did he balance his desire to preserve the Union with his well-known objections to slavery? Remember, the destruction of slavery required tremendous effort on the part of slaves, abolitionists, antislavery Republicans, the Lincoln administration, and especially the Union army. There was nothing inevitable about emancipation; it resulted from the complex and contingent developments of the war itself.

INTRODUCTION TO DOCUMENT 1

In 1859, Jackson Whitney, an escaped slave, wrote a letter to his former master, William Riley, from the safety of Canada. Whitney's words are a stark reminder of the active, even primary role that slaves took in their own liberation. Frederick Douglass, himself an escaped slave and a highly influential abolitionist, reprinted Whitney's letter in the inaugural issue of his monthly publication in 1859. You might compare this letter to Douglass's own message to his former master, reproduced as Document 1 of Chapter 11. Whitney wrote to Riley from the city of Sandwich, Ontario (later named Windsor), an important terminus on the Underground Railroad.

1. JACKSON WHITNEY'S LETTER TO HIS FORMER MASTER

FUGITIVES HOME
SANDWICH, CANADA WEST
MARCH 18, 1859

Mr. William Riley
Springfield, Kentucky

Sir: I take this opportunity to dictate a few lines to you, supposing you might be curious to know my whereabouts. I am happy to inform you that I am in Canada, in good health, and have been here several days. Perhaps, by this time, you have concluded that robbing a woman of her husband, and children of their father does not pay, at least in your case; and I

thought, while lying in jail by your direction, that if you had no remorse or conscience that would make you feel a poor, broken-hearted man, and his worse-than-murdered wife and child, . . . and could not by any entreaty or permission be induced to do as you promised you would, which was to let me go with my family for $800—but contended for $1,000, when you had promised to take the same you gave for me (which was $660) at the time you bought me, and let me go with my dear wife and children! but instead would render me miserable, and lie to me, and to your neighbors . . . and when you was at Louisville trying to sell me! then I thought it was time for me to make my feet feel for Canada, and let your conscience feel in your pocket. —Now you cannot say but that I did all that was honorable and right while I was with you, although I was a slave. I pretended all the time that I thought you, or some one else had a better right to me than I had to myself, which you know is rather hard thinking.—You know, too, that you proved a traitor to me in the time of need, and when in the most bitter distress that the human soul is capable of experiencing; and could you have carried out your purposes there would have been no relief. But I rejoice to say that an unseen, kind spirit appeared for the oppressed, and bade me take up my bed and walk—the result of which is that I am victorious and you are defeated.

I am comfortably situated in Canada, working for George Harris [another fugitive slave from Kentucky who had bought a farm in Canada]. . . .

There is only one thing to prevent me being entirely happy here, and that is the want of my dear wife and children, and you to see us enjoying ourselves together here. I wish you could realize the contrast between Freedom and Slavery; but it is not likely that we shall ever meet again on this earth. But if you want to go to the next world and meet a God of love, mercy, and justice, in peace; who says "Inasmuch as you did it to the least of them my little ones, you did it unto me"—making the professions that you do, pretending to be a follower of Christ, and tormenting me and my little ones as you have done—[you] had better repair the breaches you have made among us in this world, by sending my wife and children to me; thus preparing to meet your God in peace; for if God don't punish you for inflicting such distress on the poorest of His poor, then there is no use of *having any* God, or *talking* about one. . . .

I hope you will consider candidly, and see if the case does not justify every word I have said, and ten times as much. You must not consider that it is a slave talking to "massa" now, but one as free as yourself.

I subscribe myself one of the *abused* of America, but one of the *justified* and *honored* of Canada.
Jackson Whitney[1]

INTRODUCTION TO DOCUMENT 2

Two years after Jackson Whitney wrote his letter Abraham Lincoln was inaugurated as the sixteenth president of the United States. Although Lincoln's Inaugural Address affirmed his responsibility to protect slavery where it existed, he also rejected secession as anarchistic and illegal. He recognized the likelihood of a military confrontation and that it was impossible to disentangle the institution of slavery from such a conflict.

Many slaves understood this as well, and began to advance their own freedom, as Whitney had, at great risk to their own safety. Shortly after Virginia voted to join the Confederacy, and before any military engagements had begun, General Benjamin Butler and his troops occupied Fortress Monroe, near Norfolk. Soon, three fugitive slaves sought asylum at the fort, informing the army that they were owned by a Confederate colonel who had put them to work at a nearby harbor. In the act of approaching Butler, the fugitive slaves forced him to confront the relationship between the war and slavery: Should he take them in, knowing that the Administration had promised not to disrupt slavery in the southern states? Or should he return them, knowing they would be used to aid the Confederate war effort?

When the owner came to demand the return of his slaves, Butler refused, arguing that since Virginia had seceded from the Union, the Fugitive Slave Law was no longer in effect. Instead, the Union general classified the slaves as "contraband of war", or property used to aid the rebellion that was therefore subject to confiscation. With this act, Butler set a precedent. By June, 500 fugitive slaves were under his jurisdiction at Fortress Monroe, and soon thereafter, the number swelled to thousands. Moreover, that news spread to other areas, leading many slaves to seek out Union lines. Butler's letter (Document 2) outlines how he made this important decision, which had far-reaching consequences as the war unfolded. As you read Butler's letter, consider what it reveals about his thinking regarding slavery and the war. Does Butler see his decision as a radical and important one? Did he seem to be reacting or leading? Why was he writing directly to the Secretary of War about his decision?

2. GENERAL BUTLER ON THE CONTRABAND

HEAD-QUARTERS DEPARTMENT OF VIRGINIA FORTRESS MONROE, JULY 30, 1861

Hon. Simon Cameron, Secretary of War:—

. . . Up to and at the time of the order I had been preparing for an advance movement, by which I hoped to cripple the resources of the enemy at Yorktown, and especially by seizing a large quantity of negroes who were being pressed into their service in building the intrenchments there. In the village of Hampton there were a large number of negroes, composed in a great measure of women and children of the men who had fled, thither within my lines for protection, who had escaped from marauding parties of rebels who had been gathering up able-bodied blacks to aid them in constructing their batteries on the James and York Rivers. I had employed the men in Hampton in throwing up intrenchments, and they were working zealously and efficiently at that duty, saving our soldiers from that labor under the gleam of the mid-day sun. The women were earning substantially their own subsistence in washing, marketing, and taking care of the clothes of the soldiers, and rations were being served out to the men who worked for the support of the children. I have, therefore, now within the Peninsula, this side of Hampton Creek, 900 negroes, 300 of whom are able-bodied men, 30 of whom are men substantially past hard labor, 175 women 225 children under the age of 10 years, and 170 between 10 and 18 years, and many more

coming in. The questions which this state of facts presents are very embarrassing.

First. What shall be done with them? And, *Second,* What is their state and condition?

Upon these questions I desire the instructions of the Department.

The first question, however, may perhaps be answered by considering the last. Are these men, women, and children, slaves? Are they free? Is their condition that of men, women, and children, or of property, or is it a mixed relation? What their *status* was under the Constitution, we all know. What has been the effect of rebellion and a state of war upon that *status*? When I adopted the theory of treating the able-bodied negro fit to work in the trenches as property liable to be used in aid of rebellion, and so contraband of war, that condition of things was in so far met, as I then and still believe, on a legal and constitutional basis. But now a new series of questions arises. Passing by women, the children, certainly, cannot be treated on that basis; if property, they must be considered the incumbrance rather than the auxiliary of an army, and, of course, in no possible legal relation could be treated as contraband. Are they property? If they were so, they have been left by their masters and owners, deserted, thrown away, abandoned, liked the wrecked vessel upon the ocean. Their former possessors and owners have causelessly, traitorously, rebelliously, and, to carry out the figure, practically abandoned them to be swallowed up by the winter storm of starvation. If property, do they not become the property of the salvors? but we, their salvors, do not need and will not hold such property, and will assume no such ownership: has not, therefore, all proprietary relation ceased? Have they not become, thereupon, men, women, and children? No longer under ownership of any kind, the fearful relics of fugitive masters, have they not by their masters' acts, and the state of war, assumed the condition, which we hold to be the normal one, of those made in God's image. Is not every constitutional, legal, and moral requirement, as well to the runaway master as

their relinquished slaves, thus answered? I confess that my own mind is compelled by this reasoning to look upon them as men and women. If not free born, yet free, manumitted, sent forth from the hand that held them never to be reclaimed.

Of course, if this reasoning, thus imperfectly set forth, is correct, my duty, as a humane man, is very plain. I should take the same care of these men, women, and children, houseless, homeless, and unprovided for, as I would of the same number of men, women, and children, who, for their attachment to

Image 12.1 "Human Contraband" (1862)

These slaves were taken by Union forces as they marched up the Virginia Peninsula in the spring of 1862. By the time this photograph was taken in May, Congress had prohibited the armed forces from returning slaves to disloyal masters and allowing for the confiscation of slaves used to aid the rebellion.

Source: James F. Gibson, "Contrabands at Foller's House, Cumberland Landing Virginia, May 14, 1862." Courtesy of Library of Congress, Prints and Photographs Division. LC-B811-383

the Union, had been driven or allowed to flee from the Confederate States. I should have no doubt on this question, had I not seen it stated that an order had been issued by General McDowell in his department, substantially forbidding all fugitive slaves from coming within his lines, or being harbored there. Is that order to be enforced in all military departments? If so, who are to be considered fugitive slaves? Is a slave to be considered fugitive whose master runs away and leaves him? Is it forbidden to the troops to aid or harbor within their lines the negro children who are found therein, or is the soldier, when his march has destroyed their means of subsistence, to allow them to starve because he has driven off the rebel masters?

I have very decided opinions upon the subject of this order. It does not become me to criticize it, and I write in no spirit of criticism, but simply to explain the full difficulties that surround the enforcing it. If the enforcement of that order becomes the policy of the Government, I, as a soldier, shall be bound to enforce it steadfastly, if not cheerfully. But if left to my own discretion, as you may have gathered from my reasoning, I should take a widely different course form that which it indicates.

In a loyal State I would put down a servile insurrection. In a state of rebellion I would confiscate that which was used to oppose my arms, and take all that property, which constituted the wealth of that State, and furnished the means by which the war is prosecuted, beside being the cause of the war; and if, in so doing, it should be objected that human beings were brought to the free enjoyment of life, liberty, and the pursuit of happiness, such objections might not require much consideration.

Pardon me for addressing the Secretary of War directly upon this question, as it involves some political considerations as well as propriety of military action. I am, sir, your obedient servant,
Benjamin F. Butler.[2]

INTRODUCTION TO DOCUMENTS 3 AND 4

Butler was correct: there *were* serious political considerations to any move against slavery, for the Lincoln Administration was desperate to stop the momentum of secession and to keep as many states of the upper south—Delaware, Maryland, Missouri, and especially Kentucky—in the Union as possible. Yet Butler was not alone in his reasoning. Just a month after he wrote his letter, Congress passed the First Confiscation Act, which authorized Union forces to seize property that had been used to aid the Confederate war effort. This essentially nullified owners' claims to fugitive slaves, and while Lincoln worried about the effect this would have on the border states, he did not object.

The military situation and the antislavery sentiment in Congress continually challenged Lincoln to reconsider his commitment not to interfere with slavery. Pressure to move against slavery was also brought by abolitionists, who challenged the inviolability of the Constitution and the long history of compromises that had been forged over slavery. In Document 3, Lydia Maria Child, an advocate for women's rights and a longstanding opponent of slavery, voiced the sentiment of many abolitionists in her private letter to George Julian, an Indiana abolitionist and congressman who had pushed early on for emancipation as a war measure and the enlistment of blacks in the Union army. She was particularly thankful that Julian had protested General Halleck's decision to return a fugitive slave girl who had sought shelter with an Indiana regiment. As Child assessed the role of slavery in this conflict, she squarely considered the role of the founding fathers in enshrining slavery into the Constitution. Consider the stakes she attached to the war, even though it had been waged for less than a year by the time of her letter.

Even before the outbreak of war in the summer of 1861, federal agencies were mobilizing to gather military intelligence. The U.S. Coast Survey shifted into high gear to prepare maps and charts that would aid Union strategy. The agency was at the cutting edge of cartography, and the map shown in Document 4 was a ground-breaking attempt to translate census data into cartographic form. The map used numbers and shading to identify the ratio of slaves to the total population in each county, thereby gauging the relative strength of the Confederacy's most important and valuable resource, bond labor. It was widely copied during the war, and of special interest to President Lincoln, who used it to understand the relationship between slavery, support for secession, and Union strategy. The map confirmed and elaborated the president's understanding of the South as a complex rather than a homogeneous region with a singular commitment to secession and slavery. From your perspective, what message does the map send? What might northern generals and leaders have learned from a map like this as opposed to a traditional map of southern railways, rivers, or general topography?

---

3. LYDIA MARIA CHILD, LETTER TO GEORGE JULIAN

January 30, 1862
Mr. Julian,
Dear Sir,

. . . I feel personal obligations to you for bringing so much sound good sense and high moral courage to the aid of Freedom, in its hour of peril. I was glad you ventured to say that our fathers made a mistake at the beginning, in admitting compromises into the Constitution. It is a true word. Wholesale lauding of the Constitution has made it an object of idol-worship. It is undoubtedly a valuable document, wise in nearly all its parts. But the best feature of a Republican Government is the power to modify it, according to the needs of the people. I suppose our fathers did really believe that slavery would be short-lived in this country, yet when my reverence for them leads me to make this excuse, I never can forget the ugly fact that they legislated for the continuance of the African Slave Trade twenty years. The fact is, they were determined to have a *Union*, on *any* terms, and the South then, as now, were imperious and unprincipled in their demands. The wise and good men of that time adopted a great fallacy, when they supposed that *any* compromise of moral principles *could* be transitory in its effects. Our politicians, with few exceptions, have gone on ever since

in the same path, and whether our crooked ways will ever be made straight, God alone knows. Only seven generations have passed away since that noble band of Puritans in the May-Flower made their memorable Covenant with God. . . . If there had been anything like a general state of moral healthfulness in the Free States, they would have long ago insisted upon calling a Convention of the people to modify the Constitution. But Alas! the same year that witnessed the landing of those sturdy freemen of the Lord in the May Flower, witnessed the landing of negro slaves to wait upon the "vagabond gentlemen," who settled Virginia. It was a mysterious Providence, that brought these two antagonistic elements in juxta position in this grand new field of human progress. If we could only get *rid* of the (poisonous) virus infused throughout the blood of our body politic! But it is not an excrescence to be cut off; it has infected the whole system with disease. If *all* the Slave States had seceded, the prospects for freedom would be hopeful; but I fear the *Union* Slaveholders are dragging us all down to ruin.

As for the government, I had better say nothing; for on *that* theme, I find it difficult to keep within bounds. Never had men such a glorious opportunity to redeem a country and immortalize themselves! Never did men show themselves so miserably deficient in all the qualities, which the crisis demanded! When I see the great swelling tide of popular enthusiasm ooze away through the slimy mud of shallow diplomacy, it seems as if my heart would break.

. . . We are not *worthy* of becoming an *example* to the nations; and perhaps the best use God can put us to is to make us a *warning*.

. . . With cordial thanks for your kind expressions to me personally, I am, with truest respect and gratitude, L. Maria Child.[3]

4. MAPPING THE SLAVE POPULATION (1861)

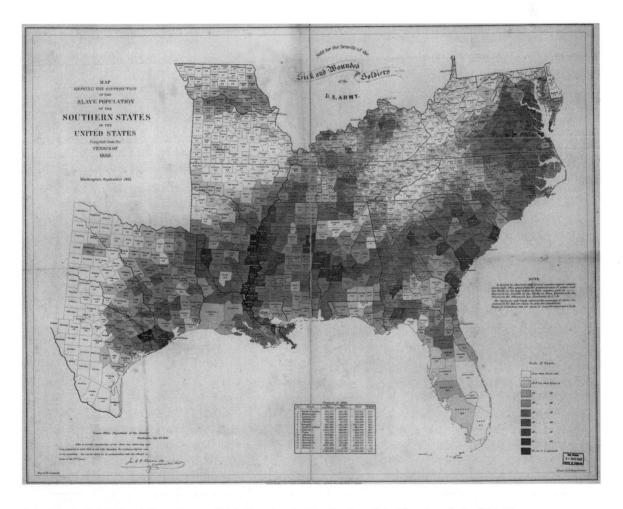

Image 12.2 United States Coast Survey, "Map Showing the Distribution of the Slave Population" (1861)

This was among the first American attempts to map Census data. For Lincoln, the map showed the South to be a complex place, with areas of strong support for slavery but also large regions where the absence of slaves might suggest weak Confederate sentiment.

Source: Library of Congress.

INTRODUCTION TO DOCUMENTS 5 AND 6

The pressure brought by Butler, Julian, and Child mattered. In March 1862, Congress adopted legislation that forbade members of the army and navy to return fugitive slaves to their owners. The following month, General David Hunter, the Union commander in the South Carolina Sea Islands, contemplated arming freed slaves for military service, an idea whose time would soon come. Congress continued to move against slavery, abolishing it in the District of Columbia on April 1862 and then in the territories later that summer. The jubilation that accompanied the end of slavery in the nation's capital, however, was tempered by the compromised circumstances of the decision, which involved compensating loyal owners and raising funds for the voluntary removal of slaves to Africa. The plan to relocate the freedmen to Africa was supported by none other than Lincoln himself, who agreed that it would correspondingly remove the source of sectional strife.

Lincoln's growing willingness to attack slavery came in part due to the military situation. The Union had won important victories in the western theater, at Forts Donelson and Henry, and especially the capture of New Orleans, which opened up about 200 miles of the lower Mississippi River to the Union. Yet the public's attention was riveted on the battlefront of Virginia, where General George McClellan's ambitious campaign to capture the Confederate capitol at Richmond stalled when Confederate general Joseph Johnston repulsed him at Fair Oaks. The failure of this campaign in June deeply frustrated Lincoln and led him to realize that the war would be harder and longer than he—or anyone else—had anticipated. Concerns abounded as well about the possibility of European nations recognizing the Confederacy. In light of these circumstances, Lincoln began to consider all means at his disposal. Slaves were the Confederacy's most valuable resource, so in July Lincoln secretly drafted an order of emancipation that could be used as a weapon of war.

At the same time, Congress passed a Second Confiscation Act, which—among other things, enabled Union forces to emancipate slaves that came within their control. Lincoln again pressed representatives of the border states to support gradual, compensated emancipation. Yet he added an important warning—if they failed to act, slavery in their states might itself become a casualty of war. Despite his urging, the border state representatives rejected his plan. That same month, Lincoln privately informed his cabinet that he would soon issue a proclamation freeing slaves in the states in rebellion against the Union. The public exchange here conveys the questions of both strategy and morality at work in the debate over attacking slavery. In Document 5 Horace Greeley—editor of the *New-York Tribune* and a vocal opponent of slavery—pressed Lincoln to act against all slaveholders, including those in the border-states. Lincoln's famous response, also public, follows Greeley's letter.

As you read this exchange, consider the following: why was Greeley so impatient with the President's policy toward the war, slavery, and the border states? What specifically does he take issue with, and were his criticisms of Lincoln valid? How did Lincoln answer Greeley? Given that he had already decided to use emancipation as a military measure in the war, why did he not make this clear in his response?

5. THE PRAYER OF TWENTY MILLIONS (1862)

HORACE GREELEY

To Abraham Lincoln, President of the U. States:

Dear Sir: I do not intrude to tell you—for you must know already—that a great proportion of those who triumphed in your election, and of all who desire the unqualified suppression of the Rebellion now desolating our country, are sorely disappointed and deeply pained by the policy you seem to be pursuing with regard to the slaves of Rebels. I write only to act succinctly and unmistakably before you what we require, what we think we have a right to expect, and of what we complain.

. . . We think you are strangely and disastrously remiss in the discharge of your official and imperative duty with regard to the emancipating provisions of the new Confiscation Act. Those provisions were designed to fight Slavery with Liberty. They prescribe that men loyal to the Union, and willing to shed their blood on her behalf, shall no longer be held, with the Nation's consent, in bondage to persistent, malignant traitors, who for twenty years have been plotting and for sixteen months have been fighting to divide and destroy our country. Why these traitors should be treated with tenderness by you, to the prejudice of the dearest rights of loyal men, we cannot conceive.

. . . We think you are unduly influenced by the counsels, the representations, the menaces, of certain fossil politicians hailing from the Border Slave States. . . . Slavery is everywhere the inciting cause and sustaining base of treason: the most slaveholding sections of Maryland and Delaware being this day, though under the Union flag, in full sympathy with the Rebellion, while the Free-Labor portions of Tennessee and of Texas, though writhing under the bloody heel of Treason, are unconquerably loyal to the Union. . . . It seems to us the most obvious truth, that whatever strengthens or fortifies Slavery in the Border States strengthens also Treason, and drives home the wedge intended to divide the Union. Had you from the first refused to recognize in those States, as her, any other than unconditional loyalty—that which stands for the Union, whatever may become of Slavery—those States would have been, and would be, far more helpful and less troublesome to the defenders of the Union than they have been, or now are.

. . . We complain that the Union cause has suffered, and is now suffering immensely, from mistaken deference to Rebel Slavery. Had you, Sir, in your Inaugural Address, unmistakably given notice that, in case the Rebellion already commenced were persisted in, and your efforts to preserve the Union and enforce the laws should be resisted by armed force, *you would recognize no loyal person as rightfully held in Slavery by a traitor,* we believe the Rebellion would therein have received a staggering if not fatal blow. . . . Had you then proclaimed that Rebellion would strike the shackles from the slaves of every traitor, the wealthy and the cautious would have been supplied with a powerful inducement to remain loyal. As it was, every coward in the South soon became a traitor from fear; for Loyalty was perilous, while Treason seemed comparatively safe. . . . The result is just what might have been expected. Tens of thousands are fighting in the Rebel ranks to-day whose original bias and natural leanings would have led them into ours.

We complain that the Confiscation Act which you approved is habitually disregarded by your Generals, and that no word of rebuke for them from you has yet reached the public ear. Fremont's Proclamation and Hunter's Order favoring Emancipation were promptly annulled by you; while Halleck's No.3, forbidding fugitives from Slavery to Rebels to come within his lines—an order as unmilitary as inhuman, and which received the hearty approbation of every traitor in America—with scores of like tendency, have never provoked even your remonstrance. We complain that the officers of the Armies have habitually repelled rather than invited the approach of slaves who would have gladly taken the risks of escaping from their Rebel masters to our camps, bringing intelligence often of inestimable value to the Union cause. . . .

. . . I close as I began with the statement that what an immense majority of the Loyal Millions of your countrymen require of you is a frank, declared, unqualified, ungrudging execution of the laws of the land, more especially of the Confiscation Act. That Act gives freedom to the slaves of Rebels coming within our lines, or whom those lines may at any time inclose—we ask you to render it due obedience by publicly requiring all your subordinates to recognize and obey it. . . .

Yours, Horace Greeley
New York, August 19, 1862[4]

6. PRESIDENT LINCOLN, RESPONSE TO HORACE GREELEY

ABRAHAM LINCOLN

EXECUTIVE MANSION, WASHINGTON
AUGUST 22, 1862

Hon. Horace Greeley:
Dear Sir:

I have just read yours of the 19th, addressed to myself through the New-York Tribune. If there be in it any statements, or assumptions of fact, which I may know to be erroneous, I do not, now and here, controvert them. If there be in it any inferences which I may believe to be falsely drawn, I do not now and here, argue against them. If there be perceptible in it an impatient and dictatorial tone, I waive it in deference to an old friend, whose heart I have always supposed to be right.

As to the policy I "seem to be pursuing" as you say, I have not meant to leave any one in doubt.

I would save the Union. I would save it the shortest way under the Constitution. The sooner the national authority can be restored; the nearer the Union will be "the Union as it was." If there be those who would not save the Union, unless they could at the same time *save* slavery, I do not agree with them. If there be those who would not save the Union unless they could at the same time *destroy* slavery, I do not agree with them. My paramount object in this struggle *is* to save the Union, and is *not* either to save or to destroy slavery. If I could save the Union without freeing *any* slave I would do it, and if I could save it by freeing *all* the slaves I would do it; and if I could save it by freeing some and leaving others alone I would also do that. What I do about slavery, and the colored race, I do because I believe it helps to save the Union; and what I forbear, I forbear because I do *not* believe it would help to save the Union. I shall do *less* whenever I shall believe what I am doing hurts the cause, and I shall do *more* whenever I shall believe doing more will help the cause. I shall try to correct errors when shown to be errors; and I shall adopt new views so fast as they shall appear to be true views.

I have here stated my purpose according to my view of *official* duty; and I intend no modification of my oft-expressed *personal* wish that all men every where could be free. Yours,

A. Lincoln[5]

The President's thinking on emancipation solidified in the summer of 1862. By the time he responded to Greeley, Lincoln had already written the preliminary emancipation proclamation, yet his cabinet advised him not to announce the decision until the military situation had improved. In September, Union General George McClellan engaged General Robert E. Lee's Confederate troops over several days near Antietam Creek in Maryland. This marked the bloodiest battle of the war, killing 20,000 men in total, and September 17 remains the single deadliest day in all of American history. Five days after Lee retreated across the creek, and Lincoln announced the preliminary Emancipation Proclamation, on September 22, 1862.

That proclamation was extremely limited in reach. It did not go into effect until January 1, 1863, giving the rebel states an opportunity to return to the Union and protect their slaves. Thereafter slaves would be subject to emancipation, but only in those areas that were not yet under Union control. Lincoln did this intentionally, for he believed that as commander in chief he only had the power to use emancipation as a military measure. To reach beyond that by attempting to liberate slaves in the border states, or in areas already occupied by the military, would be unconstitutional.

The sheer numbers killed in 1862 and 1863 shifted Union understandings of the meaning of the war—Shiloh, Chancellorsville, Vicksburg, and dozens of others, then finally Gettysburg, where 50,000 men died. The loss of life reached every corner of the Union, and generated a growing willingness to attack slavery. In the next document, President Lincoln dedicated a new cemetery at Gettysburg, Pennsylvania, in November 1863. In the course of his remarks, he attached a larger meaning to the war, framing it as a second American Revolution for liberty and equality.

7. THE GETTYSBURG ADDRESS, NOVEMBER 19, 1863

ABRAHAM LINCOLN

Four score and seven years ago our fathers brought forth on this continent, a new nation, conceived in Liberty, and dedicated to the proposition that all men are created equal.

Now we are engaged in a great civil war, testing whether that nation, or any nation so conceived and so dedicated, can long endure. We are met on a great battle-field of that war. We have come to dedicate a portion of that field, as a final resting place for those who here gave their lives that that nation might live. It is altogether fitting and proper that we should do this.

But, in a larger sense, we can not dedicate—we can not consecrate—we cannot hallow—this ground. The brave men, living and dead, who struggled here, have consecrated it, far above our poor power to add or detract. The world will little not, nor long remember what we say here, but it can never forget what they did here. It is for us the living, rather, to be dedicated here to the unfinished work which they who fought here have thus far so nobly advanced. It is rather for us to be here dedicated to the great task remaining before us—that from these honored dead we take increased devotion to that cause for which they gave the last full measure of devotion—that we here highly resolve that these dead shall not have died in vain—that this nation, under God, shall have a new birth of freedom—and that government of the people, by the people, and for the people, shall not perish from the earth.

INTRODUCTION TO DOCUMENTS 8, 9, AND 10

The next three documents—like the Gettysburg Address—illuminate the symbolic and emotional meaning of the war, and especially emancipation. Upon reading the announcement of the Emancipation Proclamation in fall of 1862, portrait artist Francis Bicknell Carpenter was struck by its historic importance. Carpenter sought to capture that moment on canvas, and the President invited him to the develop the portrait at the White House in 1864. While there, Carpenter repeatedly noticed the president scrutinizing the Coast Survey's map of slavery (Document 4). This prompted the artist to study the map in order to reproduce it clearly in the lower right corner of his iconic painting, "First Reading of the Emancipation Proclamation" (Document 8). Lincoln praised Carpenter's finished portrait and singled out the slave map as one of the most satisfying details. Carpenter's work now hangs over the west staircase of the Senate wing of the U.S. Capitol.

The symbolic weight of the Emancipation Proclamation is also powerfully captured in Document 9, a painting by William T. Carlton that depicts African Americans intently waiting for the moment that liberation would take effect, just after midnight on January 1, 1863. Entitled "Watch-Meeting, Dec. 31, 1862," the painting portrays the dramatic and emotional core of emancipation, even though few slaves were actually liberated on that day. At the center of the painting, a man holds a pocket watch, marking the onset of emancipation on New Year's Day. He is surrounded by an anxious group, creating a mood of suspense and apprehension. Thereafter, "watch-meetings" became important religious services in the African-American community, commemorating the end of slavery and the beginning of freedom. Carlton's painting was made into cartes-de-viste—small reproductions for popular consumption—and the original was given to Lincoln; it hung in the White House during his last days. In Document 10, abolitionist William Lloyd Garrison introduces a letter from the president, thanking him for that gift and acknowledging its meaning. Garrison proudly reprinted Lincoln's letter in his newspaper, *The Boston Liberator*, on February 17, 1865.

Given that both paintings found favor with the public and were widely reproduced, what can they tell us about contemporary attitudes toward Lincoln's Emancipation Proclamation? Which do you find more powerful, and why?

8. LINCOLN AND EMANCIPATION (1864)

FRANCIS BICKNELL CARPENTER

Image 12.3 "First Reading of the Emancipation Proclamation of President Lincoln to his Cabinet" (1864)
Carpenter's iconic portrait exalted the role of the president in ending slavery, though the reality was far more complicated. Note the appearance of the slave map—a favorite of Lincoln's—at lower right.
Source: Francis Bicknell Carpenter (oil on canvas, 1864), U.S. Senate Collection, Washington, D.C.

9. ANTICIPATING EMANCIPATION (1863)

Ent'd according to Act of Congress, A. D. 1863, by W. T. Carlton, in the Clerk's Office of
the District Court of the District of Mass.

Image 12.4 "Waiting for the Hour" (1863)

This image memorializes the moment that the Emancipation Proclamation took effect, just after midnight on January 1, 1863. As explained in the subsequent document, the original painting was given by abolitionists to President Lincoln as a token of gratitude and a reminder of the human dimension of the proclamation.

Source: Watch meeting, Dec. 31, 1862—Waiting for the hour. Heard & Moseley, Cartes de viste, Boston, c. 1863, Library of Congress. Based on a painting by William T. Carlton.

10. A GIFT FROM ABOLITIONISTS TO THE PRESIDENT

WILLIAM LLOYD GARRISON

LETTER FROM THE PRESIDENT

Last summer, after the public exhibition in this city of Mr. W. T. Carlton's very meritorious painting, entitled "Watch Meeting, Dec. 31, 1862—or Waiting For The Hour"—the Hour of Emancipation that the President's Proclamation of January 1, 1863—it was deemed eminently fitting that it should be purchased by subscription, and presented to President Lincoln as a mark of personal respect, and warm appreciation of his act, whereby more than three millions of fetters were broken, and a death-dealing blow was virtually given to the entire system of chattel slavery. The list of subscribers was headed by Gov. Andrew, and composed of some of our most respected citizens—the sum raised amounting to $500. The painting was duly forwarded to Washington, accompanied by an explanatory and congratulatory letter to the President; but, though the safe arrival of it at the White House was ascertained, its receipt has remained unacknowledged till now. The reason for this is satisfactorily given in the following ingenuous and appreciative letter just received by us from Mr. Lincoln.

Executive Mansion, Washington
7th February, 1865
My Dear Mr. Garrison:

I have your kind letter of the 21st of January, and can only beg that you will pardon the seeming neglect occasioned by my constant engagements. When I received the spirited and admirable painting, "Waiting for the Hour," I directed my Secretary not to acknowledge its arrival at once, preferring to make my personal acknowledgement of the thoughtful kindness of the donors; and waiting for some leisure hour, I have committed the discourtesy of not replying at all.

I hope you will believe that my thanks, though late, are most cordial, and I request that you will convey them to those associated with you in this flattering and generous gift.

I am, very truly, your friend and servant.

A. Lincoln[6]

INTRODUCTION TO DOCUMENTS 11, 12, AND 13

Aside from its political and symbolic importance, the Emancipation Proclamation provided for the enlistment of freed slaves into the Union forces, eventually adding 200,000 fresh troops to the war effort. These soldiers were especially important given that the strategy of the new commanding general, Ulysses S. Grant, was to relentlessly attack on several fronts. Black troops served honorably and valiantly, and though they were subject to inferior pay, segregation, and poor treatment, Lincoln named their military contribution "the heaviest blow yet dealt to the rebellion" in 1863.

Even with the enlistment of black soldiers, however, the war dragged on for another two years. During that time, Lincoln faced re-election in 1864 and believed for a time that he would lose to General George McClellan, who was not very successful as a military commander yet popular with northerners who wanted the war to end. Democrat McClellan campaigned against Lincoln's conduct of the war and stressed that Union victory need not bring emancipation to the southern states. The fate of slavery, in other words, was still very much in question in 1864, and had McClellan prevailed, the Civil War might carry a very different meaning today. Conversely, within the Republican Party—temporarily renamed the Union Party—momentum began to build for a constitutional amendment that would end slavery, not just in the South but throughout the nation. Without an amendment explicitly outlawing slavery, Lincoln and others worried that the end of war might leave the freedmen vulnerable to the return to bondage.

Prospects for a Republican victory improved as the Union army aggressively tore through Tennessee and Georgia. General William Tecumseh Sherman's capture of Atlanta in September boosted Lincoln's popularity significantly, as did Admiral Farragut's multiple victories in Mobile Bay. When the Republican Party won by substantial margins in November, Lincoln considered it a mandate to move forward with a Constitutional amendment to destroy slavery once and for all. The House passed it on January 31, 1865 by a vote of 119 to 56, marking not just a victory for the Republican Party and the Union cause but also a shift in thinking about the Constitution itself. Since the Bill of Rights, the Constitution had been amended only twice, relatively minor changes in both cases. The passage of the Thirteenth Amendment in December 1865 implicitly acknowledged that the Constitution was subject to substantive revisions.

The final set of documents examines the end of slavery in 1865. Document 11 is a speech by the amendment's sponsor, James Ashley, a Republican from Ohio and an ardent abolitionist. In Document 12, New York Democratic Representative Fernando Wood responds to Ashley with strong opposition to the amendment that was widely shared in his party. Wood had previously been mayor of New York City and openly expressed sympathy for the Confederacy and opposition to the war and the Lincoln administration. How did Wood and Ashley argue over the amendment, and what were the main sources of disagreement about how to proceed? How did each understand the meaning of the war?

Once the Thirteenth Amendment passed, many in the abolitionist movement believed their work was done, but Frederick Douglass urgently disagreed. He argued that the passage of the amendment and the ensuing defeat of the rebellion—immediately followed by the assassination of the president—was insufficient to ensure the rights and safety of African Americans. Without the ballot, Douglass argued, freedom was an empty gesture, simply the absence of bondage but not the achievement of social, political, or civil rights. Yet most Americans held widely different understandings of the place that freedmen would have in a postwar society. Document 13 is Douglass's address at the annual meeting of the American Anti-Slavery Society, a leading abolitionist organization, where he argued that passing the thirteenth amendment was only the beginning of freedom's work. As chapter 13 will reveal, Douglass was right to worry about the erosion of freedom for blacks after the end of the war.

11. SPEECH BEFORE THE HOUSE OF REPRESENTATIVES, JANUARY 6, 1865

JAMES ASHLEY (REPUBLICAN)

Mr. Speaker, *"If slavery is not wrong, nothing is wrong."* Thus simply and truthfully has spoken our worthy Chief Magistrate.

The proposition before us is, whether this universally acknowledged wrong shall be continued or abolished. Shall it receive the sanction of the American Congress by the rejection of this proposition [the Thirteenth Amendment], or shall it be condemned as an intolerable wrong by its adoption?

If slavery had never been known in the United States, and the proposition should be made in Congress to-day to authorize the people of the several States to enslave any portion of our own people or the people of any other country, it would be universally denounced as an infamous and criminal proposition, and its author would be execrated, and justly, by all right-thinking men, and held to be an enemy of the human race.

I do not believe such a proposition could secure a single vote in this House; and yet we all know that a number of gentlemen who could not be induced to enslave a single free man will nevertheless vote to keep millions of men in slavery, who are by nature and the laws of God as much entitled to their freedom as we are. I will not attempt to explain this strange inconsistency or make an argument to show its fallacy.

. . . That the founders of the Republic were sadly disappointed in their expectations that slavery would cease on the adoption of the national Constitution is undoubtedly true. Instead of disappearing as they confidently expected, circumstances unforeseen by them so strengthened slavery that in less than eighty years it became the dominant interest in the nation, and in 1860 openly demanded the entire control of the national Government. Because this demand was refused by the free laboring men of the North the slavemasters of the South organized this the most wicked of all rebellions, and for nearly four long years have waged this terrible war with the avowed purpose of destroying the best form of government ever vouchsafed to man, in order to establish in its stead a Government whose corner-stone should be human slavery. This is the logic of the contest.

. . . If the national Constitution had been rightfully interpreted, and the Government organized under it properly administered, slavery could not have legally existed in this country for a single hour, and practically but a few years after the adoption of the Constitution. Only because the fundamental principles of the Government have been persistently violated in its administration, and the Constitution violated in its administration, and the Constitution grossly perverted by the courts, is it necessary to-day to pass the amendment now under consideration. I say this much in vindication of the memory of the great and good men who, when establishing this Government, made a Constitution which to-day is the best known among men.

. . . Mr. Speaker, if slavery is wrong and criminal, as the great body of enlightened and Christian men admit, it is certainly our duty to abolish it, if we have the power.

. . . Pass this amendment and the gloomy shadow of slavery will never again darken the fair fame of our country or tarnish the glory of democratic institutions in the land of Washington. Pass this amendment and the brightest page in the history of the Thirty-Eighth Congress, now so soon to close, will be the one on which is recorded the names of the requisite number of members voting in its favor.

. . . The genius of history with iron pen is waiting to record our verdict where it will remain forever for all the coming generations of men to approve or condemn. . . . Let no loyal man, in such an hour as this, record his vote against this just proposition, and thus vote to prolong the rebellion and perpetuate the despotism of American slavery in this Republic.[7]

12. SPEECH BEFORE THE HOUSE OF REPRESENTATIVES, JANUARY 10, 1865

FERNANDO WOOD (DEMOCRAT)

Mr. Speaker, I presume it will not be contended that the condition of the native African is, in any regard, equal to that of the American slave. Sir, the Africans live in their native wilds as slaves. The Africans are sold into slavery by themselves. I contend that their condition in this country is in every regard improved. From barbarians they become civilized Christians; from slaves they become freemen. Admitting all the sins with which slavery is charged, it cannot be denied that it has been an instrument in the hands of God by which to confer a benefit upon that unfortunate race.

Now, sir, I contend that, if we desire to be philanthropic—if we desire to confer a benefit upon that people—let us afford every amelioration of their condition that we can under the law; but, sir, let us not forget that, evil though slavery be, there is yet a greater evil for this unfortunate country, and that is its destruction, the disunion, the consummation of the ruin now before us.

... Mr. Speaker, I had hoped that at this session of Congress there would exist a condition of public affairs that would bring about certain peace and Union; that these measures of aggression against the southern States would no longer have necessity of palliation. I had hoped that this Government would entertain propositions which have been made for a cessation of hostilities and the restoration of this Union upon the basis of the existing Constitution.

But, sir, I have been disappointed. There is no disposition to heal this quarrel at all. There is no disposition on the part of the party in power to restore the Union upon the basis of the old order of things.

I can only say further, Mr. Speaker, that I shall vote against this resolution [to pass the Thirteenth Amendment]. I shall vote against it because it is not within the power of Congress to pass it. I shall vote against it because it is unwise, impolitic at this time, if we could pass it legally. I shall vote against it because it is another step toward the eternal separation of the two sections. I shall vote against it because it would be no advantage to the negro if successful.

I shall vote against it because it is an improper intermeddling with the domestic affairs of others. I shall vote against it because I want to remove every obstacle to the peaceful solution of this great question; I want to alleviate the condition of the South as well as the North; I want to discontinue these controversies and struggles now pending between men who but yesterday were fellow-citizens of the same great country, with the same constitutional rights and privileges. I shall vote against it because I would leave to every State and every political community the entire control of their own domestic affairs. I shall vote it because I want to preserve the essence of our constitutional liberties.

I want to continue this as a Republic. I want to disseminate power from this central point instead of concentrating it here. I want to preserve the limitations of the Constitution and of the Government, as originally constructed, in theory as well as in letter and spirit, that we shall not interfere with the relation of master and slave any more than between husband and wife.

... We want the Union; we want these States back again; we want to see these men represented upon this floor; we want them to obey the laws and the Constitution; admitting they have committed a wicked folly in attempting to rebel. "To err is human; to forgive, divine. . . ."[8]

13. SPEECH AT THIRTY-SECOND ANNUAL MEETING OF THE AMERICAN ANTI-SLAVERY SOCIETY, MAY 10, 1865

FREDERICK DOUGLASS

... I take this ground; whether this Constitutional Amendment is law or not, whether it has been ratified by a sufficient number of States to make it law or not, I hold that the work of Abolitionists is not done. Even if every State in the Union had ratified that Amendment, while the black man is confronted in the legislation of the South by the word "white," our work as Abolitionists, as I conceive it, is not done. ... What advantage is a provision like this Amendment to the black man, if the Legislature of any State can to-morrow declare that no black man's testimony shall be received in a court of law? Where are we then? Any wretch may enter the house of a black man, and commit any violence he pleases; if he happens to do it only in the presence of black persons, he goes unwhipt of justice ["Hear, hear"]. And don't tell me that those people down there have become so just and honest all at once that they will not pass laws denying to black men the right to testify against white men in the courts of law. Why, our Northern States have done it. Illinois, Indiana and Ohio have done it. Here in the midst of institutions that have gone forth from old Plymouth Rock, the black man has been excluded from testifying in the courts of law; and if the Legislature of every Southern State to-morrow pass a law, declaring that no Negro shall testify in any courts of law, they will not violate that provision of the Constitution. Such laws exist now at the South. The next day, the Legislatures may pass a law that any black man who shall lift his arm in self-defence, even, against a white man, shall have that arm severed from his body, and may be hanged and quartered, and his head and quarters set up in the most public parts of the district where the crime shall have been committed. Such laws now exist at the South, and they might exist under this provision of the Constitution that there shall be neither slavery nor involuntary servitude in any State of the Union.

Then another point. I have thought, for the last fifteen years, that we had an anti-slavery Constitution—a Constitution intended "to secure the blessings of liberty to ourselves and our posterity." But we have had slavery all along. . . . Slavery is not abolished until the black man has the ballot. While the Legislature of the South retain the right to pass laws making any discrimination between black and white, slavery still lives there. [Applause] . . . Now, while the black man can be denied a vote, while the Legislatures of the South can take from him the right to keep and bear arms, as they can—they would not allow a Negro to walk with a cane where I came from, they would not allow five of them to assemble together—the work of the Abolitionists is not finished. Notwithstanding the provision in the Constitution of the United States, that the right to keep and bear arms shall not be abridged, the black man has never had the right either to keep or bear arms; and the Legislatures of the States will still have the power to forbid it, under this Amendment. . . .

. . . [L]et the civil power of the States be restored, and the old prejudices and hostility to the Negro will revive. Aye, the very fact that the Negro has been used to defeat this rebellion and strike down the standards of the Confederacy will be a stimulus to all their hatreds, to all their malice, and lead them to legislate with greater stringency towards this class than ever before. [Applause] The American people are bound—bound by their sense of honor (I hope by their sense of honor, at least, by a just sense of honor), to extend the franchise of the Negro; and I was going to say, that the Abolitionists of the American Anti-Slavery Society were bound to "stand still, and see the salvation of God," until that work is done. [Applause] Where shall the black man look for support, my friends, if the American Anti-Slavery society fails him? ["Hear, hear"] From whence shall we expect a certain sound from the trumpet of freedom, when the old pioneer, when this Society that has survived mobs, and martyrdom, and the combined efforts of priest-craft and state-craft to suppress it, shall all at once subside, on the mere intimation that the Constitution has been amended, so that neither slavery nor involuntary servitude shall hereafter be allowed in this land? . . .[9]

POSTSCRIPT

The war to preserve the Union ultimately transformed it by destroying the system of forced labor that had existed in America for centuries. That destruction was the work not just of the president but also of his party, abolitionists, black activists, soldiers, and the slaves themselves. Yet there were limits to these gains, as Frederick Douglass observed. The destruction of slavery brought great hopes in the era of Reconstruction, hopes made into laws that promised civil and voting rights to the freedmen through the Fourteenth and Fifteenth Amendments to the Constitution. Thereafter, however, the end of Reconstruction and of federal occupation in 1877 led to the collapse of freedmen's rights and ultimately their disenfranchisement. As the next chapter explores, the post–Civil War years brought an intense and violent backlash against African Americans, especially through lynching and the rise of the Ku Klux Klan.

QUESTIONS

1. How do you explain Lincoln's shift from promising to protect slavery in his first inaugural address to his decision to use emancipation as an instrument of war in September 1862? Should Lincoln be known as the "Great Emancipator?"
2. Did the Emancipation Proclamation and the Thirteenth Amendment involve a fundamental shift in how northerners thought about the war?
3. Did Horace Greeley and Lydia Maria Child criticize President Lincoln and his Union strategy for the same reasons?
4. Could the Civil War have ended without the end of slavery?
5. How do Lydia Maria Child, James Ashley, and Fernando Wood understand the Constitution in the debate over slavery?

ADDITIONAL READING

For a short overview, see William Gienapp, *Abraham Lincoln and Civil War America: A Biography* (Oxford University Press, 2002). The best single volume history of the war remains James McPherson, *Battle Cry of Freedom: The Civil War Era* (Oxford, 1988). On the opening year of the war see Adam Goodheart, *1861: The Civil War Awakening* (2011). The "original" Thirteenth Amendment, which sought to protect slavery, is deftly investigated by Daniel Crofts in *Lincoln and the Politics of Slavery* (2016). The ratified Thirteenth Amendment is definitively treated in Michael Vorenberg, *Final Freedom* (2001). On emancipation, see Ira Berlin et al., *Slaves No More: Three Essays on Emancipation and the Civil War* (1992); Louis Gerteis, *From Contraband to Freedman: Federal Policy Toward Southern Blacks, 1861–1865* (1973); Eric Foner, *Nothing but Freedom: Emancipation and its Legacy* (1983); and Elizabeth Varon, *Appomattox: Victory, Defeat and Freedom at the End of the Civil War* (2013). Regarding the failed efforts by the Confederacy to free and arm slaves, see Bruce Levine, *Confederate Emancipation* (2005). On the most important African-American voice during the war, see David Blight, *Frederick Douglass' Civil War: Keeping Faith in Jubilee* (1989). On southern women during the war, see Drew Gilpin Faust, *Mothers of Invention: Women of the Slaveholding South in the American Civil War* (1996).

ENDNOTES

1. "From a Fugitive Slave to His Master," *Douglass' Monthly* (August 1859).
2. *The Rebellion Record: A Diary of American Events*, edited by Frank Moore, Vol. 2 (New York: G. P. Putnam, 1862), pp. 437–438.
3. Lydia Maria Child Papers, Manuscript Division, Library of Congress (microfiche 51/1373).
4. *New-York Tribune*, August 20, 1862, p. 4.
5. *New-York Tribune*, August 25, 1862, p. 4.
6. "Letter from the President," *The Liberator*, February 17, 1865.
7. *Congressional Globe*, v.38, n.2, pp. 138–141.
8. *Congressional Globe*, v.38, n.2, pp. 194–195.
9. *The Liberator*, May 26, 1865.

CHAPTER 13

RECONSTRUCTION AND THE RISE OF THE KU KLUX KLAN

HISTORICAL CONTEXT

In a letter to the House of Representatives dated April 19, 1872, President Ulysses S. Grant described a "grand system of criminal associations pervading most of the Southern States." Investigations by the attorney general, by the Joint Committee of Congress upon Southern Outrages, and by local officials all revealed that a terrorist organization known as the Ku Klux Klan, or KKK, exercised enormous influence in the South and worked in defiance of federal Reconstruction. Grant alleged that members swore oaths of obedience and secrecy that they considered more binding than their allegiance to the United States. "They are organized and armed," the president declared. "They effect their objects by personal violence, often extending to murder. They terrify witnesses, they control juries in the State courts, and sometimes in the courts of the United States." Klansmen spied on, murdered, and intimidated their enemies and thereby destroyed the rule of law. Their goals, according to Grant, were

> by force and terror, to prevent all political action not in accord with the views of the members, to deprive colored citizens of the right to bear arms, and of the right of a free ballot, and to suppress the schools in which colored children were taught, and to reduce the colored people to a condition closely allied to that of slavery.[1]

The KKK, in other words, threatened the very hallmarks of democratic citizenship, as it attempted to seize by terror what the South had lost on the battlefield.

The KKK originated in informal organizations that Confederate men joined immediately after the Civil War. The agenda of these organizations became increasingly political, as Andrew Johnson's Reconstruction policies were replaced by the more stringent ones of the so-called radical Republicans in Congress. The South was now occupied by enemy troops, its cities burned, farms barren, elected officials disgraced, and population decimated. Those who had been slaves, black men and women stigmatized as ineradicably inferior, were now to be treated as equal citizens of a democracy. There was even talk of

251

confiscating southern agricultural land and redistributing it so that blacks and poor whites could become independent farmers. This plan, as it turned out, was too radical for most Republicans, whose devotion to private property—even that of former rebels—brooked few exceptions.

For African Americans, the era of Reconstruction was a time of relative freedom. Many took the opportunity to leave the land they had been bound to and sought opportunity in southern cities and even in the North. Certainly, whites feared the possible loss of their labor force. Equally threatening, the former slaves were more free to worship, work, learn, and acquire power and money than ever before. Many whites alleged that blacks were incapable of handling freedom—that black politicians were corrupt; black workers, slothful; and black masses, ignorant. But the unspoken and perhaps deeper fear was that African Americans were indeed capable of good citizenship and would compete with their former masters. In other words, the comforting idea of white superiority no longer held. If radical Reconstruction failed to secure real economic opportunity for the former slaves, it did insist that African Americans be treated as equal citizens under the law, an idea antithetical to the old southern economic and social structure, indeed to white southern identity.

But it was not just the new position of blacks that threatened white southerners. Republican rule included policies for changing the region to conform more with the tone of northern society. The "carpetbaggers" (northerners who came south after the war) and "scalawags" (southerners sympathetic to the north) generally were not corrupt individuals but people who genuinely believed that the South's salvation would come through railroads, new industries, and public schools—in short, institutions associated with economic progress in the free-labor North. Radical Reconstruction not only proposed to change racial mores but also aimed to replace the old slave system with northern-style free labor capitalism. Such drastic changes, imposed, as it appeared to many white southerners, by upstart blacks and alien Yankees, were terrifying.

The Ku Klux Klan was a response to the social, cultural, and economic changes that many white southerners found so disturbing. It might best be seen as the extreme wing of the "redeemers," those whites who sought the end of federal Reconstruction and the restoration of their wealth and power. African Americans and southern Unionists, with the aid of the federal government and the Republican Party, were able to govern several states for a few years after the Civil War, but eventually the political experience, popularity, and just plain brutality of the redeemers won the day. The Klan specialized in the latter.

Klansmen typically dressed in white robes and hoods, and they tried to convince their black victims that they were the ghosts of the Confederate dead. Blacks were intimidated, not by the transparent ghostly ruse but by the Klansmen's violence. By the late 1860s, their pattern was clear: several Klansmen would surround a victim's house at night, shoot into the windows, set fire to the structure, poison livestock, or simply drag the inhabitants out and shoot, whip, or hang them. Usually the victims were individuals who had stood up for their rights, blacks who voted, ran for office, or refused to take whites' insults. Occasionally there was open warfare between Klansmen and black militias. White citizens, too,

Image 13.1 Frank Bellew, "Visit of the Ku-Klux"
Frank Bellew's stark depiction of the Klan's use of violence against African-American freedmen stunned northern readers of *Harper's Weekly* and contributed to the crackdown on this lawless and terroristic organization.
Source: Harper's Weekly, February 24, 1872, v.16 n.791

who dared support blacks or expressed Unionist sympathies were terrorized by the night riders.

It is impossible to know how many southern men ever joined the Klan given that it was a secret organization. Yet through the late 1860s and into the early 1870s, it successfully intimidated both blacks and whites. When the federal government outlawed the organization and began prosecuting its members, the Klan lost some of its effectiveness. But by that point, violence, along with social ostracism and economic coercion, had become part of the arsenal of redeemer politics, which aimed to restore white Democratic rule to the former slave states. Redemption came to state and local government but succeeded only because the federal government lost its resolve to make sure that all citizens were treated, as promised in the Constitution, with equality. Slowly, African

Americans' rights to vote, speak out freely, and participate equally in social life were stripped away.

Just as the political disenfranchisement of African Americans that followed Reconstruction was their reduction to economic peonage. Slavery died at Appomattox, but new forms of economic and political servitude soon took its place, and they lasted for a century. In the years following the Civil War, most blacks became tenant farmers with no land of their own, and most of these sharecropped, work that offered little more freedom or material comfort than slavery. As a sharecropper, a former slave might farm a white man's land; buy tools, supplies, and food from him; and rent a shack for the family from him. Owner and renter would split the proceeds of the harvest, but the black farmer's debt for the goods that the white man had furnished would almost certainly exceed any profit. Indebted to the white planter, former slaves would be unable to leave; year after year they would have to stay on the land, trying to pay off a debt that grew ever larger.

The following documents reveal the Ku Klux Klan from various points of view. The initiation oath of the Knights of the White Camelia (a part of the Klan) reveals the style and purposes of this organization. Despite the Klan's high-toned rhetoric defending southern honor, the narratives of former slaves and their testimony in congressional hearings reveals how the Klan used violence to accomplish its goals. Note here the reasons for which the victims felt they were being attacked. Congressman Stevenson's speech summarizes the federal findings on the scope of Klan activities and shows the conflict over values and ideology between southern redeemers and northern agents of Reconstruction. Finally, *Experience of a Northern Man among the Ku-Klux* gives a good sense of how northerners viewed the South and how some of them even visualized colonizing it and remaking its society to conform to northern norms. As you read these selections, ask yourself how and why ideas about race intermingled with issues of ideology, labor, and politics.

INTRODUCTION TO DOCUMENT 1

The initiation oath of the Knights of the White Camelia reveals the appeal of such organizations. The Knights originated during the early days of the Klan in the late 1860s. Note the claims to religious faith and patriotism and the chivalric mandate: to protect the weak and defenseless against the outrages of "lawless" blacks. There was a sense of white southern manhood in this; defending home and family was the manly thing to do. Aside from the reassertion of crude white supremacy, the KKK must have been very popular for its sense of mystery, pageantry, and ritual; individuals were made to feel that they belonged to something splendid and grand.

1. INITIATION OATH OF THE KNIGHTS OF THE WHITE CAMELIA

I do solemnly swear, in the presence of these witnesses, never to reveal, without authority, the existence of this Order, its objects, its acts, and signs of recognition; never to reveal or publish, in any manner whatsoever, what I shall see or hear in this Council; never to divulge the names of the members of the Order, or their acts done in connection therewith; I swear to maintain and defend the social and political superiority of the White Race on this Continent; always and in all places to observe a marked distinction between the White and African races; to vote for none but white men for any office of honor, profit or trust; to devote my intelligence, energy and influence to instill these principles in the minds and hearts of others; and to protect and defend persons of the White Race, in their lives, rights and property, against the encroachments and aggressions of an inferior race.

I swear, moreover, to unite myself in heart, soul and body with those who compose this Order; to aid, protect and defend them in all places; to obey the orders of those, who, by our statutes, will have the right of giving those orders. . . .

The oath having been taken by the candidate, the C[ommander] shall now say:

Brother, by virtue of the authority to me delegated, I now pronounce you a Knight of the [White Camelia]. . . .

Brothers: You have been initiated into one of the most important Orders, which have ever been established on this continent: an Order, which, if its principles are faithfully observed and its objects diligently carried out, is destined to regenerate our unfortunate country and to relieve the White Race from the humiliating condition to which it has lately been reduced in this Republic. It is necessary, therefore, that before taking part in the labors of this Association, you should understand fully its principles and objects and the duties which devolve upon you as one of its members.

As you may have already gathered from the questions which were propounded to you, and which you have answered so satisfactorily, and from the clauses of the Oath which you have taken, our main and fundamental object is the *maintenance of the supremacy of the white race* in this Republic. History and physiology teach us that we belong to a race which nature has endowed with an evident superiority over all other races, and that the Maker, in thus elevating us above the common standard of human creation, has intended to give us over inferior races, a dominion from which no human laws can permanently derogate. The experience of ages demonstrates that, from the origin of the world, this dominion has always remained in the hands of the Caucasian Race; whilst all the other races have constantly occupied a subordinate and secondary position; a fact which triumphantly confirms this great law of nature. Powerful nations have succeeded each other in the face of the world, and have marked their passage by glorious and memorable deeds; and among those who have thus left on this globe indelible traces of their splendor and greatness, we find none but descended from the Caucasian stock. We see, on the contrary, that most of the countries inhabited by the other races have remained in a state of complete barbarity; whilst the small number of those who have advanced beyond this savage existence, have, for centuries, stagnated in a semi-barbarous condition, of which there can be no progress or improvement. And it is a remarkable fact that as a race of men is more remote from the Caucasian and approaches nearer to the black African, the more fatally that stamp of inferiority is affixed to its sons, and irrevocably dooms them to eternal imperfectibility and degradation.

Convinced that we are of these elements of natural ethics, we know, besides, that the government of our Republic was established by white men, for white men alone, and that it never was in the contemplation of its founders that it should fall into the hands of an inferior and degraded race. We hold, therefore, that any attempt to wrest from the white race the management of its affairs in order to transfer it to control of the black population, is an invasion of the sacred prerogatives vouchsafed to us by the Constitution, and a violation of the laws established by God himself; that such encroachments are subversive of the established institutions of our Republic, and that no individual of the white race can submit to them without humiliation and shame.

It, then, becomes our solemn duty, as white men, to resist strenuously and persistently those attempts against our natural and constitutional rights, and to do everything in our power in order to maintain, in this Republic, the supremacy of the Caucasian race, and restrain the black or African race to that condition of social and political inferiority for which God has destined it. This is the object for which our Order was instituted; and, in carrying it out, we intend to infringe no laws, to violate no rights, and to resort to no forcible means, except for purposes of legitimate and necessary defense.

As an essential condition of success, this Order proscribes absolutely all social equality between the races. If we were to admit persons of African race on the same level with ourselves, a state of personal relations would follow which would unavoidably lead to political equality; for it would be a virtual recognition of *status*, after which we could not consistently deny them an equal share in the administration of our public affairs. The man who is good enough to be our familiar companion, is good enough also to participate in our political government; and if we were to grant the one, there could be no good reason for us not to concede the other of these two privileges.

There is another reason, Brothers, for which we condemn this social equality. Its toleration would soon be a fruitful source of intermarriages between individuals of the two races; and the result of this *misceganation* [*sic*] would be gradual amalgamation and the production of a degenerate and bastard offspring, which would soon populate these States with a degraded and ignoble population, incapable of moral and intellectual development and unfitted to support a great and powerful country. We must maintain the purity of the white blood, if we would preserve for it that natural superiority with which God has ennobled it.

To avoid these evils, therefore, we take the obligation *to observe a marked distinction between the two races*, not only in the relations of public affairs, but also in the more intimate dealings and intercourse of private life which, by the frequency of their occurrence, are more apt to have an influence on the attainment of the purposes of the Order.

Now that I have laid before you the objects of this Association, let me charge you specially in relation to one of your most important studies as one of its members. Our statutes make us bound to respect sedulously the rights of the colored inhabitants of this Republic, and in every instance, to give to them whatever lawfully belongs to them. It is an act of simple justice not to deny them any of the privileges to which they are legitimately entitled; and we cannot better show the inherent superiority of our race than by dealing with them in that spirit of firmness, liberality and impartiality which characterizes all superior organizations. Besides, it would be ungenerous for us to undertake to restrict them to the narrowest limits as to the exercise of certain rights, without conceding to them, at the same time, the fullest measure of those which we recognize as theirs; and a fair construction of a white man's duty towards them would be, not only to respect and observe their acknowledged rights, but also to see that these are respected and observed by others.[2]

INTRODUCTION TO DOCUMENTS 2 AND 3

Despite the Klan's lofty rhetoric, the following testimonies by its victims reveal the terrorism for which the organization was renowned. Ask yourself who became Klan victims and why. The three statements in Document 2 were made by former slaves looking back on their experiences from a distance of several decades; the statements are taken from oral histories collected during the 1930s by the Federal Writers Project (note how the former slaves' words were rendered in heavy "Negro dialect"). The two statements in Document 3 come from testimony before a congressional committee investigating Klan violence in the early 1870s and transcribed in standard English.

2. TESTIMONY OF VICTIMS
OF THE KU KLUX KLAN (1871)

PIERCE HARPER

After de colored people was considered free an' turned loose de Klu Klux broke out. Some of de colored people commenced to farming like I tol' you an' all de ol' stock dey could pick up after de Yankees left dey took an' took care of. If you got so you made good money an' had a good farm de Klu Klux'd come an' murder you. De gov'ment built de colored people school houses an' de Klu Klux went to work an' burn 'em down. Dey'd go to de jails an' take de colored men out an' knock dere brains out an' break dere necks an' throw 'em in de river.

Dere was a man dat dey taken, his name was Jim Freeman. Dey taken him an' destroyed his stuff an' him 'cause he was making some money. Hung him on a tree in his front yard, right in front of his cabin. Dere was some young men who went to de schools de gov'ment opened for de colored folks. Some white widder woman said someone had stole something she own', so dey put these young fellers in jail 'cause dey suspicioned 'em. De Klu Kluxes went to de jail an' took 'em out an' kill 'em. Dat happen de second year after de War.

After de Klu Kluxes got so strong de colored men got together an' made a complaint before de law. De Gov'nor told de law to give 'em de ol' guns in de commissary what de Southern soldiers had use, so dey issued de colored men old muskets an' told 'em to protect theirselves.

De colored men got together an' organized the 'Malicy [Militia]. Dey had leaders like regular soldiers, men dat led 'em right on. Dey didn't meet 'cept when dey heard de Klu Kluxes was coming to get some of de colored folks. Den de one who knowed dat tol' de leader an' he went 'round an' told de others when an' where dey's meet. Den dey was ready for 'em. Dey'd hide in de cabins an' when de Klu Kluxes come dere dey was. Den's when dey found out who a lot of de Klu Kluxes was, 'cause a lot of 'em was killed. Dey wore dem long sheets an' you couldn't tell who dey was. Dey even covered dere horses up so you couldn't tell who dey belong to. Men you thought was your friend was Klu Kluxes. You deal wit' 'em in de stores in de day time an' at night dey come out to your house an' kill you.

SUE CRAFT

My teacher's name Dunlap—a white teacher teachin de cullud. De Ku Klux whupped him fo' teachin' us. I saw de Ku Klux ridin' a heap dem days. Dey had hoods pulled ovah dere faces. One time dey come to our house twict. Fus' time dey come quiet. It was right 'fore de 'lection o' Grant jus' after slavery. It was fus' time cullud people 'lowed t' vote. Dey ast my father was he goin' to vote for Grant. He tell 'em he don' know he goin' vote. After 'lection dey come back, whoopin' an' hollerin. Dey shoot out de winder lights. It was 'cause my father voted for Grant. Dey broke de do' open. My father was a settin' on de bed. I 'member he had a shot gun in his han'. Well, dey broke de do' down, an' then father he shoot, an' dey scattered all ovah de fence.

MORGAN RAY

. . . I heard a lot about the Klu Klux, but it warn't till long afterwards dat I evan see 'em. It was one night after de work of de day was done and I was takin' a walk near where I worked. Suddenly I hear the hoof beats of horses and I natcherly wuz curious and waited beside de road to see what was comin'. I saw a company of men hooded and wearin' what looked like sheets. Dey had a young cullud man as dere prisoner. I wuz too skairt to say anything or ask any questions. I just went on my sweet way. Later I found out dey acclaimed de prisoner had assaulted a white woman. Dey strung him up when he wouldn't confess, and shot him full of holes and threw his body in de pond.[3]

3. CONGRESSIONAL INQUIRY INTO KLAN ACTIVITIES (1871)

ATLANTA, GEORGIA, OCTOBER 25, 1871

Joseph Addison (White) Sworn and Examined by the Chairman:

QUESTION: What is your age, where were you born, where do you live, and what is your present occupation?

ANSWER: I am about twenty-four years old; I was born in Muscogee County, and now live in Haralson County; I have been living there ever since I was a little bit of a boy; I am a farmer.

QUESTION: During the war which side were you on?

ANSWER: I never fought a day in the rebel army; I was not in it at all.

QUESTION: Which side were your feelings on?

ANSWER: My feelings were on the side of what you call the radical party now.

QUESTION: What did they call it then?

ANSWER: I was what you call a Union man then.

QUESTION: Were your opinions well known?

ANSWER: Yes, sir; I reckon I am well known.

QUESTION: Have you seen any people, or do you know of any, in your county, called Ku-Klux?

ANSWER: Yes, sir.

QUESTION: Tell us what you know about them.

ANSWER: Do you want me to state just about all how they did?

QUESTION: Yes.

ANSWER: I will tell you how they did me. . . . My wife looked out and said, "Lord have mercy! Joe, it is the Ku-Klux." I jumped out of the door and ran. One of them was right in the back yard, and he jabbed the end of his six-shooter almost against my head, and said, "Halt! God damn you." I said, "I will give up." I asked them what they were doing that for; they said that I had been stealing. I said, "You men here know I have not." They said, "We gave you time once to get away, and, God damn you, you have not gone; now, God damn you, you shall not go, for we allow to kill you." I said, "If you do not abuse me or whip me, I will go the next morning." They said they would not abuse me or whip me, but they would kill me. I said, "Let me go and see my wife and children." They said, "No, God damn you." I turned away from the man; he jammed his pistol in my face, and said, "God damn you, go on, or I will kill you." They took me about eighty or ninety yards from there into a little thicket. The man on my right was a high, tall man; the one on my left was a low, chunky fellow. The man on my right stepped back, and said to the little fellow on my left, "Old man, we have got him here now; do as you please with him." There were some little hickories near him; he looked at them, but did not take them. They were all standing right around me with their guns pointing at me. Just as he turned around, I wheeled and run; but before I had run ten yards I heard a half a dozen caps bursted at me. Just as I made a turn to go behind some buildings and little bushes, I heard two guns fired. I must have gone seventy or eighty yards, and then I heard what I thought was a pistol fired. I heard a bullet hit a tree. I run on eight or ten steps further, and then I heard a bullet hit a tree just before me. Every one of them took after me, and run me for a hundred and fifty yards. I ran down a little bluff and ran across a branch. When I got across there, I could not run any further, for my shoes were all muddy. I cut the strings of my old shoes, and left them there. I stopped to listen, but I never saw anything more of them. I then went around and climbed up on the fence, and sat there and watched until dark. I then went to the house and got some dry clothes, and then went back where I had fixed a place in the woods to sleep in, and went to bed. That was the last I heard of them that night. They came back Sunday night before court commenced on Monday, in Haralson County. My wife would not stay there by herself, but went to her sister-in-law's, Milton Powell's wife. They came in on them on Sunday night, or about two hours and a half before day Monday morning. They abused her and cursed her powerfully, and tried to make her tell where I was. They said that if she did not tell them they would shoot her God-damned brains out. I was laying out close by there, and I stood there and heard them. They shot five or six shots in the yard; some of them said they shot into the house. They scared my wife and sister-in-law so bad that they took the children and went into the woods and staid there all night. That was the last time they were there. . . .

QUESTION: Have they ever molested you since then?

ANSWER: No, sir; they have never been on me any more since then.

QUESTION: Do you still stay there?

ANSWER: No, sir; I have done moved now. I moved off, and left my hogs and my crop and everything there, what little I made. I did not make much crop this year, for I was afraid to work, and now I am afraid to go back there to save anything.

ATLANTA, GEORGIA, OCTOBER 26, 1871

Thomas M. Allen (Colored) Sworn and Examined by the Chairman:

QUESTION: What is your age, where were you born, and where do you now live?

ANSWER: I am now thirty-eight years old. I was born in Charleston, South Carolina, and I am living here at present; that is, my family is here; I am pastor of the Baptist church at Marietta, Jasper County.

QUESTION: How long have you been living in this State?

ANSWER: I came to this State the year that James K. Polk died, about 1849.

QUESTION: How do you connect your coming here with his death?

ANSWER: I landed in Savannah at the time they were firing cannon there, and asked what was the matter.

QUESTION: Were you a slave?

ANSWER: Partly so. My father was a white man and he set us free at his death. They stole us from Charleston and run me and my brother and mother into this State. He left us ten thousand dollars each to educate us, and give us trades, and for that money they stole us away.

QUESTION: Were you kept in slavery until the time of emancipation?

ANSWER: Yes, sir; I was held as a slave; I hired my time.

QUESTION: You never were able to assert your freedom before emancipation?

ANSWER: No, sir, I could not do it. . . .

QUESTION: Have you been connected with political affairs in this State since the war?

ANSWER: Yes, sir. When the constitutional convention was called, I took an active part, and did all I could, of course. Afterwards I ran for the legislature and was elected.

QUESTION: In what year?

ANSWER: I was elected in 1868; the colored members were expelled that year.

QUESTION: From what county were you elected?

ANSWER: From Jasper County.

QUESTION: Were you reinstated in your seat in the legislature?

ANSWER: Yes, sir.

QUESTION: Have you witnessed any violence towards any of your race, yourself or any others?

ANSWER: Yes, sir. After we were expelled from the legislature, I went home to Jasper County; I was carrying on a farm there. On the 16th of

October, a party of men came to my house; I cannot say how many, for I did not see them. . . .

About 2 o'clock my wife woke me up, and said that there were persons all around the house; that they had been there for half an hour, and were calling for me. I heard them call again, and I asked them what they wanted, and who they were. . . .

They asked me to come out. At this time my brother-in-law waked up and said, "Who are they, Thomas?" I said, "I do not know." . . .

He put on his shoes and vest and hat; this was all he was found with after he was killed. He opened the door and hollered, "Where are you?" He hollered twice, and then two guns were fired. He seemed to fall, and I and my wife hollered, and his wife hollered. I jumped up, and ran back to the fire-place, where I started to get a light, and then started to go over the partition to him. I threw a clock down, and then I thought of the closet there, and went through it to him, and my wife closed the door. I hollered for Joe, a third man on the place, to come up and bring his gun, for Emanuel was killed. He did not come for some time, and then I was so excited that I could not recognize his voice. After a time I let him in. We made up a light, and then I saw my brother-in-law laying on his back as he fell. I examined him; there were four or five number one buck-shot in his breast. . . .

QUESTION: What do you know about this organization of men they call Ku-Klux?

ANSWER: I have never seen one in my life; I have seen a great many people who have seen them. I have a Ku-Klux letter here that I got on the day of the election for the constitution.

QUESTION: Will you read it?

ANSWER: Yes, sir; this is it.

To Thomas Allen:
Tom, you are in great danger; you are going heedless with the radicals, against the interest of the conservative white population, and I tell you if you do not change your course before the election for the ratification of the infernal constitution, your days are numbered, and they will be but few. Just vote or use your influence for the radicals or for the constitution, and you go up certain. My advice to you,

Tom, is to stay at home if you value your life, and not vote at all, and advise all of your race to do the same thing. You are marked and closely watched by K.K.K. (or in plain words Ku-Klux.)
Take heed; a word to the wise is sufficient.
By order of Grand Cyclops.

QUESTION: Where did you get this?

ANSWER: It was dropped in the shop the morning of the election, when I was running for the legislature. I showed it to a great many men in town; I showed it to Colonel Preston, a friend of mine. He asked where I got it, and I told him. He said, "Tear it up." I said, "No, it may be of service to my children if not to me." He said, "You need not talk so slack about it; there may be heaps of Ku-Klux in the State, and they might get hold of your talk. . . ."

QUESTION: What is the feeling of your people in regard to their personal safety?

ANSWER: They do not consider that they have any safety at all, only in the cities; that is the truth. In a great many places the colored people call the white people master and mistress, just as they ever did; if they do not do it they are whipped. They have no safety at all except in a large place like this. If I could have stayed at home I would not have been here. I left all my crops and never got anything for them. My wife had no education, and when I came away everything went wrong. There are thousands in my condition.

QUESTION: Is that the reason so many of your people come to the large cities?

ANSWER: Yes, sir, that is the reason. Mr. Abram Turner, a member of the legislature, from Putnam County, the county adjoining mine, was shot down in the street in open day. He was a colored man. They have elected another in his place, a democrat.

QUESTION: When was he elected?

ANSWER: Last fall.

QUESTION: He has been killed since?

ANSWER: Yes, sir, shot down in broad open day. . . .

QUESTION: Was he a republican?

ANSWER: Yes sir, I knew him very well; he was a good man, a harmless man; I married him to his wife.

QUESTION: Do the people of your race feel that they have the protection of the laws?

ANSWER: By no means.

QUESTION: What is their hope and expectation for the future?

ANSWER: They expect to get protection from the Federal Government at Washington; that is all. You ask any one of my people out there, even the most ignorant of them, and they will tell you so. . . . I believe that many of the jurymen, and lawyers too, are members of the Ku-Klux; I believe it positively; I would say so on my deathbed.

QUESTION: How much have you been over the State?

ANSWER: I have traveled all over the State.

QUESTION: Have you communicated pretty freely with the people of your own race?

ANSWER: Yes, sir.

QUESTION: Have you received information from them about the Ku-Klux?

ANSWER: Yes, sir, occasionally.

QUESTION: In how large a portion of the State do you find reports of Ku-Klux operations?

ANSWER: I find it in the counties of what is known among us as the Black Belt. Wherever the negroes are in the majority, there the Ku-Klux range more than in any other places. Up in Cobb County they are very peaceable. The democrats are always elected there to the general assembly. The whites have about seven hundred majority. The colored people get along splendidly there. In those counties where the whites are largely in the majority, the colored people get along very well; but go into the counties where the negroes are in the majority, and there is always trouble; for instance, in

"ONE VOTE LESS."—*Richmond Whig.*

Image 13.2 Thomas Nast, "One Vote Less"

The famous cartoonist Thomas Nast drew this image to publicize the violence used to keep blacks from the ballot box throughout the South. The words "Seymour Ratification" refer to the presidential election between Republican Ulysses S. Grant and New York Democratic governor Horatio Seymour, who supported state rights and resisted the Fourteenth Amendment's guarantee of black citizenship. The image proved so powerful with audiences that *Harper's Weekly* used it in both the 1868 and 1872 elections.

Source: Harper's Weekly, August 6, 1868

Monroe County, or Warren County, or anywhere in the Black Belt, there is always trouble between the whites and the colored people.

QUESTION: Are the colored people riotous in disposition? Are they inclined to make trouble?

ANSWER: I suppose the colored people are as peaceable as any people in the world. The colored people of Madison, when the white people went to the jail and murdered a man there, could have burned up the town and killed all the white people there.[4]

INTRODUCTION TO DOCUMENT 4

As Thomas Allen's testimony above revealed, Klan violence grew not just out of hatred and bigotry—it had particular political goals in mind. Congressman Job E. Stevenson from Ohio delivered the following address in the House of Representatives on May 30, 1872, less than half a year from the coming presidential election. Stevenson argued that the Klan was not merely brutal; it was a political conspiracy to overthrow Reconstruction and re-enslave African Americans. As you read the excerpts from his speech, note his characterization of the newly conquered South. Why did he believe that the North must stop the Klan? What arguments did he make? Note that Stevenson mentions General Forrest. He refers to General Nathan Bedford Forrest, a Confederate general notorious in the North first for the Fort Pillow Massacre in which his troops butchered hundreds of black Union troops in the act of surrendering and also for his early leadership of the Ku Klux Klan.

4. SPEECH TO THE HOUSE OF REPRESENTATIVES (1872)

HON. JOB E. STEVENSON OF OHIO

Mr. Speaker: The gravest question before Congress is the Kuklux Conspiracy, its origin and extent, character and actions, plans and purposes, condition and prospects.

ORIGIN

It originated in hostility to the Government, in enmity against the Union. It is the successor of the southern confederacy, rebellion in disguise, war at midnight. It rose like an exhalation from the unsodden grave of the "lost cause." . . .

A POLITICAL CONSPIRACY

Such being the origin . . . of this great conspiracy, we may well inquire against whom its terrors are aimed. It strikes exclusively at the Unionists of the South, principally at the freedmen. No man can deny that it is political. The oath swears the member to oppose Radicalism, to oppose the Radical party, to oppose the political equality of the races.

General Forrest said: "It is a protective political military organization. Its objects originally were protection against Loyal Leagues and the Grand Army of the Republic; but after it became general, it was found that political matters and interests could best be promoted within it, and it was then made a political organization, giving its support, of course, to the Democratic party." . . .

It appears that in the States of Georgia, Louisiana, Tennessee, and South Carolina from the spring election in 1868 to the election for President in 1868, the Republican vote was reduced eighty-five thousand by intimidation and violence.

COMMANDERS

The forces of the conspiracy are controlled by such men as Generals Gordon, Hampton, and Forrest, and under them by inferior officers, running down from grade to grade, to captains of companies, or chiefs of klans or cyclops of dens. The organization begins at the den and extends to the precinct, the county, the congressional district, the State, the South. It is compact, connected, consistent, moving as a perfect body from the head to the humblest member, as an army in the field, with sterner discipline than that of an army. . . .

AUTHORITY

These commands bind the members by an oath enforced by fear; administered with strange ceremonies, emphasized by penalty of death. At midnight the member is led blindfold to the den, and there, on his knees, hears the ritual and takes the oath. And as the bandage drops from his eyes he sees circles of men in frightful disguises armed with revolvers leveled on his head, and the Grand Cyclops says: "And this you do under penalty of a traitor's doom, which is death! death! death!" . . .

Thus members are sworn to obey their superior officers on penalty of death, and under that oath they are compelled to take the field at the command and to do any deed he may order, even to murder. Scores of members have confessed and testified that they have committed outrages and murders at the command of their officers.

OUTRAGES

The outrages vary from threats and intimidations to scourging, wounding, maiming, and killing by shooting, drowning, hanging, and burning. If we could know the whole truth it would appear that since the war this conspiracy has outraged more than thirty thousand men, women, and children—peaceful, innocent, defenseless citizens of the Republic. . . .

EXCUSES

Among the excuses made by those who control and defend this organization is that they feared the negroes; yet all Southern men of intelligence testify that the negroes of the South have behaved better than any other people ever did under similar circumstances. . . . They pretend that the Government of the United States has oppressed them, yet that Government, to which they had forfeited property, liberty, and life, spared their lives, allowed them their liberty, and returned them their property. No confiscated estates are withheld from their owners; although some abandoned property was taken, the only rebel estate remaining in the hands of the Government is Arlington [Robert E. Lee's estate], and gentlemen in both Houses of Congress propose to remove the remains of our soldiers and give that cemetery back to its rebel owners. No life has been taken for treason. Jefferson Davis is as free as the air, a citizen of the Republic. Few political privileges are denied, few leaders are unamnestied. . . .

FINANCIAL RESULTS OF RECONSTRUCTION

What has been the financial result of reconstruction? The Government and the peoples of the North forgave the people of the South and caused them to repudiate debts amounting to more than twenty-five hundred million dollars. We relieved them by constitutional amendments, and by the generosity of our people, of debts nearly double the property their own crimes had left. If the Government and the people of the North had merely withheld their hands from the South, and left the conquered rebels to their own financial devices, the South would have sunk in bankruptcy and ruin as a man thrown into the sea with a millstone at his neck. The Government and people of the North rescued them, fed them, advanced money and property, restored peace and order, and gave them the opportunity to revive their fortunes.

The white people of the South continually upbraid the colored people, saying, "The negro will not work." Yet wherever you go you see scores of white men lounging on the piazzas of the hotels, shifting their chairs to keep out of the sun, moving only to get "refreshments," while freedmen are laboring in the fields earning money to enable the whites to lounge. The laborers of the South have produced in cotton and other agricultural products since the war nearly $4,000,000,000, more than double the value of property in 1865. That is the financial result of reconstruction.

FINANCIAL EFFECTS OF KU KLUX CONSPIRACY

. . . The Kuklux conspiracy is fatal to values. It disturbs business, disorganizes labor, paralyzes industry and commerce. . . . The Kuklux conspiracy has cost the South more than all the carpet-baggers of all the States (including the Louisiana leader of the new movement), have been able to misappropriate.

DEPOPULATION

The conspiracy is driving away the people. Here is a copy of the *Freedmen's Repository,* giving an account of the emigration from this country to Liberia, showing that last fall a ship took out of the country from Virginia one passenger; from Florida, five; from North Carolina, five; from Georgia, sixty-six; and from Clay Hill, York county, South Carolina, one hundred and sixty-six. And at the head of this South Carolina party was Rev. Elias Hill, a description of whom is given here, a Baptist preacher, a cripple, whom the Kuklux scourged because he preached the gospel, taught school, and belonged to the Republican Party. He was driven with a colony of one hundred and sixty-six souls out of South Carolina, out of the United States of America, even to Liberia.

Here were two hundred and thirty-eight industrious people driven at once from the United States to Africa.

Before the war these colored people—men, women, and children—were valued by their owners at $500 each. Now they are driven out of the country by outrage, scourging, and murder; and we are told that the United States Government must not interfere to protect them. Imagine Elias Hill in the wilds of Africa, telling the bushmen how the great American Republic protects its citizens . . .

H. G. "LET US CLASP HANDS OVER THE BLOODY CHASM."—[SEE PAGE 803.]
" A Great Victory has been won in Georgia. . . . . The verdict in Georgia is certainly conclusive."—*New York Tribune, October 3, 1872.*

Image 13.3 Thomas Nast, "Let Us Clasp Hands over the Bloody Chasm"
Artist Thomas Nast frequently satirized political corruption in the Reconstruction era after the Civil War. Here he skewers Horace Greeley, the 1872 presidential candidate, for joining with conservative and anti-Reconstruction southerners to win the White House. Note that the alliance of these two camps is forged at the expense of both African Americans and the American flag, a symbol of the recent Union victory in the Civil War.
Source: Harper's Weekly, October 19, 1872. Penrose Library, University of Denver.

PRESENT CONDITION OF THE CONSPIRACY

In South Carolina the members of this organization raided in 1868, outraged and murdered Union people, and changed votes by scores of thousands. From that time until 1870 they were quiet, and then they raided again until more than three thousand outrages were committed in less than six months. The conspiracy is so organized that it may remain quiescent for a year or for two years, ready to be called into the field by the blast of the bugle, or by the click of the telegraph. Within one week this "military political" organization could throw into action a quarter of a million men, armed with the revolver, the bowie-knife, . . . with bayonets captured from State militia, and revolving rifles furnished from New York city.

ITS POWER

Shall we trust them? Are we blind—blind to the red rivers of blood they have shed; deaf to the cries of their thousands of victims? Are we mad to forget our own interests and safety? These conspirators have power, if they dare—and they are men who have dared death at the cannon's mouth—to sweep the whole South at the next presidential election; and if the result depends on the South, they can seat their candidate in the presidential chair. . . . *Whoever shall be the Democratic candidate will be the candidate of the Kuklux conspiracy. If the Democrats elect the next President it will be by Kuklux votes and violence; and the man thus elected will be the Kuklux President.*[5]

INTRODUCTION TO DOCUMENT 5

Benjamin Bryant's *Experience of a Northern Man among the Ku-Klux* argues that, while the South had been defeated, the region's way of life remained stubbornly unchanged. Bryant began with the problem of education, stating that the southern aristocracy kept both African Americans and poor whites in ignorance. The Klan had arisen to maintain this situation. Keeping the masses poor and ignorant, according to Bryant, was the Klan's main goal. Document 5 consists of excerpts from his book.

---

5. FROM *EXPERIENCE OF A NORTHERN MAN AMONG THE KU-KLUX* (1872)

BENJAMIN BRYANT

In order to better inform my readers of my intention for writing a book, I will say before entering into the main body of the work, that I have just returned from a long visit in the South, and have witnessed things which have occurred in the States late in Rebellion, and have kept a record of all, for the interest of the Northern people, and also, to give in detail the present situation of the people who are living there. . . .

As education is the great aim of every true American citizen, I will first inform you of its progress. The South has not had the advantages to aid in the development of education like the people of the North; but it has always been discouraged by the aristocracy of the South; and in so doing they have deprived the poor white people of education and other intelligences, as well as the black man. . . .

A great many freedmen are working on shares with their former masters, and are generally doing well, but are working for one-half, one-third, or one-fourth of their former pay, and are working under their master's hand, calling their former masters, "master," and denouncing the Proclamation of Emancipation. They hate that "old Northern woman" who is teaching the "nigger school," and resist all aid to free schools, and say, "I can live without education; I don't want it and will not have it."

"You are a good negro, and you may live on my land all your life-time."

That black man will work there for some time, and make one or two bales of cotton and give it to his master, as he calls him, to sell; and he will sell it and bring Tom, the good and smart negro, what he has a mind to.

Well, some day Tom will walk by the school-house and have a word or two with the teacher. Tom will tell him about his cotton. The teacher will say, "How much cotton did you have?"

"So much."

"How much money did you get?"

Tom says, "I got fifty dollars."

The school teacher will say, "Is that all? You should have more than that."

"How much more?"

"You should have twenty-five dollars more."

Tom says, "I am going to see him." . . .

[Tom's former master asked who told him he deserved more money.]

"The school teacher told me so."

"Who, that damn'd Yankee?"

"Yes sir."

"He told you that you could get more pay if you should go North, did he?"

"Yes sir. He told John, that black boy that lives with Mr. Brown, that he was free and should go to school. Yes, master, he told all the colored people to send their children and let them learn something." . . .

"Where is he from?"

"Massachusetts."

"We will fix him," says Tom's master. "Hitch up my horse; I am going away."

He will then go to the fork of the roads and tell everybody about what the damn'd Yankee school teacher told his niggers. If he stays here long he will

have every nigger in the place think that he is as good as a white man. Well, we must run him away. Send him word to leave by Monday. If not, we will fix him.

Monday has come—Tuesday has come. The nigger-school teacher has not gone yet. We must get together. (This is not talked in the presence of Tom, but Tom is in the next room and hears it all.)

"Tom, you go and tell Mr. Brown and Mr. Bond to come here, and on your way back go round by the Pugh Place and tell Mr. Pollock to come, too, and bring every one that he can."

They will all meet and talk the matter over, and agree to meet on Wednesday night at 10 o'clock, all dressed in uniform, ready to commence their secret midnight demonstration. They went to his house and took him out, and tied a large rope round his neck, and he was seen down on his knees praying. But the party who saw him was a colored man (in the woods), and he says that he could go to the spot where he was hung with his feet up, tied to the branch of an oak tree, and a log of wood round his neck, and his tongue from five to seven inches out of his mouth. This punishment will be applied to that class of Northern people who will go South and settle and have not received full information how to act. You know it is an old saying, and a good one too, when you are in Rome, act as a Roman, and when you are in the South, you must act as a Southern man. What are these actions? First, I will say, you must act with the majority, let their actions be good or bad. You must denounce all free schools for white or black children. You must not come South and pay more for labor than the established price, which is all the way from five to ten dollars per month, but an extra good hand, who has always been farming, may in some cases get from fifteen to sixteen dollars per month. Never give a black man, or a poor white man who cannot read, any advice to post themselves upon matters pertaining to their own welfare. Never speak a good word for New England, because her States demand human rights before the law, for all men. Never say anything about Bunker Hill, because that is in Massachusetts. Never express your political opinion, let it be Republican or Democratic, for we know that both parties wanted to maintain the Union. And, above all, you must hate niggers. There has been many a good enterprising Northern man driven from the newly established homestead because he did not know the existing circumstances. This organization, known as the "Invisible Empire," or Ku-Klux, does exist in the Southern States. There is a number of Northern people in both of the political parties that have manifested a strong unbelief in regard to the Ku-Klux Klans, but I will say a word on a verified fact, and truth, which is today being witnessed by every peace-loving and upright citizen.[6]

INTRODUCTION TO DOCUMENT 6

In *The Grand Army of the Republic Versus the Ku Klux Klan*, W. H. Gannon proposed that 100,000 former Union soldiers be allowed to colonize the South. These men would be given land and money, and, presumably, their example would show Southerners the value of northern industriousness and the free-labor system. Such a plan would also help alleviate the unemployment caused by swings of the business cycle. Note, however, how unspecific Gannon is. For example, would he confiscate land from southern owners? The following excerpts are taken from the chapter "How to Extirpate Ku-Kluxism from the South" in Gannon's book.

6. "HOW TO EXTIRPATE KU-KLUXISM FROM THE SOUTH" (1872)

W. H. GANNON

. . . In view of the fact, that the present phase [Reconstruction] of the difficulty between the North and the South has already continued for eight long and dreary years, whereas half that time sufficed in which to annihilate the whole of rebel armies, the conclusion is inevitable that the Northern People are making some very serious mistakes in conducting their case in its present form; and consequently, that they must make some radical change in their Southern policy, before they can hope to gain their cause at the South. . . .

(1.) That the fatal mistake of the Northern People in their Southern policy since the dispersion of the rebel armies, has been their reliance upon United States Marshals and United States soldiers, almost exclusively, to represent them at the South; (2.) that their true course to pursue towards the South is to colonize it with at least One Hundred Thousand (100,000) intelligent, respectable, and industrious Northern Working Men; (3.) that, inasmuch as the Federal Government found no very great difficulty, any time during the late war, in inducing a million of Northern men to exchange the security, peace, and enjoyment of their homes for the dangers and privations of prolonged active warfare in the face of a determined and powerful enemy at the South and to remain there year after year, until the overthrow of their antagonists left them free to return to their homes,—there are 100,000 of those same men who would gladly return South now with the implements of peace in their hands, to make their homes there, provided they had the means to enable them to do so; (4.) that One Thousand (1000) Dollars per man would be all sufficient to establish them comfortably there; (5.) that the required funds would readily enough be forthcoming, were the proper parties to ask the public for them; and (6.) that the proper parties to collect the required funds, and to select the proposed colonists, and superintend the suggested undertaking, generally, are the GRAND ARMY OF THE REPUBLIC, and the various WORKING MEN'S SOCIETIES throughout the North. . . .

All purely patriotic considerations aside, the success of this plan would, in a mere speculative and economic point of view, prove highly beneficial to the industrial and business interests of the North. Its operations, if extended to anything like National proportions, would necessarily open a vast field for utilizing the immense mass of well disposed and intelligent, but adventurous young energy now wandering aimless about the North; they would provide acceptable and remunerative employment, at the South, for multitudes of Northern working people who find it impossible to secure the means of a decent support for themselves and their families in their present abodes. For, while individual Northern enterprise in that direction is not just now advisable, yet throughout the whole civilized world, there is not another so favorable an opening for co-operative Northern enterprise, if it be united, systematic, and of a legitimate character, as the South, in its present condition, offers to it. Every associated enterprise, such as this plan suggests, if judiciously located and properly managed for developing the natural resources of the South, instead of (as some have done) plunging into mad attempts at competition with great Northern industries, would handsomely compensate the laborer for his work, besides, after the first year, paying cent-per-cent, per annum on every dollar of capital invested in it. Once settled at the South, the colonist, amidst congenial social surroundings that this plan would secure to him, could not, with a tithe of the industry, fail to secure an ample competency for themselves and their dependents, without that incessant toil which, for even a scanty and precarious support, the North exacts from every person who depends solely upon manual labor, for their livelihood within its great centers of population. Thus they would materially benefit themselves in all the relations of life, and, at the same time, leave a freer field to, and open a new market for, the industry of those of their fraternity who are established at the North. It would, also, give a new and lasting impetus to legitimate business of all kinds throughout the whole country. Therefore, leaving Southern interests and political considerations out of the question altogether, this plan deserves the serious attention of the Working men and the Business men of the North.[7]

INTRODUCTION TO DOCUMENTS 7 AND 8

The violence against southern blacks and whites engaged with Reconstruction had a deeply political character. The Democratic Party became the stronghold against Reconstruction policy, resisting reforms and working to end military occupation. The pervasive violence was extremely effective in this regard, as the following documents reveal. In Document 7 we hear form Adelbert Ames, a northerner appointed as governor of Mississippi. Ames wrote directly to President Grant, D.C. on September 8, and again on September 11, 1875, to detail the violence that had become so common against blacks in his state, particularly as a way to discourage black men from voting. Ames begged for federal assistance in the form of troops to protect the citizens, insisting that the violence was politically motivated.

The day after Ames's first letter. The chairman of the Democratic State Executive Committee telegraphed the Attorney General to declare that "Peace prevails throughout the State," arguing against federal intervention. Document 8 is the response of Grant's Attorney General, Edwards Pierrepont to Governor Ames, expressing sympathy but refusing his request. Pierrepont's letter quoted President Grant, who expressed his frustration at the extent of violence, but also underscored Ames's own responsibility as Governor for addressing it. The Mississippi election in 1875 resulted in a landslide for Democrats.

7. LETTER OF MISSISSIPPI GOVERNOR ADELBERT AMES TO PRESIDENT U.S. GRANT

SEPTEMBER 8, 1875

Domestic violence prevails in various parts of this State, beyond the power of the State authorities to suppress. The Legislature cannot be convened in time to meet the emergency. I therefore, in accordance with section 4, Article IV of the Constitution of the United States, which provides that the United States shall guarantee to every State in this Union a republican form of government, and shall protect each of them against invasion, and on application of the Legislature, or of the Executive when the Legislature cannot be convened, against domestic violence, make this my application for such aid from the Federal Government as may be necessary to restore peace to the State and protect its citizens.

SEPTEMBER 11, 1875

The violence is incident to a political contest preceding the pending election. Unfortunately, the question of race, which has been prominent in the South since the war, has assumed magnified importance at this time in certain localities. In fact, the race feeling is so intense that protection for the colored people by white organizations is despaired of. A political contest made on the white line forbids it.

8. RESPONSE OF ATTORNEY-GENERAL PIERREPONT

DEPARTMENT OF JUSTICE, WASHINGTON, D.C.

SEPTEMBER 14, 1875

To Governor Ames, Jackson, Miss.
This hour I have had dispatches from the President. I can best convey to you his ideas by extracts from his dispatches:

The whole public are tired out with these annual outbreaks in the South, and the great majority are ready now to condemn any interference on the part of the Government. I heartily wish that peace and good order may be restored without issuing the proclamation, but if it is not the proclamation must be issued.

But if it is, I shall instruct the commander of the forces to have no child's play. If there is a necessity for military interference there is justice in such interference, to deter evil-doers. I would suggest the sending of a dispatch or letter, by means of a private messenger, to Governor Ames, urging him to strengthen his own position by exhausting his own resources in restoring order before he receives Government aid. . . .

You see by the mind of the President—with which I, and every member of the cabinet who has been consulted, are in full accord. You see the difficulties, you see the responsibilities which you assume. We cannot understand why you do not strengthen yourself in the way the President suggests. Nor do we see why you do not call the Legislature together and obtain from them whatever power, and money, and arms, you need.

. . .I suggest that you take all lawful means and all needed measures to preserve the peace by the forces in your own State, and let that country see that citizens of Mississippi, who are largely favorable to good order, and who are largely Republican, have the courage and the manhood to fight for their rights, and to destroy the bloody ruffians who murder the innocent and unoffending freedmen. Everything is in readiness. Be careful to bring yourself strictly within the Constitution and the laws, and if there is such

Image 13.4 A.B. Frost, "Of Course He Wants to Vote the Democratic Ticket"

Artist A. B. Frost captured the dynamics of southern Democratic political violence just weeks before the presidential election of 1876, which effectively ended Reconstruction. The caricature reveals the degree to which the freedmen had been left to their own devices, unprotected from southern white violence and political coercion.

Source: Harper's Weekly, October 21, 1876

resistance to your State authorities as you cannot by all the means at your command suppress, the President will quickly aid you in crushing these lawless traitors to human rights.

Telegraph me on receipt of this, and state explicitly what you need.
Very respectfully yours,
(signed) Edwards Pierrepont[8]

POSTSCRIPT

The violence in Mississippi achieved its aim: in the 1875 election Democrats regained power, effectively ending the Reconstruction government. The Republican Party's razor-thin victory in the election of 1876 included a "compromise" with the South to end Reconstruction and return political control in those states to the Democratic Party. Many of these state and local governments regained control through terrorism, as depicted in Image 1.4. With this shift, life for African Americans continued to deteriorate, subject as they were to political disfranchisement, violence, and—ultimately—segregation. Not until the civil rights movement of the 1960s would the nation's attention fully return to the plight of African Americans in the South.

QUESTIONS

1. How did the Klan choose its victims? Why were whites sometimes attacked by the Klan in addition to African Americans? Which blacks were singled out?
2. What political circumstances contributed to the Klan's formation?
3. Is the Ku Klux Klan best characterized as a political organization, a terrorist organization, both, or something else entirely? Was the Klan based in race hatred? Ideology? Political power? How do you sort out its means and ends, the rational from the irrational?
4. Who were the Klan's opponents? Was stopping racism their only aim, or did they have an additional agenda?
5. What do the images reveal about the nature of violence during Reconstruction and its aftermath? Did Governor Ames, for instance, have ways of combating this threat to civic life in Mississippi?
6. Ultimately, was the Klan successful? Why or why not?

ADDITIONAL READING

On the conclusion of the war, see Elizabeth Varon, *Appomattox: Victory, Defeat, and Freedom at the End of the Civil War* (2013). On the Ku Klux Klan, see Allen Trelease, *White Terror: The Ku Klux Klan Conspiracy and Southern Reconstruction* (1971), and David Mark Chalmers, *Hooded Americanism: The History of the Ku Klux Klan* (1981). On the violence of politics in this era see Douglas Egerton, *The Wars of Reconstruction* (2015). For various interpretations of Reconstruction, see John Hope Franklin, *Reconstruction After the Civil War* (1961); Kenneth M. Stampp, *The Era of Reconstruction, 1865–1877* (1965); Eric Foner, *Reconstruction: America's Unfinished Revolution, 1863–1877* (1988); and Gregory P. Downs, *After Appomattox: Military Occupation and the Ends of War* (2015). On African Americans during emancipation, see W. E. B. DuBois, *Black Reconstruction* (1935), and Leon F. Litwack, *Been in the Storm So Long: The Aftermath of Slavery* (1979). On gender in the postemancipation South, see Amy Dru Stanley, *From Bondage to Contract* (1998), and Laura F. Edwards, *Gendered Strife and Confusion* (1997). For the era's legacy, see Jay R. Mandle, *Not Slave, Not Free: The African American Economic Experience Since the Civil War* (1992), and David Blight, *Race and Reunion: The Civil War in American Memory* (2002). On the reborn Klan of the 1920s, see Leonard Moore, *Citizen Klansmen* (1992), and Nancy MacLean, *Behind the Mask of Chivalry; The Making of the Second Ku Klux Klan* (1994).

ENDNOTES

1. President Grant, "Condition of Affairs in the Southern States," message to the House of Representatives, April 19, 1872, in House Executive Document No. 268, 42d Congress, Second Session.

2. Walter L. Fleming, ed., *The Constitution and the Ritual of the Knights of the White Camelia* (Morgantown: West Virginia University, 1904), pp. 21–29.

3. George Rawick, ed., *The American Slave: A Composite Autobiography* (Westport, CT: Greenwood Press, 1977, 1979), Supp. 1, v.5, p. 426; Supp. 2, v.4, part 3, p. 957; Supp. 2, v.5, part 4, pp. 1648–1659.

4. *Testimony Taken by the Joint Select Committee to Inquire into the Condition of Affairs in the Late Insurrectionary States* (Washington, D.C.: U.S. Government Printing Office, 1872), v.6, pp. 545–546; v.7, pp. 607–611.

5. *Congressional Record*, May 30, 1872, pp. 1–7.

6. Benjamin Bryant, *Experience of a Northern Man Among the Ku-Klux, or The Condition of the South* (Hartford, CT, 1872).

7. W. H. Gannon, *The Grand Army of the Republic Versus the Ku Klux Klan* (Boston: W. F. Brown & Company, 1872).

8. *Appletons' Annual Cyclopaedia and Register of Important Events of the Year 1875* (New York: D. Appleton & Company, 1877), p. 516.